Hart, Schaffner & Marx Prize Essays

XXII

THE TAXATION OF LAND VALUE

THE
TAXATION OF LAND VALUE

A STUDY OF CERTAIN DISCRIMINATORY
TAXES ON LAND

By YETTA SCHEFTEL

The Riverside Press

BOSTON AND NEW YORK
HOUGHTON MIFFLIN COMPANY
The Riverside Press Cambridge
1916

TO

PROFESSOR ROBERT F. HOXIE

FROM WHOSE HIGH STANDARD

OF SCIENTIFIC RESEARCH AND KEEN CRITICISM

THE WRITER DERIVED INESTIMABLE PROFIT

AND INSPIRATION

PREFACE

This series of books owes its existence to the generosity of Messrs. Hart, Schaffner & Marx, of Chicago, who have shown a special interest in trying to draw the attention of American youth to the study of economic and commercial subjects. For this purpose they have delegated to the undersigned committee the task of selecting or approving of topics, making announcements, and awarding prizes annually for those who wish to compete.

For the year ending June 1, 1915, there were offered: —

In Class A, which included any American without restriction, a first prize of $1000, and a second prize of $500.

In Class B, which included any who were at the time undergraduates of an American college, a first prize of $300, and a second prize of $200.

Any essay submitted in Class B, if deemed of sufficient merit, could receive a prize in Class A.

The present volume, submitted in Class A, was awarded first prize in that class.

J. Laurence Laughlin, *Chairman,*
University of Chicago.

J. B. Clark,
Columbia University.

Henry C. Adams,
University of Michigan.

Horace White,
New York City.

Edwin F. Gay,
Harvard University.

CONTENTS

CHAPTER I

THE TAX ON LAND VALUE

CHAPTER II

LAND TAXES IN AUSTRALASIA

CHAPTER III

AND TAXES IN AUSTRALASIA (*concluded*)

CHAPTER IV

THE TAX ON VALUE INCREMENT IN GERMANY

CONTENTS

CHAPTER V

THE ENGLISH LAND-VALUE DUTIES

CHAPTER VI

MUNICIPAL TAXATION IN WESTERN CANADA

CHAPTER VII

THE TAX IN ITS FISCAL ASPECT

CHAPTER VIII

THE TAX AS A SOCIAL REFORM

CHAPTER IX

THE TAX AS A SOCIAL REFORM (*concluded*)

CHAPTER X

EXPEDIENCY OF THE TAX ON LAND VALUE FOR THE UNITED STATES

THE TAXATION OF LAND VALUE

CHAPTER I

THE TAX ON LAND VALUE

§ 1. THE problems of tapping new sources of public revenue and of improving the present systems of taxation tend to grow more and more vital. The reason is patent. Public expenditures are increasing enormously because of the socializing tendencies of the government. Especially in urban communities where the social welfare spirit has taken root, the disbursements for public utilities, for cultural and recreational facilities, as well as for public safety and sanitation, claim a greater percentage of the budgetary requirements from year to year. When we inquire what constitute the taxable sources to meet the growing budgets in most American cities, we find some form of the property tax, supplemented by the franchise, corporation, business, or similar taxes. But since, for purposes of taxation, personal property is as elusive as the will-of-the-wisp, the burden falls mainly on real property.[1] And under the present defective system of valuation and assessment, this burden, it will be agreed, is most unequally distributed. Under these circumstances the discussion of the tax on land value, which has been proposed as a substitute, or as supplementary to the property and other taxes, is opportune.

[1] In most American cities from seventy per cent to about ninety-five per cent of the general property tax is derived from real estate, according to an estimate made from Table 34 of the Special Report of the Bureau of the Census. *Financial Statistics of Cities Having a Population of over 30,000, 1909.* For example in Brooklyn, New York, more than ninety-eight per cent of the taxes was in 1895 derived from this source. *Cf.* Seligman, *Essays in Taxation* (1913), p. 25.

§ 2. In recent years the taxation of land value has taken on a signification somewhat different from its literal meaning. Literally land has always been taxed on its value. Even in the taxation of land according to acreage, e.g., the danegeld or scutage,[1] we perceive an attempt, though a crude one, to value the land. And in this country there is no more prolific source of local revenue than the land, which is legally and supposedly assessed on its market value. Nor can "land value" mean only the full market or capital value,[2] for there are a few cities and counties — e.g., Suffolk County, Massachusetts — which claim to tax land on its actual value; nevertheless, in the modern denotation of the phrase the tax on land value does not exist in these communities.[3]

The distinctive characteristic of the tax is not alone that it is levied on the actual selling or capital value, but that it is levied on the unimproved value, on the site irrespective of the value of the buildings and other improvements thereon. In other words it is a discriminatory tax on land. Though of comparatively recent origin the tax has already assumed various forms, the heterogeneity of which will be gathered from the following. Recently the cities of Pittsburg and Scranton were probably taken aback by the newspaper pronouncement that the tax on land value had there been unwittingly instituted. That is, the Stein bill,[4] which became a law May, 1913, provides for

[1] Thus the scutage was a charge on the knight's fee corresponding to £20, annual value, a rough estimate of the value of the land. *Cf.* Dowell, *History of Taxes and Rates in England* (1888), vol. I, p. 40.

[2] By capital value of land is meant the sum which the land might be expected to realize at the time of valuation if offered for sale on such reasonable terms and conditions as a *bona fide* seller might be expected to require.

[3] In fact the question of full value assessment as an administrative improvement is at present receiving the attention of many state legislatures with the prospect of adoption, yet no country is more reluctant than ours to institute the taxation of land value.

[4] Pennsylvania H.R. Bill 967 (1913), approved May 15, 1913.

the gradual reduction of the tax on buildings in the second-class cities of Pennsylvania. This, however, is an example of only partial taxation on land value. The study of the subject makes evident the existence of the system: (1) in Australasia, in the tax on the unimproved value of the land and the exemptions of improvements; (2) in Western Canada, in the municipalities where improvements have in recent years been wholly or in part exempted from taxation; (3) in Germany, in the shape of the value-increment tax; (4) in Kiao-chau, where besides a value-increment tax of thirty-three and a third per cent, a six per cent tax is levied annually on the value of the site; and (5) in England, in the form of the land-value duties comprising the increment, reversion, the undeveloped land, and the mineral rights duties. The protean character of the tax is thus evident.

The discriminatory feature of the tax raises the question of its *raison d'être*, the analysis of which is as essential to the understanding of the system as the mode of levy itself. If we analyze the criticism and speculation which the introduction of the above taxes has evoked, we find misapprehension and confusion of thought. By some, for example, the English Lords,[1] it is regarded as an attack upon private property rights; by others, such as Adolph Wagner and the "Kathedersozialisten,"[2] as a protest against the accumulation of wealth, especially of the "unearned increment," in the hands of a few; by others, Adickes,[3] for example, as a tax on special benefit, or a special assessment; by still others, including the general

---

[1] See *Parliamentary Debates of Commons and Lords* (1909–10). Also *cf. infra*, chapter v, §§ 1, 5.

[2] Many American professors of economics so regard the tax, e.g., H. J. Davenport. See "Extent and the Significance of the Unearned Increment," in *Bulletin of the Am. Ec. Assoc.* (1911), ser. 4, vol. i, pp. 322 *ff.*

[3] Mayor of Frankfurt a. M. Like many German officials, he approved of the "Wertzuwachssteuer" because of its expediency. *Cf. infra*, chapter iv, § 9.

American public,[1] as the Single Tax in disguise, i.e., the
entering wedge to the Single Tax; while to others, notably
B. Marsh,[2] it is merely a fiscal measure, an improved
method of local taxation, to replace or supplement the
realty tax. Which is the correct interpretation? Or is
there a common ground of agreement among them?

To disclose the essence of this tax and its *raison d'être*
in the face of this heterogeneity of conception is the first
purpose of this monograph; the further purpose is to discuss the expediency of its enactment from a study of the
actual operation of the tax as well as of its underlying
principles.

§ 3. A study of the above-mentioned systems shows
that not alone in method of assessment and levy, but also
in their rationale great differences exist. From both these
standpoints therefore, tentative definitions of the tax
on land value will be attempted, comprising not so much
the systems in operation, as the hypothetical ideal common
to those systems.

From the fiscal standpoint, the tax on land value to be
herein discussed is levied on the realized, or anticipated,
capitalized income [3] accruing from the site, distinct from
all structures and other improvements upon it. Thus the
tax presumably falls on economic rent, the basis for the
assessment being either the market value of the land, or
its realized, or potential, annual rental.[4] The pith of the

[1] The writer has in mind the vehement opposition to the adoption of
the tax in Oregon, Washington, and Missouri. *Cf. infra*, chapter x.

[2] *Taxation of Land Values in American Cities* (1911).

[3] In only a few cases, e.g., the English mineral rights duty, the rental
is made the basis of the tax, but in these cases the rental bears an arbitrary ratio to the capital value. In the English mineral rights duty, for
example, the income is assumed to be two twenty-fifths of the capital
value.

[4] The annual rental is not always the criterion of the capital value of
the land. This will become evident when the English rating system is
discussed in chapter v. Whether the selling value, the net, or gross rental
is the proper taxable basis involves a subtle distinction important only
from an administrative standpoint. See chapter vii, § 7.

system from the standpoint of taxation is contained in the following principles: first, all land, whether utilized or undeveloped, whether yielding a rental at the time or not, shall be taxed at its full value, which shall be ascertained by expert assessors according to a scientific system of valuation; secondly, in accordance with the theory of the tax, all improvements and buildings shall be exempted from taxation.[1] This is its essence; the actual methods will become clearer after considering in the next section the various forms of assessment and levy.

The rationale of the tax is fourfold, ethical, economic, social and fiscal.

(a) The ethical justification of the tax is founded on the conception of the "unearned increment." The rôle played by the doctrine of the "unearned increment" as fundamental in the taxation of land value is well known. The term first employed by John Stuart Mill and based on the Ricardian theory of rent has been perpetuated by the Single Taxers. In recent years, however, when the phrase is stretched by economists to include surpluses other than those accruing from land, the term has assumed a different meaning. Value increments accruing from the land are regarded as created through certain social forces[2] and,

[1] It will be found that these requirements, namely expert valuation and exemption of improvements, are implied, if not existent in all the forms of the tax to be discussed. This is true of the value-increment duty as well (see *infra*, § 5). Practically, however, whenever the rate of tax, or the percentage of assessed value of the site exceeds that of the improvements the principle of the tax on land value may be said to be in force.

[2] To the argument that the value of all wealth is dependent upon social influences, and that value increment accrues from other forms of wealth besides land because of social causes, and not because of individual effort, the reply is given that whereas competition prevents abnormal profits falling to the capitalist and laborer, land is a monopoly by virtue of which the value of the land, increasing with the population and industrial development, accrues to the owner of the property right. All other artificial monopolies, moreover, are said to have their root in this monopoly of natural resources. *Cf.*, for example, *The Public*, September 12, 1913, pp. 868 *ff.*

therefore, it is thought, rightfully belong to the community as a whole. Since land is a gift of nature, and its value
is not attributable to individual effort, the private appropriation of such value, it is argued, is ethically unjustifi-
able. On this basis of the distinction between what is
socially created and what is privately earned rests the
chief argument of the advocates of the tax on land value.

(b) But this ethical consideration does not appear separately; the economic factor is ever present. Indeed the
phenomenon, "unearned increment," arises and can be
formulated only when scarcity appears, that is, where
economic equality is prevented either by the natural
scarcity of the commodity or through legal limitation.
Take the duty on undeveloped land or the super-assessment tax in Canada as examples: their object is to prevent
the holding of land for speculative purposes. The duty,
in other words, puts a premium upon improved land.
For instance, when the owner of vacant lots in the vicinity
of improved land receives a heavy tax bill on property
which yields him no income, he is tempted either to sell,
or to utilize the site himself.

(c) To the ethical and economic considerations should
be added the social justification which was largely responsible for the adoption of the tax in Australasia and in
Canada: namely, to discourage large land holdings and
absenteeism. Viewing the land question in these countries as less urgent than in European countries we prefer
to regard this influence as social rather than economic. In
other words, it was a union of political forces against an
unpopular class. Further, the new "social-service" view-
point, as exemplified in the theory of "socially created
increment value," seeking by means of social welfare and
public service institutions to level down the economic inequalities among the social groups, has exerted an influence
in calling the tax into existence.

(d) However much these causes may have been instrumental in promoting the institution of the tax for imperial or state purposes, they nevertheless do not appear to have determined the *raison d'être* of the local systems. In the new communities of Australasia and Canada, where the value of the land tends to rise rapidly with the influx of immigrants, and where land constitutes the chief source of wealth, the tax on the unimproved value of the land has been found fiscally preferable to the tax on capital, which is scarce and the accumulation of which it is desirable to encourage. It will appear, indeed, that while the tax for other than local purposes owes its origin chiefly to the social, economic, and ethical considerations, the local taxes on land value are predominantly fiscal in character.[1]

§ 4. Having defined and explained the rationale of the tax on land value, it is necessary to point out the various forms which the tax from the standpoint of administration has assumed: —

1. Direct levies:
   (a) Proportional taxes;
       (1) general;
       (2) specific: undeveloped land, mineral rights, timber land;
   (b) Progressive taxes;
2. Indirect levies:
   (a) Proportional;
       (1) value-increment duty (England);
       (2) reversion duty;
   (b) Progressive;
       value-increment duty (Germany).

Direct [2] taxes are periodically recurrent, that is, collected

---

[1] A possible exception is the German municipal "Wertzuwachssteuer" whose origin is discussed *infra*, chapter IV.

[2] The words "direct" and "indirect" as applied to taxes are here employed in a different sense from the customary one based on the incidence of the tax, the tax being direct if levied immediately on the ultimate bearer of the charge, and indirect if shifted by the immediate payer to the consumer, as in the case of commodities. For authority for the other

annually according to a general assessment; while indirect taxes are charged on stipulated occasions, i.e., at the time of a sale or lease, or upon the death of the owner; in other words, whenever a transfer of property occurs. The latter may be paid in the form of a stamp tax at the time the land is transferred by a deed of sale, or by a lease. By general proportional[1] tax is meant one imposed annually on all land at a uniform tax rate. We shall find this system in vogue for local purposes in those English-speaking communities [2] where the tax is in operation. When a scale of rates increases directly with the greater value of the land in addition to the ordinary charge on land, we have what is known as the progressive or graduated land tax. Thus in some cases, to the proportional levy of $1d.$ in the pound of the capital value, may be added a scale of rates, e.g., $\frac{1}{16}d.$ rising to $2d.$ on the capital value of estates ranging from £5000 to £200,000. This scale will be found levied especially for state and federal purposes,[3] in some cases as a super-tax, that is, in conjunction with the ordinary rate as in the above assumed illustration; in others as the principal levy without the ordinary rate.

The specific direct taxes are those levied on unimproved, timber, or mineral land. Whether imposed in conjunction with other forms of the land tax or as a separate levy, the specific tax is intended as an especially discriminatory land charge. This characteristic of the tax on unimproved land, for example, is shown by the methods of levy. Thus, undeveloped land may be subject to a rate

usage of the terms see Eheberg, *Finanzwissenschaft* (1911 ed.), pp. 204–05; also *cf.* Bullock, "Direct and Indirect Taxes" in *Pol. Sci. Quart.*, vol. XIII, pp. 463–65.

[1] "Proportional" is used in its technical sense of uniform rate for all property or income regardless of the amount of taxable value. In Professor Seligman's terms, "a tax is proportional when the mathematical relation between the amount of the tax and of the thing taxed remains the same." "Progressive Taxation in Theory and Practice," in *Am. Ec. Assoc. Quart.*, vol. IX, p. 565.

[2] In Australasia and Canada.   [3] Characteristically in Australasia.

one hundred per cent higher than that on improved land;[1] or unimproved land may be assessed at a value twenty-five per cent higher than its selling price;[2] or a rebate from part of the tax may be allowed the owner of improved land.[3]

Distinguished from the direct taxes are those collectible on certain occasions of transfer of property. As in the case of the direct taxes, the two types, namely, the proportional[4] and the progressive,[5] occur also as indirect levies. In the case of the duty on value increment, i.e., the difference between the value of the land on the occasion of levy and its value on a previous occasion, the tax is collectible, as already stated, at the time of a transfer of property, either by sale, lease, or at death.[6] The occasion for the collection of reversion duty[7] is at the termination of a lease, when the property reverts to the owner. In all other respects the reversion duty is a value-increment duty. As the nature of the assessment for computing the tax is complex and unique, an attempt will be made in the following section to describe and illustrate the system of taxing the value increment.

§ 5. The progressive tax on value increment, the "Wertzuwachssteuer," is essentially of German origin. In common with the other forms of the tax, it aims to appropriate a portion of the surplus or differential value of the land in behalf of the community; in the method of procedure, however, it is different from the direct levies. First, the direct tax collects its share of the value in annual installments; the tax on value increment collects a lump sum

---

[1] In the German municipalities.

[2] The super-assessment tax in Canada.

[3] The Western Australian State tax.   [4] In Kiao-chau and England.

[5] In Germany for both imperial and local purposes.

[6] There is only one more occasion for the levy of value-increment duty. That is the arbitrary occasion created, as we shall see, in the English Act for taxing corporations, namely, in 1914, and every subsequent fifteenth year. See *infra*, chapter v.

[7] Characteristically English, for it is in England that the leasing system is most prevalent.

on the particular occasions mentioned above. Secondly, and this is of vital importance, the tax on value increment falls only on the surplus, or as its name implies, on the value increment, not on the whole capital value. The government, therefore, claims a part of the owner's profit arising from the appreciation in the value of the land.

The method of valuing the increment is as follows: When a piece of property on which duty is chargeable is sold or leased, its selling price (in case of a lease, its appraised price) is compared with its purchase price, i.e., the selling price at a previous transfer when duty was paid; and the differential of the present price over that previous price constitutes the increment upon which duty is imposed. Two selling or appraised prices, then, must be known before the amount of appreciation can be computed. A moment's reflection makes it clear that the tax may be retroactive. In the German laws, in order to compute the tax the first time it is levied, an arbitrary appraisal value has in most cases been fixed. This is called the "original site value," and is ascertained for an arbitrary date stipulated in the bill.[1] To illustrate, the "Wertzuwachssteuer" in Breslau went into effect on June 23, 1907. The bill fixed January 1, 1895, as the time for which the original site value should be computed. If, then, in December, 1907, a lot was sold in Breslau for 15,000 marks which had been worth on January 1, 1895, 9000 marks, duty would have been charged on the difference in the prices, or on 6000 marks. Suppose, now, that in 1910 the same piece of land changed owners and its selling price was then 16,000 marks, the duty would be collected on 1000

[1] The details of this method of computation will be found *infra,* chapters IV and V. It may be here noted that while the German tax is with few exceptions retroactive, falling on the value increment that has accrued in the past, the English bill seeks to appropriate part of the future increment only; the latter bill provides for a valuation of all the land at the time of the enactment of the law, in this way establishing the original site value.

marks.[1] In case of a depreciation in price, of course no tax is levied. Thus, if the price of the lot in 1910 had remained 15,000 marks or had fallen below this amount no increment duty would have been collectible. It is needless to repeat that, as in the other taxes on land value, the value of the improvements and buildings would have been deducted before the value increment was ascertained.

From this brief analysis it will be observed (1) how different the modes of assessment are, and (2) how heterogeneous are the forms which the tax on land value has assumed. It will further be observed that several forms may coexist in the same community. The best illustration of this protean tax is to be found in the English system which comprises four separate duties on land. To define further the distinctive character of this tax it will be necessary to differentiate it from other land taxes.

§ 6. The pivotal distinction between the land-value tax and the other land taxes lies in the theory of incidence. In accordance with this theory, the only tax on land which cannot be shifted is one which falls on economic rent; such a tax is that on land value.

Regardless of this theory of incidence, the earliest system of land taxation made area the basis of valuation, e.g., the scutage or danegeld. In such taxes the rent, or income-bearing capacity of the land, is ignored. Survivals of this crude system are to be met with even to-day.[2] Later, product, or fertility, superseded area as the basis of assessment, e.g., in the "taille," or tallage. Product, however, theoretically represents wages, interest, profit, as well as economic rent. Hence this form of the land tax

[1] The system of assessment is more complicated because of a minimum exemption, of the deductions and additions to the selling prices, etc. *Cf. infra*, chapters iv and v.

[2] Even yet instances occur where area is made the basis of assessment. In Greece, for example, land is taxed according to area. *Cf.* Bastable, *Public Finance* (1895), p. 406. Also in Alberta, Canada, land is subject to a provincial tax based on area. *Cf. State and Local Taxation, Second Conference of the International Tax Association* (1908), p. 299.

does not satisfy the requirements of the discriminatory tax on land, the so-called tax on land value.

Another land charge which should be distinguished from the tax on land value is the apportioned land tax. As its name implies, the amount of revenue expected to accrue from its levy is apportioned by the central government among the subordinate taxing jurisdictions, each of which becomes responsible for the collection of a quota determined by the assessed value of the land at the time of apportionment. Now, were the tax frequently reapportioned in accordance with periodic "cadastral" valuations, and were the assessment made on the actual selling price of the land,[1] the tax would fall on the value of the land. As a matter of fact, however, apportioned taxes become fixed charges, the same quota being paid to the central authority irrespective of the changes in the value of the land due to the progress or retrogression of the district.[2] Thus the English land tax (instituted as far back as 1692) has yielded an almost constant sum, less than one million pounds, for about a century, in spite of the enormous appreciation in the value of the land during that time. Such taxes practically become permanent rent charges.

The prevailing form of land taxation to-day is the tax on real property. Whether we consider the English system of rating on rental, or the real estate tax on selling price in this country, they differ from the tax under consideration in their failure to accept the principle of exempting buildings and improvements, and in the system of assessment. As ordinarily levied, the tax on real property is characterized as follows: —

(1) Unused land is generally assessed at a lower value than the surrounding improved sites; thus a premium is

---

[1] More often not rent but product formed the test of value.

[2] Such taxes may, as happened in England under Pitt's redemption scheme, be redeemed by the payment of a lump sum representing the capitalized value of the tax.

given to the owners who for speculative purposes hold land
out of use.

(2) Largely because of the crude methods of assessment,
land under the realty tax is rarely assessed at its full market
value. Although this is a matter of common knowledge,
the following statistics showing the extent of underassessment are significant. Summarizing the data prepared by S. Wolff [1] from the Census Bureau Reports, real
property was assessed on an average in four of our states
at from fifteen to twenty-three per cent of its actual value,
in eight states at from thirty to forty per cent, in thirteen
states at from forty-one to fifty per cent, in seven states at
from fifty-two to sixty per cent, in five states at from
sixty-two to sixty-nine per cent, in seven states at from
seventy-five to ninety per cent. Only one county in the
entire United States (Suffolk County, Massachusetts) had
its real estate assessed at its full estimated value.

(3) With few exceptions,[2] no provision is made in this
country for the expert valuation of land, so that the surplus
or value increment, which increases rapidly in progressive
communities, for long periods remains untaxed.[3] It is
important to note that in view of this exemption of value
increment from taxation for long periods of time, the
burden of an increased rate of tax on realty is to some
extent compensated. In fact, granting the validity of the
principle of tax capitalization, whereby the capitalized
value of the tax is deducted from, or "absorbed" in, the
selling value of the land, under-assessment and inexpert
valuation reduce the burden of the tax to a minimum.[4]
For as a result of this "amortization," the tax on realty
ceases to be a tax in the proper sense of the word.

[1] *First National Conference on State and Local Taxation* (1907), p. 113.
[2] *Cf. infra*, chapter VII, § 12 *ff.*   [3] See quotation *infra*, p. 14.
[4] *Infra*, chapter VII, § 5. It seems very probable that the possibility
of the amortization of the tax, added to the Anglo-Saxon respect for private property rights, is responsible for the defective administration of the
realty tax in this country.

§ 7. Recently an improved system of taxing real estate has been introduced in a few cities,[1] with the purpose of assessing property on its actual selling value. The improvement consists in the method of assessment and valuation. To ascertain the full market value of the property a scientific system of valuation has been devised, in accordance with which the land is valued apart from the improvements. It must be noted, however, that the improvements continue to be taxed at the same rate as the site. As the system is in operation to-day, it varies from the tax on land value, first, in that buildings and improvements are not exempted from taxation; secondly, in that the assessed value is kept below the selling price of the property. Take New York City as an illustration. Efficient tax administration has indeed made the tax on selling value in that city an object of commendation.[2] Yet even there the assessment and valuation until recently failed to keep pace with the enormous growth in the value of the land. "The growth of the City of New York and the great increase in realty values since that time (1903) have been such that, in spite of the rapid marking up of values at that time, the assessed valuation to-day, taking the city as a whole, probably does not exceed seventy per cent of the market value, and in many cases is not over sixty per cent. An examination of the books for different parts of the city and for all classes of improvements, whether business houses, private dwellings, or tenement houses, leads me to believe that the assessed valuations of land lag about thirty per cent behind the extraordinary rise in values which has occurred in the last three

[1] Notably New York City, Newark, New Jersey, Houston, Texas, Cleveland, Ohio. *Cf.* also *Papers Bearing on Land Taxes and on Income Tax*, etc. (1909), *Brit. Parl. Papers* (Cd. 4750), pp. 92 *ff.*, 106. Mention should here be made of the attempt of about a dozen of our states to assess the land separately from the buildings. See *infra*, chapter VII, § 11; also *State and Local Taxation* (1907), p. 131.

[2] See *ibid.*, pp. 375 *ff.*; also (1908), pp. 237 *ff.*

years. In the case of unimproved property in many cases, the assessment is about fifty-five to sixty per cent of the market value." [1] In the interest of uniformity, the tax on land value proposes to take account of all the fluctuations in the value of the land.

§ 8. The association of the tax on land value with the Single Tax is so prevalent and the consequences of this association so serious that it is necessary to differentiate between them. There is ground for the confusion of the two. On the one hand, the opponents of the tax on land value have prejudiced the public against it by identifying this tax with the Single Tax; on the other hand, the Single Taxers exult in the introduction of the tax on land value, regarding it as the vindication of their theories, and as the entering wedge to the Single Tax.

No one will dispute the fact that fundamentally they have something in common. Both, for example, stand for an efficient, expert valuation system; both favor the exemption of improvements from taxation; both insist upon assessing and taxing land at its full value. Nevertheless, as enacted to-day, the tax on land value bears no closer relation to the Single Tax than does the recently enacted parcels post system in the United States, for example, to state socialism. England, for instance, with her value-increment duties is no nearer the Single Tax régime than is this country with her public utilities legislation near collectivism.

[1] *First Conference on State and Local Taxation* (1907), pp. 384–85. Other authorities corroborate this estimate of undervaluation. *Cf. Papers Bearing on Land Taxes*, etc. (Cd. 4750), pp. 95, 105.

Mr. Purdy, President of the Tax Commissioners of New York City, nevertheless claims that the assessment in New York City represents the full value of the land. There is abundant proof that, excellent as the work of the commissioners is, their land-value assessment is not accurately on the full value. (*Cf.* Cederstrom, *Unjust Taxation, passim.*) For example, to make the accrued rental, so long as the value of the site is less than the combined value of the land and building, the basis of computation of the selling value of the land is not to attain an accurate full value assessment. See *Seventh Conference on State and Local Taxation* (1913), p. 264.

In distinguishing between the tax on land value and the Single Tax, we are comparing a tax reform with a social philosophy. The Single Taxers are not interested in the tax as an adequate source of local revenue under existent conditions; they would employ the tax as the weapon with which to clear the way to their Utopia, the essence of which is an ideal society based on an equality of opportunity. The important, ultimate object of the Single Taxers of the Georgean type is the nationalization of the land; the method by which they propose to attain this object is through a one hundred per cent tax [1] on the value of land. In addition, these theorists claim that, with the enormous income from the public domain in the hands of society, the imposition of other taxes will be superfluous. In short, the one hundred per cent tax on land value, and the abolition of all other taxes, that is, the institution of the Single Tax, is merely the machinery necessary in the realization of their Utopian society.[2] Contrast this doctrine with the slight tax on land value, adopted in part for fiscal purposes, in part in the interest of social amelioration, e.g., to relieve congestion in urban communities, to prevent speculation in land, and, on behalf of the community, to appropriate a little of the enormous appreciations in the

[1] The writer is aware that the Single Taxers propose to leave the land in the hands of individuals who will practically act as agents of the government and who will receive a small share of the land value — about five per cent or more — as recompense. This, however, does not alter the theory as interpreted above, for the Single Tax is primarily opposed to the private appropriation of land value, hence of private property in land. As to those moderate (limited) Single Taxers who, like C. B. Fillebrown, would limit the Single Tax "to the needs of the state for an effective and economical administration of government," the theory remains unaltered. *Cf. The A.B.C. of Taxation*, p. 153. Moreover, the needs of the state, as Shearman admits, are unlimited. *Cf. Natural Taxation*, pp. 133–34.

[2] It is interesting in this connection to note that Henry George himself regarded the nomenclature "Single Tax" as a misnomer. Mr. George's son, in the *Life of Henry George*, says in a footnote (p. 496), "Mr. George never regarded the term as describing his philosophy, but rather as indicating the method he would take to apply it."

value of the land, to meet the growing budgets. Nor is the difference between them one of degree, merely; the doctrine of abolishing all taxes is as foreign to the principle of the tax on land value, as is the confiscatory feature of the Single Tax.

Having thus attempted to epitomize a complex system, it is necessary to show to what extent it is prevalent.

§ 9. Mention has incidentally been made of the several countries where the tax on land value is in operation. As early as 1873 the Canadian province of British Columbia enacted a wild-land tax, a duty on unimproved land. This tax is in force to-day. New Zealand, the pioneer in social reform legislation, in 1878 passed a measure taxing the unimproved value of the land. But the act was repealed in the following administration, and it was not until the nineties that the system was reintroduced into New Zealand and instituted in Australia. Since then the tax has gained a foothold in numerous Australasian municipalities, in its several states, and, in 1910, was made part of the federal revenue system of the Commonwealth of Australia.

An interesting experience with the tax on land value, instituted in 1898, is furnished by Kiao-chau, the German province in Asia. In Germany, the duty on value increment was first incorporated in the fiscal policies of numerous municipalities, Frankfurt a. M. taking the lead in 1904. According to Adolph Damaschke,[1] 652 local governments in Germany had by 1911 adopted the tax. The "Reichszuwachssteuer," the imperial tax, went into effect April 1, 1911.

In England, by the enactment of the "Finance Act, 1910," the new duties on land value became law. Turning to Canada, besides the wild-land taxes, a number of local authorities, notably Vancouver and Edmonton, have recently revised their realty taxes, so that they not only are taxes on land value, but constitute practically the sole

---

[1] *"Geschichte der Nationalökonomie,"* p. 549 (5th ed.).

source of local revenue. It has long been customary in these and other communities of the western provinces to assess the improvements at a lower percentage valuation than the sites. It is noteworthy, not only that the number of municipalities which exempt improvements is increasing, but that in Alberta and Saskatchewan general provincial regulations have been enacted providing for the taxation of land value for local purposes, thus assuring the extension of the tendency in that country to rate on land value.

§ 10. Summary: It will be observed that the tax on land value is of comparatively recent origin. And to judge from its protean character, it seems to have had a spontaneous growth. That is, the tax was no theory or scheme of definite form and shape, so to speak, taken over as a whole by this or that country. It would appear rather that the form or forms of the tax which were adopted in the several countries were those that seemed to be most suited to the needs and conditions of the community. That this was actually the case will be seen from the following chapters, in which the causes for the introduction of the tax in the various countries will be considered. The following chapters will also attempt to explain the nature and the working of the systems in detail, and to clear up the complexities resulting from the numerous methods of exemptions, assessment and rates.

CHAPTER II

LAND TAXES IN AUSTRALASIA

§ 1. To Australasia the Western world owes among numerous experiments in social science the system of taxation on the unimproved value of land. Although we have much to learn from an experience extending over several decades, caution must be exercised in our conclusions regarding the expediency of the tax for countries trammeled by tradition, precedent, slowly evolved social institutions, social classes, and other frictional forces. In respect to the problem in hand, for example, the attitude of the colonists toward land monopoly which has been created and fostered in their own generation, through laws for which they were themselves responsible, must be unlike that of their mother country toward an institution centuries old, upon which the very aristocracy and military glory of the country are founded. Thus, the confiscation of the "unearned increment" has less terror for those who have themselves bestowed the right or privilege to it.[1] Thus, too, it becomes comprehensible how an Anglo-Saxon people, with the deepest respect for private property rights, could embody in a recently proposed Land Bill [2] a clause limiting the ownership of land by an individual to the value of £50,000. This absence of institutions sanctioned by tradition is largely responsible for the progressive social legislation in Australasia. The untram-

[1] The Treasurer General of New Zealand, Mr. Ballance, was quoted as saying during the campaign of 1878 that it would be right to tax away the whole unearned increment. *Cf.* New Zealand, *Parl. Debates* (1878), vol. XXIX, p. 21.

[2] In a bill proposed in New Zealand, 1906, "It is made unlawful for any one to own more than £50,000 worth of land (unimproved value)." *The Australasian*, vol. LXXXI, September 22, 1906, p. 689.

meled character of the colonists is, in fact, the key to their land laws, including the land tax.

§ 2. Bearing in mind this unique attitude of the colonist toward the institution of landed property and his freedom to make and unmake laws,[1] we need only understand the needs growing out of the conditions of land tenure in Australasia to perceive the chief cause of the taxation of land value. The all-important problem which continues to confront the colonies is how to attract settlers. In the early history of the new country a sound land policy was of secondary importance. And since, as is well known, the bait that lures the venturesome to a newly opened continent remote from civilization is the possibility of becoming "land rich," [2] the inducements offered by the government at first were chiefly in the form of land grants and orders from the Crown.[3] The futility of this policy soon becoming apparent, systems of purchase and leasehold were devised, all of which, however, failed to prevent the wholesale alienation and concentration, in the hands of comparatively few settlers, of large portions of first-

[1] Cf. Vigouroux, L'Évolution Sociale en Australasie (1902), pp. 417–18.

[2] "Are we not afflicted with a land-grabbing mania, an earth hunger"? Cf. The Australian Economist, vol. I, May, 1888, p. 52. "What allures the one immigrant whom we care to welcome? The hope of settling on his own land in fee." The Australasian, June 20, 1874, p. 776.

[3] This system of free grants continued until 1831 when it was superseded by the sale of land at auction. The minimum price was at first fixed at 5s., but was increased later to 12s., then to 20s. per acre. The terms of payment were liberal and selection of the land by the purchaser before surveying was freely permitted. According to the later restrictive policies the maximum amount of country land that could be held by any one individual was, speaking generally, from 640 acres of the first-class, agricultural land to 5000 acres of pastoral, or third-class land. Besides the alienation by grants, squatter sovereignty and sales, a system of leasing for short as well as for perpetual tenure, subject to certain conditions of actual residence on the land was devised. To-day the systems of perpetual lease and of lease-in-perpetuity are much in vogue in the colonies. For a full and valuable study on the land tenure in Australasia see Epps, Land Systems of Australasia (1894). Also cf. Reeves, State Experiments in Australia and New Zealand, vol. I; Official Year Book of the Commonwealth of Australia (1901–11); New Zealand Official Year Book (1909).

class land in each of the colonies, "to the great embarrassment of the late comers." [1]

The following illustrations of the wholesale alienation of the land throw light on the lax policies of the government, and on the existent conditions of land tenure in the colonies. We read that in New South Wales one million acres were transferred to a single company at the rate of 18*d*. an acre.[2] In the middle of the nineteenth century, one squatter occupied for a £10 license more than one million acres. Again, in 1890, there were in this colony 121 freehold estates of over 40,000 acres each (comprising 11,219,484 acres).[3] In New Zealand thirteen holders occupied 165 runs, covering over 2,500,000 acres.[4] In an address before the convention of the Australian Workers' Union, in 1915, the following figures were presented to show the extent of the concentration of land holdings in Australia: 95 persons were in possession of 8,418,308 acres; 361 of 10,408,407 acres; 689 of 9,514,769 acres; 1567 of 10,754,656 acres. The holdings of these 2712 persons therefore comprised 39,096,140 acres.[5]

[1] "The frontages have been alienated, the riparian rights have been allowed to get beyond state control, and the total known sources of water supply are in the hands of individuals." *The Australian Economist*, vol. I, May, 1888, p. 53. "New Zealand had seen the spectacle, extraordinary for so young a country, of thousands of its most vigorous people going abroad in search of work and land." Lloyd, *Newest England*, p. 107. This was said also of the other colonies. *Cf. The Australasian*, August 9, 1890, p. 261.

[2] Reeves, *op. cit.*, vol. I, pp. 204 *ff*.

[3] *Australian Economist*, vol. II, June, 1890, p. 38. It is interesting to note that of this vast area only 8385 acres (not counting artificial grasses) were under cultivation.

[4] Reeves, *op. cit.*, p. 243. *Cf.* also *Papers bearing on Land Taxes*, etc. (Cd. 4750), 1909, p. 72. In 1891, 7,000,000 acres of freehold and 3,500,000 of leasehold, including much of the best land in New Zealand, according to Mr. Reeves, were held by only 584 owners. *Op. cit.*, vol. I, p. 216.

[5] *The Australian Worker*, March 4, 1915. That the sentiment with regard to the "wasted heritage" is shared generally is evident from the following passage in *The Australasian*, a conservative weekly published in Melbourne, Victoria, and opposed to the land taxes: "Within thirty years a population of about three quarters of a million will have mopped

The conditions of land tenure in relation to total area, to population, and to area under cultivation in Australia and New Zealand become further apparent from the subjoined table.

TABLE SHOWING THE PUBLIC ESTATE, AREA UNDER CROP, AND POPULATION PER SQUARE MILE IN AUSTRALASIA IN 1905 *

State	Total area in acres	Area alienated or in process of alienation	Area leased	Area under cultivation	Population per square mile
New South Wales	198,634,880	49,970,335	123,015,992	2,840,235	4.38
Victoria	56,245,760	26,346,802	17,994,233	3,219,962	13.67
Queensland	427,838,080	17,659,874	240,152,615	522,748	0.75
South Australia	243,244,800	13,467,924	89,249,487	2,255,569	0.40
Western Australia	624,588,800	12,380,035	145,769,592	364,704	0.19
Tasmania.............	16,778,000	5,338,953	1,303,383	230,237	6.57
Northern Territory	335,116,800	475,366	103,278,259	....	....
Commonwealth........	1,902,447,120	125,639,289	720,763,561	9,433,455	1.27
New Zealand..........	66,861,440	26,030,254	17,340,790	1,723,837	7.39

* Compiled from data in Anderson, *Six States of Australia and New Zealand, 1861 to 1905* (Official Statistics), pp. 1, 23, 27.

It is to be gathered from the above-mentioned facts that the land problem in Australasia is acute not because of a scarcity of land, but because of a scarcity of free, unalienated, arable land. The population of all the colonies is somewhat over five millions. Of these about one and one-half millions live in cities. The area, on the other hand, exceeds 3,000,000 square miles, of which at least one-third is good agricultural and mineral land. In 1909, the acreage of occupied land in New Zealand was over 38 millions, while in the Commonwealth of Australia more than 930 million acres were held by individuals and companies.[1]

up 33½ millions of acres in one of the finest countries of the world." Vol. xx, April 15, 1876, p. 497.

[1] Computed from data in the *Official Year Books* quoted above. Under alienated land was included land held under lease or license as well as that alienated and under process of alienation.

This makes a total of over 968 million acres or approximately one and one-half million square miles in private possession. It is noteworthy, however, that of this vast territory under private tenure only about 26.5 million acres, less than three per cent, were, in 1909, under cultivation. Of the two Commonwealths New Zealand shows the denser settlement, for about forty per cent of its occupied land was under cultivation as compared with one per cent in Australia. When we add that each of the seven states has had to pass laws providing for the public repurchase of land in the interest of denser settlement, the monopolization of land in Australasia is seen to be no mere bugbear. For more than half a century now, the government has been attempting to undo the evil perpetrated by its own legislation [1] and to bring about closer settlement, a policy which has now become a means of attracting immigrants.

§ 3. Added to the land legislation, the taxation of the large estates, as a means of overcoming the evils of land tenure, became in the seventies a popular cry. The fact that many of the large landed proprietors were absentees only aggravated the concerted agitation of the colonies.[2] The progressive land tax to "burst up the large estates" was the liberal nostrum of that time.[3] The National Re-

---

[1] A report on the working of the land system in New South Wales calls it a "huge failure, which fosters the formation of large freehold estates in the best parts of the grazing country." *The Australasian*, May 12, 1883, p. 593. "The law had made settlement hard for the bona fide selector . . . has built up large estates." *Ibid.*, April 15, 1876. The editor would have done with the "liberal land policy."

[2] The following quotation was uttered by one who regarded the tax as a confiscatory, penal tax: "Many of the latter worthies (absentees) left the country for the more promising sphere of operations that New South Wales affords, and we have not even the benefit of their ill-gotten gains being expended in the country." *The Australasian*, September 30, 1876, pp. 432–33.

[3] "The proposed tax upon absentees . . . is merely a concession like the little bit of progressive land tax to a mere popular cry." *Ibid.*, vol. xix, July 24, 1875, p. 113. "A progressive land tax is popular with a

form League, to which the university professors of economics belonged, was active in the movement of checking landed monopoly and absenteeism. Under this influence Mr. Berry [1] in Victoria and Sir George Grey [2] in New Zealand came into office. Already, in 1875, a progressive land tax [3] was proposed in Victoria, but was withdrawn. In 1877, however, the will of the people was carried out and a land tax (not on the unimproved value, however) [4] was passed by both houses of Parliament. The first tax on unimproved value was enacted the following year in New Zealand through the efforts of John Ballance, Treasurer, and Sir George Grey, Premier.

The purpose of the tax is revealed somewhat in the following citation from a speech of Mr. Ballance: [5] "And here I may take the opportunity of disclaiming and repudiating the charge which is sometimes made, that the government have in contemplation a class tax. The very contrary is the fact. We hold that the system which we propose to correct has worked unfairly in the past; that it has favored the escape of taxation of the greater portion of the wealth of the colony, and has implanted a strong sense of injustice in the minds of the wage class. The readjustment

certain class — party of anarchy and confusion — simply because it aims at the gradual confiscation of landed estates." *Ibid.*, September 30, 1876, pp. 432–33. *Cf.* also *ibid.*, February 17, 1877, p. 209.

[1] "Mr. Berry declares that he would be delighted if within twelve months every large estate was divided so that the tax did not bring in a shilling into the revenue." *Ibid.*, April 2, 1881, p. 432.

[2] Grey said, "Those who acquire land by unlawful means and so prevent its cultivation are enemies of the human race." *Ibid.*, December 23, 1876, p. 819.

[3] The proposed bill was "The Land, Property and Income Tax." The land tax was to be charged on lands, exclusive of buildings, at the rate of 1*s*, in the pound between £80 and £200 annual value, and at 1*s*. 6*d*. in cases above £200. The annual value was assumed to be five per cent on the capital value of the fee. *Ibid.*, vol. xx, March 25, 1876, pp. 400–01.

[4] The tax fell only on the large estates, and the principle of the tax on land value was violated by the provisions of valuation. See *infra*, § 10.

[5] Quoted in *The Australasian*, September 17, 1878, p. 305.

we hope to effect will tend to efface the inequalities I have referred to; and instead of promoting hostilities between classes will remove the causes which have been gradually estranging them. . . . We believe that no form of wealth is more legitimately called upon to contribute a portion of the public revenue of the colony than the value of land minus improvements, which for brevity, I shall call the unimproved value, as no other commodity increases so rapidly in value from the increase of population and the natural progress of a country. By exempting improvements, we award a premium to industry and discourage a system of speculation which thrives only upon the labor of others." The life of this measure, however, was short. With the overthrow of the liberal ministry in the following year the tax was repealed.[1]

If each law relative to the taxation of unimproved value for state purposes were reviewed, the charge of class legislation repudiated by Mr. Ballance would be found to be substantiated. Not one would be found which was not actuated by the same motive, the disintegration of the large estates and of absentee holdings.[2] It was also the avowed purpose of the "Labor Parliament" in enacting the Commonwealth tax in 1910.[3] Indeed, the provisions of the acts themselves, such as the graduated scale, the exemption of estates of less than £5000, the absentee

[1] "The great landowners trembled. They believed it was putting in the thin edge of the wedge. They rallied all their forces and in one year the tax was repealed and Sir George Grey was punished by expulsion." *Papers Bearing on Land Taxes*, etc. (Cd. 4750), 1909, p. 69.

[2] *Cf.* New Zealand, *Parl. Debates* (1878, 1891, 1893, 1896, 1907). *The Australasian*, vols. LVI, LIX, LXXXIV, LXXXVI. "With such figures as these, evidencing an earth hunger of an unhealthy character, the sooner a land tax is imposed the better will it be for the development of the colonies' resources." *Australian Economist*, vol. II, June, 1890, p. 38.

[3] Commonwealth of Australia, *Parl. Debates* (1910), vols. LV, LVI, LVII. A candidate in the election of 1910 is reported to have said: "The Labor Party's chief plank at this election is to penalize the owners of the big estates, so that it will be unprofitable to hold them." Quoted by Turner, *The First Decade of the Australian Commonwealth* (1911), p. 286.

rates, give evidence that the enactment of the tax on the unimproved value of land was directed against the holders of large estates.

§ 4. Was the land tax, then, discriminatory class legislation pure and simple? Was it mere pretense on the part of the Minister of State that the exigency of the treasury required new sources of revenue? An understanding of the fiscal policy of the colonies throws light on this question. For purposes of analysis, the fiscal problems of the federal and state governments must be kept distinct from the problem of local revenue.

The weakness of the state finances during the seventies and eighties is attributable to several causes. First, the indebtedness of the colonies and the over-expenditure for purposes of public improvements of all kinds produced an ever-increasing drain on the treasury.[1] Secondly, the remission of the tariff duties in some of the states caused a deficit.[2] Thirdly, the loss of the land fund [3] further increased this deficit in the colonies. Under these circumstances direct taxation had to be resorted to. It is significant, therefore, that synchronously with the movement to reduce the tariff duties which had obviated for a long time the necessity of direct taxation, the land taxes were either proposed or enacted.

Now, it might be argued that the fiscal needs of the state government directly brought the land taxes into

[1] About 1880 there was a deficit in the treasuries of all the colonies due to over-expenditure. *The Australasian*, August 14, 1880, pp. 208–09. Again in 1887. *Cf. ibid.*, August 20, 1887, p. 360.

[2] The land tax was proposed as a substitute for the remitted tariff in Victoria in 1875, and again in 1877, when the free traders succeeded in reducing the tariff, and when the tax was passed. *Cf. The Australasian,* August 21, 1875; January 20, 1877, p. 80; July 21, 1877, p. 80; September 7, 1878, p. 305. In New South Wales, the land tax became a law at the same time that the reduction in customs took place, in 1895. *Ibid.,* May 25, 1895, p. 989.

[3] As the land became appropriated the revenue from its sale fell off. *Cf. ibid.*, August 14, 1880, p. 208. Coghlan, *A Statistical Account of the Seven Colonies of Australasia* (1892), p. 274.

existence. This, indeed, seems plausible when the unpopularity of the income and general property taxes in Australasia is considered, for the latter usually constitute the most practical successors of the protective tariff.[1] That the land taxes, however, were not intended as substitutes for the income and general property taxes is clear from the fact that in almost all cases they are incorporated with the income tax provisions, and from the fact that the land taxes constitute but a small percentage of the total tax revenue.[2] It is difficult, therefore, to believe that the fiscal exigencies did more than offer the occasion, the opportune moment, for the enactment of a popular reform. This explains, moreover, why the land-tax propaganda was ineffective during the years of plenty and why the land-tax bill failed of passage in South Australia in 1890.[3] It also explains why it took the Labor Party a decade to enact the land-tax bill, although from the first they practically controlled the Federal Parliament.[4] So long as the treasury was filled, the propaganda was carried on in vain. For federal and state purposes, therefore, the fiscal needs

[1] So unpopular was the income tax in Tasmania that a ministry actually refused to collect it. *The Australasian*, April 27, 1907, p. 989. *Cf.* also *ibid.*, March 4, 1876; July 23, 1881, p. 113. "For bringing in revenue the property tax was an efficient instrument. It soon became, however, exceedingly unpopular, not only among Radical theorists, but among commercial men, shopkeepers and manufacturers. . . . They [the farmers] contrasted their lot with that of comfortable town-dwelling professional men whose substantial incomes went wholly untaxed, and who paid merely on savings and investments. It is necessary to draw attention to the severity and unpopularity of the property tax, for it was these which enabled the land-taxers to win the day in 1891." *Papers Bearing on Land Taxes*, etc. (Cd. 4750), 1909, p. 69. *Cf.* also New Zealand, *Parl. Debates* (1891), vol. LXXIV, p. 24.

[2] See *infra*, chapter III, § 7.

[3] There was no need of revenue. *The Australasian*, August 9, 1890, p. 261. "The revenue aspect was a purely secondary consideration." *Ibid.*, February 24, 1906, p. 455. As to the proposed federal land tax, to create a fund to carry out the pension scheme was said not to be the genuine reason. *Ibid.*, April 3, 1909, p. 849.

[4] *Ibid.*, 1904–09, vols. LXXVI–LXXXVII.

aided, but were not the cause of the enactment of the land-tax laws.

§ 5. Turning from the consideration of the land taxes for state and federal purposes to that of the local rates on unimproved value, we see that the situation is very different. Conceding that large holdings and absenteeism were thorns in the side of the general public and exerted an influence in the adoption of rating on the unimproved value of the land, we find that other more fundamental causes, chiefly fiscal, were responsible for the tax agitation in the local bodies. It is noteworthy that the local taxes on unimproved value antedated the state taxes. Already, in 1878, this system of rating was in vogue in the colonies.[1] In tracing the causes that led to the ready adoption of the tax for local purposes, it is first necessary to point out that until the nineties the local revenue in the Australasian colonies consisted chiefly of the "endowments," [2] or grants apportioned among the local divisions by the state government. Hence there was little need of levying rates, especially as education and local improvements were mainly under state jurisdiction.[3] In the eighties, however, as the expenditures of the states increased without a correspond-

[1] "It is reassuring to notice a growing feeling among municipalities in favor of rating on land, irrespective of improvements." Mr. Foxall, "The Principles of Taxation," in *The Australian Economist*, vol. I, May 12, 1888, p. 45. "It will be recollected that at the late municipal conference a resolution was carried in favor of placing municipal taxation on the unimproved value of land and in the proposed new 'Local Government Bill' municipalities are empowered on certain conditions to carry this into effect, and it is more than probable that the Legislature will endorse this power." *Ibid.*, vol. II, March 20, 1890, p. 1. See also New Zealand, *Parl. Debates* (1878), vol. XXIX, p. 17.

[2] The "endowment" is an annual subvention voted by the state government at fixed intervals to the municipality or other local body and is generally a sum proportioned to the revenue raised by the community through local rates. In other words the "endowment" is proportioned according to the fiscal needs of the local authority.

[3] Until the "Local Government Bill" was passed in New South Wales, all local improvements also were undertaken by the state government. *Cf. The Australasian*, August 5, 1905, p. 325.

ing increase in the revenue, attempts were made by some of the states to reduce the municipal "endowments." In Victoria, for example, the exigencies of the treasury, in 1880, necessitated such a reduction.[1] This policy in Victoria, however, did not involve so important a change in local government as occurred in Queensland in 1890.

The finances of Queensland were in that year in a precarious condition, and the heavy tax levied on property to pay the municipal "endowments," led to a change in the ministry. Griffith's Coalition Government came into power and succeeded in putting through the legislature the "Valuation and Rating Bill of 1890," by which the powers of the local authorities were extended to raise revenue by rating on the unimproved value of land. In this way the central government relieved itself of subsidizing the local bodies and incidentally introduced the taxation of unimproved value.[2] As to New South Wales, the motive which in 1905 actuated the central government to relinquish the state land tax in favor of the shires, and then of the municipalities, was not the fiscal need, although a fiscal problem was involved. It was the desire to shift to the local bodies some of the functions of government, e.g., the administration of local works.[3] The legislation, by which the state land tax was relinquished to the local bodies was therefore in the interest of local autonomy.

But to say that the extension of local government was the outcome of fiscal conditions explains nothing as to the cause of adopting the new system of levying rates. The reasons for choosing this tax will be found in certain advantages claimed for it in the cases where it was in use.

[1] *The Australasian*, October 30, 1880, p. 560.

[2] The deficit in Queensland amounted to £1,300,000. The Morehead Ministry had proposed an excise tax for state purposes. This proved unpopular. His successor, Mr. Griffith, had always favored the tax on unimproved value and urged it with success. *The Australasian*, August 8, 1891, p. 265. *Cf.* also *Papers Bearing on Land Taxes*, etc. (Cd. 4750), 1909, pp. 199–200; and (Cd. 3890), 1908, pp. 6 *ff.*

[3] *The Australasian*, August 5, 1905, p. 325.

These reasons are concisely summarized in the following preamble of a proposed bill of 1891:[1] "Whereas the value of land within a municipality is increased by the expenditure of rates; and whereas the benefit of all expenditure of public moneys ought to accrue to the public and not to private owners; and whereas the present assessment of rates throws the burden of municipal taxation upon industry and enriches the owners of land at the expense of the rate payers; and whereas such a method of raising rates discourages industry, prevents settlement, and is otherwise inequitable, and unsocial. . . ."

In other words, it is here argued that: (1) local taxes should be levied according to the principle of benefit; that (2) the value increment accruing from the appreciation in the value of the land is socially created and belongs to the community; that (3) industry is hampered by the taxation of improvements; that (4) under the system of *annual value* rating, land is withheld from utilization; and that (5) an unequal distribution of wealth is fostered and immigration prevented through the creation of large landed estates and absenteeism. In new democratic communities, benefit, i.e., the service which the taxpayer receives in return for his contribution, rather than ability to contribute, is regarded as the fair basis of taxation. In fact, where land is the principal source of wealth and income, and the ratepayers are the owners of land, the value of the land is not alone the measure of the benefit, but also of the ability to contribute. And the theory of "socially created land value" is but an application of the benefit theory which rests on the assumption that the expenditure and increase of population influence the value of the land. Again, in such communities it is very obvious that the taxation of improvements tends to discourage the employment of capital and to put a premium on the with-

[1] *The Australian Economist*, vol. ii, September, 1891, p. 152, Mr. B. R. Wise's bill to amend the Municipalities Act of New South Wales.

holding of unused land.[1] In fact, in a new country where capital is scarce, the rate of interest high, and land the chief source of wealth, the proposal to exempt improvements and to tax the capital value of the land will meet the approval not alone of the landless urban dweller but of the enterprising farmers as well.[2] And lastly, the resentment of the ratepayers toward the absentee owner of unimproved land [3] who escapes taxation and yet reaps the benefit of the appreciation in the value of the land, is readily comprehensible.

§ 6. But it may be asked, was not, then, the propaganda of the Single Taxers instrumental in bringing the land taxes into operation. The query is, indeed, both plausible and justified in view of the situation. First, the writings of Henry George and Alfred Wallace [4] were frequently quoted and discussed.[5] Secondly, the activity of the Single Taxers, especially after George's visit to Australasia in 1890, was unremittent. Thirdly, George's presence and his popularity strengthened the cause, "his intellectual charm" and "fine speaking powers" winning many converts.[6] Unquestionably in a country where land speculation and land monopoly were rife, and the land policy of the government was a recognized failure, the Single Taxers discovered a fertile field for their work.[7]

[1] *The Australian Economist*, vol. i, May, 1888, p. 45. Also New Zealand, *Parl. Debates* (1878), vol. xxix, p. 58.

[2] *Papers Relative to the Working of Taxation on the Unimproved Value in Queensland* (Cd. 3890), 1908, pp. 6 *ff*.

[3] New Zealand, *Parl. Debates* (1896), vol. xcii, p. 632.

[4] *Land Nationalization* (1882).

[5] *Cf. The Australian Economist*, vol. i, April 14, 1888. The taxation of land and its nationalization were frequently discussed at the meetings of the Australian Economic Association, and also in Parliament.

[6] "Mr. George's visit is bearing fruit in the shape of a very general interest being everywhere manifested in the economic problems he has so eloquently proposed and so earnestly desires to see solved." *The Australian Economist*, vol. ii, March, 1890, p. 19. *Cf.* also *ibid.*, vol. i, May 26, 1888, p. 49. *The Australasian*, April 5, 1890, p. 672; March 29, 1890, p. 628.

[7] "It is a fact well worthy of the attention of the advocates of high

Nevertheless, admitting the influence that the Single Tax leagues exerted in the movement, there is conclusive evidence that the conception of taxing on unimproved value has had a spontaneous growth in Australasia [1] and that the Utopian philosophy of the Single Tax is accepted by but a small group of devotees.[2] First, the system was in vogue before the eighties and before even the publication of "Progress and Poverty" in 1879. Second, the Victorian Land Tenure Reform League had already in 1872 embodied the Single Tax doctrine in its platform.[3] Third,

tariff that the single-taxers have made converts among the land owners themselves." *Ibid.*, November 3, 1894, p. 793.

[1] It might be argued with reason that neither George nor the Australasians were the original founders of the Single Tax doctrine, which can be traced back to Spence (*Rights of Man*, 1775), Ogilvie (*Essay on the Right to Property in Land*, 1782), Gossen (*Die Entwicklung der Gesetze des menschlichen Verkehrs*, 1854), Walras (*Théorie Critique de l'Impôt*, 1861) and others.

[2] That the Single Tax organizations are no larger than those in this country may be gathered from the following facts: (1) the guaranteed circulation of the *Liberator*, the organ of the New Zealand Land Values League, is 5000 copies per month and there are two copies monthly; (2) the total receipts for the *Joseph Fels Fund* of New Zealand from March 30 to October 15, 1913 (including all subscriptions to the *Liberator*) were only about £219. This sum is small considering Mr. Fels's offer to duplicate the amount contributed.

[3] The following quotations are from a circular of the League which appeared in 1872: —

"The land is the inalienable property of the inhabitants of every country throughout all generations."

" 'No consideration ought to be paramount to that of making the land available in the highest degree for the production of food and the employment of industry.' "

"Selling the fee-simple of the land is a political misdemeanour, as opposed to justice and reason, as it has proven injurious to the material and moral interests of society."

"The alienation of the State lands gives to the landowner the *whole improvement in value from the increase of population and national works.* The State Landlord preserves all for the benefit of the people."

"Land is the State capital, the primal source of food and wealth, and in parting with it our legislators have not only most iniquitously limited the field of profitable employment, but have burdened the people needlessly with double taxation — the one a highly unjust system to provide

the study of the taxes as enacted makes it apparent that no close analogy exists between the two systems. The numerous exemptions, low rates, progressive scales surely do not reflect the striving of the Single Taxers to make the land tax the sole tax.[1] In fact, since the enactment of the taxes, no attempts have been made as was predicted, to tighten the screw or to approach anything like the confiscation or the nationalization of the land. In those cases, where, as in New Zealand, the graduated scale of rates has been increased, the purpose has clearly been the disintegration of the large estates, nothing more. The land taxes, as well as other social legislation, are accepted by a

a general revenue; the other a direct tax on food and the necessaries of life, to enable landlords to live in idleness by the labor of others."

"A rent on State lands being light, and for a manifest benefit, would meet all the requirements of a just and desirable means of raising revenue. It would be easily and cheaply collected, and would greatly reduce the expenses of government by rendering unnecessary some of the present costly and otherwise hurtful departments."

"While strictly preserving the right of ownership in land for future generations, the greatest possible facilities for actual and productive settlement may be afforded."

"The advantages of almost free land, and the *total absence of taxation*, would ensure an unexampled condition of steady progress and general prosperity."

"*With an absolute freedom from taxation, and full and unfettered scope for industry, every inhabitant of the country would enjoy a beneficial interest from his share in the state lands, whether occupying a portion of these or not.*"

" 'The best political economy is the care and culture of men.' And such a use of the common patrimony, the gift of God to all, would not only promote to the utmost the material welfare of society, but would raise us mentally in the scale of nations, by affording the most liberal culture of which each is capable; special privileges, which should be deemed the inherent right of every member of the community."

(Italics by the present writer.) Quoted in Laveleye's *De la Propriété et ses Formes Primitives*, pp. 346 *ff*.

[1] The local rates on unimproved value even in Queensland, where they constitute practically the sole source of revenue, are low. In fact, the secret of the successful working of the tax there has been claimed to be the low rate of tax, kept so because of the constant great appreciation in land value. Cf. *Papers Relative to the Working of Taxation*, etc. (Cd. 3890), 1908, pp. 9, 20.

large number of the Australasian population, "whose tendencies are very individualistic and who contest with energy the influence of the Labor Party." [1]

Summarizing the causes which called the taxes on unimproved value into being, we may say that the land taxes for federal and state purposes owe their origin chiefly to the conditions of land tenure in the colonies, and that the local rates were adopted because of the fiscal expediency of the system. Furthermore, the fiscal exigencies merely furnished the occasion or opportunity, and the activity of the Single Taxers the necessary propaganda for the enactment of the laws.

§ 7. From the above analysis of the causes of enactment, we turn to the study of the taxes themselves. The following is a summary of the important considerations with regard to the legislation, administration and working of the land taxes in Australasia: —

(1) Rates of tax and modes of assessment.

(2) Methods of valuation and administration.

(3) Revenue yielded, and other fiscal considerations.

(4) Revisions in the laws to carry out their purpose.

(5) Social and economic effects of the taxes.

It is first necessary to point out the extent in the colonies of the system of the taxation on the unimproved value. The tax for state purposes is now levied by New Zealand and five of the six Australian states, Queensland being the only one that has never levied a state land tax. Since 1905–06 New South Wales has received only a slight revenue from the land tax, the state having relinquished the tax in favor of the shires and municipalities which have adopted rating on the unimproved value. It is important to note in regard to the state land tax that in each case it is only one out of a number of sources of public revenue. Thus customs duties, excise duties, income taxes, death duties, licenses, etc., form part of the fiscal system of each

[1] Vigouroux, *L'Évolution Sociale en Australasie*, p. 222.

of the colonies. Furthermore, the land tax is in almost all cases levied in conjunction with the income tax, i.e., under the same administrative machinery and incorporated in the same laws. Again, it is noteworthy, that, before 1910, the land taxes in both Victoria and Tasmania were levied on the capital value of the land plus the improvements.[1]

At present the local authorities empowered to levy rates on the unimproved value of the land are those in New Zealand, New South Wales, Queensland, South Australia, and Victoria. Accordingly, all the local bodies in Queensland, practically all in New South Wales, and numerous communities in New Zealand, levy taxes, called rates, according to this system. In South Australia, however, no municipality had until 1906 taken advantage of the privilege extended to it in 1893.[2] In Queensland the tax on unimproved value for local purposes is practically the single tax. So is it in those bodies in New Zealand which have adopted the system. In New South Wales all general rates in both the shires and municipalities must be levied on the unimproved value; while the levy of additional general rates in the municipalities, and of all special rates on the unimproved value is optional with the local authority. In 1914 rating on unimproved value was made optional with the local authorities in Victoria.[3]

It is difficult to measure the extent of the prevalence of the system of rating on unimproved value, for in many communities rating on this basis prevails even where the State Act has not authorized its practice. Certain it is, however, that the adoption of the system is proceeding rapidly. If, as is so generally feared, a land valuation bill

[1] In Victoria it was not the intention of the legislators to enact a realty tax, as it was in Tasmania; nevertheless, because of the peculiar method of valuation the purpose of the tax was frustrated, the tax burdening the grazing industry. See *infra*, § 10.

[2] *Papers Bearing on the Land Taxes*, etc. (Cd. 4750), 1909, p. 114.

[3] By the enactment of the "Rating on Unimproved Values Act, 1914." Victoria, 4 Geo. V, No. 2478.

is the harbinger of local rating on land value,[1] then the adoption of the system in Tasmania, with its Land Valuation Act of 1909,[2] may be predicted. In Western Australia many local bodies rate on this basis even though no State Act to the effect exists.[3] In this state, indeed, the "Roads Act, 1902" gave Road Boards the option of rating on the basis of the unimproved annual (i.e., rental), or capital, value, except in case of mining and pastoral leases to be rated on annual value exclusively. In accordance with this privilege, out of 105 Boards, 57 now rate on unimproved value, two rate partly on annual and partly on unimproved value, while the rest rate on annual value.[4]

In 1910, the land tax was made a source of federal revenue in the Commonwealth of Australia. Like the state land taxes this one constitutes a small percentage of the total tax revenue of the Commonwealth. However, taking all the systems together, federal, state, and local, the burden on land in Australasia is considerable. An analysis of the state, local, and federal systems follows.

§ 8. We may first consider the tax for state purposes in New Zealand, where it has been in operation for about a quarter of a century.[5] The changes that the provisions of the land-tax law have undergone in this colony since 1891 are noteworthy. These will be treated in the following analysis of the important provisions relating to rates and

---

[1] Cf. The Australasian, July 25, 1908, p. 229; also September 25, 1909, p. 823.

[2] Tasmania, 9 Edw. VII, No. 7.

[3] The First Annual Report of the Commissioner of the Land Tax of the Commonwealth of Australia (1912), p. 6.

[4] Ibid.

[5] The Land Tax Act of 1878, repealed the following year, was a charge of ½d. in the pound of the capital value of the land, deducting the value of all improvements. An exemption of £500 was allowed. Cf. New Zealand, Parl. Debates (1878), vol. XXIX, pp. 414–15. The Acts that govern the tax on umimproved value in this colony are The Land and Income Assessment Act, 1891, amended in 1893, 1900, 1903, 1907, and 1912. Cf. also The Valuation of Land Amendment Act, 1908, amended in 1912. For the rate of tax cf. the annual Land-tax and Income-tax Acts.

assessment, under (a) the ordinary rate, (b) the graduated scale, (c) the absentee charge, (d) the tax on mortgages, (e) the exemption of improvements.

(a) The ordinary rate which has remained unchanged is 1d. in the pound of the actual value of the land minus the value of the improvements and minus the value of any mortgages owing on the land. Land whose assessed value does not exceed £1500 is allowed an exemption of £500; if its value exceeds £1500 but is less than £2500, the exemption diminishes by £1 for every £2 of the surplus value over £1500, so that when the assessed value reaches £2500 or more no exemption is allowed.[1] In computing the amount of exemption the value of the mortgage or mortgages is not subtracted from the value of the land.[2] Thus, should the value of the land when the mortgage is included be £2500 no exemption is allowed. The only other exemption [3] from the ordinary tax provided for is that in case of an owner incapacitated by age or ill health from earning an income (except from the land) exceeding £200 per annum. In such a case the exemption may be any sum not exceeding £2000,[4] — or where the taxpayer is a widow with dependent children, not exceeding £3500,[5] — at the discretion of the Commissioner of Taxes when he is satisfied that the payment of the tax in full would entail hardship on such owner.

(b) In addition to the ordinary tax, a graduated tax is charged on all land whose value is £5000 or above. The graduated scale has undergone many revisions for the purpose of raising the rate on the larger estates. The scale began with a rate of ½d. in the pound on land valued

[1] New Zealand, 55 Vic., No. 18, Schedule A, Arts. 1, 2.

[2] *Ibid.*, Art. 2.

[3] Barring the usual exemptions of land owned by the government and used for special purposes, e.g., educational, charitable, etc.

[4] New Zealand, 55 Vic., No. 18, § 2.

[5] Amended provision in *Land and Income Assessment Amendment Act,* 1912 (New Zealand, 3 Geo. V, No. 10), § 36.

at £5000, rising to 1⅝d. on a value of £210,000, or above, the increment being ⅛d. for every £10,000.[1] Already, in 1893,[2] the scale was slightly modified so that on land of £210,000, or above, the rate was increased from 1⅝d. to 2d. A more drastic amendment was passed in 1903,[3] when the rate on all land of more than £7000 unimproved value was raised, and the scale graded to yield 3d. instead of 2d. on the largest estates. In 1907,[4] the year when the screw was put on with vigor, the progressive tax took the following form: —

RATE OF GRADUATED TAX ON THE UNIMPROVED
VALUE OF LAND, £50000 TO £40,000

Where the value is £5,000 and less than £7,000, $\frac{1}{15}$d. in the pound
"   "   "   "   7,000 "   "   "   9,000, $\frac{2}{15}$d. "   "   "
"   "   "   "   9,000 "   "   " 11,000, $\frac{3}{15}$d. "   "   "
"   "   "   " 11,000 "   "   " 13,000, $\frac{4}{15}$d. "   "   "
"   "   "   " 13,000 "   "   " 15,000, $\frac{5}{15}$d. "   "   "
"   "   "   " 15,000 "   "   " 17,500, $\frac{6}{15}$d. "   "   "
"   "   "   " 17,500 "   "   " 20,000, $\frac{7}{15}$d. "   "   "
"   "   "   " 20,000 "   "   " 22,500, $\frac{8}{15}$d. "   "   "
"   "   "   " 22,500 "   "   " 25,000, $\frac{9}{15}$d. "   "   "
"   "   "   " 25,000 "   "   " 27,000, $\frac{10}{15}$d. "   "   "
"   "   "   " 27,500 "   "   " 30,000, $\frac{11}{15}$d. "   "   "
"   "   "   " 30,000 "   "   " 35,000, $\frac{12}{15}$d. "   "   "
"   "   "   " 35,000 "   "   " 40,000, $\frac{13}{15}$d.

At the value of £40,000 the rate becomes two-fifths of one per cent, and for every additional £1000 of value the rate is increased by one-hundredth of one per cent. The rate reaches its maximum at £200,000, when it becomes two per cent for that and any higher value.[5] Furthermore, this Act stipulated that after March, 1910, an addition of twenty-five per cent to the above rate would be charged[6] in case of all estates over £40,000. It is significant

[1] New Zealand, 55 Vic., No. 18, Schedule B. This is only approximately correct, the increment being ⅛d. between £5000 and £10,000, ¼d. between £90,000 and £110,000, etc.
[2] *Papers Bearing on Land Taxes*, etc. (Cd. 4750), 1909, p. 134.
[3] *Ibid.*
[4] New Zealand, 7 Edw. VII, No. 18, Schedule.
[5] *Ibid.*, §§ 4, 5, 6.   [6] *Ibid.*, § 7.

that this additional charge was not to apply to "business premises," which were defined as "any piece of land included within the area of a building used for business purposes, together with such additional land as immediately adjoins the said building, and is used and occupied in connection therewith, and does not exceed in extent the area of the building itself." [1]

In the Act of 1912 the graduated rates are as follows: [2]

(a) From £5000 to £15,000, $\frac{1}{32}d$. in the pound, increased by $\frac{1}{32,000}d$. for each pound of the excess value over £5000.

(b) From £15,000 to £30,000, $\frac{1}{3}\frac{1}{2}d$. increased by $\frac{1}{40,000}d$. for every pound of excess value over £15,000.

(c) From £30,000 to £200,000, $\frac{2}{3}d$. increased by $\frac{3}{100,000}d$. for every pound of excess value over £30,000.

(d) Over £200,000, $5\frac{5}{8}d$. for every pound of unimproved value.

The maximum rate, it will be noted, is now about two and one-half per cent as compared with two per cent in the Act of 1907. Another change is that the twenty-five per cent additional charge on other than business premises now falls on estates of £30,000 and above, instead of beginning with £40,000. [3]

(c) The purpose of the land tax is further shown by the special rate on absentee holdings and by the amendments of that provision. According to the original Act three or more years' absence from the colony constituted absenteeism. Now, an absentee is one who has been away from

---

[1] Where the person is owner of both business premises and other land, he pays the graduated tax, without the twenty-five per cent increase, on all the land. To that tax is then added the additional charge (twenty-five per cent) "on the amount of graduated land tax that would be payable if he were not the owner of the business premises." *Ibid.*, § 7, (5).

[2] New Zealand, 3 Geo. V, No. 11, § 2.   [3] *Ibid.*, No. 10, § 44.

the colony for at least two years. More specifically, to be exempt from the absentee tax one must have resided in New Zealand at least one-half of the period of four years immediately preceding the assessment, or, if the land has been acquired within this four years, at least one-half of the period between his acquisition of the land and the time of assessment. Instead of the original super-charge of twenty per cent, the rate of the absentee tax is now fifty per cent of the graduated scale; so that, for example, if the graduated rate for a certain value be 4d. in the pound, an absentee owner of that value will be charged 6d. in the pound.[1]

(d) In computing the assessment for the ordinary tax the value of any mortgage or mortgages is deducted from the taxable value of the land, but the value of mortgages is included in the assessment for purposes of the graduated tax. That does not mean that mortgaged land escapes taxation, for the mortgage is held liable for a separate mortgage tax of $\frac{3}{4}d.$ in the pound of the value of such mortgage. Compared with the ordinary tax the mortgage has the advantage of $\frac{1}{4}d.$ in the pound.[2] For all other purposes the value of the mortgage is not deducted in computing the tax.

(e) It is interesting to note that in the original Act, for purposes of the ordinary tax, improvements were exempted only to the amount of £3000.[3] Since 1893, however, all improvements go untaxed. For purposes of the graduated tax the unimproved value only was from the first taxable. What is included under improvements will be more explicitly pointed out in the sections on valuation.[4] But it is of interest to note here the attempt not to tax value accru-

---

[1] New Zealand, 7 Edw. VII, No. 18, § 8. If an absentee taxpayer be liable for the graduated tax jointly with a non-absentee, the land is assessed jointly as if the one were not an absentee, and then the absentee tax is computed to apply to the absentee. Moreover, while a corporation is not considered an absentee, the shareholder may be so considered.

[2] New Zealand, 55 Vic., No. 18, Schedule B.

[3] *Ibid.*, Schedule A.   [4] See *infra*, chapter III, §§ 3, 4.

ing from the employment of labor and capital, as shown in the provision of 1907 [1] exempting minerals, timber, and flax which are being worked or used in good faith.

§ 9. The general character of the Australian land taxes for state purposes [2] is both like and unlike the system in New Zealand. While there is a general similarity in purpose and in definition, we note in the Australian Acts no such persistent efforts to penalize the large landowners sufficiently to bring about disintegration. This is made evident by the fact that the only Australian state which has a graduated tax is Tasmania, where the progressive scale begins with $1d.$ in the pound for land under £2500, rising to $2\frac{1}{2}d.$ on estates of £80,000 or above.[3] And yet, compared to the New Zealand scale, and considering that no ordinary or absentee tax is levied in Tasmania, the Tasmanian land tax is considerably less burdensome than the New Zealand tax. As for the taxes in the other states, the rate of tax in South Australia is $\frac{1}{2}d.$ in the pound on land valued at £5000 or less, $1d.$ on land of a greater value than £5000;[4] in Victoria it is a flat rate of $\frac{1}{2}d.$ in the pound;[5] and in Western Australia [6] it is $\frac{1}{2}d.$ and $1d.$ in the pound, respectively, according as the land is improved or unimproved. Then, too, only South Australia and Western

[1] The income derived from minerals, timber, and flax is, however, taxable under the income tax. And "if the Commissioner is of the opinion that any land containing minerals or having standing timber or flax thereon is not being worked or used in good faith and to an adequate extent for the purpose of extracting the said minerals, or of cutting the said timber or flax, such minerals, timber, or flax shall be excluded from the provisions of this section (i.e., exemption) and land tax, both ordinary and graduated, shall be assessed and paid." New Zealand, 7 Edw. VII, No. 18, § 22.

[2] Inasmuch as the tax for state purposes has been suspended in favor of the local authorities, the consideration of the land taxation in New South Wales will be reserved for the following sections dealing with the local rating systems.

[3] Tasmania, 1 Geo. V, No. 37, § 2.

[4] South Australia, 4 Edw. VII, No. 861; 5 Edw. VII, No. 894.

[5] Victoria, 2 Geo. V, No. 2327; 3 Geo. V, No. 2405, Schedules.

[6] Western Australia, 7 Edw. VII, No. 15, §§ 9, 10.

Australia have additional charges on absentee holdings; twenty per cent on the total tax in the former, $\frac{1}{2}d$. in the pound additional in the latter state. In both states absence from the Commonwealth for one year previous to the assessment constitutes absenteeism.[1]

It is significant that the amount of exemption from the tax in case of small holdings is less in the Australian states than in New Zealand. Thus no such exemption is allowed in either South Australia [2] or in Tasmania; in Western Australia land valued at £50 or less is exempt; while in Victoria land whose value does not exceed £250 is not taxable, and the exemption, in case the value of the land exceeds £250, diminishes at the rate of £1 on every £1 of such excess, leaving no exemption when the unimproved assessed value amounts to or exceeds £500.[3] Thus, when the value of the land is £275, the exemption is £225, when the value is £450, the exemption is £50, etc.

The following special exemptions should be noted. In Western Australia, a special exemption is accorded the owner of improved land used for agricultural or like purposes. In such a case a deduction of £250 from the assessed unimproved value of the land is made. This deduction is made only once in case of an owner of several estates.[4] Exempt are also in Western Australia conditional purchasers, for five years from the date of contract or date of survey, whichever is later. It is noteworthy, however, that this exemption does not apply to holders of more than 1000 acres of arable land, or more than 2500

[1] In South Australia absence from the state as well as from the Commonwealth suffices to constitute absenteeism. *Cf.* South Australia, 2 Edw. VII, No. 804, § 3; 4 Edw. VII, No. 861, § 7. *Cf.* Western Australia, 7 Edw. VII, No. 15, § 9.

[2] South Australia, 47 and 48 Vic., No. 323, §§ 8, 11. The payment of the land tax exempts the owner from the tax on income accruing from the land, except "so far as such income shall actually exceed £5 per centum per annum on the unimproved value of the land." *Ibid.*, § 12.

[3] Victoria, 1 Geo. V, No. 2284, §§ 6, 7.

[4] Western Australia, 7 Edw. VII, No. 15, § 11 (3).

acres of grazing land, or cultivable and grazing land together.[1] In Victoria, at the discretion of the Commissioner
of Taxes, a release from the tax wholly or in part may be
granted in case of serious hardship resulting from losses
by bush fires, drought, floods, or similar calamities.[2]

Other provisions to be noted are: (1) No deductions are
allowed in case of land subject to a mortgage.[3] (2) In case
of leaseholds, the owner is held liable for the tax. For
example, the South Australian Act provides that no contract or covenant should bind any person to pay the land
tax to the exoneration of any other person.[4] In Victoria,
the Commissioner is empowered to determine the amount
of tax payable by the owner and lessee, respectively, if in
the opinion of the Commissioner the interest in the land of
the legal owner is lessened by the covenants of the lease.[5]
(3) Life tenants and lessees of the Crown are deemed
owners of the fee-simple, and are therefore subject to the
tax. In such cases in computing the amount of tax account
is taken of the lessee's interest in the land. The determination of this interest, however, is often difficult and sometimes the method of computation is stipulated in the Act.
Thus, in Western Australia,[6] the unimproved value of
Crown leases, where the right of purchase is not given, is
fixed at the difference in value between the capitalized
rental under the lease and the capitalized rental if let
"under such reasonable conditions as a *bona fide* lessee
would require, assuming the actual improvements (if any)

---

[1] Western Australia, 7 Edw. VII, No. 15, § 11.

[2] Victoria, 1 Geo. V, No. 2284, § 89.

[3] In Victoria there is an exception to this provision in case of land
subject to a mortgage existing on September 30, 1910. If in that case
the land does not exceed £3000, an annual deduction from the land tax
is granted equal to one-fortieth part of the interest derived from that
proportion of the value of the mortgage as the unimproved value of the
land bears to its capital value (including improvements). *Ibid.*, § 50.

[4] South Australia, 57 and 58 Vic., No. 604, § 18.

[5] Victoria, 1 Geo. V, No. 2284, § 39.

[6] Western Australia, 7 Edw. VII, No. 15, § 2 (c).

had not been made " (the interest rate assumed to be five
per cent). (4) The attempt to penalize the owner of unimproved land is clearly shown in the Act of Western Australia which allows a rebate of one-half the tax to the owner
of improved land.[1] This provision necessitates a definition
of improved land which under that Act is as follows: (*a*)
agricultural land to be considered improved must have
improvements upon it equal to the value of one pound to
every acre of the land or equal to one-third of the unimproved value of the land; (*b*) urban land to be deemed
improved must have improvements on it equal to an
amount not less than one-third the unimproved value of
the land or equal to £50 per foot, etc.

§ 10. In addition to this outline of the chief provisions
of the land-tax Acts in Australia, a brief account of the historical development of the systems will be profitable. It
must not be assumed from the account in the preceding
section that the great uniformity of levy shown above always existed in the land-tax laws of the different states.
The laws have undergone great modification, especially
those of Victoria and Tasmania. Victoria was the first
of the colonies to enact a land-tax law; this was in 1877.[2]
But although its purpose was clearly the disintegration of
the large land holdings, the tax was not on the unimproved
value.[3] This is made evident from the provision that
owners of one or more landed estates — an estate being a
parcel of land of more than 640 acres valued at more than
£2500 — pay a tax at the rate of £1, 5*s*. for every £100 of
the capital value of such estate over and above the sum of
£2500.[4] It is significant that to be taxable the land had to

[1] Western Australia, 7 Edw. VII, No. 15, § 10.
[2] *Cf.* Victoria, 54 Vic., No. 1107 (Revised Statutes).
[3] The reason, however, cannot be said to have been ignorance of the
principle of the taxation of unimproved value for, as we mentioned above,
a tax on the unimproved value had been proposed in the Parliament of
Victoria as early as 1875. See *supra*, p. 24, and footnote.
[4] Victoria, 54 Vic., No. 1107, §§ 3, 4.

extend more than one square mile and to have a value
above £2500. That made practically all urban land, as well
as all land of the poorer holders, exempt from the land tax.

That the tax did not fall on the unimproved value of the
land was due to the peculiar and crude system of valuation provided for in the Act. The land was classified into
four categories according to its grazing capacity. Thus
land capable of carrying two or more sheep to the acre was
returned as first class, valued at £4 to the acre; land capable of carrying three sheep to two acres and less than two
sheep to the acre was valued at £3 to the acre; land capable of carrying one sheep to the acre and less than three
sheep to two acres was third class and valued at £2; and
land not capable of carrying one sheep to the acre was
valued at £1 per acre.[1] It was held that such a system
worked in the interest of the speculative holder who allowed his land to remain fallow, and that it acted as a discouragement to the grazing industry because it penalized
the more industrious graziers.[2] In spite of its ineffectiveness this $1\frac{1}{4}$ per cent tax on estates over 640 acres whose
value exceeded £2500 remained in force for about a quarter of a century, until the enactment of the Land Tax
Act, 1910,[3] which is modeled after the existing systems of
taxation on the unimproved value.

The land tax in Tasmania shows even more clearly a
development from (1) a part of the general property levied on the annual value, to (2) a realty tax levied on capital value, to (3) a tax on the unimproved value of the land
itself. The earliest charge on land was imposed in 1880
under the "Real and Personal Estate Duties Act." [4] The

---

[1] Victoria, 54 Vic., No. 1107, § 15.

[2] "The land tax meant to hit the larger holders of property, and it has
hit twice as hard the men of moderate means." The tax fell on industry.
Cf. The Australasian, April 2, 1881, p. 432.

[3] Victoria, 1 Geo. V, No. 2284.

[4] Cf. First Annual Report of the Commissioner of the Land Tax of the
Commonwealth of Australia (1912), p. 6.

rate of tax was 9d. in the pound on the annual value (rental) of all lands. Occupiers other than owners were made liable for the payment of the tax with power to recover from the owners. The value of mortgages was not exempt, but the mortgagors were empowered to recover from the mortgagees 9d. in the pound, calculated on the annual amount of interest paid. Persons in possession of Crown land under contract of purchase were liable according to the amount of purchase money actually paid by them.[1] In 1882 the rate of tax was reduced to 6d. in the pound, but was increased to 9d. again in 1885.

In 1888 [2] the basis of levy was changed from the annual to the capital value of landed property including improvements, the rate being $\frac{1}{2}d$. for every pound of value. This Act underwent much revision in its minor provisions; but in 1905 the proportional tax was replaced by a graduated tax levied on the capital value of real property.[3]

In 1909 a super-charge, an additional levy of one-fourth part of the tax collectible under the previous Act, was imposed.[4]

The change to the taxation on unimproved value took place in 1910. In the accompanying table is set forth a comparison of the graduated scales of rates charged under the Acts of 1905 and 1910, respectively.

It must be borne in mind in examining the table that, in 1905, the rate was on both land and improvements; in 1910, on the unimproved value. It will be noted that the rate is now more than double the rate under the Act of 1905, and that this increase falls most heavily on vacant land, without at the same time alleviating the burden on the improved land.

---

[1] Cf. First Annual Report of the Commissioner of the Land Tax of the Commonwealth of Australia (1912), p. 6.

[2] The Land Tax Act (1888), Tasmania, 52 Vic., No. 31.

[3] Cf. Tasmania, 59 Vic., No. 21, § 3; 5 Edw. VII, No. 4, §§ 8, 21.

[4] Tasmania, 9 Edw. VII, No. 10 (The Land Tax Super-Charge Act, 1909).

TABLE SHOWING THE RATES OF TAX IN TASMANIA
UNDER THE ACTS OF 1905 AND 1910[1]

Capital value			Rates of taxation	
			Land and improvements, 1905	Unimproved value 1910
	under	£2,500	$\frac{1}{2}d.$ in the pound	$1d.$ in the pound
£2,500 and	"	5,000	$\frac{1}{2}d.$ " " "	$1\frac{1}{4}d.$ " " "
5,000 "	"	15,000	$\frac{5}{8}d.$ " " "	$1\frac{1}{2}d.$ " " "
15,000 "	"	30,000	$\frac{3}{4}d.$ " " "	$1\frac{3}{4}d.$ " " "
30,000 "	"	40,000	$\frac{3}{4}d.$ " " "	$2d.$ " " "
40,000 "	"	50,000	$\frac{7}{8}d.$ " " "	$2d.$ " " "
50,000 "	"	80,000	$\frac{7}{8}d.$ " " "	$2\frac{1}{4}d.$ " " "
80,000 "	above		$1d.$ " " "	$2\frac{1}{2}d.$ " " "

Turning from the Tasmanian system to that in South
Australia, it is noteworthy that the land tax was from the
first levied here on the basis of the unimproved value. The
Act of 1884 imposed a tax of $\frac{1}{2}d.$ in the pound on the value
of the land.[2] An additional tax on estates exceeding £5000
and an absentee charge were levied in 1894.[3] Slight
changes in rate were made from time to time fluctuating
from $\frac{1}{2}d.$ to $\frac{3}{4}d.$ in the pound plus the super-charge and
absentee rate. The details of the rates have been epito-
mized as follows: [4]

1885–1894 ......$\frac{1}{2}d.$ in the pound on the unimproved value.
1895–1902 [5]......$\frac{1}{2}d.$ in the pound on the unimproved value, plus a fur-
        ther $\frac{1}{2}d.$ in the pound on land over £5000, plus
        absentee tax, 20 per cent extra.
1903 [6]......$\frac{3}{4}d.$ in the pound, plus a further $\frac{1}{2}d.$ additional above
        £5000; absentee tax as formerly.
1904 [7]......$\frac{1}{2}d.$ in the pound, plus $\frac{1}{2}d.$ extra above £5000, with
        absentee tax as formerly.

[1] Tasmania, 5 Edw. VII, No. 4, § 8; 1 Geo. V, No. 37, § 2.
[2] South Australia, 47 and 48 Vic., No. 323, §§ 8, 11.
[3] *Ibid.*, 57 and 58 Vic., No. 604.
[4] *Papers Bearing on Land Taxes*, etc. (Cd. 4750), 1909, p. 130.
[5] South Australia, 2 Edw. VII, No. 804.
[6] *Ibid.*, 3 Edw. VII, No. 838.   [7] *Ibid.*, 4 Edw. VII, No. 861.

1905 [1] ......¾d. in the pound, plus ¾d. extra above £5000, with the
        absentee tax, 20 per cent of total tax.
1906–1912 [2] ......½d. in the pound, plus ½d. extra above £5000, absen-
        tee tax 20 per cent of total.

Another revision made in the South Australian law was
with regard to the definition of absenteeism. Under the
Act of 1894 an absentee was any one who had been absent
for at least two years immediately prior to the levy of the
tax.[3] It was stipulated that when at least three-fifths of the
interest in a company which owns land, or when at least
three-fifths of the interest in any land is held by absentees
the land should be considered as owned by absentees; but
any non-absentee shareholder should be entitled to a re-
fund of the amount overpaid by him. The Act of 1902
and the subsequent Acts have revised this section, substituting for the period of two years, one of twelve months.

The last state in Australia to introduce direct taxation
and the tax on unimproved value of land was Western
Australia (1907).[4] The chief provisions of the Act modeled
on the other laws have already been reviewed.[5]

§ 11. The systems of local rating on unimproved value
in Australia and New Zealand lack the discriminatory
features of the state levies and reveal their purely fiscal
character. The following, from a report on the "Unimproved Land Value Taxation in Queensland," [6] contains what may be termed the inception and evolution
of the idea of exempting improvements from taxation as it

   [1] South Australia, 5 Edw. VII, No. 894.

   [2] *Ibid.*, 1 Geo. V, No. 1007.

   [3] "Except in the case of life assurance societies doing business in
South Australia on the mutual principle, or in cases in which the whole
of the income from the land is paid to or for public or charitable purposes
in the colony." *Cf.* South Australia, 57 and 58 Vic., No. 604, § 3.

   [4] Western Australia, 7 Edw. VII, No. 15 (*Land Tax and Income Tax
Assessment Act*, 1907).

   [5] See *supra*, § 9.

   [6] *Papers Relative to the Working of Taxation on the Unimproved Value
of Land in Queensland* (Cd. 3890), 1908, p. 20. Mr. Corrie, the author of
the report, was President of the Queensland Institute of Architects and
was for twenty-one years architect and valuer in Brisbane.

presented itself in the legislature in Queensland. It is a system "educed, as the gradual development of legislation proves, more or less subconsciously from the germ of the idea . . . that a premium should be held out, or at worst, no discouragement offered, to the improvement of the unexploited lands of a new country. It is a system . . . intended to provide for some reasonable advantage accruing to the land taxed." The conception, however, lay dormant until 1890,[1] when, for the purpose of meeting an emergency measure to relieve the consolidated revenue of the state government, the local authorities were empowered to levy rates on unimproved value.

The most significant characteristic of the Queensland system is that practically all the local revenue is raised from this source. All rates, general, special, and separate,[2] are levied on the unimproved value. The adoption of this system of rating is moreover obligatory. The general rates must not exceed $3d.$ in the pound; nor may they be less than $\frac{1}{2}d.$ in the pound. The Act provides, furthermore, that the total amount of special rates (excluding all separate rates) shall not exceed $3d.$ in the pound.[3] Certain special rates, for example, Special Water Rate, Special Health Rate, Special Cleansing Rate, Special Loan Rate, may be levied on the basis of the unimproved value of the land, or upon some other basis so that the burden will be distributed according to the benefit rendered.[4] The minimum at which any separate portion of ratable land shall

[1] Mr. Corrie traces the beginning of the exclusion of improvements from taxation to the "Divisional Boards Act of 1879." *Cf. Papers Relative to the Working of Taxation,* etc., pp. 5 *ff.*

[2] Special rates are levied to defray the cost of local improvements and utilities and fall on all the land of the community; a separate rate is one levied for a special benefit of some particular part of the locality and the tax falls on that section alone. A special rate may also be a separate rate, i.e., a "special assessment" but applicable to all the land. Queensland, 54 Vic., No. 24; 1 Edw. VII, No. 27; 2 Edw. VII, No. 19.

[3] Queensland, 2 Edw. VII, No. 19, §§ 209–23. Under the Act of 1890 (54 Vic., No. 24, § 29) the maximum rate was $2d.$ for municipalities.

[4] *Ibid.,* §§ 216–22.

be valued is £30 per acre in case of town and £20 in case of shire land; but in case the same person is the owner of two or more parcels of unoccupied land adjoining each other, they shall be valued as one parcel.[1]

Unique is the system of taxing public utilities corporations by means of the land tax. Private companies operating tramways, gas mains, electric lines, hydraulic mains, are taxed on the land or public roads utilized by them; but the basis of taxation is not the value of the land. For example, for the operation of tramways a tax of £1 10s. on every £100 of the gross earnings of the vehicles of the company running upon the lines is charged. In case the lines extend over into another area the tax is made proportionate to the mileage of the route under each local authority.[2]

In considering the operation of this single tax on land for local purposes, it must be remembered that the municipalities in Queensland exercise fewer functions of government than the municipalities of our country for example. Poor relief, orphanages, education, public libraries, police, criminal prosecutions and prisons, hospitals and asylums, death registration and like functions, are under state jurisdiction, paid for out of the consolidated revenue fund of the state government.[3] It is important to note, on the other hand, that the local governments of Queensland receive but a trifling "endowment" from the state government[4] as compared with the local governments in the other Australian states.

§ 12. The "Rating on Unimproved Value Act" which

[1] Queensland, 2 Edw. VII, No. 19, § 195 (6, 7).

[2] *Ibid.*, §§ 196 *ff.* It is interesting to read the following proviso: "The earnings from the running of special vehicles on any car route for the conveniences of work-people may, at the discretion of the Local Authority, be exempted from the provisions of this section, if the rate charged per passenger does not exceed ½d. per mile."

[3] *Papers Relative to the Working of Taxation on the Unimproved Value of Land in Queensland* (Cd. 3890), 1908, p. 14.

[4] See *infra*, chapter III, § 9.

passed the General Assembly of New Zealand [1] in 1896 differed from the Queensland Act chiefly in this respect; it extended to the counties, municipalities, and other local authorities the *option* of rating on the unimproved value of the land, thus making optional what the Queensland Act had made obligatory. The New Zealand measure provides for the adoption of the system by a vote of the ratepayers. The signatures of at least fifteen per cent [2] of the ratepayers are required to petition for a vote, and a majority of all the votes is necessary to institute the new measure.[3] A rescinding proposal may be carried or rejected in the same manner of voting as for adopting the proposal. A proposal to rescind may only be demanded, however, after the new rating system has been at least three years in operation. Should the rescinding proposal be carried, the old method of rating is again put into effect. After the institution of one system a rescinding proposal may not be submitted until three years have elapsed, nor may a vote be taken whether to rescind or to adopt oftener than once in three years.[4]

How have the local authorities in New Zealand responded to this privilege? Until 1914, 138 local authorities had taken a poll on the proposal to rate on unimproved value.[5] In 106 of these the measure was carried on the first poll. In 8 boroughs the proposal was rejected on the first vote, but was ultimately carried. Besides num-

[1] New Zealand, 1896, No. 5. A similar bill had been rejected several years before. In 1893, such a proposal had passed the house, but met defeat in the Legislative Council. New Zealand, *Parl. Debates* (1896), vol. xcii, p. 631.

[2] The percentage varies with the number of ratepayers in the community. It is twenty-five per cent when the roll of names does not exceed 100; twenty per cent when it does not exceed 300. New Zealand, 1896, No. 5, § 5.

[3] As amended in Act of 1900, No. 18, § 2.

[4] New Zealand, 1896, No. 5, §§ 10, 11.

[5] *Statistics of the Dominion of New Zealand*, Printed by Authority (Wellington, Mackay), 1911, pp. 659–83; *Statistics of the Dominion of New Zealand* (1913), vol. iv, pp. 63–64.

erous smaller local bodies, 27 counties, 56 boroughs and
2 cities now rate on land value.[1] In 1913, the total number
of counties in New Zealand was 124, of boroughs 115,
showing that the new system is more prevalent in the
boroughs. In nine cases the attempts to rescind the measure were rejected. In only one locality, in North-East
Valley, was the proposal to rescind carried.[2] The two
cities now rating on unimproved value are the largest in
New Zealand, Wellington with a population of about
sixty-five thousand, and Christchurch with about fifty-
five thousand.

As regards the rate of levy, the Act merely provides
that, where prior to the adoption of rating on unimproved
value a limit of rating-power was imposed upon the local
authority, the new rate should be such as to yield a revenue equivalent to that under the previous system. The
Act stipulates that the rate of 1s. on annual (rental) value
shall be deemed equivalent to $\frac{3}{4}d$. of the capital value.[3]
Until 1911 the option of rating on unimproved value did
not apply to water rates, gas rates, electric light rates,
sewage rates, or hospital and charitable rates. Upon the
vote of the ratepayers these rates may now be levied on
the unimproved value.[4]

The provisions of the South Australian Act [5] are similar
to those of the New Zealand Act. The adoption of rating
on the basis of unimproved value is made optional for any
municipality. A poll on the question may be taken upon
the petition of at least one-half the number of ratepayers.[6]
The rescission of such a proposal, after the system has been

[1] *Statistics of the Dominion of New Zealand, supra.*

[2] *New Zealand, Statistics of the Dominion* (1913), vol. IV, pp. 63–64.
Cf. also *Papers Relative to the Working of Taxation*, etc. (Cd. 3191), 1906,
pp. 25 *ff.*; also (Cd. 4750), 1909, pp. 78, 135.

[3] As amended in *The Rating on Unimproved Value Amendment Act*,
1903, No. 56, § 2 (*b*); New Zealand, 1906, No. 5, § 15.

[4] New Zealand, 1896, No. 5, § 20; also 1911 (2 Geo. V), No. 11,
§ 2.

[5] South Australia, 56 and 57 Vic., No. 573.   [6] *Ibid.*, § 11.

adopted and in operation two or more years, is made possible upon a vote of at least one-half the number of ratepayers.[1]

§ 13. The other Australian state whose experience with
rating on land value offers interesting study is New
South Wales. As pointed out before,[2] a land tax for state
purposes had been in force in New South Wales since 1895.
The movement to extend the taxing powers of the local
authorities was the outgrowth of the larger scheme of local
government. The chief purpose of the "Local Government (Shires) Act of 1905"[3] and of the "Local Government Extension Act of 1906"[4] was the organization of
the shires and municipalities in order to relieve the state
government from some of its functions. As the finances
of the state government were in a prosperous condition
and there was a surplus on hand,[5] the suspension of the
state land tax in favor of the newly created shires and
municipalities was no hardship to the state government.
Accordingly, the above-mentioned Acts provided for the
rating on unimproved value by the local authorities and
for the suspension of the land tax for state purposes as
soon as the shire or municipality had levied the first general rate under the new law.[6]

The system of local rating in New South Wales, it is
noteworthy, is intermediate between those in Queensland
and New Zealand. In respect to general rates the tax is
obligatory as in Queensland; in respect to special and other

---

[1] South Australia, 56 and 57 Vic., No. 573, §§ 30, 31.

[2] See *supra*, p. 41 footnote; New South Wales, 59 Vic., No. 15. *The
Land and Income Tax Assessment Act of 1895* provided for a tax of 1d. in
the pound of the unimproved value. An exemption of £240 (which in
the case of an owner of more estates than one was made only once) was
allowed.

[3] New South Wales, Act No. 33, 1905.   [4] *Ibid.* 40, 1906.

[5] *The Australasian*, August 5, 1905, p. 325; September 15, 1906,
p. 629.

[6] *Cf.* New South Wales, Act 33, 1905, § 33 (2); Act 40, 1906, § 65; Act
16, 1906: Parts XVIII, XIX, XX, XXI, XXII.

rates it is optional as in New Zealand. The levy of a general rate, which is compulsory, shall not be less than 1*d*. in the pound, nor more than 2*d*. in the pound in the case of shires; in the case of municipalities (Sydney excepted) the minimum rate shall be 1*d*. in the pound; while the maximum shall yield a sum not exceeding that yielded by a rate of 2*d*. in the pound on the unimproved capital value plus 1*s*. 6*d*. in the pound on the assessed annual value.[1] Beside an additional general rate which is optional with the municipality, special, local,[2] and loan rates may, at the option of the Council, be levied on the unimproved value.

The following summary shows briefly which rates under the New South Wales system are compulsory, which optional, and the manner in which the special rates may be instituted: [3]

"(*a*) Shire general rates must be only on the unimproved capital value of land.

"(*b*) Municipal general rates must be only on the unimproved capital value of land.

"(*c*) Municipal additional rates may be either on the unimproved capital value or on the improved capital value at the option of the Council subject to the right of the ratepayers to demand a poll of ratepayers on the question.

"(*d*) Both shire and municipal special, local, or loan rates may be either on the unimproved or improved capital value subject to the right to demand a poll as above."

The City of Sydney, the metropolis of New South Wales, was not subject to the rating provisions of 1906, because it is under a separate constitution and government. Until

---

[1] "The assessed annual value of ratable land shall be nine-tenths of the fair average rental of such land with the improvements (if any) thereon: provided that such assessed annual value shall not be less than 5 per cent of the unimproved capital value whether improved or unimproved." Act 16, 1906, § 134; also §§ 150, 151.

[2] Local rate is a "special assessment" rate. *Ibid.*, §§ 153–58.

[3] *Papers Relative to the Working of Taxation of the Unimproved Value of Land in New South Wales* (Cd. 3761), 1907, p. 5.

1908, all rates in Sydney were levied on the annual rental of real property. But under the "Sydney Corporation (Amendment) Act, 1908" the system of rating on the changed basis was inaugurated.[1] Accordingly, the council is authorized to levy a general rate on the unimproved value in addition to any rate already in force. That is, part or all of the revenue of Sydney may now be raised by the new method.[2] The total amount leviable shall not exceed the amount which would be yielded by a rate of 3*d*. in the pound on the unimproved capital value and 2*s*. in the pound on the average annual value taken together, of all the ratable property in the city. The general rate on unimproved value shall not be less than 1*d*. in the pound.

Thus it is evident that the major portion of the local revenue in New South Wales which is contributed by the general rates is raised by the tax on unimproved value. Except for the alienated lands within the Western Division of the state (not yet included under shire and municipality areas),[3] the state land tax stands suspended, and the "endowments" to the local governments have been reduced.

§ 14. Besides the state and local land taxes, the federal tax remains to be analyzed. In 1910, the Governor-General of the Commonwealth of Australia in his message to the Houses of Parliament then assembled proposed the taxation of land on its unimproved value in the interest of closer settlement.[4] The proposal had been in the platform of the Labor Party almost since the federation of the states in 1901.[5] The occasion, namely, the fiscal need, was, however, lacking. But when the "Labor Parliament" with a

[1] New South Wales, Act No. 27, 1908. "An Act to provide for levying rates on the unimproved value of land in the City of Sydney," etc., Part II.

[2] *Ibid.*, § 4.

[3] *The First Annual Report of the Commissioner of Land Tax of the Commonwealth of Australia* (1912), p. 4.

[4] Commonwealth of Australia, *Parl. Debates*, vol. LV (1910), p. 8.

[5] *The Australasian*, February 24, 1906, p. 455; April 3, 1909, p. 849, and elsewhere.

majority in both Houses came into power, revenue for the federal pension system,[1] as well as the encouragement of denser settlement, was made the excuse. There is no question, however, that the ulterior motive in the minds of the legislators and their constituents was the subdivision of the large estates, especially those belonging to absentees.[2]

This purpose is apparent from the provisions of the Act itself. Thus by far the most important clauses of the "Land Tax Assessment Act, 1910"[3] are those which distinguish between the rate of tax on absentee and that on non-absentee holdings and which exempt £5000 value in case of the latter holdings. "The taxable value of all the land owned by a person is —

"(a) in the case of an absentee . . . the total sum of the unimproved value of each parcel of land;

"(b) in the case of an owner not an absentee . . . the balance of the total sum of the unimproved value of each parcel of the land, after deducting the sum of £5000. Every part of a holding which is separately held by any occupier, tenant, lessee, or owner, is deemed to be a separate parcel."[4]

An absentee is one who does not reside in Australia or in a territory under the authority of the Commonwealth, and the word is defined to include a person who is absent from Australia at the time of the assessment or who has been absent more than half of the period of twelve months

[1] *The Australasian*, February 24, 1906, p. 455 ; April 3, 1909, p. 849, and elsewhere.

[2] Commonwealth of Australia, *Parl. Debates* (1910), vol. LV, pp. 16, 18, 64, 140, 144, *et passim*. "Our policy is to break up the big estates and to make room for immigrants. . . . We are desirous of breaking up these huge estates because to the people this wealth belongs," etc.

[3] Commonwealth of Australia, Nos. 21 and 22 of 1910, § 11.

[4] The High Court has interpreted this to mean that an owner may be taxed on the aggregate unimproved value of the parcels of land which he holds less the sum of £5000. *Cf. First Annual Report of the Commissioner of Land Tax of the Commonwealth of Australia* (1912), p. 14.

immediately preceding the assessment.[1] Every absentee, furthermore, must be represented by some person in Australia. In case there is no authorized agent the person who transmits income to the owner is held liable for the tax. The public officer of the company [2] is held to be the agent of an absentee shareholder who is subject to the land tax.

In accordance with the intention of the law to hold all persons who derive income from land of taxable value liable as owners, some specifications with regard to leaseholds, corporation holdings, and mortgaged land had to be made. So with respect to leaseholds, if they antedate the Act, the lessee pays the tax on the difference between the capitalized value of the rent paid by him and the actual unimproved capital value of the estate.[3] If his rent be four and one-half per cent or more of the unimproved capital value, he is not liable for the tax, the assumption being that four and one-half per cent (the average earning rate of mortgages) is a fair rental.[4] In case of a leasehold acquired since the date of the Act, the lessee is deemed the owner, although liable only to an amount proportionate to his interest in the land.[5] In order to make absentee shareholders liable, the company is required to furnish the names of the absentee shareholders and of the other shareholders

---

[1] Commonwealth of Australia, 1910, No. 22, § 3.

[2] *First Annual Report of the Commissioner of Land Tax*, etc. (1912), p. 8.

[3] In computing the unimproved value of the lessee's interest in the land, the unexpired term of the lease must be taken into account.

[4] "The assumption appears reasonable that any earning value of a property in excess of $4\frac{1}{2}$ per cent (average earning rate of mortgages) is attributable either to the improvements or the effective use made of them by the person in occupation." *Ibid.*

[5] Commonwealth of Australia, 1910, No. 22, § 27. As the commissioner of the land tax points out, the effect of this provision is that the owner of an estate leased by him to another may, in his returns, omit the inclusion of this estate with any other estates which he owns, thus evading the payment of a higher rate that he otherwise would be liable for. *Cf. First Annual Report of the Commissioner of Land Tax*, etc. (1912), p. 15.

who own more than £5000 worth of land, including other land held by them, for the amount of taxable estate, and the rate of tax varies with the kind of ownership, whether absentee or non-absentee. The practice of the commissioner of the land tax [1] is "to ascertain the unimproved value of that part of a company's land corresponding to a single share, then to require the company to supply the department merely with the names of shareholders who own shares to the number deemed worth the trouble of assessment." The company is not regarded as an absentee; hence it is taxable only when the estate owned by it is valued at more than £5000. With respect to mortgages, no deduction from the unimproved value of the land is allowed. The mortgagor is deemed the primary taxpayer except in case of bankruptcy when the mortgagee comes in possession. [2]

In accordance with the provisions of the Act, the Federal Parliament fixed the following rates: [3] (a) In case of an owner not an absentee an exemption of £5000 is allowed, above which value the rate of the tax is 1d. on the first pound of excess, increasing at a uniform rate, so that the tax is equal to an average rate of 1½d. in the pound on an estate having a taxable value of £15,000, 2d. in the pound when the taxable value is £30,000, 2½d. in the pound when it is £45,000, 3d. in the pound when it is £60,000, and 3½d. in the pound when it is £75,000. In excess of £75,000 the rate of tax is 6d. in the pound.

(b) In case of an absentee no exemption is allowed; and the rate of tax is 1d. in the pound on the first £5000, 2d. on the first pound above £5000, the rate increasing after

---

[1] *First Annual Report of the Commissioner of Land Tax, etc.* (1912), p. 9.

[2] Commonwealth of Australia, 1910, No. 22, § 31.

[3] The same schedules were readopted by the Parliament of 1911 and 1912. *Cf.* Commonwealth of Australia, 1911, No. 12, and 1912, No. 37. Toward the end of the session in 1914 the rate of the federal land tax was increased. *Cf. The Australian Worker,* January 14, 1915.

that uniformly, so that it equals an average rate of $2\frac{1}{2}d$. in the pound on the excess over £5000 when the taxable value is £20,000, 3d. in the pound when it is £35,000, $3\frac{1}{2}d$. in the pound when £50,000, 4d. in the pound when £65,000, and $4\frac{1}{2}d$. in the pound when £80,000. When the taxable value is in excess of £80,000, the rate of tax is 7d. in the pound.

Reduced to tabular form these rates are as follows: [1]

RATES OF TAX INCREASING WITH EVERY POUND OF TAXABLE VALUE

Non-absentee estate	*Absentee estate*
£5,001 to £15,000, 1d. to $1\frac{1}{2}d$. 15,000 " 30,000, $1\frac{1}{2}d$. " 2d. 30,000 " 45,000, 2d. " $2\frac{1}{2}d$. 45,000 " 60,000, $2\frac{1}{2}d$. " 3d. 60,000 " 75,000, 3d. " $3\frac{1}{2}d$. in excess of 75,000, 6d.	£5,000 or less, 1d. 5,001 to £20,000, 2d. to $2\frac{1}{2}d$. 20,000 " 35,000, $2\frac{1}{2}d$. " 3d. 35,000 " 50,000, 3d. " $3\frac{1}{2}d$. 50,000 " 65,000, $3\frac{1}{2}d$. " 4d. 65,000 " 80,000, 4d. " $4\frac{1}{2}d$. in excess of 80,000, 7d.

§ 15. Summary: Through all the variety of legislation thus far examined there run a few threads of agreement corroborating the general analysis of the purpose of the land taxes. The close resemblance which is apparent between the federal and the state taxes is evident also between the different local systems. The mode of assessment and scales of rates of the state and federal systems, moreover, are distinctly differentiated from those of the local taxes. The progressive scale of rates, the exemption of smaller

[1] It must be borne in mind that the rate changes with every excess pound of taxable value. The formulæ to compute the rate on taxable value below £75,000 and £80,000, respectively, are as follows: in case of non-absentee: Rate $= 1$ plus $\dfrac{V}{30,000}d$; in case of an absentee estate: Rate $= 2$ plus $\dfrac{E}{30,000}d$. V $=$ the taxable value in pounds; E $=$ the excess of taxable value over £5000, in pounds. *Cf.* Commonwealth of Australia, 1910, No. 21, Schedules.

estates from the tax, the distinction drawn between the absentee and the resident holder unmistakably reveal the purpose of the taxes levied by the state and federal governments. On the other hand, the uniform general rate of levy, from which practically no landowner is exempt, the abolition of other taxes, and the ordinary restrictions and conditions laid down by the superior civic jurisdiction, the state government, all point to the fiscal character of the local systems of rating on the unimproved value. The discriminatory feature of the state and federal land taxes is wholly lacking in the local rates. This does not mean that the latter method of raising revenue does not propose to penalize the owner of idle land and to make the absentee owner aid in bearing the burden of the expenditures which tend to make his land more valuable. At the same time the local rating systems on unimproved value are proof that the taxation of land value must commend itself to newly settled communities where land constitutes the chief source of wealth and tends to appreciate in value.

CHAPTER III

§ 1. FROM the very nature of the tax on the unimproved value of land, the importance of accurate valuation of the land apart from structures and other improvements is obvious; yet the difficulty implied in finding the value of the site itself, of the "original and indestructible powers of the soil," seems well nigh insuperable. Indeed, were the attempt made by the assessors to determine precisely the value added to the land by virtue of every improvement ever made thereon, the task would be a futile one and the tax would be found impracticable. How, then, is the difficulty of separate assessment of land and improvements solved, if at all? For practical purposes the intricacies and difficulties theoretically involved in the ascertainment of the actual site value are disregarded in valuing the land minus the improvements. A mean has been struck and a standard adopted which makes the system of separate valuation practicable for assessment purposes. In fact, for other than taxing purposes, valuers have often found it expedient to ascertain the value of the land separately from that of the improvements.

But, granting the insuperable difficulty implied in separate valuation, the importance of an approximately accurate appraisal of the land cannot be overemphasized in reference to a tax whose purpose it is to appropriate part of the unearned increment and part of the ever-increasing land value. Therefore, the experience with valuation of property in Australasia deserves careful consideration.

It is at first somewhat disappointing to discover that no strictly scientific system of land valuation has been evolved in Australasia after decades of practice with land taxation.

That is, instead of applying objectively certain scientific principles or rules of valuation governing land value, such as have originated in this country,[1] the taxpayers' returns are in part relied upon in a few of the Australian states, while in all the states as well as in New Zealand, revaluation is irregular and infrequent. The fact is, however, that the empirical methods of land valuation seem to work satisfactorily there and to present few of the difficulties of unequal assessments encountered in the United States. The explanation lies in the more efficient administration of the valuation departments in the colonies.

In Australasia the chief resources of the tax commissioners in valuation and in verifying the self-assessed returns of the taxpayer are: (1) the records of sale, a most reliable check; (2) publicity, for the assessment book is everywhere open to inspection; (3) disinterested assessors; and (4) the system of government loans on land on the basis of the valuation.[2]

Altogether, therefore, judging from the official reports we conclude that the system meets with general approval and satisfaction. The reason seems to lie in the fact that uniformity, if not accuracy, is attained, the latter depending upon the efficiency of the particular administrative department.

§ 2. Turning to the administration of the land tax, we find that the tax Acts lay down certain regulations regarding the organization of the department, and the methods of assessment and collection of the tax. The chief guidance of the assessor lies in the definitions in these Acts. The fact that most of the taxes were modeled after antecedent ones, after those of the New Zealand system especially, will render the description of their administration in the

[1] For example, the Somers System or the Neill-Hoffman Rule. See *infra*, chapter VII, §§ 12, 13, 14.

[2] It is said that since the government loan system came into vogue, the assessed value of land has in almost all cases exceeded the value formerly entered on the roll.

several states less complex. Speaking generally, the state
land taxes are under the direction of the Commissioner of
Taxes [1] who in all cases is the appointee of the State Governor. The Commissioner of the Commonwealth Land
Tax is the appointee of the Governor-General. The chief
valuers, district valuers, and in some cases such assessors
as may be deemed necessary in the administration of the
tax, are likewise, with few exceptions,[2] appointed by the
respective Governors of the States, Dominion, or Commonwealth.[3] Under the local systems the council generally
appoints all the assessors. The advantages of appointed
assessors responsible to one chief as compared with elected
assessors responsible to the constituents whose property
they value are well recognized. Moreover, the Governors
are the appointed representatives of the Crown (although
they act with the advice of the Executive Council) [4] so
that the tax officials are further removed from party politics. The valuers and assessors, then, work in accordance
with the system laid down by statutory enactment, are
responsible to the government alone and are disinterested
as to the value set upon the land.[5] Some of the statutes

[1] In Victoria there are three Commissioners of Taxes appointed by the
Governor-in-Council (i.e., with the advice of the Executive Council, the
Ministry). *Cf.* No. 1107, 1890, § 10; 1 Geo. V, No. 2284, § 4. In Tasmania the appointment is subject to the "Public Service Act." *Cf.* Tasmania, 2 Geo. V, No. 47, §§ 8, 9.

[2] Since 1896 the valuation department in New Zealand has been a
distinct institution, and separated from the tax and assessment department. The Valuer-General is assisted by the district valuers, who with
their assistant valuers carry on the actual work of valuation and who are
in New Zealand appointed by the Public Service Commissioner. Local
valuers may be temporarily employed by the Valuer-General. The district valuer, however, must approve of the valuation of the local valuer.
The valuer is employed at a yearly salary and is not permitted to undertake any valuation or assessment for payment by an individual except
with the written consent of the Valuer-General. *New Zealand Official Year
Book* (1913), p. 844.

[3] *Cf.* South Australia, 47 and 48 Vic., No. 323, §§ 28, 29; Western
Australia, 7 Edw. VII, No. 15, § 3; Tasmania, No. 47, 1911, §§ 8, 9.

[4] The Executive Council consists of the Ministry of the party in power.

[5] *Papers Bearing on Land Taxes*, etc. (Cd. 4750), 1900, pp. 146–47.

expressly stipulate that the valuers employed shall be expert, and shall have a knowledge of the general value of the property in the locality.[1] In New Zealand a distinct department, called the Valuation of Land Department, has been created, at the head of which is the Valuer-General. A similar department has been established by the central government of Australia.

From the standpoint of efficiency and economy, it is interesting to compare the centralized valuation system in New Zealand with the duplicated valuations by the different civic authorities in Australia. Before 1896 valuations of land in New Zealand were made separately by the two (central and local) taxing authorities as well as by other departments of government [2] and no uniformity of method existed. The state taxing jurisdiction employed a small staff of valuers whenever a new valuation seemed desirable, while the local bodies and other departments, e.g., the loan department, devised their own methods, and employed their own valuers. At present, the Valuation of Land Department under state jurisdiction supplies the valuation data for all purposes, state, local and even private. In Australia this unification has not yet been attempted. Although the state Acts provide for coöperation,

---

[1] For example, "the district valuers shall be persons of reputed knowledge of land values and improvement values," or "Assessors for the purposes of this Act shall so far as practicable be persons having a local knowledge of the value of land and of improvement values." Tasmania, 9 Edw. VII, No. 7, § 7; Victoria, 1 Geo. V, No. 2284, § 5; New South Wales, No. 16, 1906, § 137.

[2] Some purposes for which the District Valuation Roll is used are: —
(a) Advances and investments on mortgage of land by or on behalf of the New Zealand State-guaranteed Advances Office, the Public Trust Office, the Government Insurance Department, the Post Office, the Commissioner of Public Debts Sinking Fund Office.
(b) Stamp duties, etc.
(c) Claimants or Pensioners under Old-age Pensions Act.
(d) Board of Land Purchase Commissioners, etc.
(e) Maori Land Board and Native Land Court.
(f) Crown renewable leases.

New Zealand Official Year Book (1913), p. 852.

authorizing the use of the local assessment rolls and other records, and although the Commonwealth Land Tax Department "supplies free of cost to state governments and municipalities information as to the improved and unimproved values returned by landowners" [1] and is authorized in turn to seek information from any subordinate government division, a taxpayer in Australia may be called upon to make returns to all three authorities, local, state, and federal. And because of differences in definition, in law, and in method, no uniformity as regards valuation is possible.

The valuer is supplied with data found in the Land Transfer and Deeds Registry Office and with other evidence affecting the value of the land. From these and other information which he gathers he estimates the unimproved value, the value of the improvements, and the total or capital value of the land. For the purpose of obtaining the needed information the commissioners and valuers are empowered to inspect any documents, such as records of sales, pertaining to the value of the land. They may obtain detailed reports from local valuers, and may inspect the land and elicit any information that they may deem necessary. [2] From the returns of the taxpayer, supplemented by information from other available sources, the assessment book is prepared. [3] The following

[1] *First Annual Report of the Commissioner of Land Tax of the Commonwealth of Australia* (1912), p. 12. "Negotiations are in progress with the State Governments with the view to obtaining regular statements of transactions relating to transfers of land." *Ibid.*, p. 12. In the new "Rating on Unimproved Values Act" of 1914, the Victorian (state) land tax assessment roll is to be used for local rates. *Cf.* Victoria, 4 Geo. V, No. 2478.

[2] "Every classifier appointed under this Act shall for the purpose of executing his duties under this Act have power to enter at all reasonable hours in the daytime into and upon any land and do such matters and things thereon as may be reasonably necessary and may put to any person in occupation or charge of any land . . . any questions which may be necessary," etc. Victoria, 1890, No. 1107, § 13.

[3] In Victoria this book is known as the Land Tax Register, 1890, No. 1107, § 31.

are the usual particulars recorded on the assessment roll: [1]

1. A short description of, or reference to the land assessed,
2. The actual value of the land assessed,
3. The unimproved value of the land assessed,
4. The amount of land tax,
5. The names and description of the taxpayers in respect of the land assessment, so far as such names and descriptions can be readily ascertained.

In general the assessment book contains both the improved and unimproved value of the land in separate columns.[2] Both South Australia and Western Australia provide for additional assessment books to be prepared annually. These, called in South Australia the Additional Land Tax Register and the Absentee Land Tax Register, contain the assessments upon which the additional and absentee taxes are paid.[3] The commissioner is empowered to make any alterations in the assessment, if he is of the opinion that it is not correct. The taxpayer is notified of the amount of assessment and the assessment book is then made accessible for inspection. This feature of publicity is of great importance in case of local assessment books, since it enables the ratepayers to compare their own assessments with those of their neighbors.

Should the owner or taxpayer dissent from the assessed value of the land recorded on the assessment roll, he may have recourse to the courts provided for in the Acts. These courts, known by different names in the several

---

[1] *South Australia*, 47 and 48 Vic., No. 323, § 37.

[2] The Tasmanian statute requires the following particulars to be recorded: (1) consecutive number; (2) description; (3) situation; (4) name of owner; (5) name of occupier; (6) area; (7) value of improvements; (8) unimproved value; (9) capital value. Tasmania, 9 Edw. VII, No. 7, § 11.

[3] South Australia, 57 and 58 Vic., No. 604, § 6; Western Australia, 7 Edw. VII, No. 15, § 34.

states,[1] are specially created courts of appeal, the judges of which are appointed by the Governors,[2] as are the tax commissioners. The Victorian statute, for example, requires the court to consist of three members, one of whom shall be a Judge of County Courts, or a Police Magistrate, while the other two shall be persons possessing a knowledge of the value of land and improvements.[3] This court is empowered to summon witnesses and to select a convenient place for its sittings. Except on questions of law, the decisions of the court of appeal are final. When the point at issue is a purely legal one, however, an appeal to the Supreme Court is possible. In New Zealand, indeed, an appeal to the Supreme Court may be made even on a question of fact, if the judge of the Magistrate's Court is satisfied that the amount of tax *bona fide* in dispute between the objector and the commissioner exceeds £200.[4]

§ 3. More important than the procedure of assessment discussed above is the question of accurate valuation of the land. With regard to the frequency of appraisal no uniformity exists among the several states. The Local Government Act of New South Wales provides for annual valuations,[5] while in Sydney the law provides for one valuation at least every five years.[6] Annual returns are made in New Zealand [7] but actual valuations of the land are in-

[1] In Victoria, called the Assessment Court; in Western Australia, Tasmania, and New South Wales, the Court of Review; in Queensland, the Valuation Court.

[2] In New Zealand, one member of the Assessment Court may be appointed by one or more local authorities of the district whose roll is under dispute, but the appointee must not be a member of those local bodies. *New Zealand Official Year Book* (1913), p. 854.

[3] Victoria, 1 Geo. V, No. 2284, § 23.

[4] New Zealand, 3 Geo. V, No. 10, § 24.

[5] New South Wales, No. 16, 1906, § 135.

[6] *Ibid.*, No. 27, 1908, § 6. The now suspended law in New South Wales (1895) provided for quinquennial valuations of the land and annual valuations of income.

[7] In New Zealand no general valuations of land have been made since 1897, the practice being to have portions of the Dominion revalued from time to time. *New Zealand Official Year Book* (1913), p. 858.

frequent, while in Queensland and South Australia valuations are triennial. The latter state in 1902 amended the provision for quinquennial valuations.[1] But in accordance with the provisions elsewhere noted,[2] additional valuations for the absentee tax and for the additional rates must be made annually in South Australia. In the other states valuations take place at the discretion of the commissioner, although in Victoria two years at least must have elapsed between general valuations.[3] The Commonwealth Act authorizes the commissioner, "if, as, and when he thinks fit," to cause valuation of any land to be made.[4] The commissioners of Victoria will make a valuation for public departments at their request, and for owners also, provided the latter pay the fee of the valuer.[5]

In providing specifically for returns by the taxpayer, instead of for an objective appraisal of all the land, i.e., *in rem*, some of the states have retained the antiquated method of land assessment. That this method facilitates inaccuracies and inequalities in assessment among the different states and that it allows personal influences to enter, is unquestioned. True, the valuers employ certain checks [6] against undervaluations; nevertheless, the system is unscientific and does not prevent inaccuracies. A very important provision to check gross undervaluation is that by which the government reserves the right to purchase from the owner at the assessed valuation when the latter is dissatisfied with the commissioner's estimate. Unquestionably under the New Zealand and the Commonwealth Acts which provide for such acquisition, the owner is deterred from undervaluing his estate and from appealing from the commissioner's estimate, lest the government

---

[1] *Cf.* South Australia, 47 and 48 Vic., No. 323, § 36, and 2 Edw. VII, No. 782, § 3.

[2] See *supra*, chapter II, § 10, chapter III, § 2.

[3] Victoria, 1 Geo. V, No. 2284, § 15.

[4] Commonwealth of Australia, 1910, No. 22, § 17.

[5] Victoria, 1 Geo. V, No. 2284, § 72.   [6] See *supra*, § 1.

offer to purchase the land. In case of an appeal by the owner, "if the Justice (1) is satisfied that the owner has understated the unimproved value of the land to the extent of twenty-five per cent or more, and (2) is not satisfied that the undervaluation was not made with a view of evading taxation, he shall make the declaration applied for," namely, to purchase the land on behalf of the commissioner.[1] Under the Commonwealth Act the priority of purchase is allowed the state in which the land in question is situated. In New Zealand also the owner has the option of accepting the higher value or of selling the land to the government at that value, just as the government retains the right of purchasing the land in case of an undervaluation by the owner. For example, if the appeal of the owner against the assessment fails to be sustained by the assessment court, the owner may "within fourteen days of the hearing, require the Valuer-General either to reduce to the value which he considers to be the fair selling value, or else, to purchase the property *at that value*." [2] On the other hand, the Department, regardless of the decision of the assessment court, may offer to purchase the property if the owner refuses to accept the estimate of the valuer. As an alternative another course of action is open to the owner. He may ask for a revaluation of his land, which is granted provided he pays the fee for such a valuation. But in this case, if the last value fails to tally with the previous one, regardless whether it is more or less than the first, the last appraisal is substituted on the roll as the correct value.

§ 4. The considerations discussed in the preceding sections are, however, incidental details compared with the fundamental problem of ascertaining an accurate valuation of the site apart from all the improvements upon it. For this purpose the chief guides of the assessor are the

---

[1] Commonwealth of Australia, 1910, No. 22, § 48.
[2] *Papers Bearing on Land Taxes*, etc. (Cd. 4750), p. 155.

definitions of "capital value," "improvements," "value of improvements," and "unimproved value," the definitions embodied in the Acts.

"Capital value," by which is always understood the improved capital value of land, means "the sum which the owner's estate or interest therein, if unencumbered by any mortgage or other charge thereon, might be expected to realize at the time of valuation if offered for sale on such reasonable terms and conditions as a *bona fide* seller might be expected to require." [1] This is in other words the selling or market price, which the assessor can often ascertain from the records of sale and from inquiries from realty dealers. The capital value differs from the capitalized annual rental, the rental actually paid; [2] and it is obvious that the rental yielded by a dilapidated structure on first-class land, for example, is by no means a criterion of the selling value of the site. Likewise with unoccupied land which yields no rental at all. It is with reason, then, that the taxation on "capital" is superseding the taxation on "annual" value. But the adoption of the principle of capital value as the basis of taxation involves some difficulty as regards leaseholds, especially those of long duration. In such cases an adjustment must be made in consideration of the encumbered condition of the property. What the method of adjustment is will be considered hereafter.

Assuming that the capital value can be ascertained, it follows from the definition that if you deduct the value of all the improvements from the improved capital value, the result is the unimproved capital value, and that is the taxable value. What, then, constitute improvements and how is their value to be ascertained? To quote a few definitions: "'Improvements' on land means all work done or mate-

[1] New Zealand, 3 Geo. V, No. 15, § 3; *Cf.* also Victoria, 1 Geo. V, No. 2284, § 3.

[2] In Australasia, this is called annual value.

rial used at any time on or for the benefit of the land by the expenditure of capital or labor by any owner or occupier thereof in so far as the effect of the work done or material used is to increase the value of the land, and the benefit thereof is unexhausted at the time of valuation; but does not include work done or material used on or for the benefit of the land by the Crown or by any statutory public body, except so far as the same has been paid for by the owner or occupier either by way of direct contribution or by way of special rates or loans raised for the purpose of constructing within a county any road, bridge, irrigation works, water-races, drainage works, or river-protection works: Provided that the value of improvements made out of loan moneys raised for the purpose of constructing within a county any road . . . shall not exceed the amount of principal estimated by the Valuer-General to have been repaid by the owner in respect of any such loan by way of special rates." [1]

" 'Improvements' include houses and buildings, fencing, planting, excavations for holding water, wells, ringbarking, clearing from timber, or scrub, or sweet briar, or noxious weeds, or laying down in grass or pasture, and any other improvements whatsoever the benefit of which is unexhausted at the time of valuation." [2]

Very similar definitions appear in all the Acts, but there is no uniformity as to whether minerals,[3] timber, and other products are to be included under improvements, that is, to be deducted from the value of the land. For example, the Victorian statute provides that the value of minerals shall not be taken into account in estimating the value of the land, meaning by minerals, "all minerals, metals, coal or precious stones existing on or beneath the surface of the

[1] New Zealand, 3 Geo. V, No. 15, § 3.

[2] New South Wales, 59 Vic., No. 15, § 67.

[3] The question whether minerals, a wasting asset, should be considered as part of the value of the land or whether they should be deducted as other products is of more than theoretic importance as will be shown later.

land." [1] Likewise, New Zealand exempts minerals as well as timber and flax. But this proviso is made: "if the commissioner is of opinion that any land containing minerals or having standing timber or flax thereon is not being worked or used in good faith and to an adequate extent for the purpose of extracting the said minerals, or of cutting the said timber or flax, such minerals, timber or flax shall be excluded from the provisions of this section and land tax, both ordinary and graduated, shall be assessed and paid." [2] Under the Commonwealth Act, however, all minerals under private ownership,[3] except gold and silver, which are specially reserved to the Crown and which can only be removed by lessees of the Crown or by special agreements with the owners, are part of the taxable, unimproved value.[4] When minerals are included under unimproved land, the difficulty of ascertaining their value is encountered, since the value of minerals before the mine has been worked can only be guessed at. In such cases the valuer must not only fix a speculative value for the unworked minerals, but must deduct from such value any expenditures incurred by the owner in boring, probing, and otherwise testing the mine.

Having defined "improvements," the next query is how to estimate their value. The "'value of improvements' means the added value which at the date of valuation the improvements give to the land." [5] Simple as this definition sounds, it involves many practical difficulties. To ascertain the unimproved value of the land it is necessary —

(a) to deduct from the capital value the expenditure for all improvements that have enhanced the value of the

---

[1] Victoria, 1 Geo. V, No. 2284, § 37.

[2] New Zealand, 7 Edw. VII, No. 18, § 22.

[3] Mines held under leasehold from the Crown are not taxable.

[4] *First Annual Report of the Commissioner of Land Tax of Commonwealth of Australia*, p. 16.

[5] New Zealand, 3 Geo. V, No. 15, § 3.

land and only in so far as they have enhanced the value, that is, should the expenditure have been made unnecessarily or wastefully without producing an appreciation in value, such outlay is not deductible;

(b) to deduct the value of the outlay, if the benefit of the improvement be unexhausted at the time of appraisal; otherwise, that is, if the improvement no longer affects the value of the site, irrespective of the original cost of such improvement, no deduction shall be allowed;

(c) not to allow for any appreciation in value due to a public improvement unless it has been paid for by a special assessment levy;

(d) to allow only the original cost of the improvement irrespective of the appreciation in excess of the cost.[1] "It is the actual improvement which is valued, not the effect of that improvement. For instance, supposing that the expenditure of a small sum in cutting an outlet for water had converted a swamp into first-class agricultural land. The fact that the swamp was capable of easy drainage would enhance its unimproved value, and the cost only of cutting the drain would be valued as the improvement."[2]

The difficulty of adjusting the relative values of the interests in the land among the owner, lessee, and often sublessee is met in various ways by the several states. In general, the principle is adhered to that the owner of the fee-simple shall be held liable for the tax. Nevertheless, to respect contracts entered into prior to the enactment of the tax, the lessee is sometimes deemed the owner. For example, where the rental of a leasehold does not change with the value of the land, and where the lessee binds himself to pay all taxes, the latter may be held liable; for

[1] "Provided that the value of improvements shall in no case be deemed to be more than the cost of such improvements estimated at the time of valuation, exclusive of the cost of repairs and maintenance." *Cf. New Zealand Official Year Book* (1913), p. 850.

[2] *Papers Bearing on Land Taxes*, etc. (Cd. 4750), 1909, p. 150.

in that case the owner, it is assumed, would be unable to recoup himself for the payment of the tax, while the lessee would pocket the appreciated land value. On the other hand, the possibility of reversion at the termination of the lease presents another aspect of the question, for from this standpoint the owner of the fee-simple may be deemed the rightful taxpayer.[1] In general, therefore, attempts are made to compute the respective interests of lessor, lessee, and sub-lessee, by taking into account (1) the unexpired term of the lease, (2) the annual rent agreed upon, and (3) the terms of the lease, as to the rights of renewal, compensation, etc.

By reason of the agreements under leasehold, the capital value of leased land must often be determined by other criteria than its unencumbered market value. For example, under the Commonwealth Act the unimproved value of leaseholds is ascertained by assuming that the actual rental paid by the lessee is four and one-half per cent of the unimproved value. This assumption is based on the average rate on mortgages, which is held to represent the earning value of the property; any excess over four and one-half per cent is attributed to the improvements or to the owner's exertions.[2] Or in Western Australia, the unimproved value of land held under any leasehold estate or interest from the Crown, without the right of purchase, is computed at a sum "equal to twenty times the excess of the amount of the fair annual rent at which the land would let under such reasonable conditions as a *bona fide* lessee would require, assuming the actual improvements (if any) had not been made, above the annual rent . . . reserved by the lease." [3]

[1] New Zealand, 3 Geo. V, No. 10, § 39; Victoria, 1 Geo. V, No. 2284, §§ 39, 40.

[2] *First Annual Report of the Commissioner of Land Tax of the Commonwealth of Australia*, p. 8. In New Zealand "the fair market annual rental of any property is assumed under the Act to be five per cent of its total value." *New Zealand Official Year Book* (1913), p. 857.

[3] Western Australia, 7 Edw. VII, No. 15, § 2.

To complete the series of definitions laid down for the guidance of the valuer, the meaning of "unimproved value" is quoted from the New South Wales' Act of 1895.[1] " 'Unimproved value' means, in respect of land, the capital sum for which the fee simple estate in such land would sell, under such reasonable conditions of sale as a *bona fide* seller would require, assuming the actual improvements (if any) had not been made, and in case of conditionally purchased land, of which no grant shall have been issued, after deducting also the balances or amount of purchase money due to the Crown in respect of the same: Provided that the unimproved value of lands reclaimed from the sea, or from any harbor or river, or made fit for building purposes by leveling or quarrying, or by the erection of retaining walls, or by any similar operations or works, shall be the capital sum for which the said land would sell under reasonable conditions, after deducting from such sum the cost of reclamation or making, as well as all other improvements."

It is clear from the above definition that "unimproved value" means neither the "prairie" value of the land, nor the present value of the bare land, regardless of the general progress of the locality, of the public improvements, and of the utilization of the adjoining area. All these influences indeed do affect the unimproved values of the district. In seeking to ascertain the unimproved value of some particular parcel of land, then, the valuer should view it in relation to the surrounding land, assuming that the parcel under consideration was alone unimproved. And the amount by which the capital value of the property exceeds the site value constitutes the value of the improvements.

§ 5. Summarizing the general system of valuation, it is necessary to point out that there are two methods of procedure in estimating the unimproved value of the land. The one is to deduct the value of the improvements from

[1] New South Wales, 59 Vic., No. 15, § 67.

the selling value; the other is to appraise the unimproved value of the land directly, without regard to the value of the improvements. To what extent the first, which is the simpler and less scientific, process of computation, is practiced, it is impossible to say. The second method, however, is theoretically the more correct one, and the one to which the New Zealand Valuation Department aims to conform. The valuer is there expected to ascertain separately the unimproved value, the value of the improvements, and the capital value of every parcel of land.[1] With these three values before him, he can check up his estimates. If, for example, he finds that the combined estimates of the unimproved value and the value of the improvements do not equal the estimated selling or capital value, he must readjust those values, bearing in mind that the value of the improvements is the difference between the selling and the unimproved values of the parcel. In this way there is more prospect of attaining an accurate valuation than by the first method referred to above.

There appears also in the Queensland statute [2] a suggestion that the second method may be there employed. The clause reads: "Except as hereinafter otherwise provided the value of any ratable land shall be estimated at the fair average *value of unimproved land of the same quality held in fee-simple in the same neighborhood*." Elsewhere, also, there is a recognition that the unimproved value of any piece of land is related to the value of the other land in the community. "It is, however, assumed," says the federal Commissioner of Land Tax, Mr. McKay,[3] "that the property under valuation has its present day environment and is subject to all communal influences that affect value. *Whatever is due to such communal influence is tax-*

[1] *New Zealand Official Year Book* (1913), p. 846. The valuer is expected to regard each piece of land "as if it *alone* had not been improved at the date of the valuation."

[2] Queensland, 2 Edw. VII, No. 19, § 195. (Italics mine.)

[3] *First Annual Report of the Commissioner*, etc., p. 14. (Italics mine.)

able as part of the unimproved value." And yet, in spite of this recognition of "community value," no "cadastral" system of scientific valuation based thereon has been developed in Australasia such as is beginning to be employed in this country.[1]

To what degree of accuracy the valuers attain under the system of valuation in Australasia it is difficult to say. Much depends upon the efficiency of the administration. According to the official reports [2] the system of valuation in New Zealand is said to be efficient. Several factors, as already noted, have operated to produce this result. First, the assessments are used not only by the government in granting loans, but by "trustees, executors, private lenders and purchasers," and for other purposes. Second, the government retains the option of purchase in case of disagreement between the owner's and the commissioner's estimated value. Third, the assessment roll is used for local purposes and is open to the owners for inspection and comparison of one another's valuations. Fourth, the valuing department is centralized and the officials are responsible to the department, not to party constituents.

Nevertheless, that the system in South Australia does not attain accurate returns is attested by the following statement from the report of the First Commissioner of Taxation.[3] "There has throughout been no straining after *high* values. Valuators have been instructed to give fair and uniform values, founded as far as possible on sales, and on values generally recognized in each particular locality. This is the principle that has been aimed at, and

[1] *Cf. infra*, chapter VII, § 12.

[2] *Cf. Papers Bearing on Land Taxes*, etc. (Cd. 4750), 1909, pp. 146–47. Also pp. 78–79. "Although there has been a considerable rise in assessments generally since the valuing department has been fully organized, there does not appear to be any widespread discontent with, or distrust of it. The Treasury and the municipal bodies have received better returns, but there is no reason to suppose that the property owners have been oppressively assessed."

[3] *Papers Bearing on Land Taxes*, etc. (Cd. 4750), 1909, p. 129.

the fact that the assessment for the city of Adelaide comes out at £9,558,452, being £5,467,548 *or more than one-third less* than the latest Parliamentary estimate for it, may, I think, be taken as some evidence that, at all events, extreme values have not been resorted to." The Commissioner of the Commonwealth Tax reports as follows concerning the first valuation made: [1] "The fact remains that some of the shire unimproved values are, in the opinion of the departmental valuers, far below the actual sale value of the land, which is the true taxing value. The land-owning class is often directly represented on the shire council, and there is a tendency on the part of bodies so constituted to limit the values, and the consequent tax, for local government purposes." The evidence is general that the system of land valuation, taking Australasia as a whole, lacks scientific accuracy and expertness, although uniformity in valuation, and therefore a certain degree of efficiency, is there attained.

§ 6. The consideration of the administration of the land tax raises the question of its fiscal importance. It is a well-known paradox that an evident incompatibility exists between the fiscal and social interests when taxation is employed to check or prevent a social ill. For example, the federal tax of ten per cent on note issues of state banks is prohibitive and wholly unproductive as a source of revenue. Or, a protective tariff, if wholly effective, would yield a comparatively trifling revenue. So in judging of the efficacy of the land taxes from the revenue receipts we must bear in mind the purpose of the taxes. [2] According to the analysis in the preceding chapter, the purpose of the state and federal taxes was not the same as that of the local systems, the former aiming at disintegration, the latter at

[1] *First Annual Report of the Commissioner of Land Tax,* etc. (1912), p. 10.

[2] The following quotation shows this incompatibility well: "Mr. Berry declares that he would be delighted if within twelve months every large estate was divided so that the tax did not bring in a shilling into the revenue." *The Australasian,* April 2, 1881, p. 432.

revenue. This fact must be borne in mind in treating of the fiscal aspect of the taxes.

It may well be, however, that a tax may prove at one and the same time a productive source of revenue and an agent of social reform. Thus, the Australasian graduated land tax may not have disintegrated the large estates, nor the absentee tax prevented absenteeism; nevertheless, it may have acted as a discouragement to both and have made the large estates bear a heavier burden so long as they endured. At the same time the tax may have established itself as a permanent part of the fiscal system. In the following sections, then, we shall attempt to discover the expediency of the tax on unimproved value as a fiscal measure.

§ 7. Tables I and II below show the revenue yielded over a period of sixteen years by the land taxes levied for

TABLE I. RECEIPTS FROM THE DOMINION LAND TAX IN NEW ZEALAND [1]

Year	Ordinary tax	Graduated tax	Absentee tax	Total receipts	Per cent of total land tax to total tax revenue
1897–98...	£193,348	£73,353	£586	£267,287	..
1898–99...	231,871	83,220	962	298,053	..
1899–00...	215,955	76,683	990	293,628	10.16
1900–01...	222,353	71,406	825	294,584	9.68
1901–02...	233,545	78,214	1,076	312,835	10.05
1902–03...	217,307	77,832	923	296,062	9.03
1903–04...	232,774	98,681	3,536	334,991	9.18
1904–05...	254,727	94,703	3,425	352,855	9.40
1905–06...	277,144	104,949	3,663	385,756	10.04
1906–07...	317,176	125,929	4,237	447,342	10.49
1907–08...	346,166	186,000	5,680	537,846	11.58
1908–09...	389,844	209,248	5,809	604,901	13.82
1909–10...	417,668	220,044	4,558	642,270	15.13
1910–11...	416,426	209,493	2,804	628,723	12.99
1911–12...	439,398	205,114	2,503	647,015	12.21
1912–13...	475,281	251,275	2,080	728,636	13.

[1] Compiled from the following sources: *Papers Bearing on Land Taxes*, etc. (Cd. 4750), 1909, p. 74; *New Zealand Official Year Book* (1909),

TABLE II. REVENUE FROM THE STATE LAND
TAXES IN THE AUSTRALIAN STATES [1]

Year	N.S. Wales	S. Australia	W. Australia	Victoria*	Tasmania*
1897–98...	£364,131	£81,508		£115,451	£37,226
1898–99...	253,901	77,622		108,745	37,577
1899–00...	286,227	78,404		108,722	38,866
1900–01...	288,369	79,908		97,948	38,915
1901–02...	301,981	76,350		97,862	39,337
1902–03...	314,104	105,024		92,867	41,862
1903–04...	322,246	77,369		106,445	50,881
1904–05...	332,530	115,032		97,840	54,151
1905–06...	336,785	94,374		103,556	54,776
1906–07...	345,497	90,200		92,438	56,065
1907–08...	178,889	93,762	£11,140	89,496	57,742
1908–09...	80,794	92,158	33,120	85,559	59,651
1909–10...	9,066	94,126	34,344	114,357	79,021
1910–11...	7,438	135,614	37,871	210,640	64,932
1911–12...	6,479	118,725	45,166	293,823	81,234

* The land tax in Victoria and Tasmania was levied on the improved value until
1910–11.

state purposes. In Table I, we note an increase, during
the interval, 1897–1913, of about 145 per cent in the ordinary tax, of about 242 per cent in the graduated tax, and
of about 255 per cent in the absentee tax, while the total
receipts from all three taxes in New Zealand show an increase of about 172 per cent. In considering the increase
in the receipts of the ordinary tax, which of course constitutes the most substantial portion of the land tax, it is
significant to note that the appreciation in the unimproved
value of the land upon which the tax is levied was during
the same period over 152 per cent.[2] This shows a rough

p. 691; *New Zealand Official Year Book* (1912 and 1913); *Statistics of the
Dominion of New Zealand* (1910).

[1] Compiled from the following sources: *Official Year Book of the Commonwealth of Australia*, vol. I (1901–07), and vol. v (1901–11); Coghlan, *Statistical Account of Australia and New Zealand* (1903–04); *Victorian Year
Books; Statistical Register of the State of South Australia*, for years 1903–11.

[2] The unimproved value was, in 1897, £84,401,244; in 1913, £212,-
963,468. *New Zealand Official Year Book* (1913), p. 859.

correspondence between receipts and the value of the land, the rate of tax having remained the same. Again, keeping the changes in the rate of the graduated and absentee taxes in mind, the rise in yield of the graduated tax, in 1903–04, and from 1907–08 on (see column 3), is noteworthy, for in those years the tax rate was increased. A comparison of the total receipts since 1907–08 [1] (column 5) makes clear the heavy burden which now falls upon the large holders and which they prefer to bear rather than to dispose of their estates. On the whole the receipts from the graduated and absentee taxes show great fluctuations and are unlike the more steady increase of the ordinary tax. The fact that the revenue from the graduated tax has increased may be regarded as proof of the inefficacy of the tax to disintegrate the large holdings. But the effect on absenteeism, judging from the receipts from absentees, is significant. Since 1910, when the absentee rate of tax was increased from twenty per cent to fifty per cent, the receipts as shown in column 4 have been growing less. This may signify that the number of absentee owners of the very large estates, at any rate, is decreasing as a result of the heavy burden of the discriminatory tax.

From the last column of the table, showing the proportion that the total receipts of the land tax bear to the total tax revenue of the central government, it is clear that the land tax constitutes but a small proportion of the tax receipts, and a very much less proportion of the whole budget.[2] The slight variations in the proportion which on the whole tends to increase show, however, that the land tax has become an integral and permanent part of the fiscal system. Compared with the yield of the income tax, the land tax is, indeed, more productive; for example,

---

[1] The great increase in receipts for 1909–10 can be explained only by the fact that the additional rate came into effect on March 30, 1910, before the fiscal year had ended.

[2] The revenue derived from taxation was, in 1911, £4,837,322, the total revenue £10,297,273. *The New Zealand Official Year Book* (1912), p. 763.

in 1908–09, the revenue of the land tax was almost double that of the income tax, £604,901, as compared with £321,044.[1]

Turning to Table II we fail to note the same steady increases in receipts in some of the states as were found in New Zealand. The fluctuation in receipts shows in part the effect of the revisions in the Acts. For example, the fall in yield in New South Wales since 1907–08 is obviously attributable to the suspension of the tax in favor of the local governments. With regard to the great increases in revenue in South Australia, in 1902–03 and 1904–05, it will be recalled that an additional rate was levied in those years. The explanation of the enormous increase in 1910–11 over all previous years is that there was a new assessment in 1910 and the ratable value of the land had increased from £68,214,887 in 1910 to £75,943,584 in 1911.[2] Land "booms" and the subsequent depressions in value may be responsible for some of the fluctuations noticeable, e.g., the proceeds for 1898–99 show a decided decrease in land value in New South Wales, South Australia, and Victoria. Compared with the total tax revenue for the year 1906–07, the last year before the suspension of the tax, the land tax in New South Wales constituted about twenty-five per cent of the total tax receipts, in South Australia about twenty-two per cent, and in Western Australia (1910–11) about eleven per cent. When we consider, however, that all tax receipts form a very small percentage of the total revenue, 7.42 per cent in New South Wales, 13.05 per cent in South Australia, and only 8.45 per cent in Western Australia,[3] the insignificance of the land tax, fiscally considered, becomes obvious.

The revenue receipts shown in the table for Victoria and

---

[1] *The New Zealand Official Year Book* (1909), p. 691.

[2] *Official Year Book of South Australia* (1913), p. 168. *Statistical Register of the State of South Australia* (1911), pt. VI.

[3] *Official Year Book of the Commonwealth of Australia* (1901–11), p. 815.

Tasmania until 1910–11 represent the yield of the realty tax, not of the tax on unimproved value. The change to the latter mode of taxation has brought some interesting variations in receipts. It is noteworthy that in 1910–11, the first year of the tax on land value in Victoria, the revenue nearly doubled, and that in the last year shown in the table, the increase over the preceding year was more than 39 per cent. This is to be accounted for by the provision abolishing the liberal exemptions formerly allowed. In Tasmania, the exemption of improvements, formerly taxable, caused a diminution in the taxable base, reducing the yield of the tax in spite of the increase in the rates of the graduated scale. But, the decrease in receipts was slight in view of the fact that a special super-tax had been levied in 1909–10.[1] The following year, however, the deficit was more than made up, as will be noted. In both states the change to the new system has been fiscally advantageous. As regards the tax in Western Australia, its steadily increasing yield is noteworthy, but as has been shown, it constitutes a very small percentage of the whole budgetary revenue.

§ 8. From the fiscal standpoint the federal land tax is as unimportant as the state taxes. Since its levy the tax has yielded the following revenue:[2]

1910–11	£1,404,969
1911–12	1,445,260
1912–13	1,385,024

Comparing these receipts with the total revenue receipts of the Commonwealth, we find that the land tax constituted (1911–12) about six per cent of the whole.

The following report of the particulars of the land-tax assessment is for our purpose very significant:[3]

[1] *Statistics of the State of Tasmania* (1913–14), p. 332.

[2] *Commonwealth of Australia, Official Statistics*, Monthly Bulletin No. 12 (December, 1912), p. 31; Bulletin No. 24 (1913), p. 40.

[3] *Official Statistics, Commonwealth of Australia*, Monthly Bulletin No. 12 (December, 1912), p. 34; Finance Bulletin, No. 5 (Summary 1901–11), p. 13.

TABLE SHOWING THE NUMBER OF OWNERS OF TAXABLE ESTATES, THEIR UNIMPROVED AND TAXABLE VALUE, THE RECEIPTS COLLECTED IN RURAL AND URBAN DISTRICTS, AND THE YIELD PER POUND OF TAXABLE VALUE IN EACH OF THE AUSTRALIAN STATES FOR THE YEAR ENDING JUNE 30, 1911

State	No. of returns assessed	Unimproved value as ascertained by department	Taxable balance after deductions	Tax assessed			Yield per pound of taxable value
				Town	County	Total	
New South Wales —							
Resident	4,514	£79,188,969	£58,762,042	£194,037	£495,004	£689,041	
Absentee	548	2,073,068	2,063,032	12,419	11,780	24,199	3.07d.
Total	5,062	81,262,037	55,825,074	206,456	506,784	713,240	
Victoria —							
Resident	4,218	49,111,863	28,723,902	133,014	209,119	342,133	
Absentee	772	1,427,246	1,423,047	6,794	12,500	19,294	2.88d.
Total	4,990	50,539,109	30,146,949	139,808	221,619	361,427	
South Australia —							
Resident	1,665	17,768,929	10,686,550	36,785	87,206	123,991	
Absentee	334	659,196	656,946	2,259	8,847	11,106	2.86d.
Total	1,999	18,428,125	11,343,496	39,044	96,053	135,097	

TABLE SHOWING THE NUMBER OF OWNERS OF TAXABLE ESTATES (Continued)

State	No. of returns assessed	Unimproved value as ascertained by department	Taxable balance after deductions	Tax assessed			Yield per pound of taxable value
				Town	County	Total	
Queensland —							
Resident	1,709	£15,513,613	£10,298,928	£39,131	£75,335	£114,979	
Absentee	288	452,518	461,792	2,298	1,677	3,975	2.65d.
Total	1,997	15,966,131	10,750,720	41,429	77,525	118,954	
Western Australia —							
Resident	540	£6,110,661	3,971,244	22,874	18,310	41,184	
Absentee	201	312,883	312,574	1,509	896	2,405	2.44d.
Total	741	6,423,544	4,283,818	24,383	19,206	43,589	
Tasmania —							
Resident	342	5,592,343	3,057,039	6,732	24,160	30,882	
Absentee	140	235,409	234,676	290	1,490	1,780	2.88d.
Total	482	5,827,752	3,291,715	7,012	25,650	32,662	
Total for Commonwealth —							
Resident	12,988	173,286,378	110,499,705	432,563	909,647	1,342,210	
Absentee	2,283	5,160,320	5,142,067	25,569	37,190	62,759	2.92d.
Grand total	*15,271	£178,446,698	£115,641,772	£458,132	£946,837	£1,404,969	

* A taxpayer owning land in more than one state is represented in this return in each state in which he held land. The actual number of taxpayers in the Commonwealth was 13,887.

It will be noted that the tax charged on rural land was more than twice the amount collected on urban land. It is in the country, of course, where the large holdings exist. There were in all 13,387 [1] taxpayers and of these about one-sixth were absentees. The area owned by these 13,387 persons was 72,528,271 acres, giving an average of 5418 acres to the person. There were 146 owners, the un-improved value of whose estates taken individually ex-ceeded £100,000. Of the total revenue, it will be noted, New South Wales paid more than half, 50.8 per cent, the percentage of taxable area in that state to the whole tax-able area being 58.4.[2] Although New South Wales has the largest population of all the Australian states, its terri-tory is about one-half that of Queensland and about one-third that of Western Australia, showing that the con-centration of land in the hands of comparatively few is greater in New South Wales than elsewhere in the Com-monwealth. The conditions of tenure in relation to the land-tax assessment are shown in the accompanying table on page 87.

The average rate of tax was 2.92*d*. in the pound (not quite one and one-fourth per cent); and it will be recalled that all resident owners were allowed an exemption of £5000. Considering that the total number of taxpayers was about three-tenths per cent of the entire population of the Australian Commonwealth, the discriminatory character of the tax becomes apparent.

A very important consideration in judging the expe-diency of a tax is the cost of collection and administration. It is interesting to note, therefore, that the cost of collec-tion of the Commonwealth land tax, the first year of its operation, was one and one-fourth per cent of the revenue collected; while the entire cost of its administration, much

---

[1] See footnote to table, p. 85.

[2] *Monthly Summary of Australian Statistics*, Bulletin No. 12 (December, 1912), pp. 34–35.

COMPARISON OF TENURES, TAXABLE AREAS AND TAX PAID IN EACH OF THE AUSTRALIAN STATES[1]

State	Total area (acres)	Per cent of total area	Area of alienated land (acres)	Per cent of total area	Area in process of alienation (not taxable — acres)	Per cent of total area	Area included in taxable returns (acres)	Per cent of total area	Per cent of total tax paid
New South Wales	198,638,080	10.4	36,153,068	37.3	15,614,036	36.0	42,597,020	58.4	50.8
Victoria	56,245,760	3.1	23,442,000	24.2	5,094,000	11.7	8,962,888	12.5	25.8
Queensland	429,120,000	22.6	15,460,352	16.1	7,971,342	18.2	7,012,417	9.6	8.4
South Australia	243,244,800	12.7	9,017,493	9.3	} 1,846,875	4.3	6,741,298	9.3	9.6
Northern Territory	335,116,800	17.6	473,809	0.5	}				
Western Australia	624,588,800	32.8	7,202,696	7.4	11,843,236	27.3	4,713,039	6.5	3.1
Tasmania	16,777,600	0.8	4,992,276	5.2	1,104,379	2.5	2,701,659	3.7	2.3
Commonwealth	1,903,731,840	100.0	96,681,694	100.0	43,473,868	100.0	72,528,271	100.0	100.0

[1] First Annual Report of the Commissioner of Land Tax of the Commonwealth of Australia (1912), p. 23.

of which expenditure will of course never recur, was three and one-half per cent.[1] When we consider the vast extent of territory under the jurisdiction of the Commonwealth Land Office, this amount is, indeed, very trifling. In New Zealand, for the year 1908–09, the cost of valuation and collection of the Dominion land tax was 3.82 per cent of the total yield; while the administration and assessment of the income tax was 2.05 per cent.[2] It will be remembered in this connection that the yield of the land tax was nearly double that of the income tax, while the number of taxpayers of the land tax was nearly three times the number of those who were liable to income tax.[3]

§ 9. As will be surmised, the fiscal problems presented by the system of rating on unimproved value in the local bodies in Australasia are unlike those dealt with above. As we have shown, the state governments depend upon other sources of revenue besides direct taxation; the local divisions, on the other hand, are in the main dependent for approximately the entire budget upon the rates levied. When, therefore, a community adopts a *single* tax on the unimproved value of the land for local revenue, the questions which at once arise are: Is the tax a sufficient source of revenue? Is it convenient, certain, elastic?

In order to be able to compare the working of the Single Tax on unimproved value with the fiscal systems in the other local authorities, some important data relative to the fiscal policy in the several states are presented in the following table: [4]

The chief difference to be noted in the above systems of

---

[1] *First Annual Report of the Commissioner of the Land Tax of the Commonwealth of Australia* (1912), p. 25.

[2] *The New Zealand Official Year Book* (1909), p. 691.

[3] There were 30,855 payers of land tax, and 10,839 of income tax in 1908–09. *Ibid.* (1913), p. 783.

[4] *Official Statistics, Commonwealth of Australia*, Finance Bulletin No. 4 (1901–10), p. 29.

LOCAL GOVERNMENT FINANCE (1909)

| State | No. of local authorities | Local revenue receipts including loans | | | | | Valuation of ratable land | | |
| | | Rates | | Government grants | Loans and other sources | Total | Capital | Annual | Unimproved |
		General	Other						
New South Wales	394	£1,135,623	£80,232	£339,891	£664,094	£2,219,840	··	£9,260,759	£146,706,720
Victoria	206	916,449	105,080	175,601	474,686	1,671,816	£252,066,618	13,564,488	··
Queensland	162	343,567	126,403	5,274	116,641	591,885	··	··	47,314,811
South Australia	176	152,592	44,939	125,419	91,613	414,563	63,849,055	3,190,041	··
West Australia	150	143,469	41,010	89,683	223,617	497,779	17,544,977	1,340,496	*1,120,691
Tasmania	51	112,778	60,674	44,293	92,245	309,990	27,705,040	1,385,252	··
Commonwealth	1,069	£2,804,478	£458,338	£780,161	£1,662,896	£5,705,873			

* Three municipalities in Western Australia rate on unimproved value.

local finance is in respect to the taxable value upon which
rates are levied, New South Wales and Queensland rating
on the unimproved, the other four states [1] on the capital
or annual value of both land and improvements. New
South Wales has the largest budget, Queensland coming
third. It will be observed that the government grant to
Queensland is very small, and while that to New South
Wales is yet the largest endowment, there is reason to believe that the tendency will be to reduce the grants when
conditions permit.[2] The "other sources" of revenue are
from public works, licenses, fees, rents, etc. But in New
South Wales and in Queensland, besides the rates and endowment, the only additional revenue comes from public
works.

Turning to the consideration of the local revenue systems
of the particular states, we present in the following table
some important data bearing on the source and yield of the
local tax in Queensland. The elasticity of yield is very
significant. While the value of the property had increased about 19.5 per cent, from 1903 to 1911, the revenue
had increased 92.3 per cent during the same period. It
is interesting to note that the revenue of the shires had
increased more rapidly than that of the urban communities. In 1910, the prevailing general rate in the cities and
towns was 3d. which was the highest rate levied. The
lowest was $1\frac{1}{4}$ d. In the shires the general rate averaged
much less than 3d. in the pound, the maximum levied,
while the minimum rate was as low as $\frac{1}{2}d.$[3] The system of
"differential rating" whereby each minor civic division,

[1] In Victoria rating on the unimproved value was made optional in
1914.

[2] Cf. supra, chapter II, pp. 29, 55. Under the provisions of the Shires
Bill (Act No. 33, 1905) the endowment to the shires for the first three
years was on such a scale that no shire would need levy a higher rate than
1d. in the pound. Cf. Papers Relative to the Working of Taxation, etc. (Cd.
3761), 1907, p. 10.

[3] Statistics of the State of Queensland (1910), pt. VI.

TABLE SHOWING THE RECEIPTS FROM RATES AND THE
VALUE OF RATABLE LAND IN QUEENSLAND FROM
1903 TO 1911 [1]

| Year | Capital value of unimproved land | Revenue from rates, general and others | | |
		Cities and towns	Shires	Total
1903	£44,149,974	£191,975	£118,127	£340,102
1904	43,651,241	216,133	160,759	376,892
1905	42,358,173	216,283	161,198	377,481
1906	43,178,545	217,168	170,617	387,785
1907	43,817,870	226,948	187,397	414,345
1908	45,025,085	233,622	202,722	436,344
1909	47,314,811	247,433	222,536	469,969
1910	49,797,830	278,300	253,398	531,698
1911	52,788,079	..	..	654,125
1912	54,991,920	357,550	342,481	700,031

e.g., a ward, or division of a shire, fixes its own rate of tax,[2]
seems to solve a serious objection to the rating on unimproved value.[3] If the same rate were charged on town as
on rural land, as the value of land in the country is generally more than that of the improvements, it would impose
a greater hardship upon the rural community and would
violate the principle of "benefit," since the expenditure of
a town is generally greater than in the country. Altogether, the expediency of a system which has remained
practically without change in legislation since its inception in 1890, which is in operation in all the local bodies,
which is practically the sole source of local revenue, which
is not oppressive, and which fulfills the criteria of elastic-

[1] Compiled from data in the *Official Year Books of the Commonwealth
of Australia* (1901–07, p. 843, and 1901–11, p. 1017); *Official Statistics*,
Finance Bulletin 5 (1901–11), p. 28; *Statistics of the State of Queensland*,
1910, pt. VI; *A.B.C. of Queensland Statistics* (1913).

[2] Cf. *Statistics of the State of Queensland* (1910), pt. VI.

[3] *Papers Relative to the Working of Taxation on the Unimproved Value
of Land in Queensland* (Cd. 3890), 1908, p. 16.

ity, economy, and certainty, seems to be established for the local governments of Queensland.

Compared with the Queensland system, rating on unimproved value in New South Wales is still in the experimental stage, not because there is any prospect of change to the former system, but because the results are not yet conclusive. Nevertheless, the general tendency is illustrated by Sydney. Until 1908 rating was on annual value; in that year rating on unimproved land value was made optional with the city council. The question was made a party issue, until on April 30, 1916, the Sydney city council voted in favor of exempting all improvements from taxation.[1] The efficiency of the present system of local rating as compared

GENERAL RATES COLLECTED IN THE LOCAL BODIES OF NEW SOUTH WALES [2]

Year	Shires		Municipalities (Sydney excepted)		Sydney *	
	Receipts	Per cent to total revenue	Receipts	Per cent to total revenue	Receipts	Per cent to total revenue
1907.........	£287,635	53.7	..	..	..	..
1908.........	382,336	60.9	£544,339	77.4	..	..
1909.........	374,540	52.5	558,811	79.3	£202,272 } 78,723 }	78.0
1910.........	421,596	53.0	573,600	77.5	206,461 } 83,569 }	80.6
1911.........	463,501	52.3	642,630	78.8	221,450 } 98,183 }	77.6
1912.........	517,025	51.7	720,419	78.2	226,688 } 100,267 }	76.0

* In 1912 rating in Sydney was still mostly on the annual value. Only the required rate of 1d. (see *supra*, p. 55) was levied on the unimproved value. The upper figure in the table represents the amount raised on annual value, the lower that on the unimproved value. *Official Year Book of New South Wales* (1913), pp. 617, 619.

[1] *Land Values*, July, 1916, p. 46. *The Public*, April, 28, 1911, p. 393.
[2] *Official Year Book of New South Wales* (1909–13); *Official Year Book of the Commonwealth of Australia* (1901–11), p. 980.

with the former land tax for state purposes is shown in the table above, where it will be observed that the receipts from general rates in the shires alone have exceeded, since 1908, the entire revenue accruing from the state land tax. Although attributable in part to the elimination of the minimum exemption of £240, the great increase in yield shows the possibilities of the system and the advantages of the local as compared with the state administration of the tax.

It will be recalled that the receipts do not represent the full amount collected from the rates on unimproved value, for special, local and loan rates and, in the case of municipalities, the additional general rates may be levied on the unimproved value at the option of the council subject to a poll vote of the ratepayers. In connection with the increase in the yield of the tax in all the local bodies it is interesting to observe the increase in the value of the ratable land as shown in the following data: [1]

UNIMPROVED VALUE OF RATABLE LAND IN NEW
SOUTH WALES

Year	Municipalities	Shires
1909	£63,255,186	£83,464,446
1910	63,529,322	89,936,000
1911	69,844,477	94,190,000
1912	72,276,447	97,461,000

As the yield of revenue in the shires has increased somewhat more rapidly than in the municipalities, so has the value of the land. It will be noted that the yield in the municipalities exceeds greatly that in the shires although the value of the land in the latter communities exceeds that in the former. The explanation is to be found in the fact that the rate of tax in the municipalities is much higher

[1] *Official Year Book of New South Wales* (1911), p. 723; (1913), p. 622.

than in the shires, the latter relying more upon the endowment from the state government to supplement the budgetary requirements. The endowments are fixed every third year, the amount depending upon various criteria, as the size of the shire, the revenue accruing from a $1d.$ rate, the necessary expenditure, the extent of roads and other public works,[1] etc. The endowments fixed for the triennium, 1910–12, were based on the general rates collected in the shires in the preceding years. They are as follows:[2]

1st class	27 shires	No endowment
1st "	41 "	Up to 10s. in the pound on General Rate
2d "	10 "	" " 15s. " " " " " "
3d "	9 "	" " 20s. " " " " " "
4th "	7 "	" " 25s. " " " " " "
5th "	14 "	" " 30s. " " " " " "
6th "	26 "	Not less than 40s. in the pound on General Rate

Compared with the government endowments to the municipalities (1909) of £6953, the shires received £261,-029 or 36.4 per cent of the total revenue. The rates of tax levied in 1910 in the shires are shown below: —

General rate in the pound	No. of shires	Unimproved value of land
$\frac{1}{2}d.$	1	£1,472,826
$\frac{5}{8}d.$	2	1,691,054
$\frac{3}{4}d.$	4	4,626,443
$1d.$	75	54,027,624
$1\frac{1}{8}d.$	2	696,157
$1\frac{1}{4}d.$	23	13,109,370
$1\frac{1}{2}d.$	20	10,322,122
$2d.$	7	3,990,316
	134	£89,935,912

Besides these general rates, local (special assessment) rates were levied, the scale ranging from $\frac{1}{4}d.$ to $2d.$ Of the

[1] *Official Year Book of New South Wales* (1909–10), p. 601.
[2] *Ibid.* (1911), pp. 737–38.

nineteen cases of local rates in the shires only one was levied on the improved value; the others were on the unimproved value.

In New Zealand, of the total revenue from rates collected by the local authorities, amounting, in 1907–08, to £1,356,257, thirty per cent was levied on unimproved value.[1] In 1910 the proportion was thirty-three per cent.[2] In considering these percentages it must be remembered that at least one-third of the local bodies now rate on unimproved value.[3]

In this section the productiveness and elasticity of the tax on unimproved value for local purposes have been shown. The convenience and certainty of land taxes in general are too well known to need discussion. In respect to the taxes in the local governments of Queensland, New South Wales, and New Zealand, the general satisfaction with the system demonstrates the fiscal adequacy, convenience, certainty, and elasticity of the land tax.

§ 10. To sum up the effects and working of the different land taxes from the fiscal standpoint: —

(1) There are three principal tax jurisdictions in Australasia, and the same land is in some of the colonies subject to all three levies. There is, therefore, a duplication of the administrative machinery involving an additional cost of collection.

(2) The receipts of the tax levied for state and federal purposes constitute a small percentage of the total revenue.

(3) The land tax is well established in the fiscal system of the state and local governments. By this is meant that for the most part the tax is no longer a party measure.[4]

(4) The cost of administration and collection of the tax constitutes a very small proportion of the revenue collected.

---

[1] *The New Zealand Official Year Book* (1909), p. 198.
[2] *Ibid.* (1912), p. 313.
[3] *Supra*, chapter ii, § 12.   [4] See *supra*, § 7.

(5) The tax for state and federal purposes is a designedly discriminatory charge, falling on a small class of owners.

(6) The yield of these discriminatory taxes, state and federal, fluctuates according (a) as the rate is a graduated one, (b) as the rate of tax changes, (c) as the system is effective in its work of disintegration of the large holdings.

(7) The fiscal returns in the local bodies show the adequacy and elasticity of the yield of the tax.

(8) The rates on unimproved value form the chief source of local revenue in Queensland and New South Wales, and constitute the sole tax in the localities of the former state.[1]

(9) However adversely the value of land may be affected upon the introduction of the tax, the value of the land tends to rise in both the urban and rural communities, often making a higher rate of tax unnecessary to meet the growing budgets.

(10) The local system fulfills the fiscal requirements; while the state and federal taxes aim to right a social ill. Unlike the latter the local taxes are applicable to all land at a uniform rate of tax.

§ 11. Knowing the purpose of the progressive land taxes of Australasia, the question of their fiscal importance becomes subordinate to the inquiry: how has that purpose succeeded? Has the tax caused the large landed estates to be broken up?

After more than two decades since the introduction of the tax on unimproved value, Australasia is still the country of large land holdings. Only in a few states has a reduction in the size or the number of large holdings occurred. To illustrate: in New Zealand the average area held by owners of 10,000 acres and upwards in 1889 was 30,009

---

[1] That is the sole tax for local purposes. The people of Queensland, of course, contribute to the taxes levied by the state and central governments. Moreover, the "endowment" comes from other sources than the land taxes.

acres; in 1892 the average had been reduced to 29,924; in 1902 to 28,312; in 1906 to 23,061 acres; and in 1910 to 20,523 acres. The number of holdings of 10,000 acres and above has likewise considerably decreased, as appears from the subjoined data: [1]

NUMBER OF FREEHOLDERS IN NEW ZEALAND OWNING 10,000 ACRES OR UPWARDS, 1883–1910

1883	1886	1889	1892	1902	1906	1910
247	259	250	262	216	204	171

The effect of the amended Acts of 1903 and 1907 is apparent. The reduction since 1906 shows the process of disintegration. In Victoria similarly the number of such holdings has fallen from 195, in 1906, to 175, in 1910, and to 151 in 1913.[2] In New South Wales, on the other hand, there was a slight increase in the number of estates covering 10,000 or more acres, from 703 to 706 in a decade.[3] The same has occurred in Western Australia, the large holdings having increased from 74 to 110.[4] In addition, when it is considered that the legislation in the interest of closer settlement has been unremittent, and that the governments have exercised their power to repurchase land,[5] and thus to aid in the work of disintegration, the effect attributable to the land tax could have been but insignificant.

The enactment of the tax, however, has often been accompanied by an increased number of land transfers

[1] *Papers Bearing on Land Taxes*, etc. (Cd. 4750), 1909, p. 75; *New Zealand Official Year Book* (1914), pp. 567–68.
[2] *Official Year Book of the Commonwealth of Australia* (1901–11), p. 328; *Victorian Year Book* (1913–14), p. 713.
[3] *Official Year Book of the Commonwealth of Australia* (1901–11), p. 327.
[4] *Ibid.*, p. 328.
[5] In this way the famous Cheviot estate in New Zealand was subdivided and sold.

through sales. Subdivision was said to have been common
in New Zealand prior to the Act of 1907.[1] Similarly in
anticipation of the Commonwealth Act many sales of
large holdings took place. Between June and September,
1910, the law allowed the owner the right to deduct from the
taxable value the value of any estates about to be sold. In
that period 699 sales, aggregating £2,712,775 in value,
were reported to the tax commissioner; and the land thus
subject to sale was not included in the assessment of
the remaining land of these owners.[2] Then, since the enactment of the law, from October 1, 1910, to June 30, 1911,
the following sales and purchases of land transacted by
payers of the Commonwealth land tax, were reported at
the different land tax offices:[3]

State	Sales		Purchases	
	Number	Unimproved value	Number	Unimproved value
Central Office* and Victoria..............	7,032	£7,684,221	1,601	£3,798,275
New South Wales.......	7,134	6,931,090	1,151	3,496,973
Queensland............	1,109	1,027,206	166	511,328
South Australia.........	2,059	1,798,545	744	1,135,069
Western Australia......	656	391,555	107	121,022
Tasmania..............	298	355,676	105	203,839
Total...........	18,288	£18,188,293	3,874	£9,266,506

* The Central Office deals with estates that include property in more than one state.

It would seem, indeed, that at the same time that subdivision was taking place there was likewise an acquisition

[1] *The Australasian*, October 5, 1907, p. 888.

[2] *First Annual Report of the Commissioner of Land Tax of the Commonwealth of Australia* (1912), p. 24.

[3] *Official Statistics, Commonwealth of Australia*, Monthly Summary,
Bulletin No. 14 (February, 1913), p. 35.

of new estates of taxable value. But it is reported that "as a rule those who have relieved themselves of the tax are taxpayers subject to the highest scales, but the buyers of land, as a rule, are those subject to lower rates or are wholly exempt from the tax." [1] Altogether, however, allowing for the deterrent effect of the tax on the concentration of large tracts of land in the hands of comparatively few owners, the actual disintegration of large estates, except in New Zealand, has been slight.

§ 12. The reasons for the inadequacy of the land tax as a means of breaking up the large estates are traceable to certain provisions in the legislation. The recognition of this by the state governments is shown through the revisions which the Acts, especially in New Zealand, have undergone. These amendments will be discussed under the following heads: (1) evasions; (2) rates of tax; (3) valuation systems.

(1) The excessive exemptions and the progressive scales have induced evasions to a greater extent than is usual with taxes on real property. Among some common methods practiced to escape the burden were bogus partnerships, one-man companies, false sales and leases, nominal gifts, etc. [2] To form a fictitious partnership was an expedient, perfectly legal and successful, for before the amended provisions of 1907, partners were assessed separately. Or it was a simple matter, an expedient very prevalent in New Zealand, to divide the estate nominally among the members of the immediate family to avoid paying the highest rate of tax. Not only did the Dominion of New Zealand incur great losses through such evasions, but the graduated scale weighed less heavily on the large owners. Consequently, in 1907, the following clauses were inserted in the New Zealand Act to put a stop to the practices men-

---

[1] *First Annual Report of the Commissioner of Land Tax of the Commonwealth of Australia* (1912), p. 24.

[2] *Papers Bearing on Land Taxes*, etc. (Cd. 4750), 1909, p. 75.

tioned above.[1] Similar provisions have been incorporated in the laws of the other states:[2]

1. Life tenants are liable as if owners of fee-simple.
2. Lessees are liable as if owners (except lessees of the Crown, Native, or exempt land . . .).
3. Shareholders are liable as if owners of the company's land in proportion to their interest in the paid-up capital.
4. Two companies having practically [3] the same shareholders are deemed one.
5. Joint owners are assessed jointly as if the whole land was owned by a single person, and, in addition, the joint owners are liable for their interests in the joint estate taken in conjunction with any lands owned by them in severalty. . . .
6. Persons occupying land jointly are liable as if owning jointly, as if the whole land was owned by a single person. . . .
7. The buyer in possession is liable, although conveyance has not been executed.
8. The seller remains liable until 15 per cent of the purchase money is paid or the settlement has been agreed upon, except in case of agreement of sale made five years before the passing of the Act, or made by a seller not the owner of more than £40,000 unimproved value.

---

[1] "It is generally admitted that the bill is a clever piece of draughtsmanship, elaborately contrived to prevent the nominal conveyances, mortgages, trusts and other devices by which payment of the graduated tax has been evaded in the past." *The Australasian*, October 19, 1907, p. 1019.

[2] *Cf.* Victoria, 1 Geo. V, No. 2284, §§ 38–52; Tasmania, 2 Geo. V, No. 47, § 19.

[3] New Zealand, 7 Edw. VII, No. 18, §§ 11–21. The Victorian statute provides that two companies shall be deemed one "if not less than three-fourths of the paid-up capital of each is held by or on behalf of the shareholders in the other." 1 Geo. V, No. 2284, § 41 (2).

9. No disposition is to be effective so long as possession is retained.
10. Tax payable by buyer may be deducted from the amount payable by seller. . . .
11. Equitable owners are liable as if legal owners.
12. Trustees are liable as if beneficially entitled to the land.
13. Mortgagees in possession of the land are liable as if lessees.

(2) A second cause of the failure of the tax to accomplish its purpose is the rate of tax, which, speaking generally, is too low to be effective. The ordinary tax on unimproved value for state purposes ranges from $\frac{1}{2}d$. in the pound in Victoria and South Australia to $1d$. (.41 per cent) in New Zealand, Western Australia, and Tasmania. Then, it will be recalled that in Victoria and Western Australia the ordinary tax is the only one charged, that is, there exists no progressive tax in those states; that in South Australia, the additional tax on estates of over £5000 is only $\frac{1}{2}d$. in the pound, a uniform rate; and that in Western Australia one-half of the slight charge of $1d$. is remitted to the owner of improved property. The graduated scale of rates in Tasmania on land exceeding £2500 ranges from $1\frac{1}{4}d$. to $2\frac{1}{2}d$. (about one per cent). Such rates surely are not excessive, and thus far the income of the landowner has not been touched sufficiently to make the holding of his estates unprofitable.

In New Zealand, however, when the ineffectiveness of the tax was realized, the graduated scale was revised from time to time to tighten the screw, until, in 1907, a supercharge of twenty-five per cent of the new graduated scale was added on all estates of £40,000 or above, the rates ranging from $\frac{1}{16}d$. in the pound on land £5000 to two per cent on estates of £200,000 or above; since 1910, when the additional tax of twenty-five per cent came into force, the graduated scale has ranged from $\frac{1}{32}d.$ on land £5000 to about two and a half per cent on the largest estates. The estimated increase is concretely shown in the following table: [1]

COMPARISON OF PAYMENT UNDER PRESENT AND FORMER SCALES OF GRADUATED LAND TAX

On unimproved value (not business premises)	At rate in 1903–06	At rate in 1907	At rate in 1910	At rate in 1912
£5,000	£1.3	£1.3	£1.3	£.65
40,000	145.	160.	200.	211.
75,000	410.	562.	702.	807.
100,000	677.	1000.	1250.	1467.
130,000	1083.	1690.	2112.	2517.
150,000	1407.	2250.	2813.	3374.
210,000	2625.	4200.	5250.	6380.

Add to this graduated tax the ordinary rate of $1d.$ in the pound, and, if the owner is an absentee, fifty per cent of the graduated tax besides, and the burden becomes considerable.[2] Disintegration under these circumstances seems inevitable. "Even now analysts are found who are at pains to prove that the landowners will be able to pay the tax of 1910 and hold out against it as stubbornly as they defied its predecessors. In two years, however, the land tax has increased nearly £160,000, and . . . the inducements to break up the greater properties will, after next year, be very strong indeed." [3]

In the Commonwealth of Australia, the federal tax added to the state land taxes makes the burden in some cases heavier even than in New Zealand. The expectations with

[1] *Papers Bearing on Land Taxes*, etc. (Cd. 4750), 1909, p. 77.

[2] "I know one owner absent for his health, who will be called upon to pay £7000 for the year. . . . Of course this is confiscation pure and simple, and it will compel the owner to sell." *The Australasian*, August 24, 1907, p. 502.

[3] *Papers Bearing on Land Taxes*, etc. (Cd. 4750), 1909, p. 77.

regard to subdivision, therefore, apply equally to Australia as to New Zealand.

(3) Defective valuation systems have helped to frustrate the purpose of the land tax. Enough has been said concerning the systems of valuation based on self-assessment and assessments made infrequently and *in personam*. The crude scheme of valuation according to the grazing capacity of the land, which existed until 1910 in Victoria, could not be made effective in the work of disintegration. Indeed, it was estimated that the nominal valuation of land in that colony (1902) at £9,949,429 was so much below the actual value that about £100,000,000 value of private estates escaped taxation.[1] With the amended laws to prevent evasion, with the additional rates and duplicated taxes, with more efficient systems of land appraisal, some changes in the social effects of the land tax may be looked for in Australasia.

§ 13. But with all these defects in legislation the purpose of the land taxers was not wholly frustrated. To some extent they succeeded in shifting the burden upon an unpopular class. Not to mention the popularity of the land tax with the urban landless population, the tax was acceptable and favored by certain classes of landowners even. This is to be explained by another feature of the legislation, namely, the liberal exemptions; for only a small percentage of the proprietors pay any land tax at all for state purposes. In New Zealand, for example, only 30,855 owners, out of a total number of 143,243 (including Crown tenants), in 1909, were subject to land tax.[2] The exemptions are equally liberal in the other colonies. Thus only 41,000 out of a number of 170,000 landed proprietors in New South Wales in 1902 paid any land

[1] Coghlan, *Statistical Account of Australia and New Zealand* (1903–04), p. 674.

[2] It was estimated by one authority that about six-sevenths of those holding land in New Zealand escape the state land tax. *Cf. Papers Bearing on Land Taxes*, etc. (Cd. 4750), 1909, p. 70.

tax;[1] while in Victoria all city landholders as well as all
rural estates less than 640 acres were until 1910 released
from the tax. As has been already pointed out, only
13,387 land owners in all the six states were, in 1910–11,
liable for the Commonwealth tax.

Besides the minimum exemption of land value ranging
from £50 in Western Australia to £5000 under the Commonwealth Act, there are special exemptions allowed at the
discretion of the Commissioner; as, for example, the petty
owner in New Zealand, whose income does not exceed
£200,[2] etc., in which case the amount of exemption may
reach as much as £3500; or the exemption of all improved
agricultural land to the amount of £250 in Western Australia; or the exemption in Victoria of the tax when, in
cases of loss by fire, storm or other accident, the charge
would create a hardship upon the owner.

The following exemptions from the Victorian statute,
though more inclusive than those in the other states,
further limit the application of the progressive land tax:[3]

1. Land, the property of His Majesty which is unoccupied or used for public purposes.
2. Land used exclusively for . . . commons, mines,
   public worship, mechanics' institutes, art galleries,
   public libraries, cemeteries, agricultural show grounds,
   public gardens, primary free schools, charitable purposes, the purposes of any club for cricket, football,
   golf, etc., public technical and working men's schools
   and colleges, the University of Melbourne.
3. Land vested in or held in trust . . . for: any municipality or council thereof; any waterworks; trust local
   governing body; any church or religious denomination.
4. Land vested in: The Victorian Railways Company;
   the Minister of Public Instruction; the Board of

---

[1] Coghlan, *op. cit.*, p. 672.   [2] *Cf. supra*, p. 37.
[3] Victoria, 1 Geo. V, No. 2284, § 9.

Land and Works; the Commissioner of the Melbourne Harbor Trust, etc.; the Commissioner of Savings Banks . . . ; trustees for any Friendly Society or Trade Union or Trade Union Institution; any public corporation . . . if exempted from land tax by the Governor in Council.

Thus the taxpayers of the state and federal land taxes are comparatively few in number, and constitute a group, it is popularly believed, that can best bear the burden.

§ 14. However, to say that even the progressive land tax had for its purposes merely to disintegrate the large land holdings and to shift the burden of taxation on the recipients of the unearned increment would be erroneous. Indeed, other social and economic influences were expected to result from the levy of the state and federal taxes, as well as from the levy of the local land tax. Owing partly to the identification of the land tax with the Single Tax, great stress was laid upon these effects. Would it destroy the market value of land and finally put an end to private ownership of land? Would it prove the panacea for all social ills, even to the eradication of poverty? The apprehension that the existing social order would be more or less subverted was general. That is why, when the tax was first proposed, its opponents regarded it as a confiscatory, revolutionary, socialistic measure; that is why, they said of the amended Acts that they were "giving an extra turn to the screw." [1] That is why, also, rating on unimproved value was termed "experimental legislation," and great uncertainty was felt as to the weighty consequences of the system. [2] We may, therefore, inquire, how these various expectations have materialized.

[1] New Zealand, *Parl. Debates* (1893), vol. LXXXII, pp. 240, 375–77. *Cf.* also *The Australasian*, April 3, August 21, 1875; February 17, 1877; December 4, 1880, *et passim*.

[2] "It is now becoming the law that the system of taxation should be upon the unimproved value, but I have no doubt but experience will en-

The experience with the tax for over two decades has both allayed the anxiety of its adversaries and dissipated the extravagant hopes of its most ardent adherents. Nevertheless, some influences, social and economic, have been traced to the land tax. Following the questionnaire of the British Government [1] with reference to the working of the land tax, we shall consider its effect on: (1) the building trade; (2) land speculation; (3) the incidence on house property and vacant sites, and (4) rent.

For two reasons great caution must be exercised in weighing the evidence pro and con in respect to the effects of the tax. The first is, that the rate of tax has hitherto been too slight a burden to occasion great changes; the second is, that the influences tending toward the development of the Australasian colonies, aside from all the reform measures including the land tax, have been numerous. For example, to attribute the prosperity, the general steady rise in the value of land, the increase in building operations, etc., to the land tax or to any other particular social legislation would be erroneous, for the great development of the country, as is well known, is largely the result of specially favorable circumstances which enable it to compete in the world market, of certain climatic and economic advantages which attract more settlers to its soil, and of other causes operating in every newly settled country.

§ 15. These facts with reference to the development of the colonies must be borne in mind especially in examining

lighten us very quickly as to its effects. Whether those who advocate this system are right in saying that its effects will be the gradual extinction of capital value of freehold land, . . . we shall see and before many years are over many of us will have learnt a new lesson in political economy." *Papers Relative to the Working of Taxation on Unimproved Value of Land in Queensland* (Cd. 3890), 1908, p. 10.

[1] In its important and thoroughgoing investigation concerning the taxation of land value the British Government, in 1906, sent requests to various countries for information. The replies of the officials in Australasia are not all of the same tenor. There is, nevertheless, an agreement concerning the effects which is noteworthy. We propose, for the most part, to summarize their evidence in the following sections.

the effect of the land tax on building operations. The stimulus given to the use of capital employed in the building trade is more or less emphasized by the officials of the respective colonies. The expenditure on improvements in New Zealand since 1893 was said to have been so great "that the supply of labor and materials could scarcely keep pace with the demand."[1] This effect is generally and logically attributed to the exemption of improvements from taxation; nevertheless, it must not be forgotten that it is only since the nineties that New Zealand has recovered from a long period of depression and that general conditions have been especially prosperous. One official, indeed, traces the earlier relief from the depression of 1893, in Queensland, to the exemption of improvements, which greatly encouraged building operations.[2] In New South Wales, the suburban development that has taken place has been attributed partly to the tax, partly to the improved transportation facilities.[3] So also in South Australia the effect of the tax is said to have been beneficial to the building trade and to the development of the suburbs.[4]

---

[1] *Papers Bearing on Land Taxes*, etc. (Cd. 4750), 1909, pp. 134–35; also (Cd. 3191), 1906, p. 25. "The effect on urban and suburban land has been very marked. An owner of land occupied by buildings of little value finding that he has to pay the same rates and taxes as an owner having his land occupied by a valuable block of buildings must see that his interests lay in putting his land to its best use. The rebuilding of this city (Wellington) which for some years past has been rapidly going on is largely attributable to the taxation and rating on land values, so that the supply of building materials could not at times keep pace with the demand." *Ibid.* (Cd. 4750), pp. 136–37.

[2] *Papers Relative to the Working of Taxation on Unimproved Value of Land in Queensland* (Cd. 3890), 1908, pp. 4, 17.

[3] *Papers Bearing on Land Taxes*, etc. (Cd. 4750), 1909, p. 133.

[4] *Ibid.*, p. 116. The following quotation from the report of the Commissioner of Taxes in New Zealand, is significant because his conclusions are based on replies from fifty-two local authorities relative to the effects of the tax: "The effect has certainly been to greatly stimulate the building trade. The object and tendency of this system of taxation is to compel land being put to its best use, so that the greatest amount of income may be derived from it, and rendering it unprofitable to hold land for

Although the statistics of the housing conditions in Australia bear out the testimony of the officials with regard to the increase in building operations, they tell us little about the influence of the land tax on such operations. From the subjoined table the number of dwellings is seen to have increased more rapidly than the population in each of the colonies except Western Australia. From the standpoint of congestion, the housing conditions not only are good, but they have tended to improve from decade to decade.

TABLE SHOWING THE INCREASE OF INHABITED DWELL-INGS IN THE AUSTRALASIAN COLONIES FROM 1901 TO 1911 [1]

Colony	1901		1911		Per cent of increase 1901–11	
	Number of inhabited dwellings	Proportion to 100 of population	Number of inhabited dwellings	Proportion to 100 of population	Dwellings	Population
New South Wales	252,502	18.3	332,841	19.6	31.8	23.3
Victoria.........	241,410	19.9	273,495	20.4	13.2	10.6
Queensland......	98,737	19.4	126,834	20.3	28.4	22.7
South Australia..	69,856	19.4	84,437	20.1	20.8	16.0
Western Australia	48,506	25.0	70,319	23.9	44.9	51.9
Tasmania.......	34,165	19.5	40,111	20.7	17.4	10.4
New Zealand....	158,898	20.1	215,425	21.0	35.5	30.1

In New Zealand, for example, the average number of persons to an inhabited dwelling had decreased from 5.17

prospective increment in value. It has been the direct cause of much valuable suburban land being cut up and placed on the market and thus rendered more easily available for residential purposes, and of the subdivision of large estates in the country, resulting in closer settlement " (p. 136).

[1] Compiled from data in *Census Bulletin No. 17, Commonwealth of Australia* (1911), and in Coghlan, *A Statistical Account of Australia and New Zealand* (1903–04), p. 853.

in 1886 to 4.82 in 1906 and to 4.66 in 1911. Moreover, the percentage of the population in houses constructed of better materials had increased from 95.83 per cent in 1891 to 97.64 per cent in 1911; while the improved accommodations were mainly in the five to six room houses, which constituted the largest class of dwellings. There were 89,275 houses of five to six rooms in 1911, an increase of 20,885 in five years.[1] As to Australia, dwellings with five and six rooms predominated also in New South Wales, Victoria, and Queensland, in 1911; those with three and four rooms constituting the largest group in South Australia, Western Australia, and Tasmania. Wooden houses continue to predominate in all the colonies excepting South Australia, where, in 1911, stone buildings were about sixty-two per cent of all the dwellings. At the same time the number of brick houses had increased considerably, the increase being least in Queensland and South Australia.[2]

But are these favorable housing conditions attributable at all to the tax on unimproved value? Since some form of the tax is levied in each of the colonies, it is difficult to draw positive conclusions from a comparison of conditions in the several states. Nevertheless, such a comparison is suggestive, if not conclusive. Bearing in mind that of the four largest cities in New Zealand, Wellington and Christchurch rate on the unimproved value, and Auckland and Dunedin on the annual value, the changes in housing in these cities set forth in the accompanying table on page 110 deserve consideration.

It is noteworthy that Christchurch, in spite of its very rapid growth of population, has the least congestion, and that the average number of persons per dwelling has tended to decrease in Wellington more than in Dunedin; while

---

[1] *Report on Results of the Census of New Zealand* (1911), p. 24.
[2] *Census Bulletin No. 17, Commonwealth of Australia* (1911), p. 7; Coghlan, *op. cit.*, 1903–04, p. 853.

TABLE SHOWING THE AVERAGE NUMBER OF PERSONS TO EACH INHABITED DWELLING IN THE FOUR PRINCIPAL CITIES OF NEW ZEALAND, 1891–1911[1]

Borough	Population 1911	Per cent of increase in population 1891–1911	Average number of persons to dwelling		
			1891	1901	1911
Auckland.........	40,536	41.6	5.09	5.17	5.47
Wellington........	64,372	107.5	5.50	5.51	4.96
Christchurch	53,116	227.4	5.41	5.09	4.60
Dunedin..........	41,529	85.6	5.11	5.06	4.71

Auckland shows an increase in congestion rather than a decrease as in the other cities.

The optional rating system in New Zealand permits of further comparison. If the exemption of improvements from taxation encourages building and improvement, then it would seem that for towns of approximately the same population, the value of improvements would tend to be greater in the towns that rate on the unimproved value. Nevertheless, both because of the influence of other factors,[2] and because of the comparatively few cases presented in the subjoined tables, the effect of the rating system on building operations is not apparent from the table. The value of improvements exceeded the value of the land in fifteen (sixty-eight per cent) out of the twenty-two boroughs represented as rating on unimproved value, and in only nine (forty-three per cent) out of the twenty-one boroughs rating on capital or annual value. When, however, we find equally large increments of value in improvements in boroughs that do not rate on unimproved value as in those

---

[1] *Report on Results of the Census of New Zealand* (1911), p. 25.

[2] Everything that affects the site value, e.g., the general conditions of business, or the land tax even, will change the ratio of building to land value. For that reason the data presented for comparison are inadequate, but are the best available.

I. TABLE SHOWING THE RELATIVE VALUE OF LAND
AND IMPROVEMENTS IN CERTAIN BOROUGHS RATING
ON UNIMPROVED VALUE IN 1913 [1]

Borough	Population in 1913	Unimproved value of land	Value of the improvements	Per cent value of improvements to capital value	Per cent increase in value of improvements 1906-11
Devenport........	7,501	£654,513	£874,318	57.2	84
Grey Lynn.......	8,491	511,038	711,385	58.2	151
Gisborne.........	9,317	1,428,720	1,133,327	44.3	102
Dannevirke......	3,527	381,859	387,517	50.4	170
Palmerston North.	11,709	1,653,845	1,272,403	43.5	49
Masterton	5,585	572,750	680,620	54.3	30
Lower Hutt......	4,440	862,406	569,537	39.8	42
Petone..........	7,010	688,609	701,581	50.4	40
Onslow..........	1,969	270,022	271,981	50.1	79
Wellington.......	66,338	11,438,441	10,114,152	46.9	64
Karori...........	1,534	318,645	196,720	38.1	
Miramar.........	1,739	514,648	303,321	37.0	
Greymouth.......	5,560	270,534	557,722	67.3	
Christchurch	55,098	6,145,614	7,145,802	53.8	
Woolston........	3,699	172,641	303,938	63.7	
Spreydon........	3,560	235,360	342,070	59.2	
New Brighton....	1,990	167,585	186,569	52.6	
Sumner..........	1,987	272,690	255,987	48.4	
West Harbour....	2,119	74,788	129,517	63.3	
Maori Hill.......	2,278	184,000	244,642	57.0	
Invercargill......	13,590	1,274,361	1,793,723	58.4	
Campbelltown....	1,865	98,570	181,887	64.8	

that do (see last column of tables I and II), the efficacy
of the land tax in stimulating building cannot be judged
from the foregoing data.

With regard to the alleged tendency of the tax to encourage overbuilding, the following data of the number
of vacant dwellings (see table on page 113), though
equally inconclusive as the foregoing, are nevertheless of
interest.

Considering that some of the early dwellings must have

[1] *Statistics of the Dominion of New Zealand* (1913), vol. IV.

II. TABLE SHOWING THE RELATIVE VALUE OF LAND
AND IMPROVEMENTS IN CERTAIN BOROUGHS RATING
ON CAPITAL OR ANNUAL VALUE IN 1913 [1]

Borough	Population in 1913	Unimproved value of land	Value of the improvements	Per cent value of improvements to capital value	Per cent increase in value of improvements 1906–11
Whangarei *	2,790	£344,221	£287,758	45.6	129
Birkenhead *	2,073	319,415	266,605	45.5	188
Northcote	1,537	183,008	143,155	43.8	
New Market	3,127	370,569	295,560	44.3	80
Mount Eden	10,078	752,359	1,169,372	60.8	118
Mount Albert	7,878	791,660	734,600	48.1	
Auckland	47,783	11,429,684	6,987,325	37.9	73
Onehunga	4,872	514,137	497,128	49.1	
Waihi	6,740	150,063	273,535	64.5	119
New Plymouth	7,575	1,332,112	872,703	39.5	84
Napier	10,910	1,496,121	1,366,489	47.7	63
Wauganui	13,380	1,686,113	1,106,359	48.9	123
Nelson	8,465	845,223	899,720	51.5	48
Lyttelton	4,151	265,510	693,447	72.3	
Timaru	12,048	1,120,531	1,117,759	49.8	
Oamaru	5,405	290,531	542,802	65.1	
Dunedin	48,988	4,209,061	6,227,536	59.6	
Mornington	4,917	190,541	404,368	67.9	
St. Kilda *	4,486	305,045	544,585	64.0	
Green Island	1,991	60,925	173,751	74.0	
Invercargill South	1,549	136,394	122,706	47.3	

* Adopted rating on unimproved value in 1913.

been abandoned by the owners as unfit for habitation, the
figures do not indicate much overbuilding. New Zealand
had the largest proportion of vacant houses, Queensland
the least. When it is considered that urban property in
1901 largely escaped the state land taxes, and that the
system of rating on unimproved value was most prevalent
in Queensland, the very low percentage (one and six-tenths
per cent) of vacant houses in the latter colony is note-

[1] *Statistics of the Dominion of New Zealand* (1913), vol. IV.

TABLE SHOWING PERCENTAGE OF VACANT HOUSES AND
HOUSES IN CONSTRUCTION TO THE TOTAL NUMBER
OF DWELLINGS, 1901 [1]

Class of dwelling	New South Wales Per cent	Victoria Per cent	Queensland Per cent	South Australia Per cent	Western Australia Per cent	Tasmania Per cent	New Zealand Per cent
Uninhabited	5.5	4.5	1.6	7.4	4.4	6.3	6.3
In construction.....	.53	.24	..	.47	.39	.50	.50

worthy. The following figures of the proportion of vacant
houses in the four principal cities of New Zealand again
fail to furnish any conclusive evidence of the effect of the
tax on building. In 1901, when all the above-named cities [2]
rated on the annual value, the proportion of the uninhabited dwellings to all the dwellings in three of the four
cities was less than a decade later. Wellington and Christchurch show a considerable increase in the number of vacant houses, but so does Dunedin, where rating is still
on the annual value.

In this connection it has been urged against the system
of taxing land value, that the exemption of buildings from
taxation will induce the owners to utilize all the available
space to the detriment of sanitary dwellings; also that all
open spaces, recreation centers, would be built upon to
the detriment of the public welfare. A New Zealand cor-
respondent claims that this overbuilding tendency has
actually occurred in Christchurch where rating on unimproved value is in operation.[3] The evidence on this point

[1] Coghlan, op. cit., 1903–04, p. 853.

[2] Wellington adopted rating on land value in 1901, Christchurch in
1902.

[3] "It is causing open spaces in the towns to be cut up and built upon;

TABLE SHOWING PERCENTAGE OF THE UNINHABITED
TO THE TOTAL NUMBER OF BUILDINGS IN THE
PRINCIPAL CITIES OF NEW ZEALAND, 1901 AND 1911 [1]

| City | 1901 | | 1911 | | Number of houses in build-ing, 1911 |
	Number of vacant houses	Percentage of total	Number of vacant houses	Percentage of total	
Auckland....	237	3.4	220	2.9	29
Wellington...	266	3.2	941	7.2	77
Christchurch.	134	3.7	661	5.7	99
Dunedin.....	105	2.0	488	5.5	48

is, however, insufficient. But from the housing conditions
in Australasia, as described above, it is clear that the one
family house continues to prevail generally and that the
evils of congestion are not imminent there.

Returning to the evidence of the Australasian officials,
we find it claimed by many of them that the land tax
has had a deterrent effect on speculation in land, that to
some extent it has caused the "fictitious" value of land
to decline. Upon the introduction of the tax the tendency
has perhaps been for land to fall in value; [2] but with the

and there is every inducement, of course, for the owner to crowd as many
houses as possible on a section for letting purposes; seeing that he pays
the same rates whether he has one house or ten on an acre of ground. It
has been most injurious from this point of view in the cathedral city of
Christchurch, long the admiration of visitors as the 'Garden City' of
New Zealand. Land is fairly cheap there, and almost in the center of the
town were large and beautiful gardens. . . . These were additional
'lungs' for that city and added much to its picturesqueness. The new
system of rating, however, has made it ruinous for the owner to keep these
gardens and so they are being cut up and covered with more or less jerry-
built houses. To this extent the change is not for the better, and there is
no doubt that in towns the system, without any safeguards, directly tends
to the creation of slums." The Australasian, May 19, 1906, p. 1168.

[1] Report on the Result of the Census of New Zealand (1901), p. 23; Results
of a Census of New Zealand (1911), p. 27.

[2] "One of the immediate effects of the new local government law . . .

ordinary development of the country and the growth in population the value of the land has soon advanced again. In general it is held that while speculation in land is still rife in the colonies, the burden on those who have kept their land undeveloped in the hope of appropriating the increments, has induced many to part with their land. But the purchasing of land for residential and business purposes has been stimulated.[1] In South Australia, the subdivision and sale of land by speculators became perceptible only after the additional and absentee charges were levied in 1895. "For years past there has been a gradual closing up of all vacant land around the city, a great deal of which may be attributed to the land tax, more particularly since the application of additional and absentee land taxes, in conjunction with the increased rates of income tax imposed at the same time; but much of the movement would have occurred irrespective of taxation, with the gradual growth, and advancement of the State." [2] The tendency of speculators to dispose of the land because of the burden of the tax was noticeable also in New South Wales, but as in South Australia other influences coöperated in this movement.[3] The disintegration process now going on in New Zealand and in the Commonwealth of Australia is the strongest evidence

is a sharp fall in land values in the suburban districts. . . . None the less, property owners are alarmed. . . . Meanwhile, the slump in suburban land values approaches in violence to something of the kind that happens after boom bubbles have burst. One leading Sydney auctioneer and land valuer gives a most pessimistic account of the suburban land market. He fears a permanent decline in values." *The Australasian*, June 27, 1908, p. 1614.

[1] "There is less incentive to expend money in land in Queensland than anywhere else, owing to the unimproved value of land having to bear all the local tax." *Papers Relative to the Working of Taxation on Unimproved Value in Queensland* (Cd. 3890), 1908, pp. 18, 19; also *Papers Bearing on Land Taxes*, etc. (Cd. 4750), 1909, p. 133.

[2] *Papers Relative to the Working of Taxation*, etc. (Cd. 3191), 1906, p. 5.

[3] *Papers Bearing on Land Taxes*, etc. (Cd. 4750), 1909, p. 133.

that a heavy land tax checks speculative land holdings. According to the Commissioner of Taxes of New Zealand,[1] where both the legislation and administration of the tax has been most efficient, land speculation is now practically confined to suburban property for building purposes, and "the form of speculation in land unused and held for a prospective increment is rarely met with in recent years." The most that can be claimed for the tax in regard to its effect on speculation is that it discourages the withholding of land from use, and tends to steady the value of land.

The experience with the tax on unimproved value is thought to bear out the theory of the incidence of this tax; the land tax, generally speaking, is not shifted by the owner of the land. The farmers, as taxpayers, are said to be burdened heaviest by this system, for in rural communities the value of improvements which go untaxed is insignificant compared with that in cities. As regards the tax for state purposes, however, the small farmer, as we have seen, is exempt for the most part; while as regards local rates, unless the differential system under which the rate of the urban and rural divisions respectively is different and adjusted according to the needs of each division,[2] rating on unimproved value will impose a greater hardship, relatively speaking, upon rural communities.[3]

In view of this general consensus of opinion on the incidence of the land tax, the following results of a comparison of rentals in towns that rate on the unimproved value and

[1] The evidence of Mr. Heyes is especially noteworthy because of the investigation which he himself caused to be made among the local authorities, whose testimony he printed verbatim in his report published in *Papers Bearing on Land Taxes*, etc. (Cd. 4750), 1909, pp. 137–40.

[2] *Cf. supra*, pp. 90–91.

[3] The following is the report of a local body in New Zealand with reference to the incidence of the tax: "Township mostly agricultural land, and complaints made that rates fall heavily on these lands as compared with township residences, hotels," etc. *Papers Bearing on Land Taxes*, etc. (Cd. 4750), 1909, p. 138.

AVERAGE WEEKLY RENTS FOR DWELLINGS IN SELECTED
BOROUGHS IN NEW ZEALAND CLASSIFIED ACCORDING
TO THE RATING SYSTEM, 1911[1]

Class of boroughs	3 rooms	4 rooms	5 rooms	6 rooms	7 rooms	8 rooms	9 rooms*	10 rooms*
Twenty-two boroughs rating on unimproved value..	8s.	10.1s.	12.5s.	14.4s.	17.4s.	19.8s.	21.3s.	26.9s.
Twenty-four boroughs rating on annual or capital value....	6.9s.	9.1s.	11.5s.	13.6s.	16.2s.	19.0s.	22.0s.	24.7s.

* Seventeen out of the forty-six boroughs considered had no nine-room and twenty-two
had no ten-room dwellings. This fact may in part explain the divergence from the general
trend of averages in the other columns.

those that do not are somewhat startling. Nevertheless, in
viewing the table it must be borne in mind that although
the boroughs were selected at random, the only basis of
comparison was the system of rating, and that other influences very likely entered in to account for some of the
difference in rental. As shown above the average weekly
rental in the twenty-two boroughs which had by 1911
adopted the tax on the unimproved value was approximately one shilling higher (except in the case of the nine-
and ten-room dwellings) than in the twenty-four boroughs
under the old system of rating.[2] Attention must, however,
be called to the fact that the inordinately high rentals in

[1] The names and the population of the towns under consideration are
given in the tables *supra*, pp. 111–12. The averages were computed from
data in the *Report on the Results of a Census of New Zealand* (1911), p.
26. It is necessary to mention that in the computation of the averages
the fractions of a shilling were disregarded.

[2] Three of the twenty-four boroughs have since adopted rating on the
unimproved value.

Wellington, whose population is considerably above that of any city in the other class of boroughs, raised the average of the group of towns rating on the unimproved value. Moreover, that the effect of the tax is not gauged by the comparison of rentals is clearly shown in the subjoined comparison of the four principal cities of New Zealand.

If the rating system and population were the sole determinants of the variation in the rentals of the four cities, the lower rental in Dunedin than in Auckland for dwellings of from three to six rooms would not be explainable. The population of Dunedin was in 1911, 48,988, of Auckland 47,783, while both cities had the same rating system. Nor is the lower rental in Christchurch, with a population of 55,098, and the higher rental in Wellington, with a population of 66,338, as compared with Auckland to be explained by the tax on land value. The preceding tables, nevertheless, are significant in dispelling the claim that the tax on the unimproved value has reduced rents.

Only a few authorities reporting to the British Com-

AVERAGE WEEKLY RENTALS IN THE FOUR LARGEST
CITIES OF NEW ZEALAND IN 1911 [1]

Class of dwellings	Boroughs rating on unimproved value		Boroughs rating on annual value	
	Wellington	Christchurch	Auckland	Dunedin
	£ s. d.	£ s. d.	£ s. d.	£ s. d.
3 Rooms....	11 5.83	7 11.16	8 5.88	7 9.29
4 "	14 4.26	10 5.97	10 9.94	10 6.01
5 "	17 1.88	13 2.88	13 5.48	13 1.04
6 "	1 0 11.58	15 5.22	16 2.80	15 11.21
7 "	1 5 1.15	18 10.48	18 10.51	19 1.29
8 "	1 9 3.96	1 0 8.82	1 2 4.08	1 4 0.22
9 "	1 15 8.99	1 2 11.69	1 4 8.46	1 6 6.50
10 "	1 19 5.10	1 6 6.75	1 11 10.32	1 7 8.87

[1] *Report on the Results of a Census of New Zealand* (1911), p. 26.

mission mentioned a fall in rental; in general the effect on rents seems to have been slight; and where, as in New South Wales, rents were reported to have declined, the cause of the depreciation was attributed to some other factors besides the tax.[1]

But one may well inquire why rents should not have fallen. For it might be expected, as a result of the check in land speculation, of the better utilization of vacant land, of the exemption of improvements from taxation, and of the added stimulation given to building operations, that more houses would be available and that rents would decrease. The reason for the stability and in some cases the increase in rents may be found either in the failure of the tax to reduce speculation and to stimulate building operations; or in the rapid influx of immigrants, which has tended to counteract the putative tendencies of the tax and to enhance the value of the land. For, although immediately upon the enactment of the legislation the realty market may experience a depression (without a change in rents), the upward tendency of land value soon asserts itself again.

Summary: In so far as the efficacy of the land tax can be gauged at all, the results of the levy have been more or less beneficial economically and socially. Housing conditions continue to improve in the colonies in spite of the increase in population. Had the rates of taxes been considerably higher the effects on land speculation, perhaps too on rents, would have been more notable. To what extent the exemption of business premises from heavy

---

[1] "Rents of large residences have declined considerably, but to what extent the Land Tax has been a lever it is difficult to say. It has certainly operated to some extent, but there have been other factors at work." *Papers Bearing on Land Taxes*, etc. (Cd. 4750), 1909, p. 133. "The taxation of the unimproved value of land in any area," reports an official of Queensland, "omitting altogether a tax on improvements, necessarily lightens the burden in the instance of improved properties. This should and does enable the rent charge to be lessened." *Ibid.*, p. 210.

taxes has in turn stimulated business can only be inferred.

In conclusion, two significant facts are to be noted. First, in no case has there been a repeal of the tax except to extend its operation; in other words, after its adoption, however great the opposition may previously have been, the levy of the tax ceased to be a party measure. Indeed, the opponents of the tax seem to have become reconciled to its existence; at best they have attempted merely to disprove the beneficent results predicted by the sanguine supporters of the land tax.[1] Secondly, the adoption of the tax by one state after another, by the local bodies,[2] and recently by the federal government of Australia, argues in its favor and for its expediency in that country.

[1] This appears to be the attitude of such an opponent of the tax as the editor of *The Australasian*, from which we have quoted.

[2] There was a movement on foot in Tasmania to introduce rating on the unimproved value of land. Land Valuation Bills were before the Assemblies in Victoria and Tasmania, and as pointed out before, the former state now rates on land value. *Cf. The Australasian*, July 25, 1908, p. 229; September 25, 1909, p. 823.

CHAPTER IV

THE TAX ON VALUE INCREMENT IN GERMANY

§ 1. LIKE the adoption of the land tax in Australasia, the spread of the tax on value increment in Germany has been rapid; within the last decade, it is noteworthy, the tax has appeared as a local, state, and federal measure. In Germany the local increment tax laid the foundation and became the model of the state and imperial taxes. Hence, in spite of the suspension practically of the local and state systems since the introduction of the "Reichs-zuwachssteuer" (the imperial increment tax), the local taxes must nevertheless be studied in order to understand the causes, purpose, form, and expediency of the present system.

At the outset we are confronted with certain differences, both in form and character, between the German local tax and the local system studied in the preceding chapters. The latter is a direct, the former an indirect levy; in one case, the tax falls on the selling value, in the other, on the value increment; the one is a proportional, the other a progressive tax; the one tends to become a single tax for local purposes, the other to be merely a supplementary source of revenue. How are these differences to be accounted for? The explanation is to be found in the radically diverse fiscal systems of German and Anglo-Saxon communities respectively.

In England the development of the present system of rating on real property in the local bodies can be traced from the Elizabethan law of direct taxation on property. This system has not only remained uniform and unchanged in England, but has been taken over and is in vogue in her colonies generally. In contrast with this method of rating, local taxation in Germany comprises many kinds of taxes, is less uniform in the different states, and has undergone numerous revisions. Indeed, as the development of Germany in general has been a tardy one, so the development of her fiscal policy has lagged behind that of other nations.[1] If we may be permitted to summarize the local fiscal systems, rendered complex on account of the different civic divisions of local government,[2] on account of the variety of need in different sections of the country, and on account of the variety of legislation of the separate states, local revenue in Germany is, speaking generally, derived both from the levy of indirect and direct taxes. The former consist mainly of excises on consumption commodities, the latter comprise in the main, the land, building, and business taxes, the income tax and the tax on interest.[3] Thus the systems of local taxation followed the same development as the state fiscal policies; indeed, the taxes levied by the local authorities are often supplemental rates, or percentages added to the state taxes. The principle of taxation conforming to this complex system, and consciously formulated in some of the local tax laws, is that of faculty ("nach seinem Vermögen und mit seinen Kräften")[4] in contrast to that of benefit, the principle of *quid pro quo* to which, many would hold, the English rating system conforms.

But, since we are concerned with a land tax, it is necessary to note the rôle that land plays in Germany as a source of local revenue. The land, house and business taxes displaced the old general property tax of Prussia in 1861. A revaluation of the land on the basis of the average net

[1] *Cf.* Wagner, *Finanzwissenschaft*, 2 Aufl., 3 Tl., § 93.

[2] Gemeinden, Districte und Kreise, in Prussia; Gemeinden and Körperschaften, in Baden; etc.

[3] Grund-Gebäude-Gewerbesteuern, Einkommen- und Kapitalrentensteuern. The systems have been simplified recently by the enactment of the Prussian "Kommunalabgabengesetz" of 1893, and similar state measures.

[4] *Cf.* Wagner, *op. cit.*, 4 Tl., § 26.

product of the land was then made and the land tax was apportioned among the local bodies, and has since then remained a fixed land charge. The defects of this tax are admitted by all authorities.[1] The tax on houses which is a separate tax is levied on the basis of the average annual rental during the ten-year period preceding the valuation. The assessment is subject to revision only once in fifteen years. This tax likewise weighs unequally on different taxpayers. That land has contributed little to the local receipts can be seen from the following data showing the percentage of the total tax receipts collected from the "Grund- und Gebäudesteuern" in 1889, in the following important German cities: [2]

	Per cent		Per cent		Per cent
Altona	49.20	Kassel	16.80	Breslau	10.16
Stuttgart	28.53	Wiesbaden	16.34	Magdeburg	8.93
Nürnberg	21.86	Dresden	16.18	Mülhausen i. E.	8.45
Karlsruhe	21.05	Darmstadt	15.27	Strassburg i. E.	5.66
Mannheim	20.88	Frankfurt a. O.	15.18	Metz	4.44
München	20.54	Berlin	14.84	Frankfurt a. M.	0.
Mainz	17.81	Augsburg	13.31		
Leipzig	18.58	Cologne	11.69		

With few exceptions (Altona, Stuttgart) land was not a very important source of income, contributing about one-fifth of the local revenue in four cities and less in the others. Frankfurt a. M., it will be noted, levied no land and house taxes. Instead, a rental tax (Mietsteuer) was levied in that city as well as in other cities (Berlin, for example). In some of the above-mentioned municipalities, Altona, Frankfurt a. M., Leipzig, and Dresden, a tax on land transfer is charged. On the whole, however, in comparison with Anglo-Saxon countries, the burden of taxation on land is a light one.

[1] Wagner, *op. cit.*, 4 Tl., § 13. *Cf.* Adickes, "Über die Weitere Entwicklung des Gemeinde-Steuerwesens auf Grund des preussischen Kommunalabgabengesetzes vom 14 Juli 1893." *Zeitschrift für die gesamte Staatswissenschaft*, vol. L (1894), p. 585.

[2] *Ibid.*, p. 415.

From this brief sketch of the local tax systems it will be readily seen that in Germany a direct proportional tax on the unimproved value of land, such as was developed in Australasia, would have been anomalous and revolutionary.

§ 2. Having shown why the German land-value tax had to assume an essentially different character from the tax on unimproved value, we shall in the following sections attempt to account for the form it did assume. The epoch-making reform in local taxation was the Prussian "Kommunalabgabengesetz" of July 14, 1893. Its importance lies not so much in the increase of taxing powers granted to the local governments,[1] as in the division of revenue sources between the state and local authorities. The Act is significant, moreover, not because it empowered the communities to levy direct and indirect taxes on property and land [2] (taxes they already levied), but because it took from the communities the power (1) of raising income taxes (except as percentages added to the state income taxes [3]) and (2) of introducing excise duties on meat, grain, flour, pastry, potatoes and fuel; and where these taxes already existed, the rate of tax could not be increased.[4] These restrictions, it is clear, have made the local bodies more dependent upon property for revenue and have aided in the endeavor to make local fiscal policy conform with the benefit principle of taxation.[5]

The "Kommunalabgabengesetz," in fact, did more. In

[1] Local autonomy in taxation dates back to very early times in German history; but all taxing powers were taken from the local governments by Friedrich Wilhelm I (1738) and only restored to them in 1808. *Cf.* Wagner, *op. cit.*, 4 Tl., § 26.

[2] *Preussisches Kommunalabgabengesetz vom 14 Juli 1893*, §§ 13, 20, 23, 24.

[3] *Ibid.*, § 36.   [4] *Ibid.*, § 14.

[5] This tendency to simplify local taxes in conformity with economic principles is shown in the recent legislation of the other German states. Saxony had relegated the land tax to the local governments as early as 1873. *Cf. Verhandlungen des Vereins für Sozialpolitik* (1911), pp. 14 *ff.*, 18.

authorizing the communities to levy special land taxes (besondere Steuern vom Grundbesitz) and to tax building sites (Bauplätze) at a higher rate than other property,[1] the Act opened the way for the levy of a discriminatory tax on land. These taxes which took the form of the "Bauplatzsteuer" and "Steuer nach dem gemeinen Wert" were indeed the precursors of the tax on value increment. Among these antecedent attempts to discriminate against land in taxation the "Umsatzsteuer" must be included. We turn to the consideration of these land taxes.

§ 3. The "Umsatzsteuer" collected on the occasion of a transfer of real property very probably developed out of the prevailing practice of charging a fee for registering and transferring the deed of sale.[2] That it was originally intended as a fee appears from the names of the charges. Thus in Emden (as early as 1670) it was known as "Siegelgeld," seal money;[3] in Danzig, as "Kaufschoss," stamp duty on conveyance; in Hildesheim (1374), as "Litkaufsgeld," originally drink-money.[4] Whether the fiscal expediency of the charge, or some other cause, led to its development into a tax, the "Umsatzsteuer" must now be regarded as a tax, instead of a fee, for the following reasons: —

(1) The amount of tax is a percentage of the selling price of the property; the charge is, therefore, not proportioned to the expense of the service as in the case of a fee.

(2) In most cases (Leipzig, Dresden, and Chemnitz are exceptions), no charge is paid when the exchange of prop-

---

[1] *Preussisches Kommunalabgabengesetz vom 14 Juli 1893*, §§ 25, 27.

[2] The system of land registration in the "Grundbuch" is almost universal throughout Germany. *Cf. Papers Bearing on Land Taxes*, etc. (Cd. 4750), 1909, p. 12.

[3] Not only upon the sale of real property but upon the sale of ships, "Siegelgeld" was collected. *Cf.* Adickes, *op. cit.*, p. 434.

[4] The fee displaced the wine-drinking upon the close of a bargain. *Cf.* Lübben, *Mnd. Handwörterbuch*, p. 208.

erty is the result of a gift, or of a bequest; showing that the tax was intended to fall on exchanges of property involving profits.

(3) The receipts from this tax are devoted to other purposes than to cover the cost of service. Thus in Dresden the receipts are used for poor relief, schools and fire protection.[1] Similarly in other cities.

The "Umsatzsteuer" is widespread throughout Germany. Under the name of "Währschaftsgeld" this transfer tax, levied continuously since 1820,[2] is still a prolific source of revenue for Frankfurt a. M. In Prussia, all but thirteen out of the two hundred and sixty-six cities of more than 10,000 inhabitants levy land-transfer taxes.[3] The rate of tax in Prussia varies in the different cities, from one to two per cent of the value of the property including the structures and improvements. Berlin and Königsberg levy the tax, drawing a distinction between improved and unimproved land; in Berlin the rate is one per cent in case of exchanges of improved land, two per cent in case of unimproved land, while in Königsberg it is two per cent and three per cent in the city and suburbs respectively.[4]

The tax on land transfers is also prevalent in the other German states. In Hessen, for example, the "Umsatzsteuer" is levied for state purposes, but the local bodies were granted, in 1907, the option of levying supplementary rates not to exceed fifty per cent of the revenue of the state tax. This additional levy must be in accordance with the following progressive scale.[5] When the value of the property sold is less than 1000 marks, the rate is .1 per cent: —

---

[1] *Cf.* Adickes, *op. cit.*, pp. 440–41.

[2] *Schriften des Vereins für Sozialpolitik* (1910), vol. CXXVII, p. 15; *cf.* with *Papers Bearing on Land Taxes*, etc. (Cd. 4750), 1909, p. 10, where the "Währschaftsgeld" is said to have been levied as early as 1801 in Frankfurt.

[3] *Schriften des Vereins für Sozialpolitik* (1910), vol. CXXVII, p. 15.

[4] *Kommunales Jahrbuch* (1910), pp. 615–16.

[5] *Schriften des Vereins für Sozialpolitik* (Gemeindefinanzen), vol. CXXVI, p. 52.

From 1,000 to 2,000 marks, the rate is .2 per cent
" 2,000 " 10,000 " " " " .4 " "
" 10,000 " 20,000 " " " " .6 " "
" 20,000 " 50,000 " " " " .8 " "
Over 50,000 " " " " 1 " "

In 1903, the communes of Württemberg were similarly empowered to impose an "Umsatzsteuer," of which the maximum rate was not to exceed one per cent additional to the rate levied for state purposes.[1] The rate in Baden is fixed for the local governments at one-half per cent. The tax is obligatory and is levied as a supplement to the state transfer tax.[2] The local rate in Bavaria is one-half per cent, forming an addition to the state tax.[3] Similarly in Saxony, where 2400 communes levy land-transfer taxes at rates varying from eight-hundredths per cent to one per cent. The state tax is limited to a minimum rate of one-half per cent of the selling price of the property.[4] It is noteworthy, that in contrast to these low rates of tax, the state "Umsatzsteuer" in Alsace-Lorraine is five and one-half per cent (including the fee for recording of deed). This shows the influence of France where the exchange tax is unusually high, being over six per cent.[5]

The importance that the "Umsatzsteuer" has assumed in Germany is due in great part to the propaganda, since the seventies, of men like Adoph Wagner who have urged the expediency of the tax on the ground that the community is entitled to share the profits accruing from the great appreciation in land value in urban communities. The recognition of the evils that speculation in land occasions, and of the enormous profits reaped by individuals by virtue of their ownership, not toil, is general. Hence the "Umsatzsteuer."

---

[1] *Schriften des Vereins für Sozialpolitik*, vol. cxxvi, pp. 88–89.
[2] *Ibid.*, p. 119.   [3] *Ibid.*, p. 221.   [4] *Ibid.*, p. 262.
[5] Adickes, *op. cit.*, pp. 441–42. For the prevalence of the "Umsatzsteuer" in Germany *cf.* also Birnbaum, *Die Gemeindlichen Steuersysteme in Deutschland.*

§ 4. But by itself the "Umsatzsteuer" was ineffective. And under the slight burden of the "Grundsteuer" speculation continued and great fortunes were made through the enormous appreciation in the value of the land following the industrial awakening of Germany after 1871. And as the budget of the municipalities grew with the development of the cities, it became more and more evident that the urban landowners who benefited most through the growth of the city were not contributing their full quota to the revenue. To make them do so, it was necessary to tax their land on the basis of its selling price, or capital value, not as formerly on its product. This was the origin of the "Steuer nach dem gemeinen Wert." Like the old land tax this is a direct levy, but the basis of valuation is now the market value of the land. The rates vary from two to four per cent of the value of the property (improvements are generally included).

The first attempt to substitute "capital value" for product as the basis of taxation was made in Bremen. The Act passed in 1874 changed the rate of the old tax from one and a half to two mills, and provided for the assessment of urban property on the basis of its selling value.[1] In answer to the protest, which the latter provision aroused, the "Senatskommissär" replied that "in his opinion the selling value was the correct basis of valuation. In the case of purely agricultural land under cultivation the selling value was identical with the produce value (Ertragswert). In case of land used for agricultural purposes but which could be sold for building sites, the selling value exceeded the usufruct value. It was, therefore, proper that the selling value be made the basis of valuation. The selling value of land was a profit which accrued to the owner not by virtue of his own labor but through the labor and toil of many persons. Therefore, it was proper that the community demand a tax from this source."[2] As already mentioned, this senti-

[1] Adickes, *op. cit.*, p. 599.   [2] *Ibid.*

ment was voiced not only by the economists but by public men in the Prussian Parliament and in the "Verein für Sozialpolitik." [1]

But while this first attempt failed and the Bremen Act was repealed (1878) because of the difficulties of valuation,[2] the movement spread. Thus, in Prussia, twenty-seven cities out of the thirty-four with a population exceeding 75,000 had, in 1908, levied such a tax. Three more, Kassel, Frankfurt a. M., Posen, made the selling value the basis of the valuation of undeveloped land, but rental the basis for valuing improved land. Only Altona, Halle, and Hannover of the largest cities persist in taxing the usufruct instead of the land value.[3] So do also the smaller communities especially in Eastern Prussia. The reason is that they are chiefly rural and the selling value of the land corresponds closely with the value on the basis of productivity. In Hessen, Saxony, and Baden the tax on selling value is in force. In Baden the law even provides that the tax commissioner of urban communities should make an *annual* valuation of the building land and should increase the assessed valuation, as soon as the value had appreciated at least ten per cent above that of the preceding year.[4] Indeed, the expediency of the "Steuer nach dem gemeinen Wert" for urban property is everywhere acknowledged.[5]

§ 5. In making the taxation of land on the basis of capital value optional with the local governments,[6] and

---

[1] Adickes, *op. cit.*, pp. 612–13.

[2] Because of the "fictitious" land values due to overspeculation, the assessors had overvalued the land for assessment purposes. Great reductions had to be made when the appeals were heard. *Cf. ibid.*, p. 601.

[3] *Schriften des Vereins für Sozialpolitik*, vol. CXXVII, p. 13.

[4] *Ibid.*, vol. CXXVI, pp. 26–27, 256, 136–37.

[5] *Ibid.*, pp. 14, 15. "Die Besteuerung des Grundeigentums, das schon Baugelände geworden ist, oder es in absehbarer Zeit zu werden verspricht, nach seinem gemeinen Wert und nicht nach seinem Ertrag wird auch heute kaum noch ernstlich bekämpft." *Ibid.*, p. 27.

[6] *Preussisches Kommunalabgabengesetz* (1893), § 25.

in sanctioning the discriminatory tax on building sites,[1] the "Kommunalabgabengesetz" of 1893 aided greatly the movement of land-value taxation. The government recognized thereby the serious problems, fiscal and social, which the political and economic changes had brought to pass. The question of the best means by which the local bodies might appropriate part of the "unearned increment" accruing from land was the vital point at issue. Two possibilities presented themselves. First, in conformity with § 27 of the Act, a direct tax on land might be introduced, differing from the old land tax (Grundsteuer) as follows: (1) instead of rental value as the base of the tax, the selling value might be substituted; (2) instead of treating all land alike, the property might be divided into several classes, each class subject to a different rate of tax, or to a different basis of assessment.[2] The objections to such a tax, however, were serious. Not only would the classification be arbitrary and difficult to make, but the valuation system for which no scientific precedent existed in Germany, would incur such inequalities in assessment as in the Bremen experiment. Moreover, a revision of the old apportioned land tax, it was feared, would weigh heavily on mortgaged property[3] and on the *bona fide* owner as compared with the speculator.

Secondly, an indirect tax to fall only on the "unearned increment" might be levied. Already, the expediency of the "Umsatzsteuer" was generally recognized. And from this tax to the tax on value increment was a short step. Even

[1] *Preussisches Kommunalabgabengesetz* (1893), § 27: "Die Steuern vom Grundbesitz sind nach gleichen Normen und Sätzen zu verteilen. Liegenschaften, welche durch die Festsetzung von Baufluchtlinien in ihrem Werte erhöht worden sind (Bauplätze), können nach Massgabe dieses höheren Wertes zu einer höheren Steuer als die übrigen Liegenschaften herangezogen werden. Diese Besteuerung muss durch Steuerordnung geregelt werden."

[2] Under § 27 uniform tax rates and uniform assessment bases within each class are required. *Cf.* Note 1, *supra.* This bars out a progressive scale from the direct land tax. *Cf.* Adickes, *op. cit.*, p. 633.

[3] Adickes, *op. cit.*, p. 444.

the progressive scale was applicable to the "Umsatzsteuer" as we saw in the case of Hessen.[1] This latter tax, then, was the origin of the "Wertzuwachssteuer."

The close relation between the transfer and increment taxes will be clear from the following analysis of the tax on value increment. The characteristics peculiar to it are the following: —

(a) The tax is charged on specific occasions of transfer of real property.

(b) The tax falls on the increment, that is, on the differential between the prior purchase price and the selling price on the occasion of the transfer.

(c) The basis of assessment is the selling value.

(d) The tax falls on the land apart from the improvements.[2]

As regards (a) and (c), the form of tax and basis of assessment, the tax on value increment does not differ from the "Umsatzsteuer." But as regards (b), the base of tax, there is a deviation from the "Umsatzsteuer." This distinctive feature of the tax on value increment is, however, not without precedent. Under the income taxes in Germany, it is noteworthy, profit made in any "Konjunktur" transaction or through the exchange of property is taxable as a form of income.[3] In Hamburg, for example, the In-

---

[1] The justice of progressive taxation was considered greater in the case of the unearned increment accruing from land than in the case of the income tax. *Ibid.*, p. 642. It is interesting, as showing the close relationship between these taxes, that R. Eberstadt (Entwurf einer Bauplatzsteuer) proposed a progressive "Umsatzsteuer" instead of the "Zuwachssteuer." *Cf. Preussische Jahrbücher* (1893), vol. LXXIV, p. 480. In Bavaria too the property transfer tax is progressive. *Cf.* Birnbaum, *op. cit.*, p. 203.

[2] It has been asserted that the "Wertzuwachssteuer" is a tax on real estate, not on pure land value. *Cf.* Seligman, *Essays in Taxation* (ed. 1913), p. 515. This is correct in so far as it applies to the imperial tax, but is the result of the partisan influences brought to bear on the legislation of that tax. See *infra*, § 13.

[3] *Cf.* Fuisting, *Die Preussischen direkten Steuern* (6th ed.), vol. I, pp. 61 ff. *Cf.* also § 12 of the Einkommensteuergesetz vom 24 Juni 1891, "Einkomen aus Kapitalvermögen."

come Tax Law of 1903 provides for the assessment of the
"profit made on any transaction of sale of real property . . .
the amount taxable being the difference between the selling price and the purchase price, expenditure on permanent improvements being added to the purchase price in
making the calculation." [1]

The validity of the last characteristic (d) may at first
be questioned because, apparently, the selling price of the
property (improvements included) is made the basis of
assessment just as, for example, in the "Umsatzsteuer."
In reality, however, it is the purpose of the deductions and
additions to the selling and purchase prices,[2] to exempt
the value accruing from the investment of capital and labor.
In fact, it is the method of computing the value increment,
not the principle, which is in question. The system of
scientific valuation of land apart from improvements has
made little progress in Germany,[3] even though the land and
house taxes have long been separately assessed. The principle of exempting the structures and improvements from
the increment tax, however, cannot be separated from the
principle of the "Zuwachssteuer" itself, because (1) the
value of the buildings and improvements does not increase
with time, and (2) any value of the property due to such
improvements, it is reasoned, is the legitimate return from
capital and not to be placed in the same category with
the "unearned increment."

§ 6. To show further the correlation between the tax on
value increment and the "Umsatzsteuer," the first "Zuwachssteuer" enacted will here be examined. The Frankfurt a. M. Act, as well as the laws of Cologne,[4] Gelsenkirchen,

[1] Cited in *Papers Bearing on Land Taxes*, etc. (Cd. 4750), 1909, p. 16.
[2] See *infra*, § 13.
[3] *Cf. Verhandlungen des Vereins für Sozialpolitik in Nürnberg* (1911),
in *Schriften des Vereins für Sozialpolitik*, vol. cxxxviii, p. 97.
[4] The Cologne law provides that when the seller has paid an increment
tax, the purchaser may deduct the amount of the tax from the transfer
tax payable by him; but the amount so deducted must not exceed fifty

Magdeburg, Görlitz, Hannover, Berlin, is a compound of the land-transfer and the progressive value-increment taxes. The tax on value increment is merely supplemental to the land-transfer tax. The Frankfurt ordinance in which both taxes are incorporated is the "Währschaftsgeldordnung" of 1904. It comprises, in reality, three taxes: —

(1) An ordinary transfer tax of two per cent of the selling price.

(2) A progressive transfer tax collectible in addition to the ordinary transfer tax, in case of land which has not changed hands in more than twenty years. This additional tax is chargeable only when the selling price on the occasion of levy exceeds the last purchase price by an amount greater than the amount of the additional tax.[1] The base of the tax is the selling price of the property; and a distinction is drawn between improved and unimproved land, as the following scale of rates shows: —

(a) For *improved* estates, if there has elapsed, since the last preceding change of ownership, —

More than 20 years,	but not more than	30 years,	1	per cent
" " 30 "	" " " "	" 40 "	1½	" "
" " 40 "			2	" "

(b) For *unimproved* property, if there has elapsed, since the last preceding change of ownership, —

More than 20 years,	but not more than	30 years,	2	per cent
" " 30 "	" " " "	" 40 "	3	" "
" " 40 "	" " " "	" 50 "	4	" "
" " 50 "	" " " "	" 60 "	5	" "
" " 60 "			6	" "

per cent of the whole transfer tax. (§ 1.) Moreover, it is provided that whenever the tax on value increment reaches a sum greater than 400,000 marks, the rate of the transfer tax shall be reduced by one-half of one per cent; when it reaches a sum greater than 800,000 marks, the reduction of the rate of the transfer tax shall be one per cent. (§ 15.) *Cf. Kommunales Jahrbuch* (1909), vol. i, p. 575. The law is translated in *Quarterly Journal of Economics*, vol. xxii, pp. 106 *ff.*

[1] Revised ordinance, 1906, § 3. Translated in *Papers Bearing on Land Taxes*, etc. (Cd. 4750), 1909, pp. 20 *ff.* To ascertain whether the property has appreciated in value, the expenditures on permanent improvements, including new buildings, or alterations to buildings, must be added to the previous purchase price.

(3) The third tax embodied in the ordinance is the tax on value increment. This is likewise an additional charge collectible only in case of land which has changed hands within less than twenty years. The base in this case is the value increment, ascertained by taking the difference between the last purchase price and the present selling price. In computing the value increment, however, the following additions to the purchase price are made: —

1. The expenditure of permanent improvements, including cost of street construction and sewer charges, the cost of new buildings or alterations; [1]

2. Five per cent of the previous purchase price as compensation for the cost incurred in connection with the previous transfer; this includes the stamp duty, transfer tax, court charges, etc.;

3. In case of unimproved land, not used for purposes of agriculture or industry by the vendor, four per cent of the purchase price, excluding compound interest, as compensation for capital invested.

Moreover, the increment tax is not levied if the value increment is less than fifteen per cent of the purchase price (the above additions included).[2] The progressive scale of rates is as follows: —

2% of the increment, if the increment is 15 to 20% of the purchase price
3% " "   "   " "   "   " 20 " 25% " "   "   "
4% " "   "   " "   "   " 25 " 30% " "   "   "
5% " "   "   " "   "   " 30 " 35% " "   "   "

And so on, one per cent for every five per cent of increment until the maximum rate of twenty-five per cent tax is reached. And this increment tax is paid in addition to the land-transfer tax.

§ 7. Such was the origin, from a fiscal standpoint, of the "Wertzuwachssteuer." Let us now consider the underlying principles of the tax, in so far as they have evolved

---

[1] Revised ordinance, § 4. To the extent to which such expenditures are covered by insurance, however, no account shall be taken of them.

[2] In the original Act of 1904 an increment of less than 30 per cent was exempt.

out of German conditions and out of the needs of the time. These principles will be considered under the main heads of "unearned increment," "German Sozialpolitik," and "benefit" in taxation.

One reason the "unearned increment" concept has until recently been associated chiefly with the income from land is the fact that the gains accruing from urban land holdings have been extraordinarily striking. Especially true has this been in Germany.[1] Until the Franco-Prussian War Germany was predominantly an agricultural country. But after the seventies, as a result of the competition of America and Australasia in the European market, the decline in agricultural production set in, and the wretched condition of the peasantry, especially in eastern Germany, where the large estates prevailed, began to arouse the concern of the statesmen. Strange as it may seem, it is to this apprehension, which engendered the policy of fostering superior workmanship and commercial enterprises, that the industrial awakening of Germany must be traced. This development followed hard upon the victory over the French and the consolidation of the German Empire. Rural districts and villages rapidly changed into urban and industrial communities. The growth in urban population was phenomenal. The following table shows something of the increase: [2]

[1] Dr. Miquel, Prussian Minister of Finance in 1893, pointed out the enormous rise in the value of urban land in Germany, which he claimed had appreciated in value more than in England. *Cf.* Adickes, *op. cit.*, p. 624.

[2] Compiled from data in the *Statistisches Jahrbuch für das Deutsche Reich* (1911), p. 22, and the *Statistisches Jahrbuch deutscher Städte* (1907), p. 44. The following table (from *Archiv für Soziale Gesetzgebung und Statistik*, 1893, p. 433) shows the rapid rise of urban communities: —

Class of towns	1871		1890	
	Number	Population	Number	Population
Population —				
Over 100,000	8	1,968,537	26	6,302,883
20,000 to 100,000	75	3,147,272	124	4,500,520
5,000 to 20,000	529	4,588,364	683	6,054,629
2,000 to 5,000	1716	5,086,625	1951	5,805,893

TABLE SHOWING THE INCREASE OF POPULATION IN CERTAIN GERMAN CITIES

City	Population		Percentage of increase
	1871	*1910*	
Berlin..........................	826,341	2,070,695	150.6
Gelsenkirchen.................	7,820	169,530	2068.0
Schöneberg...................	3,412	140,992	4023.0
Bremen.......................	122,402	298,736	144.1
Hamburg......................	338,974	1,015,707	199.6
Frankfurt.....................	113,936	414,598	264.0
Lübeck.......................	52,158	116,533	123.4

For our purpose the important fact to be noted is that this development was accompanied by an even greater appreciation in land value. For example, Dr. Mangoldt [1] estimated that the rental of occupied land in the city of Berlin had appreciated as follows: —

1830............................	17 million marks	
1840............................	38 "	"
1850............................	45 "	"
1860............................	229 "	"
1870............................	530 "	"
1880.........................	1,042 "	"
1890.........................	1,890 "	"
1898.........................	2,118 "	"

Comparing the percentage of increase in rental in Berlin from 1870 to 1898, with that of the growth of population as shown in the table, it is as 285 per cent [2] to 150.6 per cent. Or, take the statistics for Bavaria. The average rise in the value of the land for the decade, from 1897 to 1907, was estimated at 600 per cent for Bayreuth, 640 per cent for Kaiserslautern, 976 per cent for Aschaffenberg, 1500 per cent for Behringserdorf, etc. For a longer period of

---

[1] *Die städtische Bodenfrage*, p. 31.

[2] Were the figures for 1910 available, the difference would be even more striking.

time — from 1867 to 1907 — the average increases in land value were as follows:[1]

Mosach.......2307 per cent	Landshut..........5737 per cent
Erlangen......2703 " "	Fürth.............6566 " "
Bamberg.....3200 " "	Nürnberg..........6900 " "
Würzberg....4900 " "	Kaiserslautern.....8900 " "

It is needless to multiply examples of this common phenomenon dealt with so copiously in German literature. From the seventies to the end of the century was the time when peasants, in Roscher's phrase,[2] were transformed over-night into millionaires by virtue of their land ownership.

This enormous growth in the value of the land has brought in its train two so-called social ills; first, it has aggravated the speculation in land; and secondly, it is held responsible for the housing problem. Already in the sixties and seventies speculation in urban land became active, enriching many even of those who had been born serfs; in these decades the "Millionenbauern" formed a distinct social group.[3] The victory in 1871 and the economic changes succeeding that year gave a new impetus to land speculation. Realty and building companies were formed, whose watered stock found purchasers on the stock exchange and whose purpose was by no means the development of the urban communities.[4] There are but few large cities in Germany, it is asserted,[5] whose building operations are not controlled by one or more building and realty corporations (Terraingesellschaften). According to Adolph Damaschke [6] there are seventy-three such corporations in Berlin. They are generally comprised of speculators who

[1] *Kommunales Jahrbuch* (1909), vol. I, p. 561.

[2] *Grundlagen der Nationalökonomie* (1906 ed.), p. 261.

[3] Volgt, *Grundrente und Wohnungsfrage in Berlin und seinen Vororten,* p. 109.

[4] For their methods of operation see *ibid.*, pp. 114 *ff.*

[5] This is the position of the "Bodenreformer," but is maintained also by a host of other writers.

[6] *Jahrbuch der Bodenreform* (1907), vol. III, p. 168.

make a specialty of erecting tenements (Mietkasernen) in communities scarcely urban. For example, in Charlottenburg, Schöneberg, and other more recently settled communities, apartment houses of immense size were erected long before any need for them appeared. By this method and in other ways, these corporations have succeeded in driving up the market price of land far beyond what is warranted by the law of supply and demand.[1] Recently, investigations public and private have revealed serious unsanitary housing conditions and especially conditions of overcrowding. One example must suffice here. In greater Berlin 600,000 people live in dwellings in which each room is occupied by five or more persons.[2]

Under these conditions the ethical justification of the private appropriation of the "unearned increment" has been questioned. With one group, indeed, the "Bodenreformer," private property in land has been repudiated altogether; with another group, the "Sozialpolitiker," such restriction of urban land ownership has been sought as would enable the community to share the "unearned increment." The "justice" of this position is based on the fact that the community, with the concentration of population and its increasing functions of government, not the individual owner, creates the value increment; but also on the fact that social expediency requires the restriction of ownership of urban land.

§ 8. This policy of restriction which the adoption of the increment tax sanctioned marks no radical change in prin-

---

[1] Eberstadt, *Die Spekulation im neuzeitlichen Städtebau; Cf.* also *Verhandlungen des Vereins für Sozialpolitik in Nürnberg* (1911), in *Schriften des Vereins für Sozialpolitik*, vol. cxxxviii, p. 46.

[2] *Soziale Praxis* (1911–12), vol. xxi, p. 666. For other examples see *infra*, chapter ix, pp. 390–91. In the light of this discussion the following recent statement in the *Chicago Daily Tribune* (June 20, 1913, p. 16) is interesting: "A severe collapse in the real estate and building markets has been averted only by the concerted action of the banks. Overspeculation in flat buildings in Berlin has left the city with 80,000 small flats for which there are no tenants."

ciple. For the development of private property in land, in Germany, bears the stamp of that "Sozialpolitik" — social regulation — which since the organization of the "Verein für Sozialpolitik"[1] has become the consciously accepted state policy. It is true that with the break-up of the feudal system and with the advent of the capitalistic era, land became a commodity, subject to private ownership, in Germany as elsewhere. There remained, nevertheless, a great deal of communal land, the property of the states and communes. Especially in western and southwestern Germany, survivals of the old land system are to be found, for example, in the Allmenden and Domänen (the commons).

The state in which the public domain even yet plays a great rôle is Baden, where the revenue from the land is said to have exempted 121 rural communities from all taxation.[2] It is furthermore noteworthy that the largest cities in Baden in the last two decades have sought to increase their municipal holdings. In Mannheim, for instance, the land owned by this city constituted, in 1870, 23 per cent of the whole territory, in 1905, 36.8 per cent; in 1891, the unimproved land owned by the community (excluding the streets) was valued at about 22 million marks, in 1905, at nearly 50 millions,[3] an increase of about 127 per cent. The details of the city's growth cannot be entered into here. Suffice it to say that from 1890 to 1906, the budget had grown from 2,806,200 marks to 10,622,860 marks, and that nearly sixty per cent of this amount was in 1906 covered by non-tax revenue.[4] The other cities in Baden show a slower but similar development with respect to their land policy (Bodenpolitik). It is significant that the seven

[1] Organized at Eisenach in 1872, the "Verein für Sozialpolitik" has exercised an unusually powerful influence on state legislation.

[2] Damaschke, *Geschichte der Nationalökonomie* (3 ed.), p. 363.

[3] *Schriften des Vereins für Sozialpolitik* (1908), vol. CXXVI (Gemeindefinanzen), p. 140.

[4] *Ibid.*, p. 145.

largest cities are in possession of a net capital value of about 190 million marks, more than half of which comprises land value.[1]

This "Bodenpolitik," moreover, is not peculiar to Baden alone. Numerous German cities now vie with one another in this policy.[2] Many other cities draw a considerable revenue from the public lands, and many have established special funds to acquire more land.[3] Thus, it is very significant that in the following cities more than twenty per cent of the land is communal: —

PERCENTAGE OF LAND (STREETS AND ROADS EXCEPTED) WITHIN THE CITY UNDER PUBLIC OWNERSHIP [4]

*Frankfurt a. M....	49.0 per cent	Mannheim.........	32.4 per cent
*Stettin...........	45.5 " "	Darmstadt........	30.8 " "
*Kiel..............	36.4 " "	Ulm..............	24.7 " "
*Aachen...........	36.0 " "	*Breslau...........	24.5 " "
Leipzig...........	32.7 " "	Stuttgart.........	23.2 " "
*Wiesbaden.......	32.4 " "	Crefeld...........	21.0 " "
*Magdeburg.......	22.6 " "	*Hannover.........	20.7 " "
*Recklingshausen...	22.5 " "	*Bielefeld..........	20.5 " "

The states also draw a considerable revenue from their public lands, in pursuance of this policy. Prussia, for example, in 1908, received a net profit of 92.27 million marks from its forests, mines and other land.[5]

Under the influence of this principle of "Sozialpolitik," the legal restriction of land ownership has proceeded recently in Germany to an extent which, from the standpoint of the inviolability of private property rights, as conceived of in Anglo-Saxon countries, appears revolutionary. We refer to the law passed in 1902 with respect to the re-

---

[1] *Schriften des Vereins für Sozialpolitik* (1908), vol. CXXVI (Gemeindefinanzen), p. 150.

[2] *Soziale Praxis*, vol. XVII, pp. 867, 1315; vol. XVIII, pp. 957, 1373, *et passim*.

[3] *Statistisches Jahrbuch deutscher Städte* (1909), pp. 18, 19.

[4] *Kommunales Jahrbuch* (1909), vol. I, p. 550. The asterisk denotes that the city has adopted the tax on value increment.

[5] *Statistisches Jahrbuch für den Preussischen Staat* (1908), p. 225.

distribution (Umlegung) of property in Frankfurt a. M.[1] In accordance with this law, it is possible to redistribute property in districts predominantly undeveloped, in case the public interest requires such readjustment, either in opening up new building land or in laying out sites of suitable shape.[2] The method by which this redistribution takes place is noteworthy. All the land in question is massed together, the land necessary for streets and squares is then marked off, and the remainder is distributed among the owners in portions proportionate to their interest in the whole land; and compensation is paid for any loss incurred.[3]

In a country where private land ownership is subject to restriction in so far as the public welfare requires, the introduction of the "Wertzuwachssteuer," whereby the German government does not hesitate to recognize the "unearned" character of the land-value increment,[4] is consistent with the general policy of German "Bodenpolitik."

§ 9. Compared with the potency of the above-mentioned social principles on the enactment of the increment tax, the influence of the principle of benefit in taxation, i.e., that the tax is payment for services rendered by the state, could be of but minor importance. The reason is clearly because the system of local taxes in Germany as we have shown [5] does not lend itself to that principle. Nevertheless, in justifying the taxation of the "unearned increment," German writers have from the first employed as argument the fiscal principle of benefit. Already in 1866, Alexander

---

[1] *Gesetz vom 28 Juli 1902, betr. die Umlegung von Grundstücken in Frankfurt a. M.*

[2] *Ibid.*, § 1.

[3] *Ibid.*, § 10.

[4] The imperial law declares that the tax is to fall on the *unearned* increment ("der ohne Zutun des Eigentümers entstanden ist"). *Reichszuwachssteuergesetz vom 14 Februar 1911*, § 1. In this connection it is interesting to point out that in the British Parliament the proposal to call the increment *unearned* was promptly dismissed.

[5] See *supra*, p. 122.

Meyer contended [1] that, more than in the case of other commodities, the value of land was created and determined by society and by the governmental expenditure for the protection and improvement of property, adding that "local taxes are the basis of the community, the community the basis of remunerative labor, remunerative labor the basis of high land value. Local taxes accrue to the land owner to an ever increasing degree." Likewise Wagner and Adickes defended the taxation of the "unearned increment" on the ground that the landowner in the city had a special advantage, the value of his land being the result of and depending on the development of the state and the community.[2]

The influence of the principle of benefit or compensation in taxation as an argument for the value-increment tax in Germany can be further seen from the application, or elaboration, of the principle made by Köppe. He attempts to justify the state and imperial taxes on value increment as well as the local increment taxes on this ground. Thus, admitting the effect of the services and expenditures of the local government on the value of land, Köppe reasons that without a powerful central government, i.e., the imperial government, this beneficent influence of the commune on real property would be impossible. For, says he, all imperial legislation is equally a source of benefit to the land-owner.[3]

It is, of course, evident that such an application of the principle is untenable as the principle is generally interpreted. For it is only when the benefit between government and subject is reciprocal, and at least roughly measurable,

---

[1] *Preussische Jahrbücher* (1866), vol. xviii, p. 170. Cited by Adickes, *op. cit.*, p. 444.

[2] *Verhandlungen des Vereins für Sozialpolitik* (1877), in *Schriften des Vereins für Sozialpolitik* (1878), vol. xiv, p. 16. *Cf.* Adickes, *op. cit.*, pp. 444, 590, 618 *ff.*

[3] "Das Schicksal der Reichszuwachssteuer," in *Annalen des deutschen Reichs* (1910), vol. xliii, p. 670.

that the principle of benefit applies at all. That is why it is considered applicable to local taxation, for here the incidence of the tax is more easily determined (under the English rating systems, for example), and the relation between certain services and local expenditure is more commensurable than between the more general services and expenditures of the state and imperial governments. Nevertheless, Köppe's attempt to justify the increment tax on this principle is noteworthy.

As regards both the local and imperial increment taxes, however, social causes operated more potently than the fiscal principle of benefit in the enactment of the tax measures. Additional factors which stimulated legislation were the activity of the "Bodenreformer," and in case of the imperial increment tax the fiscal exigency.[1]

§ 10. For popularizing the principles underlying the increment tax, the propaganda of the "Bodenreformer" (Single Taxers), since their organization in 1898, has exerted a strong influence. That their organization came later than in England and Australasia was due to the fact that the needs mentioned above had not become acute, or made themselves felt, earlier.[2] The widespread influence of the "Bodenreformer" may be gathered from the fact that in 1910 the number of societies was 542, and the membership about 750,000 persons.[3] Of course, the publications of the society, "Die Bodenreform," "Soziale Fragen," and the quarterly, "Das Jahrbuch der Bodenreform," all under the efficient leadership of Adolph Damaschke, undoubtedly reach a larger number of readers than is represented by the membership. On the whole, the opportunism of the leaders has directed the energy of the

[1] See *infra*, § 11.

[2] Of course, the movement to tax urban land value had started in the seventies. Adolph Wagner may well be called the pioneer in that movement; earlier and contemporaneous exponents were Herman Gossen, Adolph Samter, Karl Arnd, Flürscheim and Hertzka.

[3] *Soziale Praxis* (1910–11), vol. xx, p. 188.

society to other reforms besides the tax on land value. Thus, their activity has been extended to obtaining legislation with reference to mines, hereditary building leaseholds (Erbbaurecht), housing, and to colonization work, etc. Then, too, their opportunism as regards the tax itself has commended itself to persons who are not Single Taxers.

§ 11. Already in 1894, under the direction of Adickes, the mayor of Frankfurt a. M., a bill was introduced in that city to tax the value increment of land, but ten years elapsed before the opposition to the measure was overcome. In 1904, then, the ordinance was first passed in Frankfurt.[1] This started the ball rolling, for in the following year Cologne and Gelsenkirchen adopted the tax. Then followed in rapid succession, Essen (1906), Dortmund (1906), Gross-Lichterfelde (1906), Pankow (1906), Weissensee (1906), Breslau (1907), Hessen (1907), Kiel (1907), Hamburg (1908), Berlin (1910), and a host of others. The number of local governments in Germany which had adopted the tax before the enactment of the imperial tax was 652.[2]

The history of the enactment of the "Reichszuwachssteuer" is enlightening. The fiscal stringency of the imperial government has received a great deal of attention from German writers. In fact, the imperial government, in 1909, had reached a serious stage of fiscal stress. The growing budgets, it was felt, had to be met by other than by additional income and excise taxes.[3] The "Agrariar," the reactionary party, were, of course, opposed to any further property taxes. Indeed, so antagonistic were they also to the revision of the inheritance tax,[4] that from one of

[1] Although Frankfurt is generally regarded as the first city to introduce the "Wertzuwachssteuer," several small communes in Saxony, Oetzsch and Helbersdorf, are said to have taxed the value increment since 1902–03. *Cf.* Becher und Henneberg, *Das Zuwachssteuergesetz vom 14 Februar 1911*, p. viii.

[2] Damaschke, *Geschichte der Nationalökonomie* (5th ed.), p. 549.

[3] Beusch, *Die Reichsfinanzen und die Steuerreform*, p. 117.

[4] The proposal was to make the tax fall on direct as well as on collateral heirs. *Cf.* Linschmann, *Die Reichsfinanzreform von 1909*, pp. 123–29.

their own members on the Finance Committee came the proposal of substituting the "Wertzuwachssteuer" on securities (Wertpapiere) and land transfers for the proposed revisions in the inheritance tax.[1] After extended discussion in the committee the "Wertzuwachssteuer" was rejected by the government, on the ground that the great practical difficulties involved in the tax required a more carefully prepared bill.[2] Instead, a slight tax on land transfers, one third of one per cent of the selling price, was imposed, while the partisans of the increment tax succeeded in inserting in the same bill ("Reichsstempelgesetz," 1909) the following provision: [3]

"Before April 1, 1912, an imperial tax on the unearned increment of land shall be enacted, which shall be so regulated as to produce an annual revenue of at least 20 million marks. . . . The bill shall provide that to those local governments where the increment tax was in force on April 1, 1909, the average yield of the tax shall be turned over for a period of not less than five years after the enforcement of the imperial tax. Such a bill shall be submitted to the Reichstag before April 1st, 1911."

In accordance with this provision the "Reichszuwachssteuer" was passed February 14, 1911.

It is important to note that with the enactment of the imperial increment tax, the local and state taxes were repealed, except in so far as the local bodies retained the option of levying additional rates to the imperial tax.[4]

---

[1] The Social Democrats accused the conservative proponents of the increment tax, in preference to the inheritance tax, of selfish motives, since the increment tax would fall chiefly on urban landowners. *Cf.* Köppe, "Das Schicksal der Reichszuwachssteuer" in *Anna lendes deutschen Reichs* (1910), vol. XLIII, p. 674.

[2] *Cf.* Köppe, *op. cit.*, p. 673.

[3] *Reichsstempelgesetz vom 15 Juli 1909*, § 70.

[4] *Reichszuwachssteuergesetz vom 11 Februar 1911*, § 59. *Cf. infra*, § 16. By the amendment of the law in 1913, the revenue accruing from the "Wertzuwachssteuer" was relegated entirely to the states and local authorities. It is, therefore, an imperial tax in form only. See *infra*, § 21.

§ 12. Because of the suspension of the increment tax laws for local and state purposes, we shall first analyze the imperial law and then compare the same with the provisions of the antecedent measures. The provisions of the "Reichszuwachssteuergesetz" will be studied under the following heads: —

(1) The method of assessment and levy.

(2) The exemptions.

(3) The scale of rates.

(4) The division of the revenue among the imperial, state, and local governments.

(5) The administration of the tax.

By far the most important provisions of the law and those involving the most perplexing problems of theory and practice are those relating to the object taxed and the mode of assessment. "On the occasion of a transfer of land lying within the country there shall be levied in accordance with the provisions of this Act a tax on the value increment which has accrued through no effort on the part of the owner (der ohne Zutun des Eigentümers entstanden ist)." [1] For practical purposes this criterion of the taxable object, "unearned increment," is of no importance, since the Act later defines specifically the method of assessment.[2] The section has, however, given rise to much legal controversy involving the validity of the Act.[3]

"The difference between the previous purchase price and the present selling price shall constitute the taxable value increment." [4] In order that the tax may fall only on the increment accruing from land value, not on improvements, certain deductions from the price of the property are stipulated. Thus, the amount of encumbrances assumed by the seller, the cost of the machine equipment and other

[1] *Reichszuwachssteuergesetz vom 19 Februar 1911*, § 1.

[2] *Ibid.*, §§ 8–23.

[3] *Cf. Amtliche Mitteilungen über die Zuwachssteuer*, Jg. 1912, Nr. 8, pp. 133, 200.

[4] *Reichszuwachssteuergesetz*, § 8.

fixed capital, and also the value of the growing crops are to be deducted from both the purchase and selling prices.[1] But that is not all. All outlays for improvements and other expenditures incurred on the taxable land must be taken into account. Hence the previous purchase price and present selling price must undergo the following modifications before the taxable value can be computed: —

(a) To the previous purchase price shall be added:[2]

(1) Four per cent of the purchase price to cover outlays incurred by the transaction of sale.[3]

(2) Expenditures for buildings, repairs, and other permanent improvements, including such as have to do with agriculture and forestry; expenditures also for exploration and permanent equipment in mining;[4] and five per cent additional of the calculable value of these expenditures, or, if the seller is a builder or a building workman and has himself erected the buildings, fifteen per cent additional.[5]

(3) Expenditures and special assessments for public utilities and improvements incurred in the period of time for which the tax is calculated. Interest shall be allowed, calculated at four per cent of the expenditures for every complete year of this period, not to exceed fifteen years.[6]

(4) Two and one-half per cent interest on the total amount of the purchase price (i.e., the above additions, (1), (2) and (6) included), so far as this amount does not exceed 100 marks per *are* (100 square metres), or in case of

---

[1] *Reichszuwachssteuergesetz*, § 10.   [2] *Ibid.*, § 14.

[3] In case a higher commission was paid by the purchaser, the latter amount shall be substituted.

[4] These expenditures have no reference to such as were noted under fixed capital expenditures, nor serve for the current maintenance of structures, nor for the current utilization of land, so far as the buildings and improvements shall still exist. Moreover, if the expenditures are covered by insurance they are not deductible. *Ibid.*, § 14 (3).

[5] This does not apply if the builder is a company, or association not composed exclusively of building contractors or building workmen.

[6] On demand of the seller, instead of this interest addition, there may be substituted an amount equal to the addition under (4) or (5), etc. *Ibid.*, § 14 (4).

vineyards 300 marks per *are*, for every year since the last transfer of the property.[1]

(5) Two per cent, in case of unimproved land, one and one-half per cent, in case of improved land (for every year since the last transfer of the property) of the differential between the actual purchase price plus additions and the calculated value in (4). If not more than five years have elapsed since the last transfer, the addition in case of the unimproved land shall be reduced by one-half.[2]

(6) In case the property had been acquired at a bankrupt sale by the mortgagee, then the amount of his defaulted claims or losses incurred by him may be added.[3]

(*b*) To ascertain the value increment, furthermore, there shall be deducted from the present selling price: [4]

(1) The cost of sale and conveyance if incurred by seller (the commission customary in the locality included).

(2) Upon demand of seller, that amount by which (for every year since the last transfer but not for more than fifteen consecutive years) the annual income from the land can be shown to have been less than three per cent of the previous purchase price plus additions [(1), (2), and (6)] noted above.

(*c*) Furthermore, to the selling price shall be added: [5]

(1) Any compensation paid the seller for any depreciation in the value of the land.[6]

(2) The amount of the increment tax if the purchaser, instead of the seller, had agreed in the contract of sale to pay the tax.[7]

§ 13. Before discussing the purpose of the additions and reductions, a concrete illustration of the method of procedure in computing the taxable value will help elucidate the complex system. Suppose a parcel of unimproved land,

---

[1] *Reichszuwachssteuergesetz*, § 16 (1).   [2] *Ibid.*, § 16.
[3] *Ibid.*, § 14 (2).   [4] *Ibid.*, § 22.   [5] *Ibid.*, § 23.
[6] § 23. Provided that the claim for such compensation has arisen since January 1, 1911, and provided it is proved that the amount has not been expended for the repair of the property.
[7] *Ibid.*, § 24.

10,800 *are*, was bought in 1893 for 1,000,000 marks. A house worth 400,000 marks was constructed thereon, and the property was sold, January 1, 1913, for 2,600,000 marks. Suppose further that the income averaged 50,000 marks annually, except during 1906–10, when it averaged only 30,000 marks. The method of ascertaining the amount of increment tax is as follows: —

(*a*) Previous purchase price............................1,000,000 mk.
    To which is added: [1]
    (1) 4 per cent of purchase price......... 40,000 mk.
    (2) Cost of building.................. 400,000 mk.
        Plus 5 per cent interest............ 20,000 mk.
    (3) (No expenditure made or special as-
        sessment paid)
    (4) $2\frac{1}{2}$ per cent for twenty years of the
        value of the land calculated thus:
        100 mk. × 10,800 *are* = 1,080,000
        mk. $2\frac{1}{2}$ per cent of 1,080,000 mk..540,000 mk.
    (5) $1\frac{1}{2}$ per cent for twenty years on (the
        difference between 1,440,000 and
        1,080,000 mk.) 360,000 mk.......108,000 mk.
        Total additions...........................1,108,000 mk.
        Total purchase value .... 2,108,000 mk.

(*b*) Present selling price...............................2,600,000 mk.
    From this sum shall be deducted: —
    (1) Cost of transaction................. 5,000 mk.
    (2) Amount of deficit in income (1906–
        10) for five years: 43,200 mk. (3
        per cent of 1,440,000 mk.) − 30,000
        mk. = 13,200 mk. × 5 ....66,000 mk.
        Total deductions......................... 71,000 mk.
        Selling price.............................2,529,000 mk.
        Deducting total purchase price...........2,108,000 mk.
        Value increment (= 19.9 per
           cent of total purchase price.).............421,000 mk.
        Rate of tax [2] is 11 per cent.
        Amount of tax 11 per cent of 421,000 mk. ... 46,310 mk.
        Deductions (§ 28, 2)[2] $1\frac{1}{2}$ per cent for twenty
          years.................................. 13,893 mk.
        Tax collectible.......................... 32,417 mk.

---

[1] The items correspond to the additions referred to in the preceding section and are numbered as they were there.

[2] See *infra*, § 15, for explanation of rate and reduction.

Obviously the purpose of the allowances noted above is to reach the "unearned increment" and to exempt any increment in value which is attributable to the investment of capital and labor. How, then, has this purpose succeeded?

First, as regards the additions to the original purchase price, the expediency and equity of adding the various sums of cost and compensation to the previous purchase price or of deducting them from the selling price gave rise to much discussion in the Finance Committee.[1] Before pointing out the principles involved, it will be necessary to show by a concrete example the difference in receipts which the two methods produce. If, in the case assumed above, the 1,108,000 marks expenditure and compensation were substracted from the selling price, 2,529,000 marks, instead of being added to the purchase price, the value increment would again be 421,000 marks, to be sure;[2] but, now, the previous purchase price would be 1,000,000 marks, of which 421,000 marks are 42.1 per cent. This change would subject the value increment to a higher tax rate, twelve per cent instead of eleven per cent in this case; hence the revenue would be greater. Various writers have pointed out that,[3] not alone for fiscal reasons, but likewise in accordance with the principles of the tax, the method followed in the imperial law is reprehensible. The only practical way to ascertain the pure "unearned increment" accruing from land is to deduct the value of the improvements from the selling value of the property, allowing for its depreciation; this the law does not do. Moreover, it furnishes the speculator an escape from an otherwise heavy burden, for in Germany the land speculator and building

[1] Cf. C. Miller, Reichsgesetz über die Zuwachssteuer, p. 40.

[2] As a matter of fact the value of the buildings at the time of sale would probably be less than its original cost, and when deducted from the selling price would make the value of the increment on which the tax is chargeable still greater.

[3] Cf. Boldt, Die Wertzuwachssteuer, p. 57; Köppe, op. cit., pp. 722 ff.

operator are in the main one and the same person. Thus the "Terraingesellschaften" that erect the huge apartment houses (Mietskasernen) to further their speculative operations [1] could frustrate, in a measure, the purpose of the tax. For, the excessive cost of the buildings when added to the original purchase price of the land would lessen the value increment on which the tax is payable.

Secondly, there is no provision in the Act to deduct any depreciation in the value of the improvements which constituted part of the original purchase price.[2] For example, suppose a house and lot, valued respectively at 400,000 marks and 500,000 marks were sold in 1885, and sold again in 1910 for 1,000,000 marks. Suppose the house had deteriorated, was valueless, and was ready to be torn down. What in such a case shall be considered the value increment, 100,000 marks or 500,000 marks? Under the imperial law the original purchase price is 900,000 marks and the increment value only 100,000 marks. It is clear that in accordance with the principle and definition of the tax on land value, the value only of those improvements that are unexhausted, and to the extent that a value still attaches to them, shall be included in the original purchase price. In this respect, although the question was discussed in the Committee, the Committee granted the landowners a concession, disregarding the principle involved.

Thirdly, the expediency and justice of some of the allowances have been questioned. What is the "fair" interest or compensation to be allowed the seller on his investment? The question cannot be answered absolutely; but let us note the possible effect of the allowance under the

---

[1] See *supra*, § 7. *Cf.* Voigt, *op. cit.*

[2] Under the local systems, only that of Dortmund recognizes this principle. The Dortmund ordinance provides that in case of brick houses, which deteriorate quickly, three per cent of the expenditures for the buildings shall be deducted, for depreciation. *Cf.* Boldt, *Das Interesse als Grundlage der Gemeindebesteuerung,* in *Schriften des Vereins für Sozialpolitik,* vol. CXXVII, p. 119.

imperial law. An income of at least three per cent is assured the owner of the property.[1] Inasmuch as improved land and even agricultural land, generally speaking, yields a greater profit than three per cent, this provision favors especially the owner of unimproved land and the speculator. As Köppe points out,[2] for holding a parcel of land worth 100,000 marks out of use for a period of fifteen years (land which yields no income), a reduction of 45,000 marks [3] will be made from the selling price, thus reducing the amount of the tax. And, inasmuch as income bears the greatest burden of taxation in Germany, this same owner of vacant land is subjected to the least taxation; hence speculation in vacant land, in spite of the increment tax, is profitable and is furthered. Again, it is noteworthy that in allowing two and one-half per cent interest in case of agricultural land, and two per cent of the excess [4] (if more than five years have elapsed since the last transfer of the land) in case of unimproved land, and one and one-half per cent in case of improved land, the vacant land held for a long period has the advantage over the improved land. The expediency also of allowing five per cent interest on the cost of the permanent improvements, as compensation for directing and overseeing these improvements has been questioned. In case the owner is himself the builder, there is some reason for compensating him, but not to fifteen per cent of the expenditure.

Such, then, are some of the difficulties encountered in attempting to ascertain the "unearned increment" accruing from land.

§ 14. That the taxation of value increment is not ruthlessly carried out is furthermore evident from an examination of the exemptions. Improved land whose selling price is not above 20,000 marks and unimproved land not ex-

---

[1] Köppe, *op. cit.*, p. 726.   [2] *Ibid.*
[3] Three per cent of 100,000 marks × 15.
[4] *Cf. supra*, pp. 147–48.

ceeding 5,000 marks are exempted from the tax.[1] But the exemption is allowed only in case the income of the husband and wife had not exceeded 2000 marks the year previous to the sale of their property, and provided neither was engaged in realty operations as a business.[2] Transfers of land by inheritance or gift are not subject to the increment tax,[3] unless the latter form of transfer is to evade the payment of the tax. It is necessary to point out here that properties exchanged between owners are taxable, each parcel of property being separately assessed and taxed.[4] An important provision is that which makes the transfer of rights in the property of partnerships and companies [5] liable to increment tax, so far as the property is composed of land, and the utilization of the land is one of the objects of the company, or if the company has been formed to evade the tax.

Other exemptions under the Act are: [6]

(1) The sovereigns of the separate states (der Landesfürst und die Landesfürstin).

(2) The imperial government.

(3) The states and communes within whose jurisdiction the land is located.

(4) Societies of all sorts which are not profit-making, for example, charitable institutions, internal colonization, loan and building societies in the interest of the poorer

[1] *Reichszuwachssteuergesetz*, § 1. "Unimproved land shall include also land upon which there are gardenhouses, sheds, lumber and coal yards, and similar structures serving temporary purposes."

[2] It is noteworthy that no minimum exemption, such as is found in the local Acts is allowed under the imperial Act. In Frankfurt a. M., it will be recalled, a value increment of less than fifteen per cent of the purchase price is exempted. For changes in the provision see *infra*, § 21.

[3] *Reichszuwachssteuergesetz*, § 7 (1). Such property is subject to taxation under the "Reichserbschaftssteuergesetz" of June 3, 1906. It will be remembered also that such exchanges are not taxable under most of the "Umsatzsteuern" in Prussia.

[4] *Ibid.*, § 26.

[5] *Ibid.*, § 3. This does not apply to corporations (Aktiengesellschaften).

[6] *Ibid.*, § 30.

classes, provided the dividends distributed do not exceed four per cent of the invested capital.[1]

(5) Property owned jointly by married persons, in case of the establishing, altering, continuing, or dissolving of such ownership.[2]

(6) Property acquired through contracts concluded between co-heirs for the purpose of dividing an estate, or acquired by purchase at auction for the same purpose.[3]

(7) Property acquired by descendants from parents, grandparents, and more distant progenitors.

(8) Property acquired by a company composed exclusively of the seller and his descendants.[4]

(9) Parcels of land exchanged for purposes of rearrangement or redistribution (Zusammenlegung und Umlegung) by the public authority; or in exercising the right of eminent domain in respect to forest land.

(10) Mineral land, in case of an exchange of parts of fields between adjoining mines, and in case of a merger for the purpose of the better working of the mines, but not if the merger is effected to evade the tax.

(11) Mortgages in bankrupt sales, to the value of the mortgages.[5]

(12) An increment tax which does not exceed twenty marks in amount.[6]

The purposes of these exemptions are clearly: (1) to guard against appropriating an increment attributable to labor or capital invested, as the increment accruing to the small owner is likely to be; and (2) not to interfere with exchanges and the acquisition of property that take place for other reasons than profit-making as in the case of sale. As

---

[1] The Bundesrat is empowered to exempt such societies even if the dividends are at most five per cent.

[2] *Reichszuwachssteuergesetz*, § 7 (2).   [3] *Ibid.*, § 7 (3).

[4] *Ibid.*, § 7 (5). "The obligation to pay a tax shall arise if subsequently the company is made to include a member who is not a descendant of the seller."

[5] *Ibid.*, § 14 (2).   [6] *Ibid.*, § 28.

the tax is an indirect levy, it is reasoned, the tax for this exempted property is merely postponed to such time as it will be sold.

§ 15. The next important consideration in the analysis of the imperial tax is the progressive scale of rates. The principle of progressive taxation seems well established in Germany. It is recognized in the levy of the income and inheritance taxes as well as in the increment tax, and is consistent with their predilection for the faculty principle in taxation. In the following table the progressive schedule of rates for the increment tax is shown: [1]

10 per cent tax, if the increment does not exceed 10 per cent of the purchase price

11	per cent tax, if the increment is between							10–30	per cent inclusive		
12	"	"	"	"	"	"	"	"	30–50	"	"	"
13	"	"	"	"	"	"	"	"	50–70	"	"	"
14	"	"	"	"	"	"	"	"	70–90	"	"	"
15	"	"	"	"	"	"	"	"	90–110	"	"	"
16	"	"	"	"	"	"	"	"	110–130	"	"	"
17	"	"	"	"	"	"	"	"	130–150	"	"	"
18	"	"	"	"	"	"	"	"	150–170	"	"	"
19	"	"	"	"	"	"	"	"	170–190	"	"	"
20	"	"	"	"	"	"	"	"	190–200	"	"	"
21	"	"	"	"	"	"	"	"	200–210	"	"	"
22	"	"	"	"	"	"	"	"	210–220	"	"	"
23	"	"	"	"	"	"	"	"	220–230	"	"	"
24	"	"	"	"	"	"	"	"	230–240	"	"	"
25	"	"	"	"	"	"	"	"	240–250	"	"	"
26	"	"	"	"	"	"	"	"	250–260	"	"	"
27	"	"	"	"	"	"	"	"	260–270	"	"	"
28	"	"	"	"	"	"	"	"	270–280	"	"	"
29	"	"	"	"	"	"	"	"	280–290	"	"	"
30	"	"	"	"	"	exceeds			290	"	"	

Thus, for example, the tax is ten per cent of the value of the increment, when the increment does not exceed ten per cent of the previous purchase price. Under purchase price, it will be remembered, the additions, comprising compensation and expenditure, are included.[2]

Furthermore, it is provided that for every full year since the date of the previous purchase, the tax shall be reduced by one per cent of its amount. But if the land has been

[1] *Reichszuwachssteuergesetz*, § 28.   [2] See *supra*, pp. 147 ff.

acquired prior to January 1, 1900, the rebate shall be increased to one and one-half per cent annually from the time of the purchase until January 1, 1911.[1] For example, assume that the tax is 2300 marks, the date of purchase 1902, the date of sale 1912, then ten per cent (one per cent for ten years) is to be deducted, leaving 2070 marks payable; now, had the date of the previous purchase been 1891, the deduction would have been thirty per cent (one and one-half per cent for twenty years) leaving as tax 1610 marks.

This scale of rates and the reductions were adopted out of a number submitted to the Finance Committee,[2] the controversy being centered chiefly on the reductions. Already in some of the local measures,[3] a difference in the amount of tax chargeable was made, based upon the length of ownership. The longer the period of ownership, the smaller the amount of tax. This practice, although it favors such property as that of the "Millionenbauern" (the millionaire peasants), a class whose wealth is clearly "unearned," has been justified on the following grounds: First, it is assumed that persons who hold their land for a long period of time have not speculative motives in view. Secondly, the person who has reaped a fortune in a short period of time is better able to share it with the government than one who has waited a long time for such gain and has worked the land for a livelihood.[4] Thirdly, it is a means of compensating for a change in the value of money, through a long period of time, since no account of such change is taken in computing the taxable increment. Curiously, however, this assumes a falling value of the standard, and would not apply for a period of a rising value.

In connection with the above problems involved in dis-

---

[1] *Reichszuwachssteuergesetz*, § 28.

[2] *Cf.* Köppe, *op. cit.*, pp. 728–30.

[3] See *infra*, § 19.

[4] To be consistent with this argument a distinction should have been drawn between improved and unimproved land. Such a distinction is made in some of the local laws.

tributing the burden of the increment tax equitably, the retroactive character of the imperial tax needs consideration. The *previous* occasion from which the purchase price is determined, under the imperial law, antedates the enactment of the law; hence the value increment which had accrued prior to the Act is taxable. But it is also provided [1] that, (1) in case the previous purchase took place forty years before the occasion of paying increment tax, the value which the property had forty years before such occasion shall be substituted for the previous purchase price, unless the person liable for the tax shall prove that the previous purchase price had a greater value than on the assumed arbitrary date; (2) in case the previous purchase price antedated January 1, 1885, the value which the land had on that day shall be substituted for the purchase price, unless the taxpayer shall prove that he paid a higher price than the land was worth on January 1, 1885.

It will be noted: (1) From the fiscal standpoint, the retroactive feature of the tax is more expedient than if only the future value increment were taxed. (2) By limiting the period to forty years, property held under long tenure is favored for reasons discussed above. (3) The arbitrary previous purchase value is a fictitious one, to be estimated " nach dem gemeinen Wert "; [2] that is, according to "the selling or capital value, determined by the price which would be realized in customary business transactions according to the condition of the salable property, and irrespective of any unusual or solely personal considerations." (4) The expediency of fixing January 1, 1885, has been questioned; first, because land had appreciated greatly before 1885, and there is no reason why the value increment which accrued before that date should not be equally subject to the tax; secondly, because it is more difficult to ascertain the value of the land for 1885 than it would be

---

[1] *Reichszuwachssteuergesetz*, § 17.

[2] *Zuwachssteuer Ausführungsbestimmungen* (1911), § 22.

for such a date as 1870, for example,[1] when land, generally speaking, had an agricultural value merely.

§ 16. In view of the fact that the scale of rates under the imperial law is different and in some cases lower than under the local systems, the consideration of the suspension of the local and state laws is important. With the enforcement of the imperial law, on January 1, 1911,[2] the statutes of the states and of the local bodies relative to the increment tax became null and void, except in special cases where the local tax might continue to be levied until April 1, 1915.[3] That the revenue accruing to the local bodies from the increment tax might be assured, however, the following allocation of the revenue among the several governing bodies was made. Of the proceeds of the "Reichszuwachssteuer" fifty per cent was to accrue to the federal government, ten per cent to the states in payment for the administration and levy of the tax, and the remaining forty per cent to the local bodies in whose jurisdiction the land subject to the tax was located. In case of any community where the tax had been in force before January 1, 1911, and whose average revenue from the tax had exceeded the quota now assigned to it by the imperial government, the imperial government was to pay such community the difference until April 1, 1915.[4] Instead of paying this difference in the manner described, however, the communities might continue to levy their own tax, subject to the regulations of the Chancellor, until April 1, 1915, provided the same average amount was raised by the local government as before April 1, 1911, any excess going to the central government. The determination of the average yield was to be made by the "Bundesrat" (imperial federal council).

[1] Some of the local laws, e.g., in Essen, make this date the limit of the retroaction.

[2] The law went into effect on April 1, 1911, but with retroactive force from January 1, 1911. See *Reichszuwachssteuergesetz*, §§ 72, 62. For amendments see *infra*, § 21.

[3] The exception is discussed in this section.

[4] *Reichszuwachssteuergesetz*, §§ 58, 60.

The local governments may, moreover, with the permission of the state government (Landesregierung) levy a rate supplementary to the imperial increment tax, the revenue of which accrues to the community. This additional tax shall be a percentage rate not to exceed one hundred per cent of the revenue of the subvention. Furthermore, the supplementary rate together with the imperial tax shall not exceed thirty per cent of the value increment.[1] As regards the levy of this supplementary rate, the local authorities are empowered to determine the system of taxation with respect to the kind of land, and the length of ownership. To this extent, then, the local systems, until the law was amended, existed side by side with the imperial system.

The expediency of an imperial tax on value increment *versus* the local taxes was at the time of the enactment of the "Reichszuwachssteuer" an open question. Even though the localities had not been put at a disadvantage fiscally by the imperial enactment, authorities were not agreed as to the expediency of the policy in general. On the one hand, some tax officials saw a better administration under the imperial system,[2] based on the general advantage of uniformity. According to Dr. Boldt, the communities in which the landowners were most influential had the mildest ordinances, whereas the manufacturing cities, as Gelsenkirchen and Herne, for example, had succeeded in introducing satisfactory, effective measures. From this standpoint, then, the imperial law would make the systems uniform, would remove the tax from local political influences, and would prevent the loss of revenue through unfavorable litigation.[3] The progressive form of the tax, too, would lend itself better to an imperial rather than to a local tax.

On the other hand, the partisans of local autonomy be-

[1] *Reichszuwachssteuergesetz*, § 59.
[2] "Verhandlungen des Vereins für Sozialpolitik," in *Schriften des Vereins*, vol. cxxxviii, pp. 42–43.
[3] *Ibid.*, pp. 43, 62.

lieved that, like all taxes on realty, the increment tax
should be levied by the locality and in the interest of the
locality in which the property is situated. Thus Professor
Eheberg [1] said, "I would have much preferred to see the
tax in the hands of the localities rather than in those of the
imperial government, because the relationship between
land-value increments and local fiscal policy is surely more
evident and simpler than that between the appreciation in
land value and imperial taxation." That is, inasmuch as
the community gives rise to the great appreciation in land
value through its public improvements and industrial
development, it should be the recipient of this socially
created value. To this the further argument is added, that
the local officials can best administer the tax, and that,
on account of the complexities involved in the imperial
system, the expenses of administration will, for a while at
any rate, exceed those incurred by the localities in the
collection of the tax. [2]

Judging from the amendment of the law in 1913, and
from the operation of the imperial increment tax during
two years, we can now draw definite conclusions with regard
to the relative expediency of the German imperial and
local value-increment taxes. The causes of the relegation
of the tax to the local bodies will be discussed below. [3]

§ 17. The ten per cent of the receipts from the tax that
is turned over to the state governments is compensation
for the administration of the increment tax. These governments shall establish offices for that purpose. [4] The
administration of the tax is simple. The seller, purchaser, or
other interested person shall report any transfer of land to
the delegated tax authority within one month of such
transfer. Though each one of the interested persons is
under obligation to give notice of the transaction, not more

---

[1] "Verhandlungen des Vereins für Sozialpolitik," in *Schriften des
Vereins*, vol. CXXXVIII, p. 72. (Translated.)

[2] *Ibid.*, p. 54.   [3] *Infra*, § 21.

[4] *Reichszuwachssteuergesetz vom 14 Februar 1911*, § 35.

than one such notice is required; nor is such notification necessary, if within the month, a declaration before a court or a registration of the transfer in the "Grundbuch" (Domesday Book) is made. In case of property held in joint ownership which is transferred to a part owner of the company, no tax is chargeable. But on the next occasion of transfer, the whole increment accruing since the last taxable occasion before the separation of ownership shall be liable for tax.[1] The seller or sellers shall be held liable for the tax; but if the tax cannot be collected from the seller, the purchaser shall be liable to the amount of two per cent of the selling price of the property.[2] The fee of the realty agent is taxable, and such agent is liable, jointly and severally with the seller, for such fee. In case a transaction, on which tax has been paid, has been revoked, the amount of the tax shall be returned; or, in case of a reduction in the selling price, the tax shall be correspondingly reduced and the excess refunded.[3] If the land is transferred back to the previous owner within two years after the sale, the tax must be refunded, subject to the regulations prescribed by the Bundesrat. In such case, of course, it shall be considered that no sale has occurred.

Information shall be furnished the tax authorities by:[4] (1) registries of deeds (Grundbuchämter) concerning all recorded transfers of property; (2) by the registry courts and authorities (Registerberichte-und-behörden) concerning the registration of transfers; (3) by the authorities and officials, imperial, state, and local, and notaries concerning all legal transactions regarding the transfer of property, and concerning previous collections of tax; (4) by other bodies, upon the demand of the state governments with the consent of the Chancellor.

Upon the demand of the tax authority and within a period of time named by that authority, the seller who has

[1] *Reichszuwachssteuergesetz vom 14 Februar 1911*, § 25.
[2] *Ibid.*, § 29. [3] *Ibid.*, §§ 32, 33, 34. [4] *Ibid.*, § 38.

given notice of the transaction is called upon to make a tax declaration. Objections to the declared valuation may be made by the authority, and if the required changes are not made by the taxpayer within the period of time allowed, the tax authority may make the assessment and collect the tax accordingly. The cost of the valuation must be borne by the taxpayer, in case the tax based on the assessed value exceeds by one-third the amount based on the declaration.[1] The ordinary process of assessment does not involve the payment of fees or stamp dues by the taxpayer.[2] If the immediate collection of the tax will entail undue hardship, a delay may be granted, or payment by installments may be permitted, subject to the regulations of the Bundesrat. In such cases security may be required, and when the conditions which occasioned the special treatment have ceased to exist, the privilege is withdrawn.

Objections to the assessment may be made in writing within a month after the notice of the assessment has been served. The complaint must state the court before which, and the time within which, the appeal shall be made. The proceedings are subject to the regulation of the Bundesrat.[3]

Regarding the penalties with respect to violations of the requirements of the law, the taxpayer is subject to a fine, not to exceed four times the amount of the tax, if he fails to give notice of a transfer of property, or to make declaration, or if he knowingly makes false returns. He is given a period within which he may retract his statement before penalty is applied.[4] If it shall appear that the false statement or failure to make the necessary returns was not made with the purpose to defraud, a fine not exceeding 600 marks may be substituted for the fine mentioned above. For other violations of the provisions, a fine not exceeding 150 marks may be imposed. In case of companies and cor-

---

[1] *Reichszuwachssteuergesetz vom 14 Februar 1911*, §§ 39, 40, 43.
[2] *Ibid.*, § 56.   [3] *Ibid.*, §§ 44, 45.   [4] *Ibid.*, § 50.

porations, the representatives, managers, or directors shall be liable for the fine in full.[1] It is further provided that, if the owner is a German, his property shall not, without his consent, be sold at auction in order to collect the increment tax; nor shall an owner be imprisoned for failure to pay a fine.[2] The right to an increment tax shall lapse after ten years.[3]

In general, the administration of the tax is obviously simple. The assessment becomes largely a matter of registration of sales and of mathematical computation of the tax.[4] But while it obviates very largely the need of expert valuers such as the Australasian and English systems require, the difficulties of computation of the value increment and the litigation which the law of 1911 has occasioned, have enhanced the cost of administration inordinately in proportion to the yield of the tax.

§ 18. The provisions of the imperial law analyzed in the preceding sections were in the main modelled after those contained in the local ordinances. But there are great differences in method in the various local measures; and these deserve consideration, because the efficacy of the increment tax depends largely on the methods of assessment, on the rates, and on the exemptions. Regarding the allowances for interest, for expenditures and other compensation in ascertaining the value increment, a great variety of procedure exists. For example, the state tax of Saxony was made applicable to unimproved land only, because the difficulties of measuring the "unearned increment" accruing from improved land seemed insuperable.[5] What constitutes a "fair" interest, what a "just" allowance for expenditures incurred are questions variously answered in the different

[1] *Reichszuwachssteuergesetz vom 14 Februar 1911*, §§ 51, 53, 54.
[2] *Ibid.*, §§ 49, 55.   [3] *Ibid.*, § 57.
[4] The difficulties involved in the assessment are chiefly those connected with the interpretation and legality of the provisions. *Cf. infra,* § 22.
[5] *Cf. Schriften des Vereins für Sozialpolitik*, vol. CXXVI, p. 272.

laws. For example, Göttingen allows ten per cent of the purchase price to be added as compensation for expenditures and another ten per cent for depreciation in case the land has not changed hands in ten or more years; Frankfurt a. M., Cologne, Breslau grant an allowance of five per cent for outlays; Tegel, Weissensee, Emden, Aschenleben allow five per cent when the land is improved, three per cent when unimproved. Again, the rate of interest (not compounded) allowed for the earnings on the invested capital is not uniform. Frankfurt and Cologne provide for a four per cent allowance for each year of ownership in the case of unimproved land; Gelsenkirchen only two per cent, but for a period of ownership not exceeding twenty years; [1] Bremen and Hamburg make no allowance for interest. The expediency from both the fiscal and social standpoints of allowing no interest especially in case of unimproved land has been maintained by Dr. Boldt,[2] who argues that the less compensation allowed for, the greater the revenue and the more effective the check on land speculation. The imperial law, as we have seen, follows the other system which in turn is defensible on the principle of equity in taxation.

In most of the local measures, these allowances including expenditures are added to the previous purchase price. In Gelsenkirchen and Minden, however, they are deducted from the selling price. The latter method makes the tax more productive and accords with the principle of taxing the " unearned increment."

In respect to the retroactive feature of the tax, the provisions in the local ordinances can be summarized under four general principles. First, the tax is to be moderately retrospective, probably, with the object in view to tax only speculative value increments which are thought not to accompany long tenure. In accordance with this principle,

---

[1] *Cf. Schriften des Vereins für Sozialpolitik,* vol. cxxvii, p. 120.
[2] *Die Wertzuwachssteuer.* Dr. Boldt would limit the allowance for interest to a short period, e.g., five years. *Cf. ibid.,* p. 61.

Frankfurt levies the increment tax only on land which has changed hands within the preceding twenty years.[1] Kiel and Breslau have likewise "moderately retroactive" regulations, the "original site" limit being computed from April 1, 1900, and January 1, 1895, respectively. Secondly, there are some cities that believe the community is entitled to a share of the value increment from the day of the previous purchase. They accordingly fix no limit, seeking the actual purchase price in every case. Liegnitz, Hamburg, Weissensee are examples of this category. Thirdly, by setting the limit to 1860 and 1871, respectively, Dortmund and Essen do not in practice depart from the second principle, for the land before 1871, for the most part, had only an agricultural value. The restriction, therefore, is only nominal. Fourthly, altogether opposed to retroactive taxation are Cologne and Gross-Lichterfelde, for example. These cities proposed to tax only the increment which should have accrued since the enactment of their laws. Aside from the loss of revenue which this system occasions, it necessitates a valuation of all the land at the time the law is passed. Such a valuation is expensive and gives rise to a great amount of litigation.[2] In fixing January 1, 1885, therefore, as the limit of retroaction, the imperial law followed a middle course; the result of which, according to some authorities, will be less revenue and greater difficulty arising from valuing land from an arbitrary date.[3]

§ 19. More important criteria even of the efficacy of the increment taxes are the rates, the exemptions, and the rebates allowed on the basis of length of ownership and the kind of land, whether improved or unimproved. The dif-

[1] We have seen that in case of longer tenure the land is subject only to the "Umsatzsteuer." *Cf. supra*, § 6.

[2] A great deal of litigation, where the previous purchase price is taken as the value, is obviated because the custom of recording land transfers and the prices in the "Grundbuch" is general throughout Germany.

[3] A considerable number of lawsuits have been brought already on account of the valuation "nach dem gemeinen Wert." *Cf. Amtliche Mitteilungen über die Zuwachssteuer* (1912), Nr. 11, pp. 184–85.

ferences in the scales of rates in the local statutes are noteworthy. From the following table a comparison of the rates can be made. First, we note that unless an

TABLE SHOWING MINIMUM INCREMENT EXEMPTION, RATE OF PROGRESSION, AND RATE OF TAX IN CERTAIN OF THE LOCAL SYSTEMS [1]

City	Minimum increment exempt (per cent of purchase price)	Rate of progression (as increment progresses, rate increases by 1 per cent) (per cent of purchase price)	Rates	
			Minimum (per cent)	Maximum (per cent)
Cologne	10	10 (10–20)	10	25
Frankfurt a. M.	15	5 (15–20)	2	25
Dortmund	10	10 and 5	3	15
Essen	20	10	3	15
Linden	10	10	3	17
Kreuznach	10	30 (10–40)	3	8
Marburg	10	5	3	15
Pankow	10	10	5	20
Weissensee	10	10	5	20
Lichterfelde	10	10	10	25
Zehlendorf	10	10	5	20
Reinickendorf	10	10 and 25	2	8
Berlin	10	10	5	20
Jena	10	5	5	25
Markanstadt	10	10	1	20

increment exceeding a certain minimum percentage (ten per cent of the purchase price in most of the measures) accrues, no tax is collectible. Secondly, bearing in mind that the rate of tax increases by one per cent for every additional five, ten, and sometimes thirty per cent of the purchase price (as shown in column 3), it becomes evident that the smaller the rate of progression the larger the revenue, other things being the same; thus compare the rates in Dortmund and Kreuznach, both of whose scales

[1] Boldt, *op. cit.*, pp. 80–81.

begin with a minimum rate of three per cent, yet whose revenue will vary because of the different rates of progression. The discrepancy will be seen from the following: —

KREUZNACH	DORTMUND
3% when increment is 10– 40%	3% when increment is 10–20%
4 " " " " 40– 70 "	4 " " " " 20–30 "
5 " " " " 70–100 "	5 " " " " 30–40 "
6 " " " " 100–130 "	6 " " " " 40–50 "
7 " " " " 130–160 "	7 " " " " 50–60 "
8 " " " " 160–190 "	8 " " " " 60–70 "

Taking all the different factors into consideration, the highest scale of rates in the cities considered in the table is that of Cologne and Lichterfelde.[1]

Comparing the rates under the imperial tax with those in the table above, we find that although the minimum rate of the imperial tax is ten per cent and the maximum thirty per cent, the rates as a whole are not so high as in many of the local schedules. For, while the maximum rate under the imperial measure falls on a value increment of 290 per cent or above, the maximum under the local systems is usually levied on a lower increment. Thus in Frankfurt a. M. an increment of 130 per cent of the purchase price or above is taxable at the rate of twenty-five per cent, while in Cologne, 160 per cent is taxable at that rate; under the imperial tax, however, the rate of tax on a value between 130 to 160 per cent is only from sixteen to eighteen per cent. The difference, of course, lies in the fact that while the rate of the imperial tax increases by one per cent for every twenty per cent (up to 190 per cent) and every ten per cent (from 190 to 290 per cent) increase in the increment, the local rates increase by one per cent for every five or ten per cent increase.

With respect to the exemption of a minimum increment

[1] We must bear in mind, however, that in both these cities only the future value increment is taxable, so that the productiveness of the tax is considerably reduced. *Cf. supra*, p. 165.

from taxation, the method of levy under the Cologne ordinance is exceptional.[1] Usually in the local measures, a minimum exemption is allowed only in case the increment does not exceed a certain percentage of the purchase price. When the increment is taxable, however, no minimum exemption from the tax is made. For example, assume the minimum increment exempted under the ordinance to be ten per cent, then when the increment is 250 marks, and the purchase price 3000 marks, the increment is not taxable because it is less than ten per cent of the purchase price. But were the increment 320 marks, the whole increment would be liable for the tax. In Cologne, however, the method of levy is different; in every case ten per cent of the purchase price (in the assumed instance 300 marks) would there be exempted from taxation. Hence, in the assumed case only twenty marks would be the taxable value. For purposes of ascertaining the rate of tax, however, the exempted 300 marks would be included.

The scale of rates and method of levy in Hamburg and Berlin are somewhat different. In Hamburg, the rate of tax is calculated according to the following schedules: [2]

(a) On any increase in value —

Up to	2,000	marks			1	per cent
Between	2,000	"	and	4,000 marks	1½	" "
"	4,000	"	"	6,000 "	2	" "
"	6,000	"	"	8,000 "	2½	" "
"	8,000	"	"	10,000 "	3	" "
"	10,000	"	"	20,000 "	3½	" "
"	20,000	"	"	30,000 "	4	" "
"	30,000	"	"	40,000 "	4½	" "
Over	40,000				5	" "

(b) In addition, if the increment exceeds ten per cent of the purchase price, the rate under (a) is increased by: —

[1] *Jahrbuch der Bodenreform* (1905). Section 6 of the Cologne ordinance reads: "An increase of value of ten per cent or less is *in all cases* exempt from the tax. If the value increment exceeds this percentage, the whole percentage of increment is to be counted in determining the rate of tax. (Italics mine.)

[2] *Cf. Papers Bearing on Land Taxes*, etc. (Cd. 4750), 1909, p. 17.

10 per cent, if increment is between 10– 20 per cent inclusive
20 " " "   "   "   "   20– 30 " " "
30 " " "   "   "   "   30– 40 " " "
40 " " "   "   "   "   40– 50 " " "
50 " " "   "   "   "   50– 60 " " "
60 " " "   "   "   "   60– 70 " " "
70 " " "   "   "   "   70– 80 " " "
80 " " "   "   "   "   80– 90 " " "
90 " " "   "   "   "   90–100 " " "
100 " " " "   exceeds   100 " "

The Hamburg system, it will be noted, resembling therein the imperial tax, does not allow a minimum exemption, thereby deviating from the usual practice, but insuring more productive returns from the tax.[1]

The question of rebate on the basis of the length of ownership and the utilization of the property has been treated variously by the localities. First, some cities allow no reduction whatever; such are, for example, Gross-Lichterfelde and Liegnitz. Secondly, some grant no reduction in case of unimproved land; such are, Dortmund, Essen, Pankow, Weissensee, and others. Thirdly, there are a number of cities which make no distinction between improved and unimproved land, but allow a reduction of the tax on the basis of length of tenure; thus, in Cologne, the reduction of the tax is one-third, if more than five, but not more than ten, years have elapsed since the preceding purchase, and two-thirds if the period exceeds ten years; [2] in Hamburg, a rebate of one-fourth of the tax is granted if the length of ownership has exceeded thirty years, and the tax is increased by one-fourth if the length of ownership has been less than ten years.[3] The case is slightly different in Frankfurt a. M. where no distinction is drawn between improved and unimproved land for purposes of the

[1] Köppe (*op. cit.*, p. 727) points out that there will be the incentive to sell the property in portions and piecemeal to avoid paying the higher additional rates. But this method of evasion, which is possible under all the systems, must be prevented by special provision.

[2] See *infra*, table, pp. 170 *ff.*

[3] The rates of tax in Hamburg range, therefore, from three-fourths to twelve and one-half per cent of the increment.

TABLE SHOWING POPULATION, DATE OF ENFORCEMENT OF ACT, LIMIT OF RETROACTION, RATES, REDUCTIONS ALLOWED AND YIELD OF INCREMENT TAX IN CERTAIN GERMAN CITIES *

Cities and population	Date of enforcement of tax	Time limit as to previous purchase	Tax rates (per cent)	Reduction in case of longer ownership		Yield of increment tax (marks)
				As regards improved land	As regards unimproved land	
Breslau: 470,000† 426,000	June 23, 1907	January 1, 1895	6–25	½ when over 5 years ⅔ when over 10 years	¼ when over 10 years ⅔ when over 20 years	1907 .. 57,946 1908 .. 195,167 1909 .. 173,161
Cologne: 428,000† 372,000	July 17, 1905	April 1, 1905	10–25	After 5–10 years ½ After 10 years		1906 .. 287,176 1907 .. 385,133 1908 .. 69,531 1909 .. 203,011
Dortmund: 175,000† 142,000	September 8, 1906 Amended February 5, 1908	No limit till January 1, 1860	3–15	After 6 years 10 per cent After 15 years no tax	No reduction	1906 .. 78,491 1907 .. 151,027 1908 .. 221,409 1909 .. 156,596
Essen: 231,000† 196,000	March 18, 1908 Previously June 5, 1906	January 1, 1871	3–20	After 10 years ⅓ for each year; no tax after 20 years	No reduction	1906 .. 90,000 1907 .. 164,225 1908 .. 141,802 1909 .. 467,462
Frankfurt a. M.: 334,000† 288,000	February 19, 1904 Amended September 11, 1906	20 years	2–25	After 20 years no tax; taxes as follows:— After 20–30 years 1 per cent After 30–40 years 1½ per cent	only additional transfer taxes as follows:— After 20–30 years 2 per cent After 30–40 years 3 per cent	1904‡ .. 228,480 115,536 1905‡ .. 833,629 353,065 1906‡ .. 1,104,997 632,084

* Reproduced from Boldt, *Die Wertzuwachssteuer*, pp. 120–27. The last column compiled from *Kommunales Jahrbuch* (1910), p. 645.
† The upper figure is population of 1905, the lower of 1900.
‡ Upper figure, the increment and additional tax; the lower figure, the increment taxes only.

(170)

TABLE SHOWING POPULATION (continued)

Cities and population	Date of enforcement of tax	Time limit as to previous purchase	Tax rates (per cent)	Reduction in case of longer ownership			Yield of increment tax (marks)	
				As regards improved land	As regards unimproved land			
Frankfurt a. M.: 334,000 288,000	February 19, 1904 Amended September 11, 1906	20 years	2–25	After 20 years no tax; only additional transfer taxes as follows:— After 40 years 2 per cent	After 40–50 years 4 per cent After 50–60 years 5 per cent After 60 years 6 per cent		1907† .. 1908† .. 1909 ..	498,183 295,535 257,443 95,663 283,825
Kiel: 163,000* 121,000	August 16, 1907	April 1, 1900	5–25	After 5 years 25 per cent; after 7 years 35 per cent; etc. 5 per cent increase of reduction for every year, until 70 per cent is reached with 14 years ownership			1907 :: 1907 :: 1908 ::	83,826 167,727 103,583
Gross-Lichterfelde: 34,000* 23,000	December 29, 1906	April 1, 1906	10–25	No reduction			1906 :: 1907 :: 1908 :: 1909 ::	8,900 29,416 52,080 46,115
Liegnitz: 59,000* 54,000	February 14, 1907	Unlimited	8–18	No reduction			1907 :: 1908 :: 1909 ::	48,787 42,123 73,784
Malstadt-Burbach: 38,000* 31,000	August 1, 1907	August 1, 1907	5–20	After 5 years ¼ After 10 years ½	No reduction		1907 :: 1908 ::	14,250 9,000
Mulheim a. Rhein: 51,000* 45,000	August 1, 1907	Improved land April 1, 1907; unimproved April 1, 1896	10–25	No tax if property acquired before 1907	No tax if acquired before 1896		1907 :: 1908 :: 1909 ::	1,105 16,761 5,034

* The upper figure is population of 1905, the lower of 1900.
† Upper figure, the increment and additional tax; the lower figure, the increment taxes only.

(171)

TABLE SHOWING POPULATION (continued)

Cities and population	Date of enforcement of tax	Time limit as to previous purchase	Tax rates (per cent)	Reduction in case of longer ownership		Yield of increment tax (marks)
				As regards improved land	As regards unimproved land	
Pankow: 29,000* 21,524	October 30, 1906	Unlimited	5–20	After 5 years ½	No reduction	1906 ... 23,169 1907 ... 146,374 1908 ... 86,380 1909 ... 263,744
Reinickendorf: 22,000* 14,779	April 1, 1907	January 1, 1885	2–8	After 5 years ½	After 10 years ⅜; When increment exceeds 200 per cent tax is 8 per cent	1907 ... 124,229 1908 ... 82,577 1909 ... 94,000
Weissensee: 37,000* 34,000	August 17, 1906	Unlimited	5–20	After 5 years ½	No reduction	1906 ... 26,920 1907 ... 252,000 1908 ... 319,000 1909 ... 108,953
Hamburg: 874,000* 768,000	January 1, 1908	Unlimited	1–12½	After 30 years ¾	After 30 years ¾	1908 ...1,500,000

* The upper figure is population of 1905, the lower of 1900.

(172)

increment tax. But instead of a reduction, the rate of the increment tax is changed to the rate of the additional "Umsatzsteuer," if the ownership exceeds twenty years.[1] Fourthly, in some cities, the reduction is based on both criteria, length of ownership and condition of the land; thus, Breslau collects, when the land is improved, two-thirds of the tax in case of a tenure of over five years, one-third of the tax in case of a tenure of over ten years; when the land is unimproved, however, the reduction is one-third when over ten years, and two-thirds when over twenty years.

In contrast to these methods, the system of reductions under the imperial tax, one per cent and one and one-half per cent for each year according to the length of ownership, is novel. The principle underlying the reductions, however, is the same, the longer the period of ownership the more liberal the reduction. But in this provision of the imperial law, no distinction is drawn between improved and unimproved land.

§ 20. The effects of this variety of legislation are well seen in the fiscal returns from the local increment taxes. From the above table (see pp. 170–72) this relation between law and fiscal effect is readily traceable. The last column shows the revenue raised by the tax in some of the localities where the system is in operation. The most significant facts that the figures present are: (1) the smallness of the yield; (2) the fluctuating amounts, as in Frankfurt a. M., for example; (3) the disproportionate proceeds viewed from the standpoint of the size of the cities.

In considering these facts it must be borne in mind that most of the communities are exceptionally small (see column 1), that the tax has been in operation but a short time (see column 2), and that the tax is an indirect one, collectible upon certain occasions. Bearing in mind that the

---

[1] But under this "Umsatzsteuer," the rate is different for improved and unimproved land. *Cf. supra*, § 6.

yield of the increment will fluctuate from year to year according to market conditions, the industrial prosperity of the city, and other conditions, we nevertheless discover from the figures a close relationship between the provisions of the statutes and the proceeds of the tax. For example, taking the average receipts for the three years (1907–09), it is significant that Breslau, with a population three times that of Dortmund, raised only about eighty per cent of the revenue yielded by the tax in Dortmund; or that Weissensee, with a population less than one-tenth that of Cologne, raised on an average, during the same period, a greater sum than the latter city.

The explanation will be found in comparing columns 3, 4, and 5. The tax in Weissensee is retroactive without limit, and allows no reduction in case of unimproved land; in Cologne, on the other hand, only those increments that have accrued since the enactment of the ordinance are taxable, and the same reductions are made in the case of unimproved as in that of improved land. A striking instance of effectiveness due to legal provision is furnished by Pankow, a town of only 29,000, and just turning urban in character so that speculation is especially rife there. It is noteworthy that, in 1909, the receipts from the increment tax exceeded those of Breslau and Cologne, and came close to those of Frankfurt a. M. And so in the other cities, leading us to the conclusion that from a fiscal standpoint some of the German local systems were more effective than others, according as the reductions were fewer, the scale of rates higher, and the retroaction longer.

Another cause for the fluctuating and slight yield of the local taxes can be traced to the excessive litigation which the different laws have given rise to. The legality of the "Wertzuwachssteuer" has been questioned, especially its retroactive feature. The validity of the Frankfurt ordinance was established, however, by the decision of the

Prussian court in 1906.[1] Nevertheless, the local authorities have sustained many losses on account of the litigation.[2] For example, in Schöneberg, 500,000 marks had been collected as tax from one of the "Millionenbauern." He contested the legality of the law, on a technicality, with the result that the money had to be returned to him.[3] Indeed, the comparatively smaller yield of the tax, in 1908, in Cologne, is attributed to the decisions of the court in favor of the appellants.[4]

In connection with the fiscal aspect of the local increment taxes, it is important to point out some of the uses to which the revenue from the tax has been put in the cities. It is the general belief that the value increment is socially created, that is, attributable to the growth of the community through public improvements, protection, and increase in population. Hence the utilization of the tax for social welfare work, sanitation, educational and recreational facilities, and public utilities generally (items which consume an ever-growing percentage of the local budgetary funds), has found favor in many communities. For this reason and probably, too, because of the fluctuations in the yield of the tax, some of the cities have established special funds out of the proceeds. In Frankfurt, for instance, the fund is devoted to school building purposes and to the erection of other educational institutions. In Markran-

[1] Boldt, *Die Wertzuwachssteuer*, p. 15. The legality of the imperial tax has been upheld by the imperial court. *Cf. Amtliche Mitteilungen über die Zuwachssteuer* (1912). (Entscheidungen der obersten Gerichtshöfe.)

[2] Boldt, *Die Wertzuwachssteuer*, p. 128. The experience of Dortmund has been more favorable, since out of 225 assessments only thirteen complaints were voiced.

[3] "Verhandlungen des Vereins für Sozialpolitik," in *Schriften des Vereins*, vol. cxxxviii, p. 43.

[4] *Cf. Papers Bearing on Land Taxes*, etc. (Cd. 4750), 1909, p. 19. It will be recalled that in Cologne a valuation of the land was necessitated by the provision for taxing only the future value increment. By unifying all the measures through the imperial law, it is hoped the excessive losses of revenue through litigation will cease.

stadt, it is devoted to street building; while in Marburg it constitutes the communal land purchase fund.[1]

§ 21. How, then, were the local bodies which already taxed the value increment of land affected by the enactment in 1911 of the imperial law? Until 1915, under the provision of the Act, such communities were to sustain no fiscal loss. First, where the average yield of the tax prior to the Act had amounted to more than the forty per cent subvention under the new law, the community profited by the difference in comparison with the local bodies that had no increment tax. In Prussia the number of such "Gemeinden" was one hundred and sixty.[2] Secondly, the local governments were permitted to retain the old system of levying the increment tax. But until 1913 only seven cities had taken advantage of this permission, namely, Hamburg, Lübeck, Emden, Erfurt, Essen, Frankfurt a. M., and Gelsenkirchen. Thirdly, additional rates could be levied by any "Gemeinde" to the value of one hundred per cent of the imperial tax. Sixty-six local bodies had taken advantage of this privilege.[3] Finally, all the other communities profited by the introduction of the "Reichszuwachssteuer," receiving forty per cent of the receipts from all the taxable land transfers in their jurisdiction.

The proceeds from the imperial tax until the amendment of the Act, July 3, 1913, were for the fiscal years 1911–12 24.2 million marks, and for the following year nearly double that amount. Of these receipts the central government received 10,069,340 marks the first year, and 20,021,897 marks the second fiscal year.[4]

By the amendment of the Act of 1911, adopted July 3, 1913, the central government relinquished its quota of the

---

[1] *Kommunales Jahrbuch* (1909), vol. i, p. 551.

[2] Berthold, *Ergebnisse der Wertzuwachssteuer*, p. 22.

[3] *Ibid.*, pp. 21–22; *cf. Kommunales Jahrbuch* (1914), p. 740.

[4] *Annalen des deutschen Reichs* (1912), vol. xlv, p. 780; *Jahrbuch der Bodenreform*, vol. ix, p. 239.

tax, so that the levy of the value-increment tax on land will henceforth belong to the local and state governments. The communities shall continue to impose the tax in accordance with the Act of 1911, or shall adopt another system of increment tax subject to state regulation and in conformity with state law. The communities that received the excess amount over the forty per cent subvention will be permitted until April, 1915, to raise enough revenue to cover the excess; while the seven cities [1] that had retained their old systems of levy may continue to raise the tax thus with the consent of the state government, and to keep the excess over the designated average yield. A minor provision permits the tax officials, with the consent of the state government, to refrain from assessing and collecting a small increment tax, the amount of which is disproportionate to the cost of the assessment. [2]

§ 22. The history of the virtual repeal of the imperial tax on land value throws light on the important question of the fiscal, social, and economic effects of the tax. The proposal to raise more revenue for defence by means of an imperial value-increment tax on *all property* directed the discussion in the Reichstag in June, 1913, to the increment tax on land. The repeal of the latter was sought on these grounds: (1) The enactment of the more general increment tax would occasion double taxation if the increment tax on land were retained. (2) The cost of administration of the tax was out of all proportion to the yield. (3) The appeals involved endless litigation. (4) The tax imposed a hardship on the small owner. (5) The various needs and conditions in the different communities were not taken into account. (6) The effect of the tax on the realty market and the loan market was deleterious.

On two points there seemed to be a general consensus of

[1] *Cf. supra*, p. 176.

[2] "Gesetz über Änderungen im Finanzwesen," printed in *Jahrbuch der Bodenreform*, vol. IX, p. 237.

judgment in the Reichstag including even the radical parties.[1] First, the Act of 1911 was defective in the framing and had inflicted considerable hardship on other than speculative landowners. Secondly, it was desirable and expedient for the municipalities and other local bodies to continue to levy the increment tax. These facts and the widespread unpopularity of the tax, rather than the argument of double taxation were responsible for the repeal practically of the imperial law. Among the defects of the Act are the complex provisions which make the valuation difficult, and the costliness of the assessments of the smaller estates in proportion to the tax revenue derived from them. This is appreciated when we learn that in Berlin 64.1 per cent of all the transfers of property in 1911, and in Charlottenburg 68 per cent, were exempt from the increment tax; and that the percentage of exempt transfers is similarly large in other cities.[2] A member of the Reichstag told how in Fulda the expense incurred for the salaries of the tax officials exceeded the amount of tax accruing to the Empire.[3] Coupled with the costliness of administration was the expense of the excessive and prolonged litigation occasioned. Other complaints arose from the difficulty of ascertaining the unearned increment and from the hardships imposed upon the seller of heavily mortgaged property who was without ready money to pay the tax.

The relegation of the tax to the localities after two years' experience with the imperial levy was a decided victory for the advocates of the tax for local purposes, and for the principle of benefit in taxation. The imperial law failed to take into account local conditions. The difference between urban and rural property and between large and small

---

[1] The Social Democrats had voted against the "Reichszuwachssteuer" bill in 1911; in 1913, however, they were opposed to its repeal, but their leaders admitted the defectiveness of the law.

[2] Berthold, *op. cit.*, p. 68 *ff*.

[3] See Extracts from the proceedings of the Budget Committee and in the Reichstag in *Jahrbuch der Bodenreform*, vol. IX, p. 199 *ff*.

municipalities, the effect of public improvements on property in town and country, etc., are factors to be considered in framing a law for the taxation on land value. It was also argued that only the immediate community is in a position to decide the expediency of the tax.[1] Then, too, the failure of the central administration to save expense and to prevent excessive litigation further justified the change in the law.

In considering the social and economic effects of the tax, it is important to note that, in spite of the action taken with regard to the increment tax, the principle of the tax was very generally upheld and accepted. "The socio-political significance of the tax on value increment lies in the change of public opinion which formerly decried the tax as socialistic and confiscatory, but which now, as a matter of course, regards it as a supplement to the income and property taxes."[2]

We find the same expectations and apprehensions current in Germany when the tax was proposed as in the case of the Australasian colonies. The chief hope of the partisans was that speculation in land would be suppressed, especially the speculation which develops when the agricultural prairie value of the land is converted through social forces into building-land value.[3] The other benefits expected to accrue, such as building reform, lower rentals, industrial prosperity, centered about the checking of speculation in land. It was believed that if the speculators did not keep land ripe for building out of use, and if the "Terraingesell-

[1] See Extracts from the proceedings of the Budget Committee and in the Reichstag in *Jahrbuch der Bodenreform*, vol. IX, p. 233.

[2] *Soziale Praxis*, vol. XIX, p. 760.

[3] In a speech on fiscal problems, in 1904, Professor Wagner touched upon this point when he said, "Now, when urban land has become the common object of speculation and changes hands as readily as a banknote, now, when the owner mortgages his property to about three-fourths of its value, . . . [another kind of tax] on the value increment is necessary." *Schriften der Gesellschaft für Soziale Reform* (1904), Heft 15, pp. 27–28, 30.

schaften" in the cities did not monopolize the building trade as well as the land, the housing evils would disappear, building operations and industry would prosper, and as a result of the increase in the supply of land and houses, the market price of land would fall to the normal value, while the capitalized rental, and therefore rents, would be reduced.[1]

On the other hand, some of the opponents, agreeing that the tax would cause a decline in the market value of land, feared the consequences; for example, the stagnation in land sales. Others argued that the effect would be to raise rent because the tax would be shifted to the purchaser and by him to the tenant. And, consequently, the market price of land would tend to appreciate. As regards building operations, it was claimed by some that overbuilding would result, that by putting a premium on improved land, even garden and other open spaces would be built upon to the detriment of social health and welfare; by others, that the supply of houses already filled the demand, that there is no land actually ripe for building which is kept out of use, that, therefore, no increase in building operations is possible.

To what extent experience with the tax justifies the contentions outlined above, we shall show from three sources of evidence, the results of two official investigations and of the valuable study by Dr. Berthold. The latter throws light on the working of the imperial tax, the two former on that of the local systems.

The following statements from municipalities were received by the Mayor of Kiel in answer to his inquiry with regard to the practical working of the tax: [2]

Frankfurt a. M.: "The expected decline in land transfers, which was feared on the part of some, has failed to materialize. There has been no noticeable stagnation, nor retrogression in the development of land-value increments."

---

[1] Cf. Jahrbuch der Bodenreform, vol. IX, pp. 217–18.
[2] Soziale Praxis (1907), vol. XVII, p. 322. (Translation by writer.)

Cologne: "Retarding influences as regards land sales due to the introduction of the increment tax have not thus far set in."

Gelsenkirchen: "Regarding the practical enforcement of the law, no unusual difficulties have presented themselves. . . . Nor has a decline in land transfers or in building operations resulted therefrom. The new tax bill has undoubtedly justified itself, and will continue to constitute a very valuable supplement to the local tax system."

Dortmund: "Notwithstanding the fact that, prior to the enforcement of the tax, speculators had consummated all the land transfers possible in anticipation of the law, the tax has, nevertheless, yielded a revenue of 263,000 marks. There have been 150 land sales, and of these 149 represented purchases by the larger estate holders and by speculators."

Prior to the enactment of the "Reichszuwachssteuer" the Imperial Finance Committee caused an investigation to be made inquiring into the effects of the tax in the localities. Replies from more than three hundred communities were received. Only three reported that there had been a decrease in building operations since the introduction of the tax. In three towns the tax was said to have induced the "Terraingesellschaften" to build. Only ten claimed that rents had decreased on account of the tax, seven that the tax had caused rents to increase; while eleven reported that the tax was shifted in whole or in part to the buyer.[1]

The study of Dr. Berthold was directed to determine from official data the effect of the imperial tax on the realty market during the two years' operation of the tax.[2] His tables comparing the number and value of the transactions in real estate from 1909 to 1913 show conclusively

[1] *Jahrbuch der Bodenreform* (1910), Heft 4, pp. 315 *ff*. Berthold, *op. cit.*, p. 13.
[2] *Ibid.*

that in the majority of the towns there were fewer transactions in 1911 and 1912 than in the two preceding years.
They also show that the introduction of the tax was not
the primary cause of the stagnant conditions of the market.
The depression in realty operations during 1911–12 is
traceable to the general unfavorable business conditions, to
an excess of vacant houses, to the tight money market,
and to local conditions. Dr. Berthold, however, does not
deny that the agitation relative to the enactment of the
"Reichszuwachssteuer," as well as the practical impossibility of calculating before the sale the amount of tax, may
have added to the general depression.

A second point of inquiry, less conclusively established,
however, was with regard to the incidence of the increment
tax. Only where the property is indispensable for business
purposes will the seller be able to shift the tax. But in such
cases the seller might have charged the higher price irrespective of the tax. In certain communities attempts
were made to shift the tax, but not always successfully.[1]
As yet the problem of the incidence of the "Zuwachssteuer"
has not been solved through any careful research. Authorities are, nevertheless, agreed that experience confirms the
theory that the tax burdens the seller only. Neither the
market price of land nor rentals have risen, according to the
testimony of officials and others. Admitting the absence of
any far-reaching evidence on the subject of incidence, Dr.
Boldt,[2] for example, attempts to show that in Düsseldorf
where no increment tax is in operation, the average rental
and value of the land are higher than in either Essen
or Dortmund, cities of the same industrial type and of
approximately the same size, but which levy an increment tax. There is, indeed, little evidence to show that
the tax has been shifted to the buyer; on the other hand,

[1] Berthold, *op. cit.*, p. 114.
[2] "Verhandlungen des Vereins für Sozialpolitik," in *Schriften des
Vereins*, vol. cxxxviii, p. 46.

theory holds that the possibility of so shifting the tax is slight.[1]

One of the causes attributed by Dr. Berthold to the stagnant condition of realty operations was the difficulty of obtaining mortgage loans, especially where the security was a second mortgage. This scarcity of loan funds, added to the higher rate of interest on mortgage loans,[2] hindered the acquisition of property and interfered with building operations. Nowhere, however, does the above-named writer relate this scarcity of mortgage loans to the introduction of the increment tax, nor does he seek to discover whether any causal relationship exists between the two. Nevertheless, the losses incurred by mortgagees through foreclosures and the hardships that the payment of increment tax imposes on the seller of property heavily mortgaged may have had some deterrent influence in the loan market on such security. In this connection the argument of another writer [3] who favors the "Zuwachssteuer" deserves mention. He opposes the retroactive feature of the tax on account of its deleterious effect on the mortgage market and its interference with credit.

This question brings us to the consideration of the effect of the tax on speculation in land. Because of the general dependence of land and building speculators in Germany on mortgage loans, a weeding out process of the insolvent operators, those who operate on borrowed capital, was observed during the depression of 1911 and 1912. If, then, the tax on value increment has been effective in checking second mortgage loans, it has at the same time hindered speculation, i.e., those operations which are carried on almost entirely with borrowed capital. Moreover, the payment of the tax has in many such cases forced the seller into

---

[1] *Cf.* Weyerman, "Die Überwälzungsfrage bei der Wertzuwachssteuer," in *Annalen des deutschen Reichs* (1910), vol. XLIII, pp. 881 *ff.*

[2] Berthold, *op. cit.*, pp. 97, 103 *et passim.*

[3] Freudenberg, *Die Wertzuwachssteuer in Baden*, pp. 3-4.

bankruptcy. Thus, whether the depression in the mortgage
loan market can be attributed to the tax or not, the tax is
said to have actually hindered the most undesirable kind of
speculation in land. This effect of the tax may indeed
account for the inordinate activity of the "Terraingesellschaften" and the pressure brought to bear upon the government by them to repeal the imperial tax.[1] The rate of
tax, however, has been too slight to restrain speculative
dealings to any considerable extent in cities where the
value of the land has appreciated a hundredfold or more,
and where the process of appreciation continues.[2]

§ 23. *Taxation of land in Kiao-chau.* The justification
for treating of the Kiao-chau experience with land taxation in this chapter lies not in the similarity of the systems
of taxation so much as in the political status of the Far Eastern province with respect to Germany. There are those,
indeed, who would trace the local increment taxes in Germany to the Kiao-chau experiment, but, as has been shown
in the previous sections,[3] there is slight cause for such a
hypothesis. After all, the system of taxation in Kiao-chau
is undoubtedly part and parcel of the larger scheme of German "Sozialpolitik" with respect to this province.[4]

Kiao-chau situated in Eastern Asia was acquired by
Germany in 1898, and according to a treaty with China was
to remain under German protection for ninety-nine years.

---

[1] *Cf.* the speech of Dr. Jaeger in the Reichstag printed in *Jahrbuch
der Bodenreform*, vol. IX, pp. 217–18.

[2] "Many persons hope that the tax will quicken the utilization of
building sites. In my opinion, however, that is an illusion, for just as
it is unlikely that a comparatively small increase in the tax will cause
the suburban owner to give up his gardens, so it is also unlikely that the
land speculators in rapidly growing towns will be compelled to any extent
to sell their land, which will after a longer period of waiting reimburse
them manyfold for the burden of the tax." Ephraim, "Zur Einführung
der 'Steuer nach dem gemeinen Wert' in Oldenburg," in *Zeitschrift für
die gesamte Staatswissenschaft* (1910), p. 151.

[3] See *supra*, §§ 3–6.

[4] *Denkschrift betreffend die Entwicklung des Kiautschougebiets* (1904–
05), p. 8.

The natives, numbering 187,000, are Chinese. Of Europeans there are over 4000.[1] Since the German occupation, railways, roads, and other improvements have been built, and the province is said to be developing industrially and commercially.

The naval authorities in charge of Kiao-chau, with a knowledge of the land situation in other Eastern provinces, in 1898, introduced a bill in the Reichstag designed to prevent land speculation and to help pay the vast sums expended by the government for public improvements.[2] This Act authorized the government to buy up from the natives any land needed for building purposes. The price was to be a nominal one, i.e., what the land was worth before the German occupation, and this land was to be sold again to the highest bidders, the government reaping the profit of the increased value. No one was to lease, use, or sell land for any purpose whatsoever without the permission of the government.[3] In fact, this land policy is unique in its restrictions of private property in land.

§ 24. At the same time that the land bill was passed, the following tax scheme for Kiao-chau was enacted. An annual direct tax of six per cent is levied on the land which the government has sold.[4] It was provided that for pur-

[1] Tsingtau, the chief town, had, in 1902–03, besides soldiers 962 Europeans, 108 Japanese, and 28,144 Chinese. *Denkschrift betreffend*, etc. (1902–03), p. 23. *Statistisches Jahrbuch für das deutsche Reich* (1914), p. 449.

[2] ' After the acquisition of Kiao-chau it was to be expected that the value of the land would appreciate considerably. Hence it was feared that the native Chinese would dispose of their property to a greater or less degree for a little temporary profit. It was a question, therefore, of protecting the landed interests of the Chinese, to defend them against themselves, and to prevent a dispossession of the Chinese by the white population." Translated from Gaul, *Finanzrecht der d. Schutzgebiete unter besonderer Berücksichtigung der Steuergesetzgebung*, p. 163.

[3] *Denkschrift betreffend*, etc. (1903–04), p. 8.

[4] The land which the government did not buy from the natives remained subject to the slight tax prevalent before the occupation. The tax is on an average 200 cash (about 30 pfennige) for 614 square metres. *Ibid.*, p. 6.

poses of assessment, the price paid for the land was to constitute its value until 1902; after that year and at regular intervals, the land was to be revalued. Besides this direct tax the Act provided that, whenever the land should be sold, thirty-three and one-third per cent of the net profit, or value increment, should revert to the government. An allowance, or compensation for improvements, of six per cent was to be deducted from the gross increment. In every case, moreover, the government retained the option of purchase at the price demanded by the owner.

Bearing in mind that these taxes, as well as the policy as a whole, were to prevent land speculation and to provide more dwellings, we may note that the government was confronted with the problem of making the purchasers improve the land which they had acquired. In other words, the tax and restrictions did not prevent owners from keeping their land in an unimproved condition, apparently for speculative purposes. The fact was, however, as is very often the case in urban communities, that the land remained undeveloped, either because the owner lacked the means to build, or because the time was unfavorable for building. But this frustrated the purpose of the government. The authorities were accordingly authorized to repurchase any unimproved land at one-half the price which the owners had paid for it. This provision was found ineffective, since the authorities lacked the ready funds to repurchase the land.[1] In 1903, therefore, the plan was conceived of increasing the annual tax so long as the land remained undeveloped. This is said to have had the desired effect. According to this scheme which was not to be enforced until 1906, land not utilized for the purpose for which it had been purchased was made liable to an annual tax of nine per cent instead of the usual six per cent; if three years

[1] *Jahrbuch der Bodenreform* (1908), vol. IV, p. 132; *Cf. Denkschrift betreffend*, etc. (1902–03), pp. 9–10.

passed after this increased rate became effective, the tax was raised to twelve per cent; and this three per cent increase was to continue with every three years until an annual tax of twenty-four per cent had been reached. The Act provided, furthermore, that whenever the land should be built upon and improved, the tax should be reduced to six per cent.[1]

Another provision in the Land Act of Kiao-chau restricting the property rights to land even more is the following. The government not only retains the right of repurchase, but in the case of land which has remained unsold within twenty-five years, the land becomes subject to revaluation and a tax of thirty-three and one-third per cent is levied on the value increment.

§ 25. What has been the effect of such limitations of the right of private property on the real estate market? While no overcapitalization of the value of land under such restrictions is conceivable, both the land market and the values are sound in Kiao-chau. Land transactions occur and land has risen in value.[2] An official describes the first public sale of land as follows: "In spite of all the restrictions necessary to nip speculation in the bud, there was no lack of solvent buyers ready unhesitatingly to bid higher than the government's estimates, showing thereby that the merchant class did not question the healthy development of the colony." [3]

In considering the proceeds from the land taxes as shown in the table below, it should be borne in mind: (1) that the population of Kiao-chau is small; (2) that land is exceedingly cheap compared with European countries; (3) that

---

[1] *Jahrbuch der Bodenreform* (1908), vol. IV. p. 132 ; *Cf. Denkschrift betreffend,* etc. (1902–03), pp. 9–10.

[2] In a decade land is said to have increased from 200 to 300 per cent: from $50 for 921 square meters the value had risen to about $150 or $160, while orchard land was worth in 1908 about $200. *Denkschrift betreffend,* etc. (1908–09), pp. 37–38.

[3] *Jahrbuch der Bodenreform,* March, 1911, p. 37. (Translated.)

sales are comparatively few; [1] and (4) that some of the land has not advanced in price. Thus, there were only thirty-one transfers of property in 1908–09; yet they yielded no value-increment duty.[2]

TABLE SHOWING YIELD OF THE LAND AND INCREMENT TAXES, RENTS FROM LEASEHOLDS, AND PROCEEDS FROM LAND SALES IN KIAO–CHAU [3]

Year	Land Tax (Marks)	Rents from lease-holds (Marks)	Govern-ment land sales (Marks)	Value-increment duty
1898–99	22,170	5,870	..	..
1899–00	31,371	21,910	..	..
1900–01	52,765	31,049	..	..
1901–02	62,956	23,305	..	..
1902–03	63,961	19,676	24,422	..
1903–04	79,212	34,113	63,857	$1,128.90
1904–05	87,498	60,910	195,975	1,474.70
1905–06	139,935	83,013	149,389	417.34
1906–07	117,591	91,686	87,865	2,103.66
1907–08	112,861	75,877	73,332	301.28
1908–09	121,017	59,401	33,069	000.00

It is necessary to point out that the government must rely on other sources than the land for the budget. Taking the revenue from the land taxes, plus that from the rents and from the public land sales, we find that it constituted, in 1906–07, about twenty-seven per cent, while, in 1908–09, only nine per cent of the total expenditures.[4]

[1] The following show the number of purchasers of land: —

1902–03,	143	Europeans,	151	Chinese
1903–04,	158	"	162	"
1904–05,	197	"	174	"
1905–06,	210	"	194	"

[2] *Denkschrift betreffend*, etc. (1908–09), p. 12.

[3] Data given in *Denkschriften betreffend die Entwicklung des Kiautschougebiets.*

[4] The total revenue for 1906–07 amounted to 1,546,489 marks; in 1908–09, to 2,365,931 marks. *Ibid.* (1908–09), pp. 66–67.

It is, however, not so much from the standpoint of revenue as from that of a sound land policy that the Kiao-chau experiment offers interesting study. And yet, in considering the land policy and the taxes on land value in operation since 1898 in that province, we must bear in mind the exceptional circumstances under which the government acquired possession of the land. The problem in older countries, where the principle of private ownership of land is deep-rooted, is far more complex.

CHAPTER V

THE ENGLISH LAND-VALUE DUTIES

§ 1. The enactment of the duties on land value which constitute Part I of the Finance Act, 1909–10, marks a decided departure in the fiscal policy of England. This fact, aside from the controversy with the House of Lords over the measure, has evoked widespread criticism and interest among students and statesmen. The latter, indeed, regarding the new taxes as social reform, not fiscal, legislation, have questioned the propriety of incorporating the land taxes in the budget. Nevertheless, whatever foundation there exists for the prevailing impression that Parliament was carried away by the whirlwind of socialism and other "isms" which were sweeping the country, a study of the attempted legislation prior to the enactment of the Finance Act reveals the fact that the change in fiscal policy was inevitable.

To set forth the fiscal causes of the new taxes which are generally overlooked, and to demonstrate their unprecedented character, it is important both to show the relation between landownership and land taxation in the United Kingdom, and to trace the movement toward land-value taxation.

The history of landlordism and land taxes throws light on the strenuous opposition of the Lords to the Finance Act which in 1909 threatened the abolition of the Upper House of Parliament. In view of the fact that the Lords are in the main the landowners of England, the small extent to which land contributes to the support of the government is significant. Property owners contribute to the following sources of public revenue. First, there is the so-called annual land tax which since Pitt's redemption scheme in 1798 has yielded less than one million pounds,[1] or less than half its yield in 1692 when instituted.[2] This nominal land charge, it will be recalled, is based on a valuation made more than two centuries ago, and is unequally apportioned among the counties of England. Secondly, there is Schedule A of the income tax charged on the gross rental of real property.[3] Thirdly, under the system of rating by the local authorities, land and its improvements, including buildings, not only yield over eighty per cent of the local tax receipts, but also form the principal source of local revenue.[4] In addition to the rates, tithes are still levied on real property in some parts of the United Kingdom. Fourthly, land in conjunction with other property is subject to death duties, or inheritance tax, levied for imperial purposes. Only in this case is the basis of assessment the capital value of the property.

To estimate to what extent the English landlords are burdened by these charges, it is necessary to analyze the methods of assessment and levy of these taxes so as to ascertain their incidence.

In the first place, it was estimated by the Commission of 1901 that ratable property (including structures and other improvements) contributed about seventeen and one-half

[1] Cf. Dowell, *History of Taxation and Taxes in England*, vol. ii, pp. 239-40. In 1907-08 the net receipts were £710,000. *Cf. Parl. Debates* (1908), vol. cxcviii, p. 2075.

[2] Originally this was a general property tax imposed (1) on those possessing personal property, (2) on those holding any public office or employment of profit, (3) on those possessing land, but because of the evasion of the first two from assessment, the burden fell on land alone. *Cf.* Dowell, *op. cit.*, vol. iii, pp. 93-97.

[3] *Parl. Debates* (1909), vol. ii, p. 1870. There is a maximum reduction of one-eighth of rental in respect of agricultural land and one-sixth in respect of buildings.

[4] In 1909-10 the rates constituted forty-nine per cent of the total revenue of the local bodies of England and Wales, not counting the loans. *Statesman's Year Book* (1913), p. 49.

per cent to the imperial tax receipts; to the local budgets, eighty-two per cent of all the tax revenue.[1] But from the standpoint of incidence, it is important to differentiate between the proportions falling on land and improvements respectively, for according to the best authorities on taxation,[2] the tax on buildings is more likely to fall on the occupier than on the landowner or building-owner. The proportion that falls on land, irrespective of the buildings, has been variously estimated and differs in Scotland and Ireland from the proportion in England and Wales. According to Bastable, land under Schedule A yielded about twenty-three and one-half per cent, houses seventy-six and one-half per cent (1900), while under the local systems about one-sixth of the rates was derived from land, and five-sixth from houses.[3] He furthermore estimated that land in the United Kingdom (including all improvements other than houses) contributed (1900) about £12,500,000, which constituted about nine per cent of the total tax revenue for imperial and local taxation.[4]

Then, when we consider the possibility of capitalization and amortization in cases of taxes on real property, the burdensomeness of taxation on the landowners appears even less. For according to the theory of amortization the whole tax on land or so much of the tax as exceeds the general burden of taxation on all capital or income is capitalized and the value deducted from the selling price of the property, so that the purchaser through this reduction in price becomes exempt from the tax, while the seller loses the whole amount of the capitalized tax. In case of taxes of

[1] *Parl. Debates* (1909), vol. i, p. 892.

[2] According to Seligman, *Shifting and Incidence of Taxation* (ed. 1899), p. 307, even Schedule A must be treated as a tax on real property to ascertain the incidence of that part of the income tax.

[3] Bastable, *Public Finance* (ed. 1903), pp. 431–32.

[4] *Ibid.* The percentage was computed with the aid of data from the *Statesman's Year Book* (1900), pp. 45, 55; the total tax revenue, local and imperial, was given for the United Kingdom as £134,821,081.

long standing, therefore, the present owner is burdened only by any increase in rate since he came into ownership. The doctrine is especially applicable to the imperial nominal land tax in England, since the assessment has not only remained unchanged for several centuries, but the tax has either been redeemed or has long since been "absorbed" in the selling price, because the apportionment of the quota among the counties has not changed. It is held by Blunden [1] that even the local rates have to some extent been thus capitalized and ceased to be a burden. Whether this is true or not, there are, as we shall show below, further reasons for believing that but a small part of the rates are borne by the landowners.

Again, inasmuch as it is upon the rates that the local governments chiefly depend for revenue, and inasmuch as ratable property is heavily burdened for local tax purposes,[2] it is of importance in this conection that the burden falls mainly upon the occupier, not upon the landlord. The reasons are: (1) The occupier pays the tax in the first instance, and through various causes which we need not dwell upon,[3] he is unable to recoup himself for the tax by deducting it from his rent. The following table (Distribution of the Burden of the Rates in England and Wales in 1891, on page 194) shows that only 15.31 per cent of the rates on land and houses, in 1891, fell on real property, or rather, on the land owners and lessees.

---

[1] *Local Taxation and Finance*, p. 43. "But there appears to be good grounds for the conclusion that the burden is mainly, as Dr. Giffen suggested in 1871, 'on the property, and not on the individuals who have incomes from it.'"

[2] The average rate per pound on ratable rental increased from 3s. 3¼d. to 5s. 7½d. from 1882 to 1902. *Cf.* Armitage-Smith, *Principles and Methods of Taxation*, p. 161.

[3] See Seligman, *Shifting and Incidence of Taxation*, pp. 246 *ff.*

DISTRIBUTION OF THE BURDEN OF THE RATES IN ENGLAND AND WALES IN 1891 [1]

	On real property (per cent)	On personal property (per cent)	On occupiers' income (per cent)	On consumers' income (per cent)
Lands and tithes	15.31	..	..	..
Houses	..	..	56.4	4.29
Railways	..	14.00	..	..
Other property	3.59	2.82	..	3.59
Total	18.90	16.82	56.40	7.88

(2) Since the lessee almost always contracts to pay the taxes, any increase in the rate of tax will be borne by the lessee, at least until the expiration of the lease. Now, in England, the builder is very often a lessee and cannot recoup himself for any increase in the rate until his lease expires. (3) Non-income-bearing land, irrespective of its value, is exempt from rating. Thus, in spite of the enormous increase in urban values, land in England and Wales contributed, in 1894, a smaller percentage of the whole tax than in 1814, as shown below: —

CONTRIBUTION OF PROPERTY TO THE TOTAL ASSESSMENT OF THE LOCALITIES, 1814–1894 [2]

	1814 (per cent)	1843 (per cent)	1868 (per cent)	1894 (per cent)
Land	69.28	49.10	33.20	20.9
Houses	27.84	41.44	47.27	63.7
Railways and other property	2.88	9.46	19.53	15.4

[1] Blunden, *op. cit.*, p. 62. There is no reason to think that conditions of incidence have changed much since 1891, for the method of assessment is the same.

[2] Data gathered from Goschen, *Report on Local Taxation*, p. 23; and from *Report of the Royal Commission on Local Taxation* (Cd. 9528), 1899, pp. 44–45.

Furthermore, this system of assessment on rental rather than on capital value, which exempts the owner of undeveloped land from taxation, has contributed most to the evasion by the landowner of a burden of taxation proportionate to his ability or his benefit. The influence of this class, in fact, is seen in their resistance to taxation on the basis of capital value. Thus it was not until 1894 that the death duties were made to apply to real property in the same way as to personal property, that is, on the basis of capital value assessment.[1] And until the enactment of the Finance Act, 1909–10, the death duties were the only tax on real property assessed on capital value.

Finally, the special treatment of agricultural land is noteworthy. The exemption in recent years of about £2,000,000 annually from the tax on agricultural land under Schedule A is generally considered to have been a boon to the landlords, rather than to the farmers whom it was intended to relieve.[2] The cause of the remission of that amount is of course the decline in the value of agricultural land. But this decline, which has made the actual rent paid by the tenant farmer exceed the economic rent, the rent warranted by the produce obtained, has shifted the burden of the taxes from the landlord to the tenant.[3] A remission of the taxes, therefore, is only apparently a

[1] For the opposition of the landowners to this measure see Wagner, "Die Englische Erbsteuerreform von 1894" in *Zeitschrift für Volkswirtschaft, Socialpolitik u. Verwaltung* (1899), p. 323.

[2] See Agricultural Rates Act (1896).

[3] *Parl. Debates* (1909), vol. v, p. 627. *Cf.* also Seligman, *Shifting and Incidence of Taxation*, p. 307. The condition of agricultural production in England is peculiar. The depression has caused the land to become depreciated, so that the farmers, because of the immobility of the capital invested and their own inability to enter other employments readily, are paying more than the usual rack rent or economic rent; hence the tax paid by them in the first instance is not shifted to the landowner. "Although the farmer has been struggling to adjust his rent to lower prices, the process has been a slow one; and the fall in actual rents has not kept pace with the fall of economic rent due to these lower prices." Seligman, *ibid.*, p. 232.

relief to the farmer; in reality the position of the landlord, when a renewal of the lease is sought by his tenants, is thereby strengthened, and the landlord can resist a reduction of the rent which conditions would otherwise warrant.[1]

Thus it is clear that in singling out the landowning class for special taxation, and in choosing land taxes, the incidence of which is supposedly certain, the Lloyd George Budget is a departure from precedent and from the tax legislation hitherto favorable to the landowning class.

It remains to show, further, that the enactment of the land-value duties was not the revolutionary, unreflected measure of a socialistic parliament. The problem of taxing land value had been well deliberated upon, and the arguments pro and con thoroughly weighed by the various Select Committees who, since 1891, had been delegated by Parliament to investigate the intricate problem of local taxation. The anomalous feature in this movement is, rather, that the outcome of the agitation among local authorities for land-value rating should have resulted first in an imperial rather than in a local tax.

§ 2. Discontent with the rating system by which the landowners largely escaped taxation, while the occupiers bore the heavier burden, early asserted itself. The reform movement, after years of agitation, became concentrated upon the following demands: (1) the division of rates between occupier and owner;[2] (2) the taxation of land value; (3) "special assessment" taxation.[3] We are concerned here with the second reform advocated.

The expediency of taxing land value was raised by the

---

[1] Cf. also J. S. Nicholson, *Rates and Taxes as Affecting Agriculture,* where the incidence of the land tax is shown. Cf. also Row-Fogo, *An Essay on the Reform of Local Taxation in England,* pp. 171–82.

[2] The system whereby the owner pays one-half the tax and the occupier the other half is in vogue in Scotland and Ireland.

[3] Cf. Blunden. *op. cit.,* chapters VII, VIII, and IX.

Housing Committee in 1884.[1] In its report the committee recommended that "land available for building in the neighborhood of populous centers" be rated for local purposes at four per cent of its selling value. The purpose of the proposal was to relieve the congestion of population. In 1892, the Select Committee on Town Holdings reported unfavorably on the taxation of vacant building land as well as on the proposition of separate valuation of land and of improvements. The proposal of the Draft Report Committee to tax land on the selling value at a higher rate than buildings, because land receives an exceptional value through the growth of towns, while buildings represent an outlay of capital which is discouraged by taxation,[2] was rejected by the majority as impracticable. The following conclusions of the Select Committee, which refused to recognize the expediency of land-value taxation, were adopted: [3]

"(1) Ground rents and feu[4] duties are already taxed, as being included in the ratable value of the town holding on which they are secured. They do not constitute a fresh

[1] See *Second Series of Memoranda and Extracts Relating to Land Taxation* (Cd. 4845), 1909, pp. 71 *ff*. It is interesting to note that the late King of England, Edward VII, then Prince of Wales, was a member of that Committee. See *Report of the Housing Committee* (Cd. 4402), 1885.

[2] House of Commons Paper 214 (1892), pp. xcii, xxxvi. The arguments used in this draft report are the usual ones. "The growth of towns has added an exceptional value to town lands. Such value is maintained, and has to a great extent been created, by municipal expenditure, and it is therefore just that those who are in receipt of the annual returns from town lands should contribute a substantial proportion of it to defray the municipal expenditure of which they thus reap the fruits. . . . Buildings represent the direct outlay of capital and their return depends substantially upon their cost. Heavy rates upon buildings as opposed to land tend to stimulate the erection and use of inferior houses. . . . The annual value of land may be considered as a net return from an improving property, whereas that of buildings is a gross return from a wasting property, and it is unfair that they should be taxed at the same rate in the pound," etc.

[3] *Ibid.*

[4] Feu tenancy in Scotland is perpetual, the rent being a fixed amount.

matter of assessment hitherto untouched as is often sup-
posed. The imposition of a direct assessment upon such
ground rents and feu duties as distinguished from the
assessed value of the house itself, as at present rated,
would lead to anomalies and inequalities and has been
generally abandoned. . . .

" (2) The real as opposed to the apparent incidence of
land taxation in towns falls partly upon the owner of
the land, partly upon the house owner, and partly upon
the occupier. The proportions in which the burden is distributed are difficult to determine and depend upon a
variety of circumstances among which the demand and
supply of houses is the most important.

" (3) Owners of ground rents, with or without rever-
sions, derive no appreciable benefit from local public expenditure for current purposes. . . .

" (4) The burden of such increased land taxation as
was not in contemplation of the parties on entering into
leases falls on the lessee, unless the occupier has been unable to shift it. But as regards lessees, the unforeseen increase in the value of their properties has, in most cases,
more than made up to them for the unexpected burden
of increased rates."

Four years later the Royal Commission appointed to
inquire into the subject of local taxation reached similar
conclusions in rejecting the proposition of land-value taxation. After interviewing numerous witnesses and after an
extensive investigation their report was published in 1901.[1]
Again, a separate report on "Urban Rating and Site Values," by a committee consisting of Lord Balfour of Burleigh,[2] Lord Blair Balfour, Sir Edward Hamilton, Sir
George Murray, and Mr. James Stuart, dissented from

---

[1] *Final Report of His Majesty's Commission Appointed to Inquire . . .
Local Taxation* (Cd. 638), 1901.

[2] The same Lord Balfour of Burleigh vigorously opposed the Finance
Act, 1909–10, in the House of Lords.

the majority's findings. Their recommendations were very similar to those of the Draft Report of 1892, with this additional proposal, that the institution of site-value rating by the locality be made optional.[1]

The London County Council and the Glasgow Council were meanwhile active in discussing the question of rating on site value. In the reports of the London County Council of 1889 and 1893 the adoption of this system was recommended. The council actually undertook to make a valuation of all the land within London.[2] Similarly, Glasgow, as early as 1891, and again in 1895, drew up reports favoring the rating of land value.[3] In the House of Commons also considerable discussion took place on the subject, not only in regard to local taxation, but also in regard to Schedule A.[4] To carry out the recommendation

[1] The advantages of taxing land value were enumerated in this minority report as follows: (1) It would conduce to placing the urban rating system on a more equitable and thus sounder basis; (2) it would make the ground-owner and lessee having an interest in the land contribute somewhat more than under the old system to local taxation; (3) it should go some way toward putting an end to agitation for unjust and confiscatory measures; (4) it would enable deductions for repairs to be made solely in respect of the buildings; (5) it would tend to lighten the burdens in respect to buildings and thus aid in solving the urgent housing problem; (6) it would tend to rectify inequalities between districts and between owners. *Report*, etc. (Cd. 638), 1901, p. 176.

[2] *Cf. Parl. Debates* (1907), vol. CLXXXII, p. 46; Also, 1909, vol. v, p. 1221. *Cf. British Parl. Papers* (Cd. 9150), 1899, p. 13.

[3] For a discussion of the London County and Glasgow resolutions regarding the taxation of land value see Smart, *Taxation of Land Values and the Single Tax*, chapters II and III. Not only did the Corporation of Glasgow in 1897 pass resolutions declaring the taxation of land value "the most equitable method of removing the present inequalities of local taxation," but in the same year the Glasgow City assessor proposed an increment tax on land. See *British Parl. Papers* (C. 9319), 1899, pp. 257–58.

[4] In view of later events the following speech of Mr. Billson, M.P., containing a prophecy is interesting: "In connection with the property tax under Schedule A the law lays down that land should be charged according to what it produces, and not according to its real value. When this property tax was first put in force about fifty years ago, the conditions were somewhat different, and there is now in all our large towns a

of the minority report of 1901, Mr. Trevelyan the following year introduced the "Urban Site Value Rating Bill"
in the House of Commons. As the majority reports of the
special committees, however, had opposed the new tax,
Trevelyan's measure could only meet defeat.[1] But the
game had been started, and the following year, Dr. Macnamara presented "A Bill to provide for the Separate
Assessment and Rating of Land Values." [2] This bill failed
to secure a second reading, although by an adverse majority of only thirteen votes.[3]

The purpose of the bill, as Dr. Macnamara set forth
in the introductory paragraph, was "to give urban authorities a new source of revenue in relief of the present
rates and so to diminish the existing burdens on building
enterprise." The rate was to be one penny in the pound
and "to be levied on the capital value of all land, whether
occupied or not, as distinct from the value of any buildings or structures on the land." Again that year, a "Land
Valuation Bill" was presented in the House by a Scotch
member. It proposed to rate only unoccupied land. But
after the first reading the bill was dropped.

Then more bills followed. In 1904, another "Land Values (Assessment and Rating) Bill" was given a second
reading,[4] but no further action was taken. This was succeeded, in 1905, by still another bill entitled "Land Values
Taxation (Scotland) Bill" which proposed to empower the

---

great deal of land that escapes taxation which ought to bear taxation.
Large quantities of land lie idle and produce nothing and consequently
such land does not come within the purview of this taxation. And why
not? . . . I hope that he himself [the Chancellor of the Exchequer] will
introduce a very considerable measure for the taxation of land values, but
if he does not *some more enterprising Chancellor of the Exchequer will do so
in the future.*" *Parl. Debates* (1900), vol. LXXX, pp. 1247–50. (Italics mine.)

[1] *Ibid.*, (1902), vol. CIII, p. 475.

[2] It is significant that David Lloyd George supported this and subsequent measures to tax land value.

[3] *Ibid.*, (1903), vol. CXVIII, p. 400.

[4] *Ibid.*, vol. CXXIX, p. 480.

Town Councils of the burghs to impose a tax not exceeding two shillings in the pound on the annual rental of all land. The annual rental, however, was to be calculated at four per cent of the selling price of the land, exclusive of the buildings upon it. It furthermore proposed, diverging in this respect from the preceding bills, that the tax should be deducted by the tenant or lessee who paid it from the lessor or owner, irrespective of the stipulation of existing contracts. As was to be expected, this measure met a fate similar to the preceding ones. Its failure, however, did not deter the partisans of land-value rating from introducing another bill in the same year. The contents of Mr. Brunner's bill were not unlike those of the former measure, except for the stipulation to respect contracts. It provided that only under a lease or agreement made subsequent to the enactment of the bill, was the occupier authorized to deduct the tax from the rental. Then, too, instead of four per cent, three per cent of the capital value was to constitute the annual value for assessment purposes.[1] Although voted a second reading by a majority of ninety, nothing further was done with the proposal. Mr. Ferguson's measure,[2] the "Land Value Assessment (Scotland) Bill" was presented in the same year and was defeated. In that year, also a deputation of rating authorities waited upon the Prime Minister relative to the matter of site-value rating.

§ 3. These persistent efforts on the part of the adherents of the tax were destined to bear fruit. Thus in

[1] "Its main object," said Trevelyan, its supporter, "was to make an assessment of the land values of our towns and urban districts, to place upon the rate-book a second column, which would consist of assessments at three per cent of the selling values, and to provide that where the new assessment in the case of any piece of property amounted to a larger sum than the present assessment on the annual value the rate should fall upon that new assessment." *Parl. Debates* (1905), vol. CXLV, pp. 207–08.

[2] The sponsor of this bill, Mr. Ferguson, had been a member of the Select Committee on Town Holdings and had helped draw up the Draft Report from which we quoted above.

1906,[1] when Mr. Sutherland's "Land Values Taxation
(Scotland) Bill" was introduced before a newly elected
House, a second reading was voted by a majority, it is noteworthy, of 258, and on April 24, it was committed to the
Select Committee for consideration.[2] As the findings of
this committee were often quoted during the debate on
the Finance Act of 1909–10, and throw light on the final
enactment of this measure, an analysis of the Committee's
report is necessary. In the Draft Special Report submitted
to the Committee the disadvantages of the existing order
were set forth. It was pointed out that under the system
of taxation whereby land and improvements were treated
as a unit and that unit was assessed on the basis of its annual value, land was kept out of use and undeveloped, so
that the supply of land was restricted and its acquisition
rendered more difficult and more costly. Furthermore,
the system tended to penalize the builder and to prevent
the owner from making necessary improvements.[3]

Three important problems which occupied the attention of the committee were: (1) the practicability of separate valuation of land and improvements; (2) the cost

[1] In the same year two more bills were presented as follows: "Land
Values Assessment (Scotland) Bill," by Trevelyan, and "Land Valuation
(Scotland) Act 1854 Amendment Bill," by McCrae. See *Parl. Debates*
(1906), vols. CLII and CLIV.

[2] The thoroughness with which this committee investigated the subject
of land-value taxation deserves mention. Data were gathered from many
foreign countries, while expert, practical men and economists were sum-
moned to give evidence.

[3] The objections were summarized as follows: —

1. Rating on hypothetical capital value would create inequalities.

2. Separate taxation of site value is inequitable and impracticable.

3. Rating on land value would tend inevitably to a curtailment or suppression of gardens, and all other open spaces in private ownership.

4. The scheme interfered with private contract.

5. It would be a harsh and confiscatory proceeding against the public
and private trusts and private investors who had acquired the feu duties
simply as a form of investment.

6. Public credit and financial security would be disturbed. *Papers,*
etc. (Cd. 4845), 1909, p. 53.

of such valuation; (3) the treatment of existing contracts. As to the question of valuation the evidence was conflicting. Expert valuers differed as to the practicability of separate valuations for site and building. The reports of the previous committees that had investigated the question were quoted and discussed.[1] According to Messrs. Moulton and Harper,[2] who had testified in 1900, no difficulty in separate valuation exists and valuers actually resort to that method in their work.[3] According to others the difficulty of separate valuation was insuperable. Likewise there was a difference of opinion as to the probable cost of such valuation. Mr. Harper's estimate was the lowest.[4] An expert valuation of London County, according to him, would probably cost £40,000; according to others, such a valuation could not be made for less than a million pounds. In going over this evidence of hypothetical estimates, it is significant to note, the Select Committee of 1906 appears to have given little weight to the testimony of officials in other countries, for example, of Mr. Purdy, the Commissioner of Taxation in New York City, and to have neglected the experience of the Australasian and Canadian colonies, where the practicability of separate valuation is no longer in question.[5]

Aside from the subject of valuation, we must point out another serious objection of the Committee to the taxation on land value, namely, the interference with existing contracts. The system of leasehold in England, as is well known, makes this question of contracts a matter of vital importance. Not only are sites leased under the freehold rent charge, the 999-year leasehold, and the

---

[1] *Papers Bearing on Land Taxes* (Cd. 4750), 1909, pp. 258 *ff*.

[2] Mr. Harper is now employed by the Valuation Department as expert valuer in the great task of valuing all the land in the United Kingdom.

[3] *Cf.* Cd. 638 (1901), p. 41.   [4] Cd. 638, p. 42.

[5] See *Papers Bearing on Land Taxes*, etc. (Cd. 4750), 1909, and others on *The Taxation of Land*.

99-year systems, but subletting further complicates the situation. Thus it happens that besides the freehold purchaser and main lessor, the lessee, sublessee, and occupier may have interests in one piece of property. Obviously, were the new system of taxation adopted, the tax would fall on the lessee or occupier, because the latter had contracted to assume the burden of all taxes. Therefore if the purpose of the new system was to be carried out, and the tax made to fall on the owner of the fee simple or lessor, the contract which made the tenant liable for all charges and taxes would be violated and the rights of the landlord infringed upon. On the one hand, it is argued that such a tax would inflict a hardship upon the owner who probably, at the time when the contract was made, consented to a smaller rent because he was relieved from the tax burden. Moreover, since the lessee, until the expiration of the lease, remained the recipient of any increases in the income from the land, the exemption from the tax would be a bounty, or an additional profit. On the other hand, it is pointed out that the ground-owner, upon the expiration of the lease, not only receives back his property, but all the improvements made by the lessee; that, also, whenever a renewal of the lease occurs, the landowner exacts a higher rental due to a rise in the value of the land, often, too, as a result of the improvements made by the tenant. It is clear, therefore, aside from any prejudice in the matter,[1] why the difficulty in rendering

[1] The position of the Committee, forecasting the vehement opposition that had to be overcome before the enactment of the Finance Act of 1909–10, is shown in the following summary of the evidence: "Your Committee cannot but take cognizance of the fact that the principal evidence in support of the scheme was that of men of very extreme views, and of predatory, if not altogether confiscatory, opinions in regard to rights of property in land. In the view of such witnesses this new rate is only the beginning of a scheme of expropriation without compensation, whereby the whole burden of local and imperial charges is to be laid upon the owners of one form of property, if, indeed, any rental value at all is to be left to them. In the opinion of your Committee, a scheme,

justice to the contractual parties under such complexities was made a weighty consideration in the final decision of the Select Committee.

§ 4. The final recommendations of this Select Committee, as well as the subsequent attempts at legislation, showed that the enactment of rating on land value in face of the opposition of the House of Lords would be impossible. In reference to the Land Values Taxation (Scotland) Bill of 1906, the Select Committee recommended [1] (1) that the bill be dropped, (2) that a substitute measure be introduced making provision for a valuation of the land in the boroughs and counties of Scotland, apart from the buildings and improvements, and (3) that no assessment be determined upon until the amount of that valuation should be known and considered. Then, in accordance with these recommendations a bill "to provide for the ascertainment of the land values in Scotland" was presented in the House by the Lord Advocate, Mr. Shaw, during the session of 1907. It will be noted that this bill was merely for statistical purposes, not for the taxation of land value; nevertheless, the Opposition was apprehensive of the consequences of the proposed land valuation. The bill passed the House of Commons, only to be defeated in the House of Lords. [2] In the following year another bill bearing the title, "Land Values (Scotland) Bill of 1908," [3] was again favorably voted upon in the House of Commons, but was so amended by the Lords that the government was compelled to drop the bill. This action of the Upper House, of course, only kindled the ire of the public, who

mainly advocated by persons holding such opinions, must be regarded with suspicion by all who condemn their ultimate aims, not only as contrary to public policy, but as inconsistent with public faith." Cd. 4845, p. 52. From a report submitted by Mr. Remnant.

[1] House of Commons Paper 379 (1906), p. XIV.

[2] See *Parl. Debates* (1907), vols. CLXXIV, CLXXXI.

[3] *Parl. Debates* (1907), vol. CLXXXII, pp. 43 *ff*. As before this bill provided for the assessment in a separate column of the capital value of all the land in Scotland.

interpreted it as an undue interference with popular government.[1]

That this determined opposition of the Lords is in part responsible for the imperial taxation of land value, as embodied in the Finance Act of 1909–10, is attested by numerous utterances of the leaders in power. Thus in 1909, when Lloyd George was upbraided because no reference to the question of valuation had been made in the King's Speech, he replied:[2] "Well, we have had some experience of trying to carry Valuation Bills through Parliament. We carried a Valuation Bill for Scotland in the House of Commons and sent it to 'another place' but it came to an unfortunate end. We are bearing that in mind. We are considering whether there are not other means of dealing with that great question, especially as it has got mixed up with local and Imperial finance. . . ." The other means referred to were undoubtedly the land-value duties. Incorporated in the budget, the land-value duties would have to become law. Indeed, the Lords' opposition to this drastic reform reached a dramatic climax in that year. It

[1] In a speech of October, 1907, Lloyd George said: "The Land Values Bill, which did no more than throw upon the local authorities the single duty of valuing the land apart from the buildings upon its surface was incontinently rejected, and I say this rejection was a piece of arrogance and high-handedness which marks the extreme pretensions of the House of Lords." Quoted in the House of Lords; see *Parl. Debates* (1908), vol. CXCII, p. 15.

[2] *Ibid.* (1909), vol. I, p. 936. The following quotations express the same thought: "We do not believe that Increment Duty is at all a desirable tax. We supported it when the Budget of 1909–10 was going through on certain definite grounds. *It was the only means of getting a valuation of the land. Owing to the action of the House of Lords in refusing to pass in two Sessions in succession a fair valuation bill we had to get our valuation of the land of the country via the Finance Act of 1909–10.*" (From a speech by Mr. Wedgewood, M.P. *Ibid.* (1913), vol. L, p. 176.) "Land reformers believed that a valuation had been accomplished, a value apart from the buildings and improvements upon land by which they would finally be enabled to secure *a basis for rating and taxation fairer and more just than the basis upon which our rating and taxation now depend.*" Quoted from a speech by the Lord Advocate, A. Ure. *Ibid.*, vol. LVI, p. 404. (Italics mine.)

meant capitulation to the measure insuring a valuation of the land, or the dissolution of the House of Lords.[1] In such circumstances the Lords gave way, and thus the Finance Bill of 1909–10, providing for the taxation of land value, was finally enacted.

§ 5. Having traced the development of the principle of taxing land value as a fiscal policy, evolved from the needs of the local governments, we have yet to discover the other motives which made the budget acceptable in 1909–10. The time was ripe for the reform, and the motive existed to set the latent forces free. The budget proposal, in fact, was of a piece with the general policy of social legislation of the administration. The party in power was pledged to a number of progressive measures which it most conscientiously strove to carry out. Old-age pensions, insurance against invalidity, accident and unemployment, labor exchanges, home rule for Ireland, were on the board; likewise, the taxation of land value.

Certainly for the unusual proposals in Part I of the Budget, the fiscal exigencies — that is, the increased expenditure needed for the navy and old-age pensions — are not a sufficient explanation.[2] Indeed, the charge of the Opposition that Lloyd George favored the taxes on land value because he was "bitten with certain theories" cannot be repudiated. They pointed out with reason that the estimated yield of the tax was too insignificant to be fiscally justifiable.[3] Furthermore, when we find some Cabinet Ministers[4] pledged to the cause of the new

---

[1] Cf. Parl. Debates (1908), vol. cxcii, pp. 14, 15.

[2] Cf. Lloyd George's Budget Speech, ibid. (1909), vol. iv, pp. 477, 500. If it had been a measure of fiscal exigency the tax should have been repealed in 1911–12, when there was a surplus revenue.

[3] Cf. ibid., vol. iv, p. 758.

[4] The Lord Advocate, Mr. Ure, was honorary vice-president of the Scottish League for the Taxation of Land Values; the Secretary of the Navy, Mr. Haldane, is said to have been a member of the Single Tax League. Cf. ibid., vol. vi, pp. 79, 85. Moreover, Asquith, Lloyd George, and Ure had always supported the land-value measures that had previously been presented in Parliament.

taxes, it is not to be wondered at that this plank in the platform was inserted in the Finance Bill, where it had a better likelihood of enactment.[1] And this *coup d' état* succeeded.

Again, the form of the tax, or rather taxes, disproves their alleged fiscal character. This becomes evident if we compare the English duties with the local land taxes in Australasia or Canada. In the latter countries, taxation on the basis of capital value was the natural outgrowth of conditions;[2] and land-value taxation was there adopted, because, for local purposes, it was found most expedient fiscally. The English duties, on the other hand, like the increment taxes of Germany and the Australasian progressive land taxes, were enacted for other than fiscal reasons. Moreover, of all the forms of land-value taxation in operation, the English system bears the most studied character. It is a combination of the tax on selling value and the tax on value increment, adapted to the peculiar conditions of Great Britain. But the discriminatory feature of the English land-value duties confirms the charge of the Opposition that not fiscal need, but antagonism to the unpopular landowning class to whom the increments from the appreciation in the value of the land accrue, is responsible for the measure.

And because the tax was a transplanted system, so to speak, and the deeply-rooted principle of private property rights was felt to be infringed upon, the controversy in England was vehement and prolonged. In the debates in Parliament the bone of contention appears to have been the proposed substitution of capital for annual value assessment and the valuation of the land which this involved. From the vehemence of the Opposition, the extent to which the interests of the landlords were felt to be at

---

[1] It was well understood that the House of Lords could not reject the Finance Bill with impunity; this later events demonstrated.

[2] See *supra*, chapter II, § 5; also *infra*, chapter VI, § 1.

stake, and the extent to which their burden of taxation and rating had hitherto been evaded, now became apparent. The apprehension with regard to the valuation, however, was chiefly confined to the landowners in England. In Scotland, where annual valuation had existed since 1854, the valuation of the land apart from the buildings was in general regarded with favor.[1] In England, the unprecedented character of the reform aroused the severest disapproval. The duties were regarded by the Opposition as a confiscatory measure.[2] "This Undeveloped Land Duty," said Mr. Everett in the House of Commons,[3] "is a very remarkable one; it is the greatest innovation of all the Land Taxes proposed, and it excites a great deal of apprehension in the minds of many. It is quite exceptional and unprecedented in its character. . . ." Equally novel appeared the duty on value increment, which was modeled after the German "Zuwachssteuer," [4] and the reversion duty, which, though resembling the increment duty, was clearly adapted to the English leasehold system. As for the mineral-rights duty, so impractical and impossible did the valuation of undeveloped, unopened mines appear that the original proposal to tax mineral land was abandoned, as we shall see,[5] and a new method

---

[1] "For twenty years back in seven of the counties of Scotland, the rent and the consequent rate had been fixed upon the valuation of the land apart from the buildings and improvements upon the land. In all these counties where the custom was for the tenant to erect buildings and make improvements there was no rent charged upon them, and there was a valuation every year of land alone apart . . . with regard to urban districts . . . for upwards of half a century it had been the regular practice in Scotland to make the valuation of land and buildings separately." From a speech by Mr. Ure. *Cf. Parl. Debates* (1908), vol. CLXXXIV, pp. 891–92.

[2] *Cf. ibid.* (1909), vol. IV, pp. 811, 909; vol. VI, p. 110.

[3] *Ibid.*, vol. XII, p. 516.

[4] Lloyd George, prior to the presentation of the budget in the House, had himself traveled through Germany to investigate the subject at first hand. See *ibid.*, vol. IV, p. 1758.

[5] *Infra*, § 11.

substituted. Nevertheless, in spite of the severe controversy which the duties aroused, these "fantastic proposals which were so alarming the country" [1] became law.

§ 6. Turning to the analysis of the land-value duties,
it is necessary to point out that many of the clauses admit
of various interpretations. It is, indeed, agreed among
legal authorities that the bill was badly framed, [2] and it
has given no end of difficulty to the courts which must
interpret its meaning. The full title of the Finance Act
(the "statute with a barbarous name," [3] as it has been
called by a "truculent King's Counsel") reads as follows:
"A Bill to Grant Certain Duties of Customs and Inland
Revenue (including excise), to alter other Duties and to
amend the Law relating to Customs and Inland Revenue
(including excise) and to make other financial Provisions."
Thus, not only did the government incorporate a social
reform measure in a comprehensive fiscal proposal, but
it consigned the first part [4] of the Act to the fiscally unimportant land-value duties. It is this part that will here be
examined.

The English system of taxing land value is complex,
embracing not one tax but four different ones; namely,
(1) the value-increment duty, (2) the reversion duty, (3)
the undeveloped-land duty, and (4) the mineral-rights
duty. The first two are indirect levies, the last two are
annual, direct taxes. In the following sections we shall
attempt to interpret these several duties in the light of
recent court decisions, to explain the system of valuation

---

[1] *Parl. Debates* (1909), vol. IV, p. 1779.

[2] *Cf.* Napier, "The Valuation Scheme of the Land Clauses of the Finance Act" (1910), in the *Law Quarterly Review* (1911), vol. XXVII, pp.
441 *ff. Cf.* also Cox-Sinclair and Hynes, "Some Problems in Land Values," in *Law Magazine and Review* (1912–13), vol. XXXVIII, pp. 336 *ff.*.

[3] *Law Quarterly Review* (1912) vol. XXVIII, pp. 320–21.

[4] Part I has the following subdivisions: (1) Increment-Value Duty, (2)
Reversion Duty, (3) Undeveloped-Land Duty, (4) Mineral-Rights
Duty, (5) Valuation for Purposes of the Duties, (6) Appeals and Sup-
plemental Clauses.

of all the land in the United Kingdom as provided for in the Act, and to describe the administrative features of the new taxes.

§ 7. The value-increment duty [1] is a tax of twenty per cent of the increase in the site value of the land, calculated from the "original site value" on April 30, 1909. The occasions for the payment of the duty are as follows: [2]

(a) Whenever the land or any interest in the land shall be sold.

(b) When land shall be leased for a period exceeding fourteen years.

(c) In case of the transfer of land on death.

(d) On April 5, 1914, and in every subsequent fifteenth year, on land held by bodies corporate or unincorporate.

The next important consideration is how to ascertain the value increment. The Act defines value increment as "the amount (if any) by which the site value of the land on the occasion on which increment-value duty is to be collected . . . exceeds the original site value of the land." [3] This original site value is to be determined by making a valuation of all the land, and the value is to be estimated as on April 30, 1909.

To ascertain the site value the Act defines four values, the total, the gross, the full site, and the assessable site values. This classification, it is agreed,[4] unnecessarily complicates the system of valuation and assessment. Reduced to its simplest terms, the site or assessable value may be defined as the value which the "fee simple of the land, if sold at the time in the open market by a willing seller in its then condition, free from incumbrances, and

---

[1] It is significant that the proposal to change Section I to read "unearned increment" was voted down in Committee. See *Parl. Debates* (1909), vol. VI, pp. 1484–87.

[2] House of Commons Bill 144 (1910), § 1.

[3] *Ibid.*, § 2.

[4] *Cf. Solicitors' Journal*, vol. LV, p. 736; also Cox-Sinclair, *op. cit.*, p. 343.

from any burden, charge, or restriction ¹ (other than rates or taxes) might be expected to realize," after deducting: —

(a) The amount of any buildings and of any other structures, including fixed machinery, all growing timber, fruit trees, fruit bushes, etc.

(b) The total value of the expenditures incurred for improvements, such as drainage, leveling, advertisements, etc.

(c) The value added to the land by dedication of neighborhood land as squares, gardens, roads, open spaces for the use of the public.

(d) The value attributable to expenditure on the redemption of any land tax, fixed charges, enfranchisement of land previously of copyhold tenure, or attributable to "goodwill," etc.²

Comparing the value-increment duty with the German system, it is to be noted: —

First, as regards the occasions of levy, while the German tax is collectible only on the occasion of a sale of the land, the English law adds the transfer by lease, death,

---

¹ Bill 144, § 25. "The amount by which the value would be diminished if the land were sold subject to any fixed charges and to any public rights of way or any public rights of user, and to any right of common and to any easements affecting the land, and to any covenant or agreement restricting the use of the land entered into or made before the thirtieth day of April, 1909, and to any covenant or agreement restricting the use of the land entered into or made on, or after that date."

² We have attempted to simplify the definitions of values used in the Act, which have been called a "verbal juggle." The Act provides for the separate valuation of the total and assessable site values. To ascertain these, a roundabout method is provided for: thus the assessable site value is obtained by making certain deductions from the total value, which is itself the gross value less burdens, charges, restrictions. According to the Act, § 25 (4), however, the assessable value of land means the total value after deducting: " (a) the same amount as is to be deducted for purposes of arriving at full site value from gross value," etc. This necessitates the ascertainment of gross value and full site value. The result of this method of valuation has been sometimes very anomalous values, for example, minus values. Cf. Solicitors' Journal, vol. LVI, pp. 478 ff. Cf. also infra, § 12.

and in case of corporations, a periodic occasion of fifteen years. This last occasion for the collection of value increment is explainable by reason of the fact that a corporation has legally a permanent existence. The arbitrary period of fifteen years is therefore substituted for the occasion of the passing of land on death. While, then, the German government contents itself with sharing the increment whenever the profit actually accrues to the landowner, the English government demands a share of the increment on all occasions of transfer, whether the increment has actually accrued to the owner, or is only potentially realizable.

Secondly, the method of ascertaining the value increment is different. In the German system the actual selling prices constitute the basis of computation; in the English system, a hypothetical, fictitious value is the basis.[1] It is true that the latter is in closer accordance with the principle of the tax, that only the increment attributable to influences affecting the value of the site irrespective of the improvements should be taxable.[2] The German system, however, even though lacking in accuracy from the standpoint of principle, is simpler in administration and more practicable.

Thirdly, the English tax, which takes from the landowner one-fifth of the value increment accruing since 1909, is neither retroactive, nor progressive, as is the German imperial tax. Only the future increments will be made subject to duty. That this is fiscally less expedient has already been pointed out in the case of the Cologne ordinance.[3] First, the revenue from the value-increment duty must be trifling for a number of years to come; sec-

---

[1] It is held that the valuation provisions are applicable to the ascertainment of the occasional as well as the original site values. *Cf. Solicitors' Journal*, vol. LV, pp. 717, 710.

[2] We have, indeed, seen that in some cases the German "Zuwachssteuer" is a realty, not a land-value tax. *Cf. supra*, pp. 150–51.

[3] See *supra*, chapter IV, § 18.

ondly, the expense of the valuation for the original site value has already been enormous.[1]

Fourthly, as under some of the German local measures, a remission of ten per cent of the original site value is allowed under the English system, on the first occasion for the collection of increment duty; and a remission of an equal amount of the site value on the last preceding occasion for the collection, on any subsequent occasion for the collection of duty; with this proviso, "no remission shall be given on any occasion which will make the amount of the increment value on which duty has been remitted during the preceding five years exceed twenty-five per cent of the site value of the land on the last occasion for the collection of increment-value duty prior to the commencement of that period or of the original site value if there has been no such occasion." [2] Thus, in order to be taxable the value increment must constitute at least ten per cent of the previous site value; and then it is only the excess over the ten per cent that is taxable. [3]

Fifthly, like its German prototype, the value-increment duty is a stamp duty and is deemed paid when the govern-

---

[1] Of course, as we have shown, the valuation of all the land in the United Kingdom was to serve another purpose than the administration of the value-increment duty. See *supra*, p. 206 and footnotes.

[2] An illustration will make this complicated wording clear. A piece of land whose original site value, i.e., on April 30, 1909, let us suppose, was £600 is sold in 1911 for £660. Since the value increment does not exceed ten per cent of the original site value, no tax is payable. Suppose, now, it is sold again in 1914 for £726. Again, because the excess over the previous selling price is only £66 or just ten per cent, no tax will be imposed. Now, should this piece of land be again sold in 1916 for £800, the value-increment duty will not be charged on the £74, the difference in value since the last occasion in 1914; but on the difference between the original site value, £600, and the £800, for the amount of the value increment on which duty had been remitted during the preceding five years exceeds twenty-five per cent of the original site value. However, as a remission of twenty-five per cent is allowed in this case, the taxable value increment will be only £50. Twenty per cent will give a tax of £10. *Cf.* Napier, *The New Land Taxes*, pp. 13 *ff*.

[3] *Cf.* Bill 144, (1910), § 3.

ment stamp has been attached to the deed at the time of transfer.[1]

Sixthly, following the German precedent again, the English Act provides that, if it can be proved to the Commissioners that the site value of a piece of land at any time within twenty years prior to April 30, 1909, exceeded the original site value as ascertained under the Act, that higher value shall be substituted for the original site value. It will readily be seen that it is in the interest of the person subject to the value-increment duty to have the original site value as high as possible, unless this person be likewise subject to the undeveloped land duty.[2]

Seventhly, difficult as it is to determine the incidence of the tax, the English law nevertheless stipulates, as do the German laws, that the tax shall be paid by the transferor or lessor, and in case of a sale by the seller.[3] It would seem therefore that the conflicting interests of seller and purchaser with regard to the value of the land will tend to the registration of the actual value of the land and will tend to prevent fraud. For it is to the advantage of the seller to have the original site value estimated as high as possible, and the selling price as low as possible, so that the difference may be less. On the other hand, it is to the interest of the purchaser to have the selling value assessed as high as possible, so that the difference between that value and the value at a future transfer may be less.

Eighthly, a notable departure from the German practice is the exemption of agricultural and small holdings from value-increment duty.

The following are exempt: —

(1) Agricultural land, or rather land whose market value does not exceed the average value of land used for agricultural purposes.[4] For example, if a parcel of land used for

---

[1] *Cf.* Bill 144 (1910), § 3.   [2] *Ibid.*, § 2. See *infra*, § 9.   [3] *Ibid.*, § 4.
[4] *Ibid.*, § 7. The chief reason for exempting agricultural land is that the value of rural land in England has on the whole depreciated.

agricultural purposes could bring a higher value if sold for building purposes, the exemption would not apply.

(2) Small properties occupied by the owner, provided:[1]

> (a) the house is situated in the County of London and has an annual value not exceeding £40 (as determined for Income Tax, Schedule A); or,
>
> (b) the house is situated in a borough or urban district of 50,000 population or upward and has an annual value not exceeding £26; or,
>
> (c) the house is situated elsewhere and has an annual value not exceeding £16; or,
>
> (d) the land is used for agriculture and does not exceed 50 acres,[2] whose average total value does not exceed £25 per acre.

Other exemptions are: —

(3) Any land owned by a corporate or unincorporate body which receives no dividends or profits out of the revenue, but uses the land for games and other recreational purposes.[3]

(4) Land held by any department of government, or by or for the king. This does not obviate the valuation of Crown lands, for, to facilitate future transfers, increment duty owing on such land is assessed and deemed to have been paid.[4]

The further discussion of the value-increment duty must be reserved for later sections under the administration and working of the tax. We shall find that peculiar difficulties in administration have arisen, because the law was framed

---

[1] *Cf.* Bill 144 (1910), § 8.

[2] The owner must be resident on the land and the total amount owned by him must not exceed fifty acres. The exemption is not applicable to any land together with a dwelling house when the annual value of the house exceeds £30. See *ibid.*, § 8.

[3] *Ibid.*, § 9.

[4] *Ibid.*, § 10.

in accordance with the theory of the tax, not in accordance with experience.[1]

§ 8 The adaptation of the principle of the tax on value increment to leasehold property is characteristically English, for it is in England that the leasehold system is very widely developed. The Act provides that, on the expiration of a lease of land, reversion duty shall be charged at the rate of one pound for every complete ten pounds of the value of the benefit accruing to the lessor, by reason of the determination of the lease.[2] At first sight the reversion duty would seem to be a value-increment duty collectible on another occasion than those mentioned, that is, on the expiration of a lease. But in principle and method of assessment the two are distinct taxes and should be differentiated from each other. To illustrate: a landowner, without making any outlays, leases his land to a tenant for a term of years, frequently on a ninety-nine year lease. The tenant improves the property by erecting a building and otherwise, assumes all risks, pays all taxes, and at the expiration of the lease, the property, including improvements, reverts to the landowner. Such being the usual case, it is argued, as in the case of the value-increment duty, that to appropriate ten per cent of this "unearned" value in behalf of the government creates no hardship upon the owner of the fee simple.[3]

This reasoning has been attacked on several grounds. Unlike the duty on value increment, the reversion duty is not only retroactive, but is an infringement of the right of free contract. To illustrate this contention, assume that a person owns a parcel of land which his father had leased to a builder for a period of eighty years for a ground rent of £20 annually, plus a sum of £300, as a premium in consideration of the lease. At the expiration of the lease in 1912, the landowner recovers the house and lot. Assume

---

[1] See *infra*, §§ 12, 13.   [2] Bill 144 (1910), § 10.
[3] *Parl. Debates* (1909), vol. xii, pp. 369 *ff.*; vol. iv, p. 540.

further that the total value of the land, buildings, fixtures, etc., at the termination of the lease was £2000. Deducting from this amount the value of the consideration paid at the time of the original grant of the lease, namely £300, plus the capitalized rental at twenty-five years purchase, £500, the lessor profits by a value increment of £1200. Reversion duty on this sum at ten per cent equals £120. Suppose, now, the opponents of the tax argue, that the £20 rental was not a rack rent; suppose that the rental charged was somewhat less by virtue of the expenditure incurred by the lessee, the landlord counting on the increased value because of the improvements and the expected reversion; is it right to disappoint his expectations by levying this retroactive tax? Suppose, too, that the rental was less because of a certain stipulation in the contract as to the amount of expenditure the lessee was to incur; is it not an interference with the right of contract, to levy this tax on a false assumption that the rental charged always represents a rack rent? [1]

To meet such arguments and to avoid any possible hardships, the government has granted concessions to the Opposition, which invalidate the objections to a great extent. First, it is provided,[2] that in computing the value of the benefit accruing to the lessor, any value attributable to any works executed or outlays incurred by the lessor, as well as any compensation payable by him to the lessee on the termination of the lease shall be deducted from the total value. Secondly, the value of the land at the time of the original grant of the lease shall be ascertained on the basis of the rent paid and the payments made in consideration of the lease; and when a *nominal* rent has been charged the tenant, the value of "any covenant or undertaking to erect buildings or to expend any sums upon the property" shall be taken into consideration in calculating

[1] *Cf. Parl. Debates* (1909), vol. VI, pp. 79, 80; vol. XII, pp. 371 *ff.*
[2] Bill 144 (1910), § 13 (2).

the value of the land at the time of the original grant of the lease.[1] In regard to lessors who are themselves entitled only to a leasehold interest in the land, the value of the benefit accruing on the termination of a lease shall be reduced in proportion to the amount by which their interest is less than the value of the fee simple.

Again, in view of the liberal exemptions from reversion duty, the objection to the retroactive feature of the tax loses weight. These exemptions, however they may limit the fiscal efficacy of the tax, are in accordance with the government's general policy as regards leaseholds. Exempt are:[2]

(a) Any reversion in case of a lease made prior to April 30, 1909, which determines within forty years of the date of purchase.

(b) Any reversion of land which on the expiration of the lease is agricultural land.

(c) Any reversion in case of a lease, the original term of which did not exceed twenty-one years.

We may take note also of the following provision of partial exemption: In case of a reversion before the term of the lease expires, and in case the lessee is granted a new lease for a term extending at least twenty-one years beyond the date on which the original lease would have expired, an allowance of two and one-half per cent of the duty shall be granted for every year of the original term of the unexpired lease from the time the lease is determined. This allowance shall be treated as if it had been paid, provided that the exemption shall not exceed fifty per cent of the whole duty payable.[3]

[1] The decision in the Camden case makes this provision practically superfluous and renders evasion of part of the tax easy. The House of Lords confirmed the judgment of the Court of Appeal against the government, holding that the value of the building, £6000, was to be considered in the rental. The government held that the £125 rental agreed upon at the time of the grant of the lease in 1824 was not a nominal rent merely. *Cf. Solicitors' Journal*, vol. LVIII, p. 717.

[2] Bill 144 (1910), § 14.

[3] *Ibid.*, § 14 (3). Repealed in 1911. *Cf.* Revenue Bill (1911), § 2.

It is necessary to point out the reasoning upon which these exemptions are based. First, short lease contracts are to be exempted, because the lessor in such cases cannot demand so high a rental as for a long-term lease, in view of the improvements to be made by the lessee which will ultimately revert to the lessor. In other words, in granting a short-term lease the rental will be less in consideration of the outlays to be incurred by the lessee. On the other hand, in granting a long-term lease, as for a period of forty years or over, the owner, it is assumed, has in mind a permanent income and does not anticipate the enhanced value of the property which may ultimately revert to him. Such an enhanced value is in the nature of a "windfall," and to appropriate a share of it will not disappoint the expectations of the ground-owner. The distinction drawn between short- and long-term leases is for the purpose of discouraging the latter and to facilitate the frequent renewal of leases. That short-term leases, under which the lessee is apt to get more favorable treatment, are desirable seems to have been the sentiment of both political parties.[1]

Further exemptions from reversion duty are the following: —

    (*d*) Mining leases.[2]

    (*e*) Where the reversioner is a rating authority.[3]

    (*f*) Where reversion is held for charitable purposes.

    (*g*) Where reversion is held by a statutory company for

---

[1] In his budget speech Lloyd George argued that the exemption of short-term leases from reversion duty would have the desired effect: "I propose to make a special abatement of duty proportionate to the unexpired period of the original lease which is surrendered and have great hopes that this allowance, coupled with the fact that the value of the reversion for the purpose of duty, will be calculated upon the difference between the consideration for the old and the consideration for the new lease, will induce owners to grant renewals more readily and upon more favorable terms than at present, and so tend to remove one of the most mischievous effects of the leasehold system." *Parl. Debates* (1909), vol. IV, p. 541.

[2] Bill 144 (1910), § 22 (1). Under certain conditions. *Cf. infra*, p. 233.

[3] *Ibid.*, § 35.

the purposes of its undertaking and cannot be appropriated except for those purposes.[1]

As in the case of the value-increment duty, so with regard to reversion duty, the ambiguous wording of the clause has given rise to difficulties in legal construction and has been held up to criticism, if not ridicule, by legal authorities.[2] The clause in question reads: "On the determination of any lease of land there shall be charged . . . on the value of the benefit accruing to the lessor by reason of the determination of the lease, a duty, called reversion duty, at the rate of one pound for every complete ten pounds of that value."[3] Now, it is argued that a lease can expire, not alone by lapse of time, but by merger through a release or surrender of lease, etc. Suppose the lessee in the illustration given above, after making the improvements, had purchased the leasehold of the ground-owner, would not a benefit have accrued to the latter on the determination of the lease? And in accordance with the wording of the clause, should he not be liable for reversion duty? Again, it has been argued ingeniously, that the words "benefit" and "by reason of the determination" are ambiguous, that a benefit arising from a merger accrues by the sale, not by reason of the conveyance which reversion implies; hence the determination of the lease does not give rise to the benefit.[4] A further objection is the possibility of evading the payment of reversion duty by avoiding a

[1] Bill 144 (1910), § 38. A statutory company is a quasi-public company incorporated under a Special Act. *Cf. Report of Commissioners of Inland Revenue, 1911* (Cd. 5833), p. 151.

[2] *Solicitors' Journal*, vol. LV, pp. 104 ff.

[3] Bill 144 (1910), § 13.

[4] It has been pointed out, however, that the merger involves the determination of the lease, and gives rise to a benefit, for the value of the freehold, when the lease expires, exceeds the value of the lease and reversion. In other words there is a "dormant" value which the determination of the lease confers on the owner. "During the existence of the lease neither lessee nor lessor can deal with the property to the same advantage as if it were free from lease." *Cf. Solicitors' Journal*, vol. LV, p. 105.

merger. Thus, by assigning the lease to a trustee for the lessee, until the renewal of the lease is effected, the estate would not revert to the owner at all and no duty would be collectible.[1] The objections, however, are for the most part legal quibbles and do not affect the administration of the duty.

It is necessary to point out that when the lease expires by sale, value-increment duty, as well as reversion duty, is collectible. But to provide against the payment of double duty it is stipulated that, when value-increment duty has been paid, no reversion duty shall be charged on the same property at the same time, and *vice versa*.[2] Furthermore, whether the ground-owner actually realizes a sum of money on the determination of the lease is immaterial; the important thing is that the property shall have a higher value than at the time of the grant. The possibility of evasion of the duty has been much discussed and has led to the amendment of some of its provisions.

In regard to the rate of the tax, it is worthy of note that the reversion duty is at the rate of ten per cent, or one-half the rate of the value-increment duty. When, however, it is considered that reversion duty is a retroactive tax and that no minimum exemption is allowed as in the case of value-increment duty, the discrepancy is after all slight.

§ 9. The duties thus far considered are both indirect levies; the others, comprising the land-value duties, the undeveloped land and mineral-right duties, are direct taxes. The undeveloped land duty is a charge of one-half penny in the pound on the value of unimproved land. It is an annual tax on capital value. What constitutes undeveloped land, the following definition will make clear: "For the purpose of this Part of this Act, land shall be

---

[1] *Cf. Solicitors' Journal*, vol. LV, pp. 105–06.

[2] "The difficulty of determining, say on death in 1930, how much value increment had been included in the taxation in 1920 of benefits accruing by reason of the determination of a lease, is a little appalling." Napier, *The New Land Taxes*, p. lii.

deemed to be undeveloped land, if it has not been developed by the erection of dwelling houses or of buildings for the purposes of any business, trade, or industry other than agriculture (but including glass-houses or green houses), or is not otherwise used *bona fide* for any business, trade or industry other than agriculture. . . ." [1]

In instituting this direct tax on unimproved land the aim was to correct a social ill peculiar to most urban communities, rather than to tap a new source of revenue. The minority reports of the different select committees that had investigated the subject had called attention to the aggravation of congestion in cities arising from the fact that land was being kept out of use and held for speculative purposes. This was the grievance to which the Chancellor of the Exchequer pointed when he said: [2] "There are millions of acres in this country which are more stripped and sterile than they were, and providing a living for fewer people than they did even a thousand years ago." It was hoped that even a slight tax on non-income-bearing land would induce utilization of the land, a result much to be desired.

What then could be the objection to such a small charge on land? The fundamental objection raised against the undeveloped land duty was one of principle. This was the first time that a direct, i.e., annual, tax on capital value was imposed, a most discriminatory tax. First, therefore, the establishment of a precedent was regarded with serious apprehension. Secondly, the taxation of non-income-bearing land seemed contrary to the established principles of taxation. Receiving no income, wherewith was the owner to pay the duty? "It is a tax not upon annual value, as all other rates and taxes to which we are accustomed are, but it is a tax upon capital value, and it differs from all the other Land Taxes in that it is an annual charge. It is not a charge once and for all as the

---

[1] Bill 144 (1910), § 16.   [2] *Parl. Debates* (1909), vol. IV, p. 490.

Increment Taxes, but an annual charge upon capital value. It is a tax laid on without there being any money in hand out of which to pay it. . . . But in this case the tax is to be laid on annually on individuals who are receiving nothing and have not the wherewithal to find money unless they sell the land or draw it from some other source." [1]

Other objections to the duty on undeveloped land were raised. Thus the question was discussed in Committee as to the possibility of judging of the ripeness of vacant land for building purposes. On the one hand, it was questioned whether land was kept out of use for other reasons than that its improvement was at the time unprofitable. A tax on such land would compel the owner to make im-

[1] From a speech by Mr. Everett, M.P., *Parl. Debates* (1909), vol. XII, p. 516. Whether the new tax actually entails hardships cannot be determined from isolated instances, nevertheless the following cases, occurring after a three years' experience with the undeveloped land duty, cited by the Earl of Camperdown in the House of Lords should be noted: "The Undeveloped Land Duty is, I think, the heaviest and the most unjust of all the land taxes under the Budget of 1909–10. Undeveloped land duty is imposed on the difference between the value of the land for agricultural purposes and the assessable site value of the same land. . . . In saying that this duty amounts to 50 per cent or upwards of the highest income obtainable at the present time, I have put it at a very moderate figure, because in a great many cases it amounts to a great deal more than 100 per cent. . . . Here is one case. It concerns three acres of land. The present income is £7 10s., the capital value on which duty is assessed is £2490, and the amount of the duty is £5 4s. As against £7 10s. income the owner has to pay £5 4s. duty, and it is calculated that in fifteen years that land may be developed. That is not the only hardship, because five years hence this land will be revalued. It may not have been developed, . . . indeed, the valuer does not expect that it will be developed for fifteen years . . . but at that time the capital value may be considerably increased, and therefore the duty payable would be also considerably increased. The owner of this property has to pay £5 4s. in duty out of an income of £7 10s. until such time as the land is developed, and when it is developed, if it is found to be of a higher value than it is assessed at — if the owner receives more for the land than it is assessed at at the end of those fifteen years — he will be liable to Increment Duty on the difference." Another case cited by the Earl was of a duty of £20 levied on land used for rabbit shooting from which the income was £5. *Parl. Debates* (Lords 1913), vol. XIV, pp. 1743–44. *Cf.* also (Commons) vol. LII, pp. 913, 919–20.

provements prematurely, would force land and buildings
into the market before there was a demand for them.
Moreover, it was feared that such a duty by giving the
owner an incentive to build would have the effect of overutilization of the land; the familiar argument, that gardens,
squares, and other open spaces, the so-called "lungs" of
the city, would be built upon, to the detriment of public
health. On the other hand, the opponents also claimed that
the purpose of the duty on undeveloped land would be
frustrated, because so far as the rich estate-holder on the
periphery of growing towns was concerned, a tax of one-
fifth of one per cent would not impose a special burden upon
him to induce him to develop or sell the land.[1] Speculation
would go on and land remain vacant as before.

The question of the definition of undeveloped land
proved perplexing. To guard against special hardships,
as well as to prevent evasions the following provisions were
inserted: [2]

(a) Land which had once been improved but has become
derelict shall be exempt for a period of one year after it has
ceased to be used; after that such land shall be subject to
the duty as undeveloped land.

(b) When the owner of unused land proves that he or his
predecessors had incurred expenditures on roads, sewers,
etc., with the purpose of developing the land, such land
shall be regarded developed to the extent of one acre for
every complete £100 of that expenditure, provided, that
not more than ten years have elapsed since the outlay was
made.

(c) For the purposes of this duty, undeveloped land shall
not include minerals, nor mineral land.

(d) When value-increment duty has been paid on undeveloped land, the site value of this land, for purposes of
computing the amount of undeveloped land duty, shall be

[1] *Parl. Debates* (1909), vol. XII, p. 575 *et passim*.
[2] *Cf.* Bill 144 (1910), § 16.

reduced by a sum five times the amount paid as value-increment duty.[1]

Furthermore, to guard against the evil of overutilization of land as well as to encourage gardening and open spaces in the interest of health and recreation, the following exemptions from duty were stipulated: [2]

(a) Land, the site value of which does not exceed £50 per acre.

(b) Agricultural land, except when the site value exceeds £50 per acre; in the latter case undeveloped land duty shall be charged only on the amount by which the site value exceeds the average value of purely agricultural land.

(c) Parks, gardens, and open spaces used by the public; also land held vacant for games and recreation in the interest of the public.

(d) Land not exceeding an acre in extent occupied with a dwelling-house; or any gardens or pleasure grounds which together with the dwelling-house do not exceed twenty times the annual value of the gardens; but such land shall be exempt to the extent of five acres only.

(e) Agricultural land held under a tenancy originally created by a lease, or agreement made, or entered into before April 30, 1909.

(f) Small holdings in case of agricultural land occupied or cultivated by the owner, where the total value of the land with any other land belonging to the same owner does not exceed £500.[3]

In order to prevent the evasion of duty under exemption (c) above, which provides for the exemption of sites used for games or other recreation grounds used under some agreement with the owner, the Act stipulates that such exempted land, "shall not be built upon unless the Local Government Board give their consent, on being satisfied that it is desirable in the interest of the public that the re-

[1] This provision is to prevent double taxation.
[2] Bill 144 (1910), § 17.   [3] Ibid., § 18.

striction on building should be removed." Under such a provision, obviously, only a *bona fide* purpose will tempt the owner to seek exemption.

As we shall see later,[1] for the purpose of levying this duty a quinquennial valuation is provided for to ascertain the site value of undeveloped land. Therefore, irrespective of any changes that may occur in the value of the land, the assessed site value remains unchanged during the five year period between valuations.[2]

§ 10. Vehement as was the opposition to the enactment of the undeveloped land duty, the controversy waged fiercest about the mineral-rights duty. For here, not alone the landowners but the mining industry were deeply concerned. Indeed, of the four duties proposed, the one on mineral rights had to meet the severest criticism, especially in the early stage of the debate. Convinced of the difficulties of valuation and the uncertainty of both the incidence and yield of the tax as first proposed, the Chancellor of the Exchequer was persuaded to revise the clauses with regard to taxing mineral land.[3] As originally drafted this tax was a charge of two-tenths of one per cent on the capital value of the unworked mineral land and was in every respect correlated to the duty on undeveloped land, its supporters claiming that the duty would have the effect of opening up the mines and increasing industry. But the proposal to tax unworked minerals aroused a storm of antagonism. How was the value of minerals unworked and beneath the surface to be ascertained?

The duty which was finally adopted falls on the royalty which the lessor enjoys "without contributing anything to the rates of the district or in any way risking his money." [4] It is a charge of one shilling for every twenty shillings of the rental value of all rights to work minerals

[1] *Infra*, § 12.   [2] *Cf. Parl. Debates* (1913), vol. LVI, p. 350.
[3] *Ibid.* (1909), vol. IX, pp. 662 *ff*.
[4] *Ibid.* (1909), vol. XII, p. 587. The sentiment against the mine-owners at the time of the budget agitation ran high. At a conference

and of all mineral way-leaves.[1] A mineral way-leave is defined as "any way-leave, air-leave, water-leave, or right to use a shaft granted to or enjoyed by a working lessee, whether above or under ground, for the purpose of access to or the conveyance of the minerals, or the ventilation or drainage of his mine or otherwise in connection with the working of the minerals." [2] Like the undeveloped land duty this is a direct annual levy, but the rate is five per cent of the rental value, as compared with the one-fifth of one per cent tax on the capital value of undeveloped land.

From the standpoint of the government the amended provisions were an improvement over the original proposal rather than a concession to the Opposition. First, the change obviated the complexities involved in valuing unworked minerals, and made the administration of the tax comparatively simple. In case of a lessee — most mines are operated by lessees in England — the annual value is easily ascertained, for it is the amount of rent paid by the working lessee in the last working year. The difficulty arises in computing the annual value in case the proprietor himself is the operator of the mine. The law provides that the Commissioner shall determine the rental in such cases. He is to determine a hypothetical value, "the sum which

of Scottish miners it was estimated that the annual value of the coal in Great Britain was £120,000,000, and that of this sum nearly £10,000,000 were paid to the landowners in royalties. The mines are for the most part worked by lessees, who also protested against the exorbitant rents exacted from them. "In one important section of our industries we are already sufficiently and more than sufficiently handicapped. The country at large, however, knows very little of it, but it appeals to me very forcibly indeed. It stands up against me in every balance sheet of the various companies of the north of England with which I am connected. These companies alone during the last ten years have paid no less than £761,000 in royalties and way-leaves, an average of £76,000 per annum. Apart from my own particular interests, the Cleveland district within the period of my own life-time has yielded royalties to a sum exceeding £13,000,000 sterling." *Budget, Land, and the People*, p. 48.

[1] Bill 144 (1910), § 20.   [2] *Ibid.*, § 24.

would have been received as rent by the proprietor in the last working year if the right to work the minerals had been leased to a working lessee for a term, and at a rent, and on conditions, customary in the district, and the minerals had been worked to the same extent and in the same manner as they have been worked by the proprietor in that year." [1] Another difficulty that may arise in the administration of the duty is to ascertain the amount to be deducted from the taxable annual rental for expenditures incurred by the proprietor in boring and proving the minerals. In regard to this allowance, the Act provides that, when the rental is shown to the Commissioner to exceed the rental customary in the district, and to represent a return for expenditure on the part of any proprietor which would ordinarily have been borne by the lessee, the Commissioner shall estimate and make allowance for the excess amount of rent.

Secondly, under the revised proposal, the mineral-rights duty became a more productive source of revenue. Whereas under the original plan Lloyd George had estimated the yield of both the undeveloped land and unworked mineral duties at about £350,000 for the first year, when the change was made to the duty on rental, he set the estimate for mineral-rights duty alone at £350,000.[2]

In one respect, however, the change in the bill was said to be a surrender of principle, and a concession to the Opposition. As the bill originally stood, the tax on the unworked minerals would have, according to theory, fallen on the proprietor of the mine, the person whom it was intended to burden. Regarding the duty as finally adopted, i.e., on working mines only, although Lloyd George and others contended that it could not be shifted to the lessee nor affect the market price of the product, this contention has

[1] Bill 144 (1910), § 20. See *Parl. Debates* (1909), vol. XII, pp. 599 *ff*.

[2] *Ibid.* (1909), vol. IV, p. 540; vol. XI, p. 504. As a matter of fact the revenue yielded even the first year greatly exceeded the estimate. *Cf. infra*, § 14.

been questioned. In fact, in consenting to exempt "common clay, common brick clay, common brick earth, or sand, chalk, limestone, or gravel," the Chancellor of the Exchequer was inconsistent, for if the taxation of the above-named minerals would enhance their market price, why should it not do the same thing in the case of the other minerals? It may have been merely a concession to the Opposition. Nevertheless, the argument that upon the renewal of the lease the rental would be raised to the amount of the tax capitalized, causing a rise in the price of the raw material, has not been refuted experimentally.[1]

The complex provisions with regard to the assessment of the mineral-rights duty, arising from the conflicting or synchronous occasion for the value-increment duty on mineral lands, will be analyzed in the following section.

§ 11. When the clauses of the Finance Act relating to the mineral-rights duty are analyzed, we find in reality two duties embraced under the one name: first, the five per cent tax on the rental value of the minerals comprised in a mining lease or being worked by the proprietor at the time the Act was passed and so long as the mines continue to be so worked; secondly, a twenty per cent tax charged on the annual value increment in case of mines opened for work after the 30th day of April, 1909. Whenever the annual value-increment duty is levied, no mineral-rights duty, that is, no five per cent tax on the rental, is collectible. When the purpose of this provision is explained, the seeming complexity will disappear. In the first place, because mines are wasting assets, that is, are subject to depreciation in value when worked, they must be treated somewhat differently from other land whose tendency is rather to increase in value. Secondly, since the mineral-rights duty is charged only on mines which are being

[1] *Parl. Debates* (1909), vol. IX, pp. 666 *ff*. Of course, the law provides that the proprietor, not the operator of the mine, shall be liable for the tax. The question is whether the owner is the ultimate bearer of the duty.

worked, unworked mines would be at an advantage, or at a premium, unless they were made subject to the value-increment duty. But the value-increment duty, thirdly, on a wasting asset is impracticable, because the value increment on the occasion of a transfer could not be determined, for the value on the occasion might be found to be less than on the previous occasion, or than the original site value; and yet the rental accruing to the mine owner during the period might have included an increment. Therefore, since the indirect levy of the value-increment duty is impracticable, and since the mineral-rights duty on working mines is insufficient without the value-increment duty, the *annual* value-increment duty was devised to apply only in case of mines opened to be worked after April 30, 1909.

A few illustrations of the method of assessment will further elucidate the complicated provision: (1) Suppose A owns a mine which is unworked. He pays no mineral-rights duty on it, because the duty is inapplicable to unworked mines. The owner now places no value upon the minerals; therefore, at the general valuation made, it is recorded as of no value in accordance with section 23 (2) of the Act. Now, suppose A sells the mine in 1911 for £500. Increment duty is payable on the whole £500, and amounts to £100. Had A set a value on the mine, as he had a right to do, at the time of the original valuation, he would have been subject to less value-increment duty.[1] (2) Suppose A's mine was being worked by a lessee, B, since 1905, in payment of a rental of £200 yearly.[2] A would be liable

[1] What prevents the owner from putting a high or any value on the mines is that that value would be taken also as the sum on which he would pay rates and death duties when that occasion arose. The particulars of a contested case of assessment under this clause decided in favor of the Government are given in the *Solicitors' Journal*, vol. LVIII, p. 749.

[2] The royalty contracted for in mining leases is often made dependent upon the product mined. Thus " a usual form of mining lease reserves a dead rent to cover a certain amount of minerals brought to the surface,

for mineral-rights duty at the rate of five per cent of the rental; in this case an annual tax of £10 as long as the mine continued to be worked. (3) Assume that B who purchased the mine in 1910 for £500 leases it to C, to be worked at an annual rental of £60. B will now be liable for an annual value-increment duty of twenty per cent of the annual value increment. To ascertain this value, the law has created a hypothetical original annual value to be computed at "two-twenty-fifths part of the capital value on the last preceding occasion on which value-increment duty has been collected otherwise than as an annual duty." [1] In other words, the value increment in the illustration above is the difference between the rental £60 and two twenty-fifths of £500, or £40; at the rate of twenty per cent the annual increment tax will be £4. In this case also the duty will continue to be levied while the mine is being operated. When the mine ceases to be worked the proprietor will again have the option of placing a value upon it or not. If later the mine is sold or passes on death, while it is yet unworked, value-increment duty will be paid in a lump sum; if it is leased or recommences to be worked by the proprietor, annual value-increment duty will be payable. [2]

It is important to note that in accordance with the Act the reversion and value-increment duties are suspended

with a royalty on the excess, a power to make up shortages and a cesser of rent on payment either by rent or royalty of a certain sum being the estimated value of the minerals or the mine. In the case of such a lease it is possible, that increment-value duty may in some cases greatly exceed the dead rent, in others be nothing at all. The proprietor will often pay far more by way of increment-value duty under the provisions of this section than he would if he paid on a capital sum. But he obtains some security against paying on an unrealized increment." Napier, *The New Land Taxes*, pp. 112–13.

[1] Bill 144 (1910), § 22. This arbitrary, hypothetical annual value is on the basis of twelve and a half years purchase, which even for mineral lands is a reasonable, i.e., short period for capitalization. *Parl. Debates* (1909), vol. XI, p. 1271.

[2] Napier, *op. cit.*, pp. LXII *ff.*

with regard to mineral land only when their levy would involve the double taxation of such land. Thus reversion duty is payable in case of a non-mining lease of land even if it contains minerals, or of a lease of land containing any of the exempted minerals, such as common clay, brick clay, limestone, gravel, etc. Thus also mineral land, as we have seen, is liable to the indirect levy of value-increment duty, except while the mine is being worked. Moreover, the payment of the annual value-increment duty relieves the proprietor or lessor from the payment of mineral-rights duty only to the amount of value-increment duty paid by him in that year. Other provisions to be noted are as follows: (1) A reduction of duty is allowed when the rental represents in part a return for money expended within fifteen years by a lessor in boring or otherwise proving the minerals.[1] (2) When a mine subject to duty ceases to be worked for two years, it is regarded as an unworked mine upon which a capital value must be placed.[2] (3) Not only is a leased mine subject to duty, but likewise any way-leave.

§ 12. From the foregoing analysis of the duties, it will be clear that the administration of the new taxes is not simple. Besides the assessment and collection, the Commissioners were confronted with the colossal task of valuing all the land in the United Kingdom including Ireland, approximately eleven million hereditaments.[3] The administration including the valuation was put in the hands of the Commissioners of Inland Revenue. But so enormous

[1] Bill 144 (1910), § 22 (4).

[2] *Ibid.*, § 23. As we have already pointed out, unless the proprietor furnishes the commissioners an estimate of the capital value of the minerals, specifying the kind of minerals the land contains, the mine is assumed to have no value. The consequence of this provision will readily be perceived. It places the owner in a predicament; for while it is in his interest for purposes of value-increment duty to place as high a value as possible on his mineral land, for purposes of estate duty or local rating, it is in his interest to estimate the value as low as possible.

[3] *Report of the Commissioner of Inland Revenue* (Cd. 5833), 1911, p. 149.

was the task of establishing the machinery of the system that a new department had to be founded, namely, the Valuation Department, and the services of the Assessors of Income Tax, who are appointed for each Income Tax Parish by the District Commissioners of Taxes and who, therefore, have local knowledge of the rating assessment books, had to be employed. The help of these assessors, called Land Valuation Officers, was dispensed with, however, as soon as their reports had been turned in to the District Valuers.[1]

For the purposes of the valuation the United Kingdom is divided into fourteen Divisions, each of which is under the control of a Superintending Valuer. Each Division in turn is subdivided into Districts, under the charge of a District Valuer, a number of Assistant Valuers and a staff of clerical and technical assistants. A number of expert Mineral Valuers are also employed.[2] All the valuers are responsible to the Chief Valuer, the head of the Valuation Department. The administrative duties are performed by a staff consisting of an Assistant Secretary, four Committee Clerks and assistants. In Ireland, the valuation of the land is under the charge of the Government Valuation Department which was already in existence at the time of the passing of the Act. The work of valuation is much facilitated in Ireland because the detailed particulars regarding estates are already known to the Department.

Considering the important results, statistical and fiscal, which the leaders of the government hoped to accomplish through the valuation, the procedure should be further described. When the valuation shall be completed, the record

[1] *Report of the Commissioner of Inland Revenue* (Cd. 5833), 1911, pp. 158–59.

[2] In 1911 there were employed one Chief Valuer at a salary of £1200; 15 Superintending Valuers at salaries of £800 each; 49 Valuers of the First Class, and 107 of the Second Class at salaries of £550 and £350, respectively, and 1376 assistants, etc. *Ibid.*, p. 157.

of the value, character, and boundaries of every parcel of land will constitute another "Domesday Book," the famous undertaking of land valuation in William the Conqueror's time.[1] Each hereditament has to be classified and numbered by the Land Valuation Officers, and forms of return prepared and issued to owners in accordance with the provision of the Act. These forms have been subjected to much criticism,[2] because of the detailed particulars which the owner is called upon to give. Especially is this true of Form 4 issued for purposes of the value-increment duty.[3] From statutory companies, such as railway, dock, or other quasi-public companies, only the cost of the land to the company is required.

Having gathered the returns from the owners,[4] a provisional valuation is made and served upon the owner or any other interested party who has applied for a copy of the valuation. The unit of valuation is the hereditament, or unit of occupation as on April 30, 1909; but at the request of the owner a smaller unit may be taken if such hereditament is under separate occupation. This provision has, however, been amended allowing, under certain conditions, parcels of land if owned by one person to be valued together, provided the aggregate area does not exceed one hundred acres.[5] Unless the owner gives notice of objection to the

[1] The Commissioner mentions one case of an estate which has remained in the hands of one family from the time of William the Conqueror's Domesday Book to this day. The estate covering about 2,296 acres is now valued at about £26,748, the annual value being over £1428. *Report of the Commissioner of Inland Revenue* (Cd. 5833), 1911, pp. 149, 168.

[2] *Cf. Parl. Debates* (1913), vol. L, pp. 1527–39, 160 *ff.*

[3] Besides particulars concerning ownership, tenure, and area, the owners are required to state the annual value, the annual value of the fixed charges, of the public right of way, of right of common, of the public rights of user, of easements and covenants, etc. Additional particulars as to gross value, site value, total value, assessable site value and particulars as to how the values were arrived at may be returned, if desired.

[4] During 1910–11, about 10,700,000 forms were sent out, the number of returns was 9,600,000. *Report*, etc. (Cd. 5833), p. 160.

[5] Revenue Act (1911), § 4.

provisional valuation within sixty days, the valuation becomes permanently adopted as the original site value. This value can then be changed for a different apportionment only in case the unit of valuation is changed.

The valuation will serve as the basis of the levy of value-increment duty and of undeveloped land duty. In case of the former, a subsequent valuation of the land will be made whenever an occasion for duty arises. For this subsequent valuation, the selling price in case of a sale is taken as the "total value," and by a process of deductions the site value is obtained. Both for the original site value and for the subsequent valuations, the "total" and "site" values are to be recorded. The process of attaining these is shown by the form on the opposite page.[1]

The value-increment duty is a stamp duty. Thus, the document of transfer must be sent to the Revenue Office and the stamp affixed to the deed.[2]

For undeveloped land duty the original site value is the assessable value. As the Act provides for quinquennial valuation only, the value for purposes of undeveloped land duty remains unchanged for five years. The quinquennial valuations will serve also as the basis for levying value-increment duty in case of corporations on April 5, 1914, and every fifteenth year thereafter.[3]

A special form of return is issued for purposes of paying reversion duty.[4] All persons to whom a benefit accrues on

[1] Form of Notice of Appeal (A) Schedule to the Land Values (Reference) Rules, 1910, made by the Reference Committee for England under § 33 of Finance Act (1909-10). The complexity of procedure will be noticed.

[2] There are two other kinds of stamps, one "indicating that all particulars necessary to enable a correct assessment to be made have been furnished"; the other, the "no duty payable" stamp, where no claim for duty can arise. *Report*, etc. (Cd. 5833), p. 163.

[3] Important amendments in 1913 (Revenue Bill 175, § 13) provide for the first revaluation of the land in 1916, instead of in 1914, and make April 5, 1919, the first periodical occasion for levying duty on corporations.

[4] *Cf. Report*, etc. (Cd. 5833), Appendix II (F), p. 181.

Provisional Valuation

| County | Parish | No. of hereditament |

---

1. Gross Value

Deductions from Gross Value

(a) To arrive at Full Site Value		(b) To arrive at Total Value	
2 Difference between Gross Value and Value of the Fee Simple of the Land divested of Buildings, Trees, etc.		3. Fee Farm Rent, Rent Seck, Quit Rent, Chief Rent, or Rent of Assize. 4. Other Perpetual Rent or Annuity. 5. Tithe or Tithe Rent Charge. 6. Burden or charge arising by operation of Law or imposed by Act of Parliament.	fixed charges
		7. If Copyhold, Cost of Enfranchisement. 8. Public Right of Way or User. 9. Rights of Common. 10. Easements. 11. Restrictions under covenant or Agreement.	
Total Deductions		Total Deductions	
Full Site Value		Total Value	

Deductions from Total Value to Arrive at Assessable Site Value.

12. Deductions from Gross Value to arrive at Full Site Value (as above)
13. Works executed.
14. Capital Expenditure.
15. Appropriation of Land for streets, roads, open spaces, etc.
16. Redemption of Land Tax or Fixed Charge.
17. Enfranchisement of Copyholds.
18. Release of Restrictive Covenants.
19. Goodwill or personal elements.
20. Cost of clearing site.
Total Deductions.
Assessable Site Value.

the expiration of a lease are required to return this form
filled in to the District Valuer, who makes and reports the
valuation to the Revenue Office. For reversion duty, therefore, as for mineral-rights duty, the provisional valuation
is not necessary. Mineral land, indeed, is treated as a separate parcel of land.[1] Minerals are to be valued showing the
total or market value, and the capital value, that is, the
market value less the value attributable to any works executed or expenditures incurred. As mineral-rights duty is
for the most part charged on the actual rent paid there is
little difficulty in its collection, since the existing machinery for the assessment and collection of the Income Tax
can be employed; and the data needed for mineral-rights
duty were made accessible in that way. The progress made
by the Commissioners and the difficulties encountered will
be considered in the following section.

§ 13. The progress made in the valuation can be judged
from the fact that out of the eleven million hereditaments
in the three Kingdoms, about four and one-half millions
in the United Kingdom alone had, up to May, 1913, been
valued. The following year the total number of hereditaments valued had reached the figure, eight millions.[2]
The valuation of Ireland has proceeded less rapidly. Up
to September, 1912, about twenty-five thousand hereditaments had been reported as valued.[3] The number of
"occasion" valuations in Great Britain for collection of
value-increment duty was up to the same date 539,970.
The cost of valuation and collection to March, 1913, was
£1,390,000,[4] and it was estimated that each valuation for

---

[1] Bill 144 (1910), § 23.

[2] Statement by Lloyd George in House of Commons. *Parl. Debates*
(1913), vol. LII, p. 886; *ibid.* (1914), vol. LXIV, p. 286.

[3] *Ibid.* (1913), vol. L, p. 836.

[4] *Ibid.*, vol. LII, p. 811. The cost has been as follows :—

> 1910–11, £332,559.
> 1911–12, £355,290.
> 1912–13, £506,653.

(Estimated cost) 1913–14, £630,086.

Ibid., vol. LI, pp. 376–77; vol. LII, p. 1682.

value-increment duty costs the Government a guinea.[1]
By March, 1914, the expense of the department had increased to £2,178,397; and by 1915 to very nearly £3,000,-
000.[2] The number of officials employed in the Valuation
Department had increased as shown below:[3]

> 1910–11, 1550 persons.
> 1911–12, 2830 "
> 1912–13, 4150 "
> 1913–14, 4650 "

Over four thousand of the employees in 1914 were
temporary appointees.

When we are told, however, that only three and one-half
millions of the four and one-half million provisional valuations in 1913 had been settled or recorded as permanent,
we realize the serious problems which confront the valuers
and which have given rise to many appeals. First, as
regards the machinery provided for appeals, except in the
few instances where the Commissioners' decision is final.[4]
In the first instance an appeal may be made to a referee.
The Act provides [5] for the appointment of a Reference
Committee for each Kingdom to be composed for England
of the Lord Chief Justice of England, the Master of the
Rolls and the President of the Surveyors' Institution.
The Reference Committee in turn appoints the referees
out of a panel composed of persons admitted as Fellows of

[1] *Parl. Debates* (1913), vol. LI, p. 376.

[2] *Ibid.*, vol. LII, p. 811; (1914), vol. LXIII, p. 1605; (1915), vol. LXXII,
p. 508. Lloyd George's expectation that the valuation would be practically completed by March 31, 1915, did not materialize. Judging from
the rate of progress made in the preceding years, however, the cause may
lie in the interruption of the work occasioned by the enlistment for
the war of several thousand of the men in the Valuation Department.

[3] *Ibid.* (1915), vol. LXXI, p. 2366; (1914), vol. LVIII, p. 782.

[4] The Commissioners' decision is to be considered final in judging of
the value of the covenant entered into in determining the " total value "
under § 25 (3), and in assessing for undeveloped land duty under § 17 (3)
of the Act.

[5] Bill 144 (1910), §§ 33 and 34.

the Surveyors' Institution, or other persons having experience in the valuation of land. The referee appealed to determines all matters of valuation in consultation with the Commissioners and the appellant, or any persons nominated by the Commissioners and appellant, respectively, for the purpose. The referee is also authorized to decide who shall be liable for the expenses incurred. The owner or Commissioner may appeal from the decision of the referee to the High Court. Or in cases of disputes involving not more than £500 the appellant may have recourse to the County Court instead of to the High Court. Further appeal may also be had to the Court of Appeal.

According to Lloyd George's estimate, only one out of every 833 valuations has been subject to appeal.[1] Until February, 1913, 4466 appeals were entered against the provisional valuations, .118 per cent of the total number.[2] But only a few of these even came before the referee, the greater number of objections being adjusted between the owner and the Commissioner. Only in the case of 155 hereditaments up to 1913 did the appeal reach the referee.[3] Of twenty cases before the referee on the question of valuation, twelve were decided in favor of the valuers, in five there was a compromise, while three were decided against the Commissioners.[4] Until March, 1913, 1272 appeals were taken against the undeveloped land duty, and 123 against the value-increment duty.[5]

But it is the character of the appeals, more than the number, that in the eyes of many condemns the present system of levy of the land-value duties. This becomes evident from the fact that the collection of both the undeveloped land duty and the value-increment duty is temporarily altogether in abeyance as a result of certain judicial decisions.[6] There have occurred a few important cases,

[1] *Parl. Debates* (1913), vol. LII, p. 886. [2] *Ibid.*, vol. L, p. 1591.
[3] *Ibid.*, vol. LII, p. 886. [4] *Ibid.*, vol. L, p. 1591.
[5] *Ibid.*, vol. LI, p. 1163. [6] *Ibid.* (1915), vol. LXXI, p. 2366.

which, when the decision of the referee was unfavorable to the Commissioners, were appealed by the latter to the High Court, as test cases. One of these cases, Herbert's Trustees *versus* the Commissioners of Inland Revenue, has given rise to a great deal of criticism due to the ambiguity of the definitions of *value* under the value-increment duty clauses. The estate in question is located in Glasgow and its assessable site value was fixed at *minus* £545. This value was obtained by computing the assessable site value, in accordance with the Act, from the total value after certain deductions had been made. As in this case, it may happen that the value of the deductions to be made from the total value exceeds the total value,[1] thus resulting in a *minus* quantity for the assessable site value. The Scottish Lands Valuation Appeal court decided that a minus value could not exist, that value could not mean *minus* value;[2] but upon appeal to the High Court this decision was reversed.[3] Although a *minus* assessable value is logically admissible, for an increment in value may represent a decrease in burden as well as a positive increase in advantage, nevertheless such a value is merely hypothetical and theoretical and indicates the complexities of the Act. Moreover, a further difficulty presented itself when the *minus* value was legalized. The Court had to decide that in accordance with the provision of exempting ten per cent of the original site value, the ten per cent deduction was to be of the full site value, not of the assessable site

[1] In the case mentioned the deductions amounted to £4320, the total value to £3775, leaving −£545 for the assessable site value. "Assessable site value is something more than the value of the cleared land; as the value of a building and site on which the building stands is always something more than (different than) the arithmetical sum of the two values of the building and site." (Cox-Sinclair and T. Hynes in *Law Magazine and Review*, vol. XXXVIII, p. 336.) In other words, the difficulty of determining the value of the separate units in a compound for which both units are indispensable is here shown.

[2] *Cf. Solicitors' Journal*, vol. LVI, p. 469.

[3] *Parl. Debates* (1913), vol. LIV, pp. 2266–67.

value,[1] for to take ten per cent of a minus quantity as a deduction from duty would be absurd.

Another case which aroused the ire of the Opposition and which led to the amendment of the Finance Act was the Lumsden case. In 1911, Mr. Lumsden, a speculative builder, sold a piece of property for £750. The property had not then been valued under the Finance Act to ascertain the original site value. When the official valuation was made, some months after the sale, the original site value was fixed at £625 or £125 less than the property had sold for. Mr. Lumsden was said to have agreed that the value of the property as by a willing seller to a willing buyer was £625 as fixed by the valuer. He had nevertheless succeeded in selling it for £750 because the buyer believed he had a monopoly location for the shop which was upon the site.[2] The decision of the referee, upheld by the Court, was that the property was liable for value-increment duty on the £125. Although it seemed evident even to the government that the value of the site had not increased, the latter contended that the increment was a "fortuitous windfall" and therefore, taxable. On the other side, it was argued that the profit made by Mr. Lumsden was due to the existence of the shop and to his personal ability; hence was not taxable. It is worth noting that in spite of the favorable decision of the Court, the government introduced an amendment [3] in 1913 which will prevent the recurrence of taxing "fortuitous windfalls" in case of improved property of which the building is worth more than the site.[4]

[1] *Parl. Debates* (1913), vol. LVI, p. 319. In 1913 (see Revenue Bill 175, § 6) the amendment stipulated that where the site value on which the reduction would be calculated is less than £100, the reduction may be calculated as ten per cent of the value increment.

[2] *Ibid.*, vol. L, pp. 184, 187.

[3] The Revenue Bill (1913), § 2. This clause gives the owner of improved property, when the value of the buildings exceeds that of the site, the option of having the property valued on the basis of the hypothetical value as under the Act or on the basis of the actual selling price.

[4] The Land Union, an organization opposed to land-value taxation,

In the valuation of agricultural land also some difficulties have arisen. It is charged that the valuers include fences, roads, drains, and manuring in the site value of agricultural land. Some cases contesting this practice have arisen. Another question which was, in 1913, *sub judice*, was whether or not tenants' rights should be deducted from the agricultural value of the land. Between two and three million acres of agricultural land are liable to undeveloped land duty.[1]

In view of the serious defects in the law and of the numerous loopholes for evasion of taxation,[2] the widespread dissatisfaction with the land-value duties, even on the part of those who helped pass the measure,[3] is explainable. The valuation has been practically condemned by the Departmental Committee on Taxation [4] and in the report of the Land Conference, the latter finding such a lack of uniformity in valuation that "it could not be fairly used either for the purposes of a national tax or even for the assessment of duties imposed by the 'People's Budget' itself." [5] Nevertheless, granting that the expense of valuation has already been enormous and out of all proportion

and that has tried to get adverse decisions on the commissioners' valuations, threatened to appeal the Lumsden case to the High Court. The case did reach the House of Lords where the vote of the four judges was evenly divided. A member of the Opposition said in the House of Commons that the Government would have preferred an adverse decision in this case, because the claim of Mr. Lumsden was generally conceded, and no amendment to the law would then have been necessary. *Cf. Parl. Debates* (1914), vol. LXV, pp. 631, 672.

[1] *Ibid.* (1913), vol. L, p. 177; vol. LII, p. 1146; (1914), vol. LVIII, p. 821.

[2] *Cf. Law Quarterly Review* (1914), vol. XXX, p. 180; *Law Magazine and Review*, vol. XXXIX, pp. 326 *ff.*

[3] *Cf. Parl. Debates* (1913), vol. L, p. 176.

[4] *Ibid.* (1914), vol. LXII, pp. 477–78.

[5] Both bodies mentioned above are said to have been composed of a partisan and prejudiced majority. At the Land Conference the Surveyors' Institute, the Auctioneers' Institute, the Land Agents' Society, the Chamber of Agriculture, the Farmers' Union, etc., were represented. *Ibid.*, vol. LVIII, p. 812.

to the yield of the taxes thus far collected, granting that the herculean task of valuation will yet cost millions of pounds before completion,[1] granting also that hardships have been entailed in some cases in levying the taxes, and that difficulties have arisen sufficient to question the possibility of accurate valuation, the conclusion, nevertheless, cannot be escaped that when completed the data[2] will not only be invaluable for statistical purposes, but will have far-reaching effects fiscally and socially.

§ 14. If the valuation of the land has been subjected to ridicule, the land-value duties have fared no better. From a fiscal standpoint the powerful opposition which the land taxes encountered seems scarcely warranted. Moreover, the fact that after half a dozen years the opposition has not abated and that the law stands unrepealed confirms the conclusion expressed earlier that a social principle, not fiscal expediency, was involved in its enactment. The receipts from the land duties have been disappointing beyond measure. Already for the year 1910–11 the yield (the mineral-rights duty excepted) fell short of the official estimate.[3] And instead of increasing in amount as had been predicted, the revenue from three of the duties, as appears from the subjoined data, continues to be inconsiderable.

[1] It will be remembered that in accordance with the provisions of the amended Act a revaluation of the land in 1916 is due.

[2] The new Domesday Book will be a card catalogue of all the land in the three Kingdoms. One card is given to each unit or hereditament; it contains the particulars of the original and subsequent valuations, and bears the identification number of each parish. The cards of each parish are filed in separate cabinets and arranged in numerical order. *Report of the Commissioners of Inland Revenue* (1911), p. 166.

	Estimated receipts	Actual net proceeds
Value-Increment Duty	£50,000	£127
Reversion Duty	100,000	258
Undeveloped Land Duty	100,000	2,351
Mineral-Rights Duty	350,000	506,289
	£600,000	£509,025

This is according to the revised estimate of the Chancellor. *Cf. Parl. Debates* (1909), vol. IV, p. 542; vol. XII, p. 702.

RECEIPTS FROM LAND-VALUE DUTIES, 1910–1913 [1]

	1910–1911	1911–1912	1912–1913	1913–1914	1914–1915	Total up to March 31, 1915
Value-increment duty	£127	£6,127	£17,000	£31,000	£48,316	£106,000
Reversion duty	258	22,620	48,000	80,000	19,313	170,000
Undeveloped land duty	2,351	28,947	98,000	275,000	8,657	413,000
Mineral-rights duty	506,289	436,194	298,000	349,000	..	..
Total...	£509,025	£493,888	£461,000	£735,000	£725,000	..

How unproductive a source of revenue the duties have been is further apparent from a comparison of their total yield with the cost of their collection and valuation, the cost exceeding the receipts up to 1915. Of the four duties the mineral-rights duty has proved the most productive and promises to yield a stable annual amount. It is worth noting that the Opposition even seems reconciled to this duty, regarding it as part of the income tax.[2] The productiveness of the duty on mineral rights is attributable to its characteristics: (1) No valuation of the land is necessary for its assessment; (2) the machinery of assessment already existed at the time of the enactment; (3) it is a direct levy, not dependent upon the number of transfers of property. In contrast, the proceeds from the undeveloped land duty, as a direct, annual tax, are exceedingly trifling. This is explicable on various grounds: first, inasmuch as the duty is collected only on the unimproved land that has been valued, the true yield of the undeveloped land duty will not be known until the valuation has been completed;[3]

[1] Data taken from *Parl. Debates* (1915), vol. LXXI, p. 2366; vol. LXXII, p. 1478; *Hazell's Annual Register* (1912), p. 121; *Statesman's Yearbook* (1915), p. 48.

[2] *Parl. Debates* (1915), vol. LXXII, p. 1705.

[3] The collection of the arrears of this duty will undoubtedly create hardships on many who will be compelled to pay three or four years' duty.

and, secondly, the operation of the tax has been temporarily suspended by reason of the court decisions. The fluctuation and increase in amount are due to the inclusion of arrears from previous years. The paltry sums yielded by the indirect taxes, namely, the value-increment and reversion duty, are accounted for by the fact that the levy of the former is dependent upon the number of transfers of property, of the latter upon the determination of long-term leases. The transfer of certain kinds of property was said to have been interfered with during the stormy sessions of Parliament and even after the enactment of the Finance Bill.[1] Moreover, the taxable value increment accruing during the first troublous year and even in the few succeeding years could be but slight. Indeed, it is very likely that the market value of some land has been unfavorably affected by the duties. On the other hand, the few cases reported as liable for reversion duty during the first year are attributable, according to the Commissioners of Inland Revenue,[2] to the liberal exemptions and to the ignorance and misunderstanding of the liabilities under the Act. In the last years the amount of reversion duty has been insignificant because of the legal controversies still *sub judice*.

The above considerations show that temporary causes chiefly have tended to make the yield of the new duties inconsiderable. Whether the anticipations of the Chancellor of the Exchequer who saw in these new taxes a source of an expanding revenue for the needs of the State [3] were well founded, it is too early to predict.[4] But while final

---

[1] *Cf. Solicitors' Journal*, vol. LVII, p. 780. That this was not true of the large estates will be shown *infra*, § 15. It is necessary to point out that the ordinary transfer tax on property was doubled by the Finance Act (1909–10), § 73.

[2] *Report for 1911*, p. 164.

[3] *Parl. Debates* (1909), vol. IV, pp. 537, 539; vol. IX, p. 318.

[4] "That the possibilities of the tax are still highly regarded is, nevertheless, evidenced by the protests made by the local authorities against the provision of the Revenue Bill now before Parliament by which half

judgment concerning the fiscal expediency of the land-value duties for imperial purposes must be withheld, the possibilities of fiscal reform which the enactment of the duties has opened up must also be taken into account. The utility of the valuation itself is no longer questioned. The chief reasons are: [1] (1) the compulsory acquisition of land by local authorities will henceforth be based on the assessed value of the land instead of on the speculative value fixed by the owner; (2) it will prevent the undervaluation of land for death duty purposes; [2] (3) the valuation will greatly facilitate the adoption of local rating on land value, for which bills continue to be introduced in the House of Commons.[3]

§ 15. After all, however, considering the primary purpose of the land-value duties, the question of fiscal expediency must give way to the question of the social and economic effects. As we reflect upon the extravagant claims of the adherents and the vehemence of the opposition when the possible effects of the land duties were debated in Parliament, we may wonder at the apparently unchanged conditions, social and economic, since these duties have come into operation. To quote for illustra-

the proceeds of the taxes is to be swept into the exchequer in lieu of the value of the outdoor relief saved to the authorities by the recent extension of the operation of the Old Age Pension Act to paupers." (*Financial Review of Reviews*, April, 1911, p. 27.) In explanation of this passage it is necessary to note the provision of section 91 of the Finance Act, 1909–10, for an equal division of the revenue accruing from the land duties between the imperial and local governments. The Revenue Bill of 1911, however, repealed the provision, so that the total revenue is now devoted to imperial purposes.

[1] *Cf. Financial Review of Reviews*, April, 1913, p. 35.

[2] See *Speech by Lloyd George at City Liberal Club* (February, 1912), p. 12.

[3] Even in 1912 three "local rating on land value" bills were introduced in the House of Commons. Bill 64 (Scotland) passed a second reading; Bill 25 was withdrawn, while Bill 173 was dropped after a second reading. Very significant is the provision for a new valuation for rating purposes which Lloyd George included in his Budget Proposals of 1914. *Cf. Parl. Debates* (1914), vol. LXII, p. 478.

tion Mr. Winston Churchill's hopeful expectations: "The effect will be, as we believe, to bring land into the market and thus somewhat cheapen the price at which land is obtainable for every object, public and private, and by so doing, we shall liberate new springs of enterprise and industry, we shall stimulate building, relieve overcrowding, and promote employment." [1] The failure of these claims to materialize is not difficult to explain. First, the taxes are not yet in full operation. Secondly, the tax rates are too slight to be burdensome; that is, a tax of one fifth of one per cent on undeveloped land will scarcely check speculation and lead to the utilization of more land. Thirdly, other social forces tend to counteract the influences which the duties may exert, for example, the increasing population in urban communities. Thus, it may be argued, the salutary effects of the duties have not yet been felt.

On the other hand, facts have been presented to show that the new taxes have had a deleterious influence on the building trade. That there was a depression in building operations in England in the years following the enactment of the duties is seen from the following data: in 1910–11, only ten per cent of the number of small houses of £20 annual value and below were erected, that had been erected in each year from 1904 to 1906. [2] A member of the Opposition quoted the following figures to show the injurious effect of the taxes on building operations: [3] In 1901,

[1] *The Budget, the Land, and the People,* issued by the Budget League (1909), p. 46.

[2] The figures quoted by Mr. Peto in the House of Commons were: in 1904–06 (on an average) 107,021 small buildings had been built, in 1910–11 the total number was 10,651. *Parl. Debates* (1913), vol. L, p. 208. *Cf.* also *ibid.* (1914), vol. LVIII, p. 854.

[3] The same member, Mr. Royds, caused an inquiry to be made on his own account, and in reply to his question, "Have the Budget Land Taxes affected the building trade in your district?" received answers as follows: (1) "The provisional valuation scheme has destroyed credit and frightened mortgagees. . . . In the whole of this city I do not think there are a dozen cottages under construction." (2) ". . . the values of the official valuer have had a depressing and unnerving influence on the builder and

in the forty towns investigated there were 65,000 uninhabited houses, in 1911 the number had declined to 47,740,
and in 1913 to 24,000. In reply it was pointed out that the
high cost of building materials and of labor and the increase in the rate of interest and in local rates were responsible for the shortage of small houses; while in general the
conditions in the building trade had improved since the
imposition of the land-value duties. The last statement
was substantiated by the decrease in unemployment in the
trade since 1909, which was a year of depression, and by
the advance in wages in the building trades over and above
that in general wages.[1] Whether, as some claim, the law
has withdrawn capital from the building trade,[2] discouraged building operations and raised rents,[3] or whether the
depression was the result of the uncertainties attending
the valuation and the interpretation of the law has not
been proved.[4] Another effect which from the standpoint
of the government is favorable is that large estates are
being broken up, and that there is in consequence an
increasing number of small owners of land. This is generally admitted even by the Opposition,[5] but the result of

on the owners of property. Values of twenty per cent less than cost are
usual from the value here. . . . This has had a distressing effect upon the
investing public, who for some years have shunned property and have
not yet recovered. Its effect is entirely to upset all confidence in the
property market." *Parl. Debates* (1914), vol. LVIII, pp. 806–07.

[1] *Ibid.* (1914), vol. LVIII, pp. 824, 845–46. The percentages of unemployment were given as follows: 1906, 7.2; 1907, 7.3; 1908, 11.5;
1909, 11.7; 1910, 8.6; 1911, 5; 1912, 4.2; 1913, 3.8. These percentages,
quoted by Lloyd George, were declared misleading, because the membership of the building trade unions had decreased since 1909.

[2] *Ibid.* (1913), vol. L, p. 1558.

[3] *Ibid.*, p. 171.

[4] *Cf. ibid.*, vol. LII, p. 905. The testimony of the members of Parliament regarding the depression in the building trade, was, however, not
unanimous. Thus it was claimed by one member that building operations in towns were more active and that unemployment in that industry
was less than for many preceding years. *Ibid.*, vol. L, pp. 1551 ff.

[5] See Speech by the Earl of Portsmouth in the House of Lords. *Parl.
Debates* (Lords, 1913), vol. XIV, p. 1067.

the abnormal sale of estates is said by them to have been
that it has put the tenant farmer in an unfortunate position.[1] It should be mentioned also that the value of
land has tended to increase in spite of this tendency toward
disintegration.[2]

[1] *Parl. Debates* (Commons, 1913), vol. LVIII, p. 812.
[2] *Ibid.*, pp. 825–26.

CHAPTER VI

MUNICIPAL TAXATION IN WESTERN CANADA

§ 1. REAL estate is the prevailing and chief source of local revenue in Canada. The cause for the separation of the central, provincial, and local sources of public revenue in Canada is political rather than economic. But, since the Dominion government relies for its revenue chiefly upon customs and excise taxes, and the provincial governments upon corporation and succession duties, and railway, income, and similar taxes, little else [1] remains for the local authorities to tax besides property, real and personal. And though the personalty tax, now generally discredited in Canada,[2] is being superseded by the business or other taxes,[3] real property constitutes the main source of municipal income. So long as landed property continues to be the main source of wealth in the community, and so long as the principle of benefit, the principle of taxation which Canadian writers accept as self-evident,[4] continues to give satisfaction to the ratepayers, real estate will bear the heaviest burden of taxation.

[1] Licenses, franchises, poll, income, and business taxes are other taxes levied in the Canadian localities, but these are unimportant, subsidiary sources of revenue.

[2] The various provincial tax commissions were invariably in favor of its abolition. *Cf. Report of the Ontario Assessment Commission* (1902). Also *Sessional Papers, Ontario* (1893), No. 73, and the *Report of the Royal Commission on Taxation in British Columbia* (1911).

[3] The business tax, which has taken the place of the personal property tax in Ontario, is reported as working well. *Cf. The Municipal World,* November, 1909, pp. 272–73.

[4] For example, the alderman of Westmount, Quebec, who succeeded in introducing some reforms in the system of taxation in his city defines taxation as " a payment by the individual to the organized community for services rendered to him by it." *Canadian Municipal Journal,* June, 1914, p. 230.

That the Canadian fiscal system should have developed along lines similar to the English system is readily comprehensible. Considering the differences in the economic and social conditions of the two countries, however, it is noteworthy that the assessment on annual or rental value, as in England, was prevalent in Canada until the fifties. This method of assessment, which distributes unequally the burden of taxation by exempting unused property from taxation, was perpetuated in England by a dominant landowning class. In new and democratic communities, however, where the principle of equal distribution of the tax burden tends to be jealously observed, and the reciprocal relation between services of the government and the wealth of the individual is accepted as an article of faith,[1] the transition to assessment on capital value seems inevitable. In Canada the first departure from the traditional system is seen in the provision of the tax law for Upper Canada in the fifties, that the taxable annual value should in every case constitute the real rack rent, and if the rent be less than six per cent of the actual value of the land, the assessed rental should be calculated at six per cent of the full or capital value.[2] Shortly afterward followed the change to assessment on capital value in Ontario (1869).[3] And now, with one exception,[4] rating on capital value has become general throughout Canada.

§ 2. More recently the western provinces of Canada have departed still further from the English system by

[1] The fact that public utilities and improvements enhance the value of the vacant as well as of the improved land is cited again and again in Canada in discussions on taxation. Therefore, also "special assessment" taxes are common in western Canada.

[2] Full value is the amount at which the land would be appraised in payment of a just debt from a solvent debtor. *The Consolidated Statutes for Upper Canada*, 22 Vic., c. 55, § 28; 16 Vic., c. 182, § 12.

[3] 32 Vic., c. 36, § 30; see also *Revised Statutes of Ontario* (1877), c. 180, § 23.

[4] The city of Quebec still rates on the annual rental. *Cf.* Vineberg, *Provincial and Local Taxation in Canada*, in *Columbia University Studies* (1912), vol. III, p. 91.

exempting improvements from the real-estate tax. The tendency is even to remit all other taxes for local purposes, so as to make the value of the land the sole source of local revenue. The causes of this tendency to adopt the single tax on land value are fiscal, economic, and social. So great has been the appreciation in the value of the land in the western provinces, that the owner does not feel the burden of the taxes. As will be shown later,[1] the rise in land value has kept pace with the increased budgets without necessitating any considerable increase in the tax rate. In the eastern provinces, on the other hand, where the value of the improvements nearly equals or exceeds the value of the land, and where the value of the land is more constant,[2] the remission of other taxes and the exemption of improvements would necessitate a higher tax rate and the burden on the land would be increased.

Attention should be called to the similarity between western Canada and the Australasian colonies both in respect to the underlying economic and social conditions and in respect to the legislation resulting from those conditions. Western Canada, comprising British Columbia, Manitoba, Alberta, and Saskatchewan (omitting the Yukon and the Northwest Territories),[3] reminds one of the vastness and wildness of their sister colonies in the Eastern Hemisphere. Like Australasia, western Canada is the hope of the venturesome pioneer; both are very sparsely populated. Settled by squatters, mainly speculators, the western provinces display the same eagerness as Australasia to attract immigrants and to encourage the employment of labor and capital. Moreover, the same

[1] See *infra*, § 8.

[2] *Cf. Canadian Municipal Journal*, December, 1912, p. 490.

[3] For purposes of comparison Canada must be dismembered, for the newly opened western country is in many respects as different from eastern Canada, as Australia, for example, from its mother country. The Yukon and Northwest Territories are scarcely organized and populated. There are only about 27,000 people in about 1,500,000 square miles of territory (1912).

ideals, such as equality of opportunity, the same resentment and intolerance toward special privilege, characterize both countries. The greatest boon to the inhabitants
is, of course, the influx of immigration, and as prosperous
industrial conditions and business opportunities are the
chief incentive to settlement, it behooves even the speculators to promote improvements and business enterprises.

The land problems in the two countries differ only in
degree. The following facts throw light on the condition
of land tenure in the western provinces. Western Canada,
i.e., the three prairie provinces, was acquired by the
Dominion by purchase from the Hudson's Bay Company.[1]
But the federal government disposed of part of these lands
by liberal grants to railway companies and by sale to land
speculators. The original grant to the Canadian Pacific
Railway Company alone was 27,000,000 acres plus 17,000,-
000 acres from the absorbed roads.[2] At present it owns
about 200,000 acres in Manitoba, excluding 70,000 acres
owned by the Canadian North-West Land Company, a
child of the Canadian Pacific. In Alberta and Saskatchewan, 7,000,000 acres belong to the same company; while
in British Columbia it owns about 4,000,000 acres more.
The Esquimalt and Nanaimo Railway Company owns
nearly 1,250,000 acres on Vancouver Island alone. Besides,
there are fifteen incorporated land companies owning vast
estates in British Columbia.[3] Considering, however, that
the area of the four provinces contains more than 700,000,-
000 acres, the crown lands have by no means all been disposed of. Nevertheless, although the Dominion lands are

[1] *Cf.* Rupert's Land Act (1868), 31–32 Vic., c. cv. The Hudson's Bay
Company, by the charter from King Charles II, claimed and held possession of this whole western territory until after the Confederation of
1867. At about that time the land was ceded to the Dominion for a cash
bounty and certain fur-trading privileges, the company retaining one-
twentieth of the land as well. *Cf. An Official Hand Book of Alberta* (1907),
p. 6; also the London *Economist*, March 16, 1912, p. 573.

[2] *Ibid.*

[3] *Agriculture in British Columbia*, Official Bulletin 10 (1912), p. 96.

still extensive, they are not the most desirable lands, for the territory near and along the main railway lines is in the hands of the Canadian Pacific, while the Hudson's Bay Company's lands comprise one-twentieth part of all the fertile belt.[1]

There is still much free land in Alberta and Saskatchewan, of whose area scarcely half has yet been surveyed, while in British Columbia the Dominion Government owns 3,500,000 acres in the Peace River country and a large area in the River Belt.[2] There is less free arable land in Manitoba, except in the north and northwest.[3] The Dominion lands are open for entry to homesteaders.[4] The policy of the Canadan Pacific Railway Company, as of most of the land companies, has been to sell its holdings at

[1] *An Official Hand Book of Alberta* (1907), p. 56. The London *Economist*, March 16, 1912, p. 573.

[2] The number of acres of Dominion lands surveyed to January 1, 1913, was 154,552,067 acres, of which only 30,000,000 have yet been disposed of. The *Canada Year Book* (1912), p. 432. *Cf.* also Lawson, *Canada and the Empire*, pp. 202–03. *Bureau of Provincial Information*, Official Bulletin 10 (B.C., 1912), p. 95.

[3] *Cf. Canada Hand Book* (1915), p. 67. The following data present concisely the conditions of land tenure and of cultivation in the four western provinces in 1901 and 1911 (*Canada Year Book* (1914), p. 170): —

| Provinces | Total area (acres) | Occupied lands | | |
		Area (acres)	Improved (acres)	Unimproved (acres)
British Columbia:				
1901	236,922,177	1,497,419	473,683	1,023,736
1911	226,186,370	2,540,011	477,590	2,062,421
Manitoba:				
1901	41,169,098	8,843,347	3,995,305	4,848,042
1911	41,169,098	12,228,233	6,746,169	5,482,064
Alberta:				
1901	161,872,000	2,735,630	474,694	2,260,936
1911	161,872,000	17,751,899	4,351,698	13,400,201
Saskatchewan:				
1901	155,764,480	3,833,434	1,122,602	2,710,823
1911	155,764,100	28,642,985	11,871,907	16,771,078

[4] The applicant for a homestead of 160 acres pays a fee of $10. The conditions of entry are: (1) six months' residence in every year on the land; (2) the cultivation of at least fifteen acres for three years.

reasonable prices. It is of course in the interest of these companies to promote immigration and settlement. At the outset the Canadian Pacific sold land at $2.50 per acre with a rebate of half the amount for every acre brought under cultivation. At present, the average selling price for good land is $10 per acre without rebate for improvement, while the irrigated lands bring prices of $30 to $55 per acre.[1] Within recent years the influx of population has been very rapid and the investment of foreign capital in land, chiefly by English and American capitalists, has increased enormously.[2] The result has been a great appreciation in the value of the land, mainly an inflated valuation.[3]

Not only has the increased rural population in the west-

[1] The following data show the enormous profits reaped by the land companies from their land sales (Lawson, *op. cit.*, pp. 97, 210): —

CANADIAN LAND SALES IN THE NORTHWEST

	1893–1908		1909–1910	
	Acres	Value	Acres	Value
Canadian Pacific Railway Company....................	8,453,730	$35,062,944	655,585	$10,473,425
Hudson's Bay Company.....	1,514,153	9,484,943	104,382	1,297,454
Canadian Northern Company	1,171,400	6,638,511	285,428	2,783,010
Calgary and Edmonton Company......................	1,240,087	4,454,800	18,323	182,926
Manitoba South Western Company.................	1,153,999	4,006,301	14,501	126,950
Q'Appelle, Long Lake, and Saskatchewan Company...	1,022,915	2,017,224	106,000	964,600
Great Northern Central Company.................	213,206	990,963	571	6,863
Total	14,769,490	$62,655,686	1,184,790	$15,835,228

[2] "The speculation in city properties has largely been in the hands of foreign investors and a class of semi-professional real estate dealers resident here." London *Economist*, February 1, 1913, p. 221.

[3] Farm land in Manitoba is said to have increased ten per cent in price within the last five years, while the average increase in Saskatchewan and Alberta has been fully thirty per cent. *Ibid.*, March 9, 1912, p. 532. Near cities, like Saskatoon and Regina, Sask., unimproved land brings $40 to $50 per acre, whereas elsewhere it brings only $10 per acre. *Ibid.*, March 30, 1912, p. 686.

ern provinces caused an appreciation in the value of farm land, but the rapid growth of the incorporated local bodies has given rise to "booms" in town land. It has been estimated that of the 1,244,597 immigrants who entered the western provinces from 1900 to 1909, 31.4 per cent were represented in homestead entries. Allowing for the immigrants who became farm laborers and those who bought land from the land and railway companies, a considerable proportion must have become residents of the towns.[1] A few examples will make this evident. From 1901 to 1911, the urban population of Alberta increased from 20,623 to 141,937 (588 per cent); that of Manitoba from 70,473 to 200,365 (184 per cent); that of British Columbia from 90,179 to 203,684 (126 per cent); and that of Saskatchewan from 17,550 to 131,365 (648 per cent).[2] The following table shows the increase in the number of municipalities in Saskatchewan:[3]

	1905	1913
Rural municipalities	2	290
Villages	63	255
Towns	16	72
Cities	3	5

This development, then, has caused a prodigious value increment to accrue from realty transactions. And while speculators are seeking to attract capital to this new country in order to reap further profit from the increment in the value of the land, the taxpayer in the municipality feels himself aggrieved because the property of the absentee, held for speculation in an unimproved condition, rises in value as a result of the community's expenditure for improvements. In further explanation of the attitude of the

[1] "The Immigration Situation in Canada," in *Report of the Immigration Commission*, U.S. Senate Doc. No. 469 (1910), p. 22.

[2] *Canada Year Book* (1912), pp. 14–19.

[3] *Canadian Municipal Journal*, October, 1913, p. 412; *cf.* also *The Public Service Monthly* (Sask.), vol. II, September, 1913, p. 10; December, 1914, p. 126.

settlers toward this class of landowners, we may note that in many towns the Hudson's Bay Company and the railway companies hold large tracts unimproved.[1] To hit these non-residents and to attract capital, such is the end toward which the system of taxing the land irrespective of improvements is chiefly directed. When we add the fiscal factors, the elasticity and sufficiency of the tax, and the ethical consideration, to distribute the burden equally on those who can best bear it, we have the motives which have called the tax on land value into being.

§ 3. The history of the development of the system of exempting improvements from taxation bears out the conclusion that its adoption was prompted by fiscal and social considerations. The earliest attempt to discourage landed monopoly through taxation was the levy of the wild-land tax in British Columbia. This tax, first imposed in 1873 for provincial purposes, applied only to undeveloped land in unorganized communities.[2] The rate of tax was one per cent of the value per acre on all land except such as was improved as follows: [3]

(1) Land upon which $1 per acre was expended annually, provided such land did not exceed the value of $20 per acre.

(2) Land upon which permanent improvements [4] to the amount in value of 20 per cent of the assessed value of the land had been made.

(3) Land, not worth $5 per acre, upon which five head of cattle per 100 acres were pastured; or land, when

[1] Moreover, the lands of the Canadian Pacific Railway Company are exempt from taxation.

[2] British Columbia, 36 Vic., No. 11. Having relegated the levy of property taxes to the local governments, the provincial government reserved the right to tax property only in the unorganized districts. *Cf. ibid.*, § 1 (b).

[3] Other exemptions, such as are usual in taxation, need no mention here.

[4] § 2 defines permanent improvements as any building, fence, prospecting mining work, or reclamation of the land.

valued in excess of $5 per acre, upon which fifteen head of sheep per 100 acres were pastured.

(4) Land leased for timber cutting, or for agricultural purposes.

In 1876 this Land Tax Act was repealed and replaced by a property and income "Assessment Act" which, besides a tax of one-third of one per cent on the capital value of real estate, provided for an annual tax of five cents per acre upon all *unoccupied* land in unorganized districts.[1] This provision, though still discriminatory, made the burden on unimproved land a nominal one and in many cases represented a reduction in burden, since the tax was now based, not on land value, but on acreage.[2] Since 1900, the rate of the provincial tax on realty has fluctuated from one-half to four-fifths of one per cent; during the same period, the rate on the value of wild land has increased from three to five per cent.[3] During this time the meaning of *wild land* has become more clearly defined, and since 1905 [4] has become differentiated for taxing purposes from timber and coal lands. Wild land is such as has not existing upon it improvements to the value of $2.50 per acre, in addition to the cash value of the land itself, in territory west of the Cascade Range of mountains; and $1.25 in territory east of the Cascade. Temporary structures including machinery and other temporary equipment do not constitute improvements. The following

---

[1] British Columbia, 39 Vic., No. 8, §§ 1, 9, 10. "Unoccupied land shall mean land on which there shall not be existing improvements to the amount of $5 per acre on each parcel of land." In 1877 (40 Vic., No. 10), this provision was repealed and $2.50 was substituted instead of $5.

[2] The owner of valuable unimproved land was now liable to the same slight charge as the owner of the most worthless property.

[3] British Columbia, 64 Vic., c. 38, § 4; 3–4 Edw. VII, c. 53, § 5; 5 Edw. VII, c. 50, § 15. A reduction in case of the realty tax of one-fifth of one per cent, in the case of the wild-land tax of one-half of one per cent, is allowed if the tax is paid before a specified time.

[4] British Columbia, 5 Edw. VII, c. 50, § 15.

rates of tax on the different classes of land are in force at present:[1]

(1) On real estate (improved land), $\frac{1}{2}$ of 1 per cent.

(2) On wild land, 4 per cent.

(3) On timber land,[2] 2 per cent.

(4) On coal land, class A (being worked), 1 per cent.

(5) On coal land, class B (being unworked), 2 per cent.

(6) On unworked Crown-granted mineral claims, 25 cents per acre.

This wild-land tax, which has persisted since 1873, and which is clearly intended to discriminate against the holder of unimproved land, was until 1914 levied for provincial purposes[3] in British Columbia only. The proceeds are devoted to local improvements. In 1914 a wild-land tax

---

[1] Revised Statutes of British Columbia, 2 Geo. V, c. 222, § 9. The following statement of the annual receipts collected from the wild-land tax by the provincial government shows the increase in yield, due both to the appreciated value of the land and to the increase in rate of tax: —

		1906:	
1873	$950.79	Wild land	$73,456.41
1878	9,530.93	Coal land A	1,434.40
1883	5,162.92	Coal land B	20,038.62
1893	13,832.00	Timber land	38,150.93
1898	61,575.07		
1900	49,241.89	Total	$133,080.36
1903	71,340.50	1907:	
1905	101,607.29	Wild land	$91,098.34
		Coal land A	2,463.00
		Coal land B	21,536.00
		Timber land	46,325.97
		Total	$161,423.31
		1911 — Total	$316,130.83

(*Report of Royal Commission on Taxation (British Columbia)*, 1911, p. B 26; *Papers Relative to the Working of Taxation of the Unimproved Value of Land in Canada* (Cd. 3740), 1907, pp. 9–10.)

[2] "A royalty is reserved to the Crown on all timber cut from Crown lands, from railway subsidy lands, and from lands held under lease or license from the Crown," etc. Where the timber is manufactured or used in the province a rebate is allowed in case of the timber tax. *Year Book of British Columbia* (1911), p. 283.

[3] In Alberta there is a provincial tax on land levied at a flat rate per acre, not on the capital value of the land. Likewise, in Saskatchewan, the provincial land tax is now only one cent per acre. *Cf. The Public Service Monthly, Legislative Supplement to the February Number* (1913), p. 12; *Official Hand Book of the Dominion of Canada* (1897), p. 69.

of one per cent was adopted in Alberta.[1] As in British Columbia this charge falls on land outside the boundaries of an incorporated city, town, or village.

The latter province, it is significant, outdid her sister province to the west by the institution, in 1913, of a tax on the unearned increment of land.[2] This tax applies to land transfers in incorporated as well as in the unincorporated districts of Alberta, and the proceeds are to be devoted to provincial purposes. The rate of tax is five per cent of the value increment, which is the excess of the selling price at the time of transfer over the assessed value in 1913.[3] The tax is not collected at the transfer of land from the Crown nor on the death of the owner; while agricultural land, of which at least ten per cent has been under cultivation during twelve months preceding the transfer, is also exempt.[4]

§ 4. The taxation of real property within the incorporated local bodies was from the first relegated to them by the provincial governments of western Canada. In British Columbia, the councils of the local bodies were already in the nineties authorized to discriminate between land and improvements and to tax the latter at a lower rate. Thus, as early as 1891, the option of rating improvements at a lower value than land was extended to the municipalities of British Columbia. According to this provision it was possible to exempt improvements altogether.[5] The following year the exemption of at least fifty per cent of the value of improvements was made mandatory.[6] The

---

[1] Alberta (1914), c. 3.   [2] *Ibid.* (1913), c. 10.

[3] In case of land not within any incorporated municipality, the original site value is deemed to be $15 per acre, unless the owner within a year from the passing of the Act can prove that the land had a higher value. *Cf. ibid.*, § 4.

[4] When the area of unsubdivided land, however, exceeds 640 acres, the excess over 640 acres is subject to increment tax, but only to the extent of the excess value beyond the sum of $50 per acre of the unimproved value of the land.

[5] British Columbia, 54 Vic., No. 29, § 132; 59 Vic., c. 37, § 136.

[6] *Ibid.*, 55 Vic., c. 33, § 148.

municipalities were also empowered to levy a wild-land tax at a rate not to exceed four per cent of the assessed value of such land situated within the boundaries of the municipalities.[1] In 1910, out of fifty-one municipalities, only sixteen levied a wild-land tax. The explanation given for this small number that have adopted the tax is that, when assessed as wild land, the value of the land is less than as building land;[2] therefore, in municipalities where the vacant land has been surveyed, subdivided into small lots and assessed as building land, the tax on real property is more productive than the wild-land tax would be.[3] Only where the land is not ripe for building purposes does the wild-land tax yield more revenue. This conclusion is confirmed by the fact that only three of the sixteen municipalities which in 1910 levied the wild-land tax had more than 1000 ratepayers. Besides the wild-land tax, eleven of these sixteen municipal bodies also exempted all improvements from taxation, and four more exempted fifty or more per cent of the value of improvements.[4] Altogether, in 1914, out of the thirty-three cities in British Columbia, fifteen taxed improvements to fifty per cent of their value; fifteen exempted them entirely; while three taxed them at thirty-three and one-third, thirty, and twenty-five per cent respectively. Out of the twenty-eight district communities, twenty-four exempted improvements altogether.[5]

In the Northwest Territories, of which Alberta and Saskatchewan were a part until 1905, a similar enactment,

---

[1] The rate on real property was not to exceed one and one-half per cent, not including special and school rates; the rate on wild land was in 1896 not to exceed two and one-half per cent. B.C. 59 Vic., c. 37.

[2] In a municipality, the land nearer the center, or the business section, has a higher value than in the outlying districts. Until the place is platted and laid out in lots, one acre of land is valued with every other acre as agricultural land.

[3] *Papers Relative to the Working of the Land Taxes in Canada* (Cd. 3740), 1907, pp. 8–11.

[4] *Year Book of British Columbia* (1911), pp. 275–76.

[5] Haig, *Exemption of Improvements from Taxation in Canada and the United States*, p. 262.

in 1894, empowered the councils of the municipalities to exempt all improvements from taxation, provided such exemption should not occasion a higher rate of tax than four per cent for all local purposes, including the general, school, special and debenture rates. For the adoption of this provision a majority vote of two-thirds of the members of the municipal council, or a petition of at least one-half of the resident ratepayers, was required. In case a petition shall have been presented for two years in succession, the new system of rating becomes law permanently; rescission, however, is possible, if the same procedure of voting, or of petition, is followed as for adoption.[1] The option of rating on land value continued after the incorporation of Alberta and Saskatchewan. Indeed, under the Village Act of the latter province a Single Tax may even be raised on land value.[2] For the institution of the Single Tax for municipal purposes, it was required that a petition signed by at least two-thirds of all the ratepayers be submitted to the commissioner. The maximum rate was fixed at two per cent in 1906, but was changed to two and one-half per cent in 1908.[3] Under the city and town Acts,[4] improvements were required to be assessed at sixty per cent of their actual value; the rate on real property on this basis was not to exceed one per cent of the assessed value. The development of the movement to exempt improvements reached its final stage in the Rural Municipalities Act of 1912–13, in the provision that "land shall be assessed at its actual cash value *exclusive of any increase in such value caused by the erection of any buildings thereon, or by any other expenditure of labor or capital.*"[5]

The present status of the legislation in Saskatchewan with reference to land-value taxation is as follows: In cities,

[1] Ordinances of Northwest Territories No. 3 of 1894, Pt. IV, § 9.
[2] Saskatchewan (1906), c. 35, § 40.
[3] *Ibid.* (1906), c. 35, § 40; (1908), c. 18, § 181.
[4] *Ibid.* (1908), c. 16, § 310; c. 17, § 302.
[5] *Ibid.* (1912–13), c. 30, § 23. (Italics mine.)

towns and villages improvements shall not be taxed to more than sixty per cent of their value. Since 1911 cities and towns have the option of exempting a greater value of the improvements than forty per cent, provided that the rate of reduction shall not exceed fifteen per cent in any one year.[1] This means that any municipality which had availed itself of this provision in 1911 could exempt improvements to one hundred per cent by 1915. In villages the option of exempting improvements still exists; while in the rural municipalities total exemption is obligatory. On rural land, moreover, a surtax is charged for local purposes. The rate is six and one-fourth cents per acre and the land subject to the surtax is as follows: [2]

(1) Land not exceeding 320 acres owned by a non-resident and of which less than one-fourth is improved.

(2) Land from 320 to 640 acres, less than one-fourth of which is under cultivation.

(3) Land from 640 to 1280 acres, less than one-half of which is under cultivation.

(4) Land from 1280 to 1920 acres, less than one-half of which is under cultivation.

(5) Land of any owner or occupant exceeding 1920 acres.

The subjoined data show how the local bodies had responded, by 1914, to the permission to exempt improvements: (1) The cities had all taken advantage of the privilege. Moose Jaw in 1914 taxed improvements to forty-five per cent, North Battleford and Weyburn to thirty per cent, Regina to twenty-five per cent, Prince Albert and Swift Current to fifteen per cent. (2) Of fifty-five towns, forty-two assessed improvements at sixty per cent, the others at less than sixty per cent, two taxing improvements at twenty-five per cent. (3) About one-fourth of the 246 villages exempted all improvements, the others taxing

---

[1] Saskatchewan (1910–11), c. 18, § 15; c. 19, § 17.

[2] *Ibid.* (1912–13), c. 31, § 4. The discrimination against absentee holdings is here very apparent. An additional burden on the non-resident owner is the hail insurance tax. *Cf.* Haig, *op. cit.*, p. 34.

sixty per cent. (4) Improvements were exempted altogether in the rural and local improvement districts in accordance with the law.[1]

In Alberta, also, from an optional levy in towns and villages, the system of land-value taxation progressed, until in 1912 the exemption of improvements was made compulsory throughout the province, except for the cities incorporated under special charters.[2] Of the six cities, Edmonton, Medicine Hat, and Red Deer exempt all improvements, Calgary seventy-five per cent, Lethbridge sixty-six and two-thirds per cent, and Wetaskiwin twenty per cent.[3]

The government of Manitoba has not gone so far in her legislation as to exempt improvements from taxation in the municipalities. Nevertheless, the same tendency is at work. For example, the "Municipal Assessment Act" provides for the assessment of all land in rural municipalities, improved for farming or gardening purposes, on its unimproved value. Thus buildings and residences on farm land are exempt; while improvements on land used for other purposes are taxable. Where lands are improved for the purpose of a local industry other than farming or stock ranching, the improvements may be assessed at not less than one-half of the actual value, if the council so direct.[4] Winnipeg under a special charter taxes improvements at sixty-six and two-thirds per cent. The other three cities in Manitoba undervalue improvements although illegally.[5]

In all four provinces, therefore, the taxation of land value has received attention, and its introduction for local purposes has been furthered by provincial enactment. The system has progressed farthest in the more recently incorporated provinces, Alberta and Saskatchewan, where the exemption of improvements is more or less obligatory.

[1] Haig, *op. cit.*, p. 262.
[2] Alberta (1906), c. 63, Pt. xxxi; (1911–12), c. 3, § 252; c. 2, § 267.
[3] Haig, *op. cit.*, p. 262.
[4] Manitoba, Revised Statutes (1902), c. 117, § 28.
[5] *Cf.* Haig, *op. cit.*, pp. 19–20.

In British Columbia the total exemption of improvements is optional, but the exemption of improvements to fifty per cent of their value is mandatory. The abolition of all other taxes than that on land value is optional, with certain restrictions, in three of the provinces; in Manitoba, however, no provision to that effect has been enacted.

§ 5. In the legislation reviewed in the preceding section, the beginning as well as the development of the movement toward the single tax for local purposes in western Canada is evident. There seems to have been nothing revolutionary about the measures; that there has been a development and an extension of the system, however, cannot be doubted. We may, however, ask, what forces were behind the legislation? In view of the current belief that the Single Taxers were responsible for the introduction of the system in Canada, it is significant to read in the *Single Tax Review* that the man who drew up the plan of taxation in Edmonton, William Short, did not know who Henry George was, nor had ever heard of the Single Tax.[1] Again, in tracing the history of the legislation by the Vancouver Council and by the provincial legislature, Mr. Dicey, a Single Taxer, fails to show the influence of the Single Tax philosophy, except to point out that a few members were followers of George.[2] George had, indeed, visited Canada between the years 1885–90, and before the nineties the Toronto Single Tax Association had been organized.[3] Nevertheless, there is nothing to show that the philosophy of the Single Tax, the principle of land nationalization, had taken root in the young, thriving communities of western Canada, where land is the chief commodity, the chief cause of individual aggrandizement.[4]

[1] *Single Tax Review*, November–December, 1910, p. 48.

[2] *Ibid.*, May–June, 1911, pp. 56 *ff.*

[3] *The Public*, June 2, 1911, p. 511.

[4] The absurdity of attributing the "Single Tax" as administered in western Canada to the Georgian philosophy of the Single Tax becomes apparent, when we imagine what the effect of municipalization of the

The introduction of the tax on land value must be attributed rather to fiscal and economic expediency as shown above.[1] This deduction is corroborated also by the feebleness of the opposition which the legislation everywhere encountered. If the landowners had been hereditary landed proprietors, or if they had been drawing income regularly from tenants in a densely populated country where land has a value more or less stable, their interests would have been opposed to a tax which puts a heavier burden, or in some cases the whole burden on land. In Canada, however, landowners are primarily speculators whose chief interest lies in attracting labor and capital, that is, new settlers. At the same time they are resident landowners, and they prefer to have their improvements exempted. What wonder, then, that they so generally vote to exempt capital, which they are convinced will accumulate more rapidly if untaxed, and to increase the burden of the non-resident landowner? According to a Single Taxer,[2] the legislature of Saskatchewan was unanimously in favor of the bill exempting all improvements from taxation. The Union of Saskatchewan Municipalities in the convention of 1910 passed a resolution favoring the abolition of taxes on improvements.[3] The assessors of some of the municipalities in Alberta, Saskatchewan, and British Columbia unanimously attributed the introduction of the tax to the local fiscal and economic needs, not to any Single Tax propaganda. The following are replies of some assessors as to the causes of the adoption of land-value taxation: [4]

Medicine Hat: "The chief reason for introducing the single tax system . . . was for the encouragement of buildings, it being considered that the taxation of improvements was practically a fine upon improvements."

land, or of a tax on all the value increment of the land, would have on the settlement of the western provinces.

[1] *Supra*, §§ 2, 3.

[2] F. J. Dixon, *The Progress of Land Value Taxation in Canada*, p. 3.

[3] The *Canadian Municipal Journal*, October, 1911, p. 386.

[4] Replies received by the writer in answer to a questionnaire.

Moose Jaw: "That the burden of taxation might be borne by all parties receiving benefits therefrom."

Prince Albert: "The legislature made it optional . . . the Council favored its adoption."

Lethbridge: "First, it was a mistake to penalize those who were willing to build and to operate factories, and to penalize merchants who were willing to carry first class stocks; secondly, it is practically impossible to get an equitable assessment on anything but land values."

Red Deer: "To encourage building."

Edmonton: "Much of the land in centres of population was held by non-residents who made no improvements on it but simply held it for speculative purposes. The people actually living in these centres who were increasing the value of lands by their expenditure of time, energy and money deemed it advisable that the non-resident land-owner whose land was being increased in value by them should pay as much towards the revenue of the Municipality as they did, because these non-residents were reaping large profits on account of increased values which they did very little to bring about."

Alderman Clarke, of Edmonton, speaking before the convention of the Union of Canadian Municipalities,[1] expressed doubt as to the influence of the Single Tax or other economic theory; and said as to the motive of the tax: "I believe the real reason for the adoption of the land tax in Edmonton was that a mere handful of people who actually lived in Edmonton at the time the charter was adopted and therefore controlled the municipal government, owned all the improvements in the city; but outsiders, non-residents, owned large portions of land within the city limits, on which there were no improvements. And the motive for exempting improvements was really a very selfish desire to saddle the non-residents with the greater portion of the taxes, and not a recognition of the

[1] *Canadian Municipal Journal*, October, 1912, p. 388.

justice of the land tax in itself. . . . The agitation which led to the abolishment of the floor space [1] and business tax came almost entirely from the retailers."

Although there was surely an element of self-interest that prompted the adoption of the tax, it was accompanied by that public-spirited interest in a new community which displays itself in collectivistic legislation. In western Canada, indeed, hand in hand with the taxation of land value goes municipal ownership of public utilities.[2] There is an aversion to the granting of franchises to private corporations, and it is the boast of Edmonton that "it owns and operates its street cars, telephones, waterworks, power plant, street paving and sewer building department." [3] And like the operation of public utilities, so the exemption of improvements has been introduced as a matter of public policy.

§ 6. If further proof were needed to show that the system of exempting improvements from taxation was not the outgrowth of the Single Tax propaganda, it would be furnished by the fact that not the slightest agitation exists to make land the sole source of income for Dominion or provincial purposes. On the contrary, the opportunistic character of the system is clear from the fact that land within the municipality is considered the proper source of local revenue only; the fact that the community gives land its value is never lost sight of in these communities.[4]

---

[1] In many Canadian cities the taxation of business property valued on the basis of floor space which the business occupied superseded the personal property tax.

[2] *Canadian Municipal Journal*, October, 1912, p. 390.

[3] From a circular. Calgary likewise owns the street railway system as well as the light and power department, which are a source of profit to the municipality. "The citizens have grown up with a firm belief in municipal ownership, and the results — in the form of good service and handsome profits — justify their belief." *Canadian Municipal Journal*, September, 1911, p. 340.

[4] This principle is illustrated by the demand by North Vancouver that "taxes on land reverting to the Crown on subdivision be paid by the

Moreover, the fact that a few municipalities, and they are very few, have abolished for local purposes all other taxes besides those on land, is no indication that they were dominated by the philosophy of the Single Tax. It is important to point out, moreover, that even within the so-called "Single Tax" communities, other taxes for provincial and Dominion purposes are raised; thus, income and personal property taxes, death duties, customs duties, poll taxes, etc., in so far as they are levied by the provincial or central government, fall on the "Single Tax" municipalities as well.

Although the exemption of improvements from taxation is prevalent throughout all the western provinces and is almost universal throughout Alberta, only a few municipalities have as yet found it expedient to abolish the business, income, or other subsidiary taxes. Licenses continue to be levied even in the cities where the "Single Tax" has been introduced. But since they primarily serve a social rather than a fiscal purpose,[1] the use of licenses is not inconsistent with the purpose of the system, namely, to make land value the chief source of local revenue.

The villages, cities, and other municipalities where land serves as the sole source of public income (license fees excepted) are the following: In Alberta,[2] Edmonton, Medicine Hat, Red Deer; in British Columbia, Vancouver, Victoria, Kelowna, Westminster, Prince Rupert;[3] in Saskatchewan and Alberta, all the rural municipalities. By the Town Act of 1912, the towns in Alberta were obliged to exempt all improvements and to abolish all

government to the municipality." *Cf. Canadian Municipal Journal,* January, 1914, p. 19.

[1] For example, a saloon license or a dog license is issued not for revenue, but for health, morality, or like purposes.

[2] There was an announcement in the *Canadian Municipal Journal,* February, 1914, p. 71, that Lethbridge has postponed the adoption of the Single Tax.

[3] *Cf. Single Tax Review,* November–December, 1910, p. 50.

other forms of taxation than the land tax. The fiscal difficulties which this general enactment occasioned in some of
the towns induced the legislature to amend the Act the
following year. Upon a petition of at least two-thirds of
the members of the council, the Minister was authorized to
grant permission to the council to impose a business tax.
The tax was to be levied according to the rental value of
the business premises, was not to exceed twenty per cent
of the rental, and was to be raised for a period not exceeding three years.[1] In 1914, it is worth noting, this permis-
sive amendment was repealed, and the levy of a business
tax was made optional with the council. A two-thirds vote,
however, is necessary, and the maximum tax shall not
exceed ten per cent of the rental value; nor can the business tax be adopted for a period exceeding four years from
December 31, 1914.[2] It would seem, therefore, that the
business tax enactment is deemed a temporary, and an
emergency measure merely. As only twelve towns out of
the forty-six subject to the Town Act had in 1913 petitioned for permission to levy a business tax, it is probable
that most of the towns derive all the local revenue from
the land tax only.

It is a matter of some interest that the process of elim-
inating other taxes than that on land, and of exempting
improvements was a gradual one.[3] In Vancouver, for
example, from 1895 to 1905, improvements were assessed
at fifty per cent of their value. From 1906 to 1909, the
percentage of value exempted was raised to seventy-five;
only since 1910, therefore, has the whole value of improvements been exempt. Other taxes were gradually abolished
in Vancouver. At present, however, except for the subsidy

[1] Alberta (1913), c. 8, § 13 (1st session).

[2] *Ibid.* (1914), c. 7, § 7.

[3] Exception to this statement must be made in the case of Alberta,
where by a "blanket" enactment of the provincial legislature the system
was suddenly imposed upon the towns. For the evil effects of this measure see the discussion in Haig, *op. cit.*, pp. 129 *ff.*

from the provincial government for hospitals, schools, and similar purposes, the land tax in Vancouver suffices for all local expenditures.[1] In Edmonton, also, the elimination of the other taxes, the poll, business, and floor taxes, was gradual, although since its incorporation (1904) [2] Edmonton has exempted all improvements from taxation.[3] Or take Red Deer for illustration. Before 1912 improvements were assessed at fifty per cent and personal property was taxed. In that year the tax on improvements was entirely removed, and now land constitutes the sole source of revenue. While in all the above-named localities all rates and special assessments [4] are levied on the unimproved value of the land, there are numerous other municipalities which tend to become "Single Tax" communities.[5] That the process of change to the new system in the principal cities of the four provinces is not complete, however, can be seen from the data shown in the table on page 273.

---

[1] The subsidy comes out of the provincial taxes levied in Vancouver on personal property and income (the provincial poll tax of $3 on all males between the ages of eighteen and sixty years was abolished only in 1912). (From a letter by the Assessment Commissioner, H. J. Painter of Vancouver.) The succession duty and corporation and railway taxes are other sources of provincial revenue in British Columbia. *Cf. The Year Book of British Columbia* (1911), pp. 281 *ff.*

[2] *Cf. Ordinances of the Northwest Territories* (1904), c. 19.

[3] *Canadian Municipal Journal*, October, 1912, p. 388. The tax on transient traders, circuses, etc., has been retained "only for the purpose of regulating the holders from the standpoint of health and morality and public safety."

[4] "Special assessments," that is, the building of roads, streets, and sanitary improvements, by taxing the particular landowners whose property is improved, are very general in western Canada. In Medicine Hat, for example, the property-owners paid two-thirds of the cost of the sidewalks on streets (business section), the city one-third of the cost; on the avenues the owners paid one-third, the city two-thirds. *The Canadian Municipal Journal*, May, 1914, p. 199.

[5] *Cf. supra*, p. 270, note 2, for example.

TABLE SHOWING THE SOURCES OF TAX REVENUE IN
THE PRINCIPAL CITIES OF WESTERN CANADA [1]

City	Population (1911)	Per cent of value assessed		Other taxes for local purposes
		Land	Improvements	
British Columbia :				
Vancouver	111,240	100	..	..
Victoria	31,660	100	..	..
Manitoba :				
Winnipeg	136,035	100	66⅔	Business tax [4]
Brandon	13,839	100	50	Business tax [5]
Alberta :				
Edmonton	24,900	100	..	..
Calgary	43,704	100	25	Business tax [6]
Lethbridge	8,050	100	33⅓	Business tax, poll, superassessment tax [7]
Medicine Hat . . .	5,608	100	..	..
Saskatchewan :				
Regina	30,213	100	30	..
Saskatoon	12,004	100	25	..
Moose Jaw	13,823	100	45 [2]	Business, income, and poll taxes
Prince Albert	6,254	100	15 [3]	..

[1] *Compiled from data in Commercial Hand Book of Canada, 5000 Facts About Canada, Canadian Year Book,* and from letters by the assessors of the respective cities.

[2] The assessor of Moose Jaw writes that a reduction of the percentage by fifteen per cent will be made annually until the whole value of the improvements will be exempt.

[3] The reduction of the taxable percentage of improvements since 1911 has been at the rate of fifteen per cent; after 1913 improvements, it was hoped, would be entirely exempt.

[4] The tax is levied on the annual rental value of the premises used for business purposes. The rate is six and two-thirds per cent. Licenses also yield a considerable revenue in Winnipeg.

[5] The business tax in Brandon is based on the annual rental value of business premises; the rate is ten per cent.

[6] In Calgary, the business tax (called personal property tax) is on the basis of the value of the stock. The assessment is made on two-thirds of the average annual amount of stock. *Cf.* Dixon, *The Progress of Land Value Taxation in Canada,* p. 8.

[7] The basis of the business tax in Lethbridge is fifty per cent of the value of the stock. The poll tax is on single men only, who are not otherwise taxable and are over twenty-one years of age. The superassessment is an assessment of twenty-five per cent over and above the actual value of vacant building property.

§ 7. In such small communities as the municipalities of western Canada the system of administration and valuation does not involve many difficulties. First, as regards the administration, the council and mayor are responsible for the proper assessment and collection of the tax. They appoint the assessor or assessors [1] who prepare the assessment roll. To check up their work, the council in many of the municipalities appoints two of its members, who with the assessor constitute the assessment committee. A majority of this committee is sufficient to change the valuation of the assessor. When the roll has been corrected and supervised, notices of the assessment are sent out to the taxpayers. Any person may appeal against the assessment to the court of revision, into which the council resolves itself for the purpose of hearing appeals.[2] From this court further appeal is possible to a judge of the court having jurisdiction in that municipality. The assessments are generally made annually, although the council is empowered to vote to adopt the assessment roll of the preceding year, without undertaking a new valuation.

The law requires that the land and improvements be assessed separately, the former at its actual cash value, the latter at the cost of replacing such improvements at the time of assessment, taking into account the condition of the property, and allowing for any deterioration. In valuing the land, moreover, it is often provided that the location and the purpose for which the land is used or might be used within a reasonable time be considered. In other words, the community influences that affect the value of the land are to be taken into account.[3]

[1] In many cases the secretary-treasurer of the municipality has been appointed assessor. *Cf. The Public Service Monthly*, vol. II, September, 1913, pp. 8, 9.

[2] In British Columbia, the council or five members of the council may sit as the court of revision. One month's notice, by publication in the *Official Gazette* and a newspaper, is given of the sitting of the court of revision. The members of the court form a quorum and a majority of a quorum may decide all questions of appeal. *Year Book of British Columbia* (1911), p. 272.

[3] In the Alberta law it is even stipulated that when the assessed value

The assessors are aided in their work of ascertaining the value of the land by the records of sales, and by comparing the quality of the soil, in case of agricultural land, with an average quarter section taken as a standard, and by considering the location of the land with respect to the highway, railway, and market-places.[1] The land registry system facilitates the valuation. In British Columbia, the right of way, and the improvements thereon, of railway companies are assessed as real property within the municipality.[2] Crown land under preëmption or lease is liable for taxes as if owned.

Such is the law with respect to valuation. In actual practice underassessment frequently occurs. In some places, e.g., Saskatoon,[3] the assessors reported an undervaluation of from ten to twenty per cent. Often this was due to the rapid rise of land value. In the recent ebb tide of values, overassessment was frequent. In the Canadian municipalities, however, where the valuation is for local purposes only, uniformity in assessment is of greater importance than full value assessment.

It has been pointed out that in practice the exemption of improvements in western Canada applies to buildings, fences, trees, and other visible improvements, not to filling, grading, clearing from timber, draining, and irrigation, etc.[4] In many of the Acts, improvements include "any other

is either below or above its actual value, the assessed value shall not be changed upon appeal, if such value bears a "fair and just proportion to the value at which the lands in the immediate vicinity of the land are assessed." Alberta (1906), c. 63, Pt. xxxi, § 5. This clause has recently served an unforeseen purpose in the towns, so that an amendment was necessitated. In the fiscal exigency caused by the institution of the Single Tax, the towns interpreted the above clause as legalizing overvaluation of the land. (See *infra*, § 9.) To prevent such interpretation, this amendment was adopted in 1914, "that in no case shall an obviously excessive assessment be maintained." Alberta (1914), c. 7, § 5.

[1] *Cf. The Public Service Monthly* (Sask.), vol. ii, September, 1913, p. 9.
[2] *The Year Book of British Columbia* (1911), p. 273.
[3] Haig, *op. cit.*, p. 59.
[4] Bullock, in New York *Evening Post*, June 27, 1914.

increase in value (of the land) caused by any other expenditure of labor or capital thereon." Cases do occur of land whose value after clearing has fallen below the cost of clearing and improvement. It is recognized, however, that only so much of the cost of the improvement can be exempted as remains unexhausted at the time of valuation.[1] Whether the rule is theoretically valid or not, valuers have found it practicable.

A less common method of assessment exists in Medicine Hat. Under the Act of Incorporation, the council was empowered to set apart certain sections of the land to be known as improvement districts.[2] Within these districts, land which is not being utilized as the demands of the vicinity require, that is, unimproved land, may be subject to a superassessment. The council, in case it decides to levy such a superassessment tax, determines the proportion of overvaluation, which is, however, in no case to exceed fifty per cent of the actual value. For example, owner A has a parcel of land valued at $500 which is unimproved. The assessor, by a vote of the council enacting a superassessment of twenty-five per cent above the value of the land, enters A's land on the roll at $625. The purpose of this provision is clearly to encourage improvement and to subject the absentee holder to a greater burden of taxation.[3] Lethbridge also has had such a tax for many years. In 1913, the superassessment was twenty-five per cent above the value of the land.

When the assessment roll has been completed, the council fixes the rate of tax. The general rate, when levied on

[1] So in Australasia. *Cf. supra*, chapter III, § 4. *Cf.* also *Report of the Royal Commission on Taxation of British Columbia* (1911), p. B 25.

[2] Alberta (1906), c. 63, Pt. XXXI, § 5.

[3] The tax assessor of Lethbridge writes: "Some years ago it was noticed that a very large proportion of vacant property in the city was held by outside speculators, and the council at that time obtained permission from the Legislature to put a clause in the city charter allowing them to superassess this vacant land within a certain limit of the improved area to the extent of fifty per cent." From a letter to the writer.

land only is usually not to exceed two per cent of the assessed value. When improvements are taxed, the maximum rate is in most cases one per cent. In British Columbia where improvements are not taxed above fifty per cent of their value, the general rate may not exceed one and one-half per cent. Besides the general rate, school, park, library, hospital, health, and other special rates are leviable. A tax for paying the interest on the municipal debt may also be raised. Local improvement rates and those special rates to be expended for improvements benefiting particular areas in the municipality are raised by special assessments, that is, the cost of such improvements is charged to the particular property benefited. The principle of "special assessment" is in accord with that of land-value taxation and is well recognized in the systems of taxation throughout Canada.[1] A rebate is allowed for the prompt payment of the tax. In case of delinquency in payment interest is charged, and if the tax is not paid usually within three months of the date of notice, lands are liable for sale.[2] Lands sold for delinquent taxes may be redeemed within one year from the day of sale on payment of the amount for which the land was sold plus interest.[3]

§ 8. By far the most important fiscal consideration which the system of taxing land value presents is the adequacy or productiveness of the tax for all local expenditure. That the real estate tax constitutes an elastic source of revenue is well established. By mere regulation of the rate of tax, the required revenue can be obtained. The aim in taxation is, of course, to keep the rate of tax as low as possible. When, however, improvements are exempted from taxation, and when the land has been assessed at its full value, the rate of tax must be increased to yield the same sum of revenue as before. This increase in rate of tax is

---

[1] See *supra*, p. 272, note 4.
[2] *Cf.* British Columbia (1911), c. 170, § 278.
[3] *Cf. Year Book of British Columbia* (1911), p. 272.

obviated only under one condition, namely, when the value of the land has appreciated. An illustration will make this clear. Suppose the assessed value of the land in a municipality is $200,000, that of the improvements $50,000. To obtain a revenue of $5000, the rate of tax on real estate will be twenty mills. The following year let the improvements be exempt from taxation, and the tax rate will have to be twenty-five mills, unless in the mean time the value of the *land* has appreciated to $250,000. This was indeed the secret of the fiscal success of this system of taxation in the western provinces before the business depression that set in in 1913. Here the land actually tended to appreciate more rapidly than the expenditure of the municipalities, so that the rate of tax did not need to be raised inordinately when improvements were untaxed. Another noteworthy advantage that rendered this system of taxation more expedient in the western than in the eastern and other densely populated cities, was that in those newer communities the value of the improvements tended neither to increase so rapidly as the land nor to equal the value of the land as in older cities. For example, compare the assessed value of property in Vancouver and Calgary with that in Toronto and Montreal: [1]

ASSESSED VALUE OF PROPERTY IN 1912

	Land	Per cent of total assessment	Improvements	Per cent of total assessment
Vancouver...	$138,557,595	72.2	$53,515,295	27.8
Montreal....	377,670,560	59.2	260,351,065	40.8
Toronto.....	147,668,179	50.6	144,131,416	49.4
Calgary	102,260,915	83.0	20,813,620	16.9

[1] *Financial and Departmental Reports,* Vancouver, B.C. (1912), p. 60; *Report of Assessment Department,* City of Montreal (1912), p. 4; *Manual of Calgary; Report on Taxation of Improvements by Assessment Commissioner of Toronto* (1912), p. 11.

By exempting improvements, therefore, the added burden of taxation on land, *ceteris paribus*, would be considerably heavier [1] in the eastern than in the western cities.

The distribution of burden on the individual owners under the system of taxing land value, however, is quite another proposition. Clearly, if the rate of tax must be doubled, land with no improvements will be taxed most, land with improvements of the same value as the site will pay the same amount of taxes, while the owner of land whose value falls short of the value of the improvements will pay less than under the realty tax. The shift of burden which the exemption of improvements occasions is apparent from the following assumed cases: A, B, C, D, etc., are owners of parcels of real estate, the respective values of which and the amount of taxes payable under the different systems and rates of taxation are set forth and computed in the following table: —

Assessed value		Realty tax when	Land-value tax when	
		Rate of tax is 15 mills	Rate is 30 mills	Rate is 20 mills
A	{ Land............$15,000 } { Building......... 15,000 }	$450	$450	$300
B	{ Land............ 15,000 } { Building......... 5,000 }	300	450	300
C	{ Land............ 15,000 } { ——— .... (vacant) }	225	450	300
D	{ Land............ 15,000 } { Building......... 20,000 }	525	450	300

The above table shows the incidence of the tax under various circumstances. Assuming (1) that the same

[1] It is very significant, however, that even in an old city such as Montreal, the value of improvements does not equal the value of the land. Indeed, the assessment of 1913 shows an increase of $125,259,245 in the value of the land, and an increase of only $28,532,375 in the improvements. *Cf. Report of Assessment Department,* City of Montreal (1913), p. 4.

amount of revenue must be raised after the institution of the tax on land value as before, and (2) that the value of the improvements in the community just equals that of the land, then the new rate of tax will be thirty mills instead of fifteen mills as shown in columns 2 and 3. How will the change in the system of taxation affect the amount of taxes payable by the four proprietors A, B, C, D, each of whom owns tracts of land of the assumed value of $15,000, but under various conditions of improvement? From the table (columns 2 and 3) it will readily be seen that D whose land is best utilized will alone profit by the change from the realty to the land-value tax. His tax bill will be $75 less than before; A will be liable for the same amount; while B and C whose land is kept in a comparatively undeveloped condition will be more heavily burdened than before.

Suppose, again, that instead of being equal to the value of the land, the value of improvements in the municipality is one-third that of the land, as is the case in many of the western Canadian municipalities. Then a rate of twenty mills will suffice to yield the same revenue as before the institution of the system. The incidence of the burden in that case is illustrated in column 4. Both A and D will pay less; B will pay the same; while C will again be subjected to a higher tax. In other words, the tax on land value favors the owner of the more highly improved land as compared with the owner of the less improved land; and the less the increase in rate occasioned by the change of system, the greater, of course, is the relief to the owner of improved property.

As a matter of fact, the Canadian municipalities were unusually circumstanced in that the adoption of the tax on land value did not necessitate a great increase, if any, in the rate of tax, even in spite of the growing budgets. The reason for this is the important fact that land tended to appreciate so rapidly in value in those communities. The truth of this assertion is made evident from the following table: —

TABLE SHOWING INCREASE IN THE ASSESSED VALUE OF REAL PROPERTY IN CERTAIN SMALL COMMUNITIES, 1912–1913 [1]

Locality	Assessed value of property	Increase over preceding year
Port Coquitlam, B.C..................	$6,449,887	$1,449,887
North Battleford, Sask.[2]..............	10,034,137	4,454,740
Portage La Prairie, Man...............	4,473,612	365,267
Medicine Hat, Alta.[3]..................	20,393,950	13,381,365
Moose Jaw, Sask.[4].....................	51,997,286	8,331,988 [4]
Orillia, Ont..........................	3,429,080	500,000
Milden, Sask..........................	146,000	54,000
Bassano, Alta.[5]	1,675,360	243,290 [5]
Point Grey, B.C......................	19,911,318 [6]	5,266,730
Saskatoon, Sask......................	54,463,930	18,992,515 [7]
Broadview, Sask......................	604,094	132,421
Canora, Sask.	2,081,600	1,155,950

[1] Data collected from the "Financial Notes" columns of the *Canadian Municipal Journal* (1910, 1911, 1912, 1913), and from official letters to the writer. The accuracy of some of the above figures cannot be vouched for as they are not all official.

[2] North Battleford will introduce the tax on land value as the sole source of local revenue within two years. (*Canadian Municipal Journal*, September, 1913, p. 373.)

[3] The assessment is on land only.

[4] The assessment in Moose Jaw in 1914 fell below that of 1913, the total gross assessment being $50,651,090. Figures taken from a letter by the City Assessor.

[5] ASSESSMENT AND TAXATION OF TOWN OF BASSANO AND BASSANO SCHOOL DISTRICT FOR THE YEARS 1910 TO 1914

	1910	1911	1912	1913	1914
Assessed valuation in town municipalities.........	$293,325	$478,736	$1,432,070	$1,675,360	$1,750,435
Assessed valuation in school district	Not formed	478,736	1,432,070	3,169,760	3,373,811
Municipal rate, mills............	10	15	13	16½	18½
School rate, mills..	Not formed	15	7	2½	½

[6] The assessment is on land only.

[7] The appreciation in the value of land in Saskatoon is shown below: —

Year	Assessment on land	Tax rate (mills)
1910.............................	$8,639,760	21
1911.............................	21,525,758	18
1912.............................	35,471,415	18
1913.............................	54,463,930	18
1914.............................	54,461,350	17$\frac{1}{10}$

(Data furnished the writer by the City Assessor.)

What is thus characteristic of these smaller communities is even more strikingly characteristic of the larger cities, Edmonton, Calgary, Vancouver, and Winnipeg, as shown in the tables on the opposite page.

In spite of the growth of the towns, therefore, and of the increased expenditure which this growth necessitates, the rate of tax has not had to be increased in many cases. In many cases the rate has even been reduced, while in many more it has had to be increased but slightly.[1]

A few examples of the rate of tax in some of the cities in western Canada are shown below:[2]

Municipality	1910 (mills)	1911 (mills)	1912 (mills)	1913 (mills)
Vancouver	20	20	20	20
Edmonton	17	13.7	12	16
Calgary	15	14.5	12.5	18.75
Winnipeg	10.8	13.25	12	13
Kelowna	..	23.5	15	17.6
Prince Albert	15.26	13.33	13	11
Medicine Hat	14	11	16.5	15
Bassano:				
Municipal rate	10	15	13	16.5
School rate	..	15	7	2.5
Saskatoon	21	18	18	18
Regina	18	18.1	15.88	14
Victoria	26.25	24	21	20

The significance of the above table may be summarized thus: First, in 1913, even though the depression had set in, the maximum rate of tax did not exceed two per cent. Secondly, in five of the cities the rate was either reduced or

[1] This enormous appreciation in land value from year to year is not only responsible for the abolition of other taxes in the municipalities, but also for the excessive indebtedness incurred by the western towns because a surplus revenue leads to extravagance in public expenditure. Thus while public improvements tend to enhance the value of land, so the latter in turn becomes itself the cause of the public outlays for improvement.

[2] Data gathered from various sources, chiefly, however, from the replies to the questionnaire.

TABLE SHOWING INCREASE IN THE VALUE OF TAXABLE
PROPERTY IN CALGARY, EDMONTON, AND WINNIPEG [1]

Year	Assessed value of taxable property		
	Calgary	Edmonton	Winnipeg
1901......	$2,307,040	$1,395,912	$26,405,770
1902......	2,383,325	1,724,420	28,615,810
1903......	3,221,549	3,208,100	36,273,400
1904......	4,099,437	3,959,648	48,214,950
1905......	5,433,469	6,620,985	62,727,630
1906......	7,771,921	17,046,798	80,511,725
1907......	12,832,496	21,985,700	93,825,960
1908......	17,941,698	22,535,210	116,106,390
1909......	19,824,978	25,584,990	107,997,320
1910......	30,796,092	30,105,110	157,608,220
1911......	52,747,600	46,494,740	172,677,250
1912......	112,559,400	123,475,070*	214,360,440

* This enormous increase of nearly 200 per cent in assessable value is in part due to the
annexation to Edmonton in 1912 of the suburban town, Strathcona.

TABLE SHOWING THE PHENOMENAL GROWTH OF VAN-
COUVER IN POPULATION AND IN VALUE OF ITS LAND
AND IMPROVEMENTS [2]

Year	Population	Per cent of increase	Assessed value of land	Per cent of increase	Assessed value of improvements	Per cent of increase
1887	5,000	..	$2,456,842	..	$182,235	..
1891	13,685	174	10,477,420	326	1,501,665	724
1895	17,862	31	13,829,724	32	4,317,660	187
1899	24,000	35	12,705,099	decrease	5,011,190	16
1903	34,484	44	13,845,565	9	9,091,270	81
1907	60,100	74	38,346,335	177	16,381,475	80
1911	111,240	85	98,720,345	158	37,858,660	131
1912	122,100	9	138,557,545	43	53,515,295	41

[1] For Calgary, cf. Annual Report of City of Calgary, Alta. (1912), p. 10;
for Edmonton, City of Edmonton, Ninth Annual Report, Financial and
Departmental, p. 365; Winnipeg, Municipal Manual (1913), p. 137.
[2] Corporation of the City of Vancouver, B.C., Financial and Departmental
Reports (1912).

remained the same throughout the four years' period; in the other six municipalities only a slight increase, or slight fluctuation, in rate is noticeable. Thirdly, in the five cities relying on the land as the sole source of revenue, the maximum rate of tax was twenty mills, the minimum fifteen mills. Kelowna required a rate of fifteen mills when improvements were taxable, a rate of seventeen and three-fifths when improvements were exempt. The fact that in Vancouver, since 1906, the rate of tax continued to be twenty mills shows that the complete untaxing of improvements which was instituted in 1910 did not occasion an increase in rate. Where the value of land rises so enormously as to obviate an increase in rate of tax, the substitution of the tax on the unimproved value of the land for that on realty will not only relieve the owner of improved land, but will add only slightly, if at all, to the burden of unimproved land.

§ 9. Before the recent industrial crisis set in it would have been possible to say that the adoption of the tax on land value, even as a single tax, was highly expedient in western Canada, from the standpoint of both elasticity and productiveness. In fact, under the conditions discussed, elasticity is not an unmixed good. The unwillingness to reduce the tax rate leads to extravagance in expenditure. The tax, however, is self-sufficient, where, as in the municipalities of western Canada, the value of the land is an ever-increasing source of revenue. And it is for this reason that the other taxes, such as burden industry or labor can be dispensed with.

The results of the industrial depression have been seized upon by the adversaries of the Single Tax. We are in this section concerned only with the fiscal aspect of the land tax. What, then, has been the effect of the present "slump" in land value on the municipal tax system? [1]

---

[1] My conclusions are drawn particularly from Dr. Haig's study. The investigation was made on the spot, in 1914, during the depression. And in the first part of his book he has put the results of the study in a form which makes it in a sense source material.

To appreciate the industrial situation in western Canada, the abnormally speculative values of land before 1913 must be called to mind. Also the fact that the stagnant condition of the realty market left many realty operators with a large number of holdings on their hands, land yielding no income, yet on which taxes had to be paid. "The economic condition of Saskatoon is much more serious than the people realize. They expect the present depression to be relieved very soon; but relief will not come for many years. The fundamental richness of the country cannot be denied; but the values of the city real estate anticipate the far distant future. The distant future will take care of itself very nicely; the immediate present is another question. Many men who counted themselves rich two years ago and who did not get rid of their real estate are in real distress. An acquaintance who owns a half section laid out in lots within the city limits confided that he was greatly worried about his grocery bill. With taxes due on a piece of land assessed at $20,000, 'I, myself, do not know where in the world to get the money to pay them with.' The heavy land tax makes it difficult to carry vacant land. Every one feels it. Up to this time people have paid absolutely no attention to taxes; they have been an unimportant detail. People paid them cheerfully. There has been no public discussion about them and they have not entered into calculations. Now, for the first time, attention is being called to them. It is foolish to say that land has not depreciated in value. The bottom has entirely fallen out of the market. No prices are being quoted," etc.[1] Or, "Edmonton has not been so hard hit as other cities by the present depression. There is more building going on there than in other places. Most of the distress is being experienced by people who are loaded up with vacant property which is not good security for loans. Many people bought up the land at high prices expecting to pay but one install-

[1] Haig, *op. cit.*, p. 69.

ment and to sell at an advance before further payments became due. With the bottom out of the real estate market such people are finding difficulty in paying interest, the second installment and the taxes on their property. The Hudson's Bay Company is experiencing difficulty in its attempt to collect the second installments on the land sold in their great sale a few years ago. Many persons would gladly sacrifice their first payment if the company would take the lands off their hands; but this the company refuses to do. Some of the property in town has a value which is greatly inflated. Many of the subdivisions will doubtless decrease enormously in nominal value in the near future." [1] In Calgary also, in spite of the speculation promoted by the discovery of petroleum in 1913, the realty market has been inactive.[2]

Nevertheless, admitting the hardships created by the heavy taxation of land, especially to the owners of vacant property, the fiscal effects have not been serious.[3] In Calgary, for example, the fact of business depression is established by the decline in bank clearings from 275 millions in 1912, to 247 millions in 1913, and to 201 millions in 1914. At the same time the total tax base increased from 111 millions in 1912, to 133 millions in 1913, and to nearly 135 millions in 1914; while the total rate of tax had to be increased from 12.5 mills to 18.75 and to 20.75 mills during the same period. But this increase in rate loses significance when we consider that 12.5 mills levied in 1912 was the lowest rate since 1895, and that the rate of tax was 22 mills during 1904–06 and 21.5 mills in 1909. Moreover, the receipts from the property tax were nearly twice as great in 1913 as in 1912.[4] In Saskatoon, likewise, the net assessment (including business and income) increased from 36.8

---

[1] Haig, op. cit., pp. 105, 106, 118.   [2] Ibid., p. 110.

[3] It is necessary to point out that in New York City the realty tax has had similar serious effects during the recent depreciation in land value, and has given rise to widespread discontent with the present tax system.

[4] Ibid., pp. 111, 117.

millions in 1912 to 56.2 millions in 1913 and to 56.6 millions in 1914; the tax rate was reduced from 19.5 mills in 1912 to 18.4 mills in 1913 and to 17.55 mills in 1914; while the tax levies were as follows: $666,812, $1,014,667, and $993,037 in the three years, respectively.[1]

Turning to the three largest "Single Tax" municipalities, we find the fiscal conditions were somewhat less favorable, as appears from the subjoined table.[2] Yet only in

	Vancouver	Edmonton	Victoria
Taxable value:			
1912.............	$138,557,595	$123,475,070	$71,670,770
1913.............	144,974,525	188,539,110	89,130,150
1914.............	150,456,660	191,283,970	89,151,990
Tax rates:			
1912.............	20 mills	12 mills	21 mills
1913.............	20 "	16 "	20 "
1914.............	22 "	17.5 "	22.35 "
Tax levies:			
1912.............	$3,078,749	$1,530,205	$1,313,248*
1913.............	3,217,466	3,471,444	1,466,797*
1914.............	3,677,160	3,769,970	

* Receipts yielded by the land tax and constituting about half of the total budget. The frontage and special assessment taxes almost equaled the yield of the land tax in 1913. See Haig, *op. cit.*, pp. 225, 229–31.

Vancouver did the tax rate reach the high water mark for that city. In both Edmonton and Victoria higher rates had been levied in preceding years. The tax rate for Edmonton was 21.5 mills in 1901, for Victoria, in 1909, it was 26.5 mills. There are, however, other fiscal data to offset this favorable showing. Thus, in 1913, the first time in many years, the budget account of Vancouver showed a deficit of $223,956. In Edmonton, also, there was an excess in deficit in the general fund over 1912 by about $30,000.[3] Again, the arrears in payment of taxes have grown since 1913 to an alarming extent in some of the com-

[1] Haig, *op. cit.*, pp. 58–60.   [2] *Ibid.*, pp. 92–93; 190–95.
[3] *Ibid.*, pp. 88, 180–81.

munities, reflecting the general depression in land value.[1] Furthermore, the increase in the number of appeals against assessments and the greater value of the assessed property in 1913 and 1914 indicate an overvaluation of the land.[2] Overassessment is not an unusual occurrence in a time of transition and readjustment of values. The business depression, moreover, interfered with the contemplated public improvements and made retrenchment necessary in many communities.[3] Nevertheless, if we discount the fiscal stringency, which, we must not overlook, prevailed also in other Canadian and in American cities during the same time, the land-value tax, not as the *single tax*, however, seems to have stood the test even in a period of declining values. Nor must it be overlooked that whatever complaints may have been voiced and demands made to extend the tax base, no municipal council, nor provincial legislature, has thus far been induced by necessity to abandon the system of exempting improvements.[4]

[1] *Cf.* Haig, *op. cit.*, p. 94. Sales of property for taxes, although unpopular, were declared very generally throughout the western provinces during 1914 and 1915. The lax enforcement of law in British Columbia which permits the taxpayer to be in arrears several years before he can lose his property has been blamed for the excessive arrears recently. It was found that the redemption of properties sold for taxes in 1914 proceeded fairly and that only a small percentage was likely to be forfeited in British Columbia. At a tax sale held in North Vancouver in 1914, 276 parcels were offered for sale. Of this number all but 38 parcels were redeemed at the close of the redemption period of one year. The unredeemed parcels were worth four per cent of the total arrears, and among them were several bad titles. Again it was reported that while bidding at the sales in British Columbia was brisk on good residential property, business property in most cases fell to the municipality. *Canadian Municipal Journal* (1915), pp. 132, 240, 352, 388, 313.

[2] *Cf.* Wade, *Single Tax in Western Canada*, in *National Tax Association Proceedings* (1914), p. 428. In British Columbia, in 1915, a reduction of about fifty per cent was made in the undeveloped districts. *Cf. Canadian Municipal Journal* (1915), p. 436; also p. 313.

[3] *Cf. Ibid.*, pp. 53, 437.

[4] The fact that the Union of Alberta Municipalities in 1912 and 1913 refused to vote for the repeal of the system of land-value taxation is likewise good evidence of the expediency of the tax. *Cf.* Haig, *op. cit.*, pp. 80, 84.

The experience with the Alberta Town Act of 1912, however, proves convincingly the inexpediency of instituting the new system during a period of falling land value, or of introducing it too suddenly in static, unprogressive communities.[1] Enough has been said about the economic conditions under which the land tax can be instituted successfully to make explicable the embarrassment of the towns in Alberta when the provincial enactment was passed providing for the taxation of land value to the exclusion of all other taxes for local purposes. Of the forty-six towns affected by the legislation only one had as large a population as 3,000. In some of these local bodies the change was made without fiscal stress; in the majority of cases, however, the untaxing of buildings and the exempting of personalty necessitated a considerable increase in the tax rate. In some of the towns the tax rate had to be raised about one hundred per cent or more. For example, in Ponoka, the rate was more than doubled, from eighteen mills in 1911 to forty-five and five-tenths mills the following year; in Leduc the advance was from twenty to forty-two mills. Local conditions in these cases and in others aggravated the financial stringency that ensued.[2] Illegal means, such as overassessment, excessive frontage taxes, other special assessments, etc., had to be resorted to in order to raise the requisite revenue. In fact, the amendments to the Act in 1913, providing for a frontage tax, not to exceed ten cents per foot of frontage, and a business tax[3] are evidence of the impracticability of a general enactment which disregards the differences in local conditions and local needs. In passing judgment upon this instructive experience in Alberta, it must not be forgotten that the change involved more than the untaxing of buildings, and that the latter is yet in force in the towns.

[1] For an excellent and detailed account of the effects of this legislation see Haig, *op. cit.*, pp. 129 *ff.*

[2] In some towns, the exemption of the land owned by the railway companies was the cause of the narrow tax base. *Cf. ibid.*, p. 142.

[3] Alberta (1913), c. 8, § 13 (1st sess.); c. 22, § 14 (2d sess.).

§ 10. Granted that the fiscal adequacy of the land tax in western Canada has been established, its expediency must be tested further by the criterion of incidence. Without attempting to discuss the justice of the distribution of burden, it is necessary to point out and examine certain data widely employed to show: (1) that under the system of local taxation in western Canada a small percentage of the population, the landowners, bear the whole burden of the local budgetary requirements; [1] (2) that the untaxing of buildings shifts the burden from the more fortunate owner of the skyscraper to the owner of vacant property; (3) that the rich owner therefore profits at the expense of the poor home-owner; and (4) that the system favors the rich landlord also in that he is exempted from more taxes proportionately than the landless resident. [2]

Briefly, the first point made above is directed against the *Single Tax* feature of the system with which we are not here concerned. Whether improvements are taxed or untaxed, the number of taxpayers in a community, where, in the main, house and lot are owned by the same person, will remain practically the same. It is significant, nevertheless, that the percentage of property owners in the western municipalities is notably high. In Regina, for example, about sixty-five per cent of the houses are inhabited by the owners, in Vancouver and Saskatoon about sixty per cent, in Edmonton from sixty to sixty-five per cent, in Calgary about sixty-six per cent. [3] And since many of the tenant

[1] Wade, *Experiments with the Single Tax in Western Canada*, pp. 12, 16. "But under the so-called Single Tax only one citizen in five (in Vancouver) pays for the civic upkeep, while four in five escape the burden altogether. Twenty-two thousand pay the way for 114,200, and 92,000 comfortably escape all responsibility." The basis for Wade's comparison is surely incorrect. Had he compared the number of taxpayers with the number of voters, instead of with the total population, the ratio would have been more faithful to the facts.

[2] "In other words, about seventeen-eighteenths of the exemption is in favor of the wealthier classes, and one-eighteenth in favor of those not so well provided." Wade, *The Single Tax Failure in Vancouver*, pp. 5–6.

[3] Haig, *op. cit.*, pp. 63, 100.

occupiers may own unimproved or other property in the town the percentage of taxpayers even exceeds the high percentage of home-owners. With regard to the second contention raised, the untaxing of buildings did shift the burden of the tax from the owner of the skyscraper to the owner of vacant property. But that was exactly the purpose of the change. It was intended to make the owner of unimproved land contribute a larger quota to the local revenue, either because such owner was often a non-resident, pocketing the value increment of the land, or was a resident speculator. The latter, indeed, convinced of the beneficent effects of the system on the community, which would be reflected in the rapidly rising land values, was himself responsible for the institution of land-value taxation. As a matter of fact, in times of rising values, the speculator was affected only slightly by the added burden.

The charge that the exemption of improvements imposes a greater burden on the home-owner than under the realty tax can apply only to owners of buildings the value of which falls below the average ratio prevailing between the value of the improvements and that of the site. Where that ratio is about thirty per cent or less as in the western towns, very few resident owners have been adversely affected by the change. In fact, we have seen that in very many cases, the untaxing of buildings did not even necessitate a higher tax rate. Finally, the charge that the exemption of the wealthier class from taxation is relatively greater than that of the working class loses weight when we reflect that (1) under the Single Tax system the landless workman escapes all local taxes, and that (2) the relief from taxation afforded to owners of business premises and buildings was expected to revert indirectly to the community in the form of social and economic benefits. This leads us to inquire what the economic effects have been.

§ 11. In venturing to trace in social phenomena the effects of a tax, the general principle must not be lost sight of, namely, that numerous forces are at work in society, and that social phenomena are the resultant of the interplay of a variety of causes. This was pointed out in the case of the Australasian taxes. Indeed, so similar are the conditions in both countries, that the conclusions with regard to the social and economic effects of the tax in Australasia hold true in the case of the Canadian system. So remarkable has been the development of the towns, so great the influx of population, so favorable the industrial opportunities, so rich the natural resources, that the influences of the tax on land value, whether salutary or otherwise, have been scarcely noticeable or traceable.

Nevertheless, it is generally admitted even by the opponents of the system[1] that the exemption of improvements has given an impetus to building operations in western Canada. In the provinces this opinion is especially general; and the prodigious increase in building operations in recent years, especially in the localities where all improvements are exempt, is attributed in part to this cause.[2] A few examples showing the great expenditures made for building purposes, although not necessarily evidence of the influence of the tax system, will disclose the general situation of prosperity and rapid development of the western communities before the depression which began in 1913.

While the real cause of this unmistakable trend in building operations lies in the enormous increase in population, it is the costliness of the structures, not the number, that may reflect the influence of the exemption of improvements from taxation. Take Saskatoon, for example. In 1911, the population was about 12,000; yet the amount expended on

[1] *Cf.* Bullock, "Single Tax in Vancouver," in the New York *Evening Post*, June 27, 1914. Also Wade, *The Single Tax Failure in Vancouver*, p. 13.

[2] Letters received by the writer from Medicine Hat, Moose Jaw, Prince Albert; see *Single Tax Review*, May–June, 1911, pp. 10 *ff.*, on effect of the tax on the building trade in Vancouver, and for Edmonton, see *ibid.*, November–December, 1910, p. 48.

TABLE SHOWING THE COST OF NEW BUILDINGS IN CERTAIN PROGRESSIVE TOWNS IN WESTERN CANADA [1]

Year	Vancouver	Edmonton	Winnipeg	Calgary	Saskatoon	Victoria
1907....	$5,632,744	$2,280,210	$6,309,950	$2,094,264	$377,211	$1,490,250
1908....	5,950,893	2,549,847	5,513,700	1,004,520	115,625	1,314,240
1909....	7,258,565	2,128,166	9,226,325	2,420,450	1,002,055	1,773,420
1910....	13,150,365	2,159,106	15,116,450	5,589,594	2,817,771	2,373,045
1911....	17,652,642	3,672,260	17,550,400	12,907,638	5,028,366	4,126,315
1912....	19,388,322	14,446,819	20,563,750	20,394,220	7,640,530	10,666,206
1913....	10,424,197	9,242,450	18,593,350	8,619,653	2,553,885	4,037,092

buildings in five years, 1907–11, was over nine million dollars.[2] But especially noteworthy are the enormous sums expended on new structures during 1911–12, over $12,600,-000! These were years when the reduction was made in the assessment on improvements. But that this reduction was not alone responsible for the building activity is clear, for the activity slackened considerably in 1913 in spite of a further ten per cent reduction on the assessment of improvements.[3] The rapid development of Saskatoon is borne out also by the following quotation:[4] "The city, although only ten years of age, has gotten past the shanty stage. Brick, stone, concrete, steel are the materials used in the construction of its houses." In Vancouver, in 1910, the first year under complete land-value taxation, the increase in the number of building permits was about ten

[1] Vancouver's Financial and Departmental Reports (1912); Winnipeg's Municipal Manual (1913); Annual Report of Calgary (1912); British Columbia Year Book (1911), p. 322; Canadian Municipal Journal, July 1913, p. 252 et passim; Eighth Annual Report of the Department of Agriculture of the Province of Saskatchewan (1912), p. 135.

[2] In 1912, the population had more than doubled, 27,527 persons, and there were 1783 permits granted for new buildings. It is noteworthy that in all the municipalities of Saskatchewan, in 1912, the total value of the new buildings was $33,270,781, as compared with $17,857,308 in 1911. Eighth Annual Report of the Department of Agriculture of the Province of Saskatchewan (1912), p. 135.

[3] By that time the business depression had set in and may have been a counteracting influence in the situation. Cf. Haig, op. cit., p. 270.

[4] Canadian Municipal Journal, December, 1913, p. 484.

per cent, the growth in the value of building operations was about eighty-one per cent. The high *per capita* value of new buildings in 1912, the crest of the flush period, is shown in the subjoined table: [1]

TABLE SHOWING THE RELATION OF BUILDING OPERA- TIONS TO POPULATION AND TO IMPROVEMENT EX- EMPTION IN 1912

Municipality	Population	Value of new buildings	Taxable per- centage of improvements	Value of new buildings per capita
Vancouver.....	122,100	$19,388,322	..	$158.8
Edmonton.....	53,383	14,446,819	..	270.6
Winnipeg......	166,553	20,563,750	66⅔	123.4
Calgary	70,000	20,394,220	25	291.3
Saskatoon	27,527	7,640,530	..	277.5
Victoria	65,000	10,666,206	..	164.0

It is perhaps safe to attribute the stimulus to building, in part at least, to the exemption of improvements. What is to be said, however, of the desirability of such an effect? Statistics of the number of vacant dwellings in the western cities are not available. Nevertheless, we may agree with an authority that "Vancouver is badly over- built." [2] About the condition in the other municipalities data are lacking. Now, on the part of the building operator [3] excessive overbuilding cannot be continued indefinitely.

[1] That other factors entered in as well as the exemption of improve- ments is seen in the wonderful progress of Calgary, where although im- provements are liable to taxation to twenty-five per cent of their value, and although the population was only slightly more than half that of Van- couver, the value of its buildings exceeded by one million dollars that in Vancouver.

[2] Haig, *op. cit.*, p. 204.

[3] In western Canada the builder is usually not the speculator, as in German cities, operating except, for a small margin, with borrowed capi- tal. Loans on real estate are conservatively financed in the western provinces. *Cf. ibid.*, p. 274.

It is comprehensible how during a period of expansion the expectancy of a larger influx of immigrants, together with the relief from taxation, could induce an overproduction of structures, but as in all forms of overspeculation the collapse must follow.

From the standpoint of the tenant, on the other hand, even in Vancouver the large supply of vacant houses [1] did not prevent exorbitant rentals during the boom; nor an inordinate decline in rents during the depression. The movement of rents, indeed, must be explained on other grounds than the overstimulation of building. With the daily influx of new settlers seeking dwellings, and with speculation in property rife, the tendency for rents to increase is easily explained. [2] The opposite tendency ensued with the advent of stagnancy in the land market and with the exodus of people seeking employment elsewhere. In so far, then, as other causes operated, the tax on land value at the rates levied was ineffective in determining rents and the market price of the land. The determination of the incidence of the tax is likewise impossible, for in a time of fluctuating, inflated land value the tenant probably pays part of the artificially screwed-up value, including the tax. In a period of declining values, on the other hand, the owner is in the weaker position and is less likely to shift the tax.

Again, whether the impetus to building is to be judged salutary or deleterious will depend on the kind of construction promoted. Was the erection of residence houses

---

[1] There has been a decrease in the population of Vancouver since 1913. The number fell from 122,000 in 1912, to 114,220 in 1913, and to 106,110 in 1914. It may, therefore, be that Dr. Haig's statement and Mr. Wade's statistics of overbuilding do not apply to 1912 at all. *Cf.* Haig, *op. cit.*, pp. 204, 208.

[2] Statistics gathered from the three principal cities of Saskatchewan show an increase in the rent for an ordinary furnished room in a private house from $10 in 1910 to $12 and $14 per month in 1912. *Cf. Eighth Annual Report of the Department of Agriculture* (Sask., 1912), p. 161.

stimulated, or of tenements? And how was the general condition of congestion affected? In Vancouver there were constructed, in 1912, 217 apartment houses with a value of over six millions, and 2226 dwelling-houses costing over three millions; in the same year in Victoria were erected 1312 one- to two-story dwellings, exclusive of brick or concrete buildings, and 32 apartment houses.[1] Even without available data for comparison, the large number of new dwelling-houses in a single year would lead one to think that the incentive to residence building was no less than to apartment construction. Some evidence was quoted, e.g., the subdivision of lots, and the reduction in the number of purchasers of lots for garden and yard purposes in Vancouver,[2] to show a more economical use of land as a result of the tax. Whether this tendency of a more intensive use of the land was evident before the depression was not stated. On the other hand, the phenomenon of narrow, twenty-five foot lots in some of the cities has been attributed to local conditions. For example, "The high cost of land and the necessity of being served by local improvements has operated to cause Regina to be less scattered. . . ." In Victoria, on the contrary, a "Single Tax" city, and with a relatively smaller area and greater density of population than the other cities of western Canada, the prevailing standard lot is the fifty-foot parcel.[3] In short, congestion not being a problem in these western communities, little can be gathered with regard to this matter which reflects the effect of the land tax.

§ 12. As to the other results which logically might have been expected to follow, even less can be proved from the economic conditions in the western provinces. Taking up the question of speculation in land, we will ignore the present unfavorable status of the land market as it is causally

---

[1] Haig, *op. cit.*, pp. 200, 233-34.
[2] *Ibid.*, p. 197.
[3] *Ibid.*, pp. 48, 236.

unrelated to the land tax. Until 1913, then, it would have been impossible to show that the speculator had been deterred in his operations in western Canada on account of the land tax. For it is not surprising to find speculation rampant in a country where the appreciation of the value of land has been so extraordinary. Nor will the speculation mania [1] cease, so long as the tax fails to appropriate the entire profit. Thus, while it may be assumed that the increased building operations are a sign of the better utilization of town land, the tax has surely not been prohibitive of property in vacant land, because the enormous value increment, the result of overcapitalization of the land, makes the payment of a two per cent tax, or less, a trifling matter in the calculations of the speculator. Therefore it is not surprising that in spite of the tax there are 26,763 vacant lots in Calgary, Alberta, which have sewerage and water facilities; yet working men are compelled to go outside the city limits to buy land on the prairie for homes.[2] As an official said, at times of land "booms" and "fictitious" values, the assessment is seldom considered. Nor can the disintegration of the large landholdings, to which the following quotation is testimony, be attributed to the influence of the taxing system alone. "Many of the most fertile valleys were monopolized by a few individuals, who owned from 1000 to 30,000 acres. . . . These big estates are now being subdivided and sold in small parcels, with the result that small farms and orchards are becoming numerous on ground which was held for years as pasture or merely for purposes of speculation. The breaking-up of these large ranches is one of the most hopeful signs of the

---

[1] The treasurer of Brandon, Man., writes: "In this part of the world we are subject to periods when there is a big demand for land and very large sums of money change hands in the speculation in land. At such times as these every one is land mad and lands change hands in many cases at ridiculous prices." See also for description of enormous realty transactions, London *Economist*, May 3, 1913, p. 1039.

[2] *Canadian Municipal Journal*, August, 1914, p. 332.

times." [1] On the whole, nevertheless, speculation continued unabated as before, and in spite of the institution of the new system of taxation; but absentee owners and speculators in vacant property contributed a greater share than before to the public revenue.

The increase in wages and the unusually high rates of wages in western Canada before 1913 [2] can be only remotely, if at all, traceable to the operation of the land tax. Wages in the building trade had undoubtedly advanced on account of the activity in that trade. So had the wages of common labor, both in the towns and on the farms. However, since the prices of food and lodging had also advanced, and since labor was scarce, the increase in wages must be attributed rather to the general prosperity of the country, which the tax on land value may have slightly, if at all, furthered. On the other hand, if the building activity is attributed at all to the land tax, the latter must also bear the blame for the abnormal condition of unem-

---

[1] *Bureau of Provincial Information, Agriculture in British Columbia* (1912), Official Bulletin 10, p. 14.

[2] The following table, from the *Eighth Annual Report of the Department of Agriculture* (Sask., 1912), p. 162, shows the increase in wages in Saskatchewan since 1910: —

Trade or calling	1910	1911	1912	Per cent increase 1912 over 1910
Bricklayers	65 *h*	67½	70 *h*	15
Carpenters	40 *h*	40	45 *h*	12
Electricians	35 *h*	37½	40 *h*	14
Plumbers	50 *h*	55½	60 *h*	20
Plasterers	60 *h*	65	67½ *h*	12
Painters	35 *h*	35	40 *h*	14
Woodworkers	30 *h*	35	35 *h*	16
Building laborers	22 *h*	22	25 *h*	14
Common laborers	20 *h*	20	22½ *h*	11
Teamsters	55 *m*	55	65 *m*	18
Printers	18 *w*	19	21 *w*	17
Machine operators	22 *w*	24	25 *w*	14
Store Clerks	18 *w*	19	20 *w*	11
Stenographers	55 *m*	60	65 *m*	18
Domestics	18 *m*	18	20 *m*	11
Farm laborers	200 *y*	200	250 *y*	25

h, cents per hour; *w*, dollars per week; *m*, dollars per month; *y*, dollars per year.

ployment in the building trades that succeeded the flush of prosperity.[1]

We may conclude, then, with regard to the expediency of the tax as a social reform measure that although ineffective as a total reform, the tax may be salutary in its general influence. Its real value lies, however, in its fiscal character. As a fiscal measure, the tax has responded adequately to the needs of the communities, since it is not only a productive source of revenue, but also since it is least burdensome to industry and capital.

§ 13. The fact that the adoption of the tax in the western provinces has spread and that, even in the recent dire fiscal stress [2] no attempt to rescind the measure has anywhere been made, is further testimony of its expediency.[3] The question arises, however, will its adoption be confined to those provinces merely? Hitherto, or rather until several years ago, the older, eastern provinces stood solidly against the principle of the tax.[4] Before the depression, however, there were signs that the popularity of the new

[1] In the spring of 1913, usually the busy season for the building trades, about half the union workmen were said to be out of employment in Vancouver. *Cf. The British Columbia Federationist*, March 21, 1913.

[2] The popularity of the tax and the faith in its expediency are shown by the following incident. During the "hard times" in Vancouver recently, an alderman mustered up sufficient courage, the narrator says, to suggest a tax on twenty-five per cent of the value of improvements. But his suggestion did not meet with approval in the council. *Canadian Municipal Journal*, May, 1914, p. 172.

[3] That numerous complaints should arise against the exemption of improvements, especially in a time of falling values, is to be expected. The significant fact that cannot be overlooked is that no action has been taken to change the system, where legislation is so simple. Of all the cities, Vancouver has perhaps suffered most from the depression, and it is there that discontent with a tax which falls so heavily on the landowner should be most widespread. Yet in this city Mr. Taylor, a pronounced adherent of the system, has been reelected mayor time after time, and again in 1915, in spite of the successful effort to unseat him. (*Cf. Canadian Municipal Journal*, April, 1915, p. 132.) The fact that his opposing candidate, Hepburn, also favored the system of taxation shows all the more the general popularity of the land tax.

[4] *Cf. Canadian Municipal Journal*, October, 1912, p. 388.

taxing system was growing even in the older communities. Nevertheless, though public sentiment may be strongly in favor of exempting improvements in part at least, great opposition must be expected from the more conservative provincial legislatures. Thus in Ontario, 250 municipalities have already petitioned the legislature in vain to be authorized to reduce the tax on improvements as compared with that on land.[1] The organizations that petitioned for the change in Ontario were: The Canadian Manufacturers' Association, the Toronto Board of Trade, the Corporation of the City of Toronto, the Toronto District Trades and Labor Council, the Dominion Grange of Canada.[2] In Toronto, too, popular judgment favors the change. Thus, by a vote of twenty-three to one the city council submitted the following proposition to a referendum vote: "Are you in favor of applying for legislation to assess buildings, business tax and incomes on a lower basis than land?" The popular vote stood about four to one in favor of the proposal.[3] It is significant also in this connection that the Union of New Brunswick Municipalities adopted a resolution in 1911 favoring the land-value tax as the only source of local revenue.[4] New Brunswick, situated on the eastern coast of Canada, lacks the conditions which give rise to great land-value increments such as appear in the western provinces. For example, the increase in population during the decade, 1901–11, was in New Brunswick only 6.3 per

[1] *Canadian Municipal Journal*, October, 1911, p. 407. "In the last couple of years attempts have been made to permit any municipality to reduce the tax rate on improvements if the property owners wished it, and petitions asking for this have been presented to the Legislature . . . signed by over 250 municipalities, 200 newspapers and 300 labor organizations; they have been endorsed by most of the agricultural papers and by over 100 business firms in Toronto." A. B. Farmer, *Tax Reform*, a speech delivered before the Union of Canadian Municipalities.

[2] Taken from a circular issued by the Tax Reform League of Eastern Canada (Toronto).

[3] Dixon, *op cit.*, p. 4.

[4] *Canadian Municipal Journal*, February, 1912, p. 50, and December, 1911, p. 478.

cent, as compared with 119.6 per cent in British Columbia, 413 per cent in Alberta, 439.4 per cent in Saskatchewan, and 78.5 per cent in Manitoba.[1] Furthermore, as was pointed out by Professor Kierstadt, while land in Vancouver was worth two and one-third times the improvements, the improvements in Fredericton, N.B., were valued at one and one-half times the land.[2] The fact, therefore, that the New Brunswick municipalities favor the exemption of improvements from taxation is especially noteworthy. In Nova Scotia, a bill making the partial exemption of improvements and personalty optional with the local body passed the Lower House several times but was rejected in the Legislative Council.[3]

[1] *5000 Facts about Canada* (1913 edition), p. 8.
[2] *Canadian Municipal Journal*, December, 1912, p. 490.
[3] Bill 129 (1914), "The Optional Assessment Act." *Cf.* Haig, *op. cit.*, p. 13.

CHAPTER VII

THE TAX IN ITS FISCAL ASPECT

§ 1. AFTER the examination in the preceding chapters of the systems of land-value taxation in operation, we must proceed by synthesis to discover the common essence of the various forms of the land tax, to find its relation to the other taxes, and to set forth its underlying principles from a fiscal standpoint. To reduce the protean land taxes to a homogeneous form — to the land-value tax — is not simple. Indeed, the possibility of classing the value-increment duty with the tax on the capital value of land, or the mineral-rights duty with either of the former, may well be doubted. In one case the base of the levy is the value increment, in another the capital value, in a third the rental value; in one case the tax is direct and in another indirect; sometimes it is proportional and sometimes progressive; in certain cases it has occurred as a general and in other cases as a special, or ancillary charge. Nevertheless, it may be maintained that certain essential characteristics appear in the land-value tax under all the divergences of form. The basis of taxation in all these systems is land; the essential or common purpose is to tax the realized or realizable income accruing from the ownership of such land, and to exempt income derived from the employment of capital and labor expended for improvements. Discrepancy makes its appearance in the methods and means of assessing the income and of levying the tax.

If we inquire what has determined the choice of method, and which of the various systems is the most to be desired, it will be found, first, that the proponents of the taxes on land value in the several countries have followed the line of least resistance; secondly, that, inasmuch as social as well as fiscal considerations are often the determining factors in the introduction of the tax, fiscal expediency alone cannot determine what form will be most expedient. We shall find, for instance, that in the British colonies the taxation of the unimproved value of the land on the basis of its capital value is not only most expedient economically, but is most consistent with the democracy of those colonies; that in Germany the value-increment tax founded on the system of taxing "Konjunktur" gains [1] conforms best with the prevailing system of taxing income [2] rather than property; that in England, where the taxation of capital value has hitherto been unpopular, if not obnoxious, a plurality of duties — an almost fantastic adaptation of a transplanted system of taxation — was deemed necessary to effect the purpose in view.

Again we find that where the purpose was fiscal rather than social or economic, the proportional direct levy on unimproved value was found most productive and most expedient; that where the purpose was social, where, for example, the disintegration of large estates, and the discouragement of speculation and absenteeism were sought, the progressive scale of rates, or the especially discriminatory undeveloped land tax, was most effective; that where the ethical, or economic motive, the question of the "unearned increment" was uppermost, the indirect mode of levy, i.e., on occasions when the increment would accrue, was adopted; and that where a particular system of land tenure, such as the leasing system, had taken deep root, as in England, a new form of levy had to be devised, namely, the reversion duty.

[1] See *supra*, chapter IV, § 3.
[2] That the German system is to tax the increment which has actually accrued at the time it is appropriated is seen from the fact that the occasion of the levy of duty is on transfer of property by sale. This is in contrast with the English system which levies a duty on a hypothetical or anticipated increment, as, in the reversion duty, undeveloped-land duty, and value-increment duty in case of death, or lease, etc.

Assuming that in spite of the differences in form and purpose, these various imposts are essentially the same in principle, it is necessary to consider the tax on land value in the light of fiscal theory and of modern thought generally.

§ 2. As to the place of the land tax in the general categories of taxation, it is evident that the tax on land value belongs to the genus property tax, and to the species real property tax. As already set forth,[1] the direct, proportional tax on land value is merely a modified form of the realty tax. This was made clearly evident in the discussion of the Canadian system. As for the value-increment tax, although the method of assessment and collection varies from the usual methods of taxing real property, it is nevertheless like the realty tax in that the basis of taxation, the income accruing from landed property, is the same in both cases. But just as the real property tax is differentiated from the general property tax by the elimination of personalty from taxation, so the tax on land value is differentiated similarly from the real property tax by the exemption of improvements from taxation.

A second criterion of classification of taxes concerns their relative importance in the fiscal system — whether they are principal, subsidiary, or single sources of revenue. If by a "single source" is meant one covering at once all federal, state, and local needs, it is to be remarked that there is no single tax in existence anywhere; and according to fiscal authorities a single tax, whether the base be general income, land value, or something else, is for a variety of reasons fiscally undesirable.[2] For municipal purposes the land tax in certain Canadian and Australasian communities constitutes the chief source of public income, although not the sole source, since as we have seen, licenses and subsidies

---

[1] See chapter I, § 7.
[2] *Cf.* Seligman, *Essays in Taxation* (1913), chapter III; Bastable, *Public Finance* (1903), pp. 343 *ff*; Cossa, *Taxation* (1889), pp. 128 *ff*.

from the provincial government supplement the local revenue. As for the value-increment, undeveloped land, reversion, and mineral-rights duties, the intention has always been to make these merely subsidiary sources of revenue. In fact, the nature of these forms of the tax prevent them from becoming the prevailing taxes, since their yield is uncertain and inelastic. Thus, the revenue from the undeveloped land duty, unless the purpose of the tax is frustrated, should diminish in amount as the land becomes better utilized. It would seem that only the direct proportional tax is adapted to a general levy, that is for general purposes, while the revenue accruing from the other forms of the land-value tax has been sometimes devoted to a special fund, as, for example, for municipal improvements [1] or old-age pensions. With the exception of one form of the tax, then, the direct proportional, the tax on land value constitutes a subsidiary impost. Indeed, wherever levied, the accruing revenue constitutes a trifling proportion of the total public income.

§ 3. Taxes may further be classified according to the civic division, local, state, or national, by which and for whose use they are raised. Great emphasis is laid by authorities on public finance upon the problem of separating the sources of revenue according to their suitability for local, state, or federal purposes.[2] It is, therefore, necessary to show to what extent, if at all, the tax on land value conforms to the most authoritative scheme of separation. The tax on land value is in essence a tax on real property. Now, whatever difference of opinion there may exist with regard to the classification of the other taxes, there seems to be a consensus of opinion, in this at least, that the real property tax should be relegated to the local governments.[3]

---

[1] As in Frankfurt a. M., for example. *Cf. supra*, chapter IV, § 20.

[2] *Cf.* Seligman, *Essays in Taxation* (1913), chapters XI and XII.

[3] This position is taken primarily because it accords with the widespread practice in this country of supplying nearly all the municipal budgets by means of the realty tax.

The arguments upon which the defense of this position is based are the following: First, from the standpoint of administration, the local assessors, especially if they are civil service appointees, are most likely to know the actual value of the property, and to have an understanding of the peculiar local conditions influencing values. Secondly, there is the "situs" argument, that the property should be taxed where it is located, so that the community in which the value of the land has been created may be benefited by appropriating a part of that value. It accords, therefore, with the principle that land value is a socially created, or community value. Again, it also accords with the "benefit" theory of taxation, that the individual ought to contribute to the state in proportion to the services received by him. Thirdly, the local assessment of realty conforms with the principle of local autonomy. The levy of a property tax by the state, for example, often results in the support of the poorer sections by the more wealthy sections of the state. But under local autonomy, i.e., where each community provides its own budget from its own resources, the rural districts and the urban districts will be self-dependent. This, then, meets the objection, for example, that by the exemption of improvements, the urban communities will be relieved from some of the burden of taxation at the expense of the rural districts where the value of the land compared with the value of the improvements is proportionally greater than in cities.[1] Fourthly, it is also argued that no other tax is more appropriate or more available for local purposes than the real property tax. The income, inheritance, railway, corporation and excise taxes are held to be more suited for the other taxing jurisdictions. Moreover, to tax business or any form of capital in one locality and not in the others, is very likely to drive out the business or capital taxed, to the detriment of the industrial progress of the community. These reasons, there-

[1] *Cf.* Seligman, *Essays in Taxation* (1913), p. 85; and *infra.*, pp. 344 *ff.*

fore, favor the relegation of the tax on real property to the local governments.

In actual practice the tax on land value, in spite of its kinship to the realty tax, has been levied now by the municipality, now by the state, and again, by the federal authority. As we have seen, however, the proportional, direct, general land-value tax, such as is levied in the Canadian municipalities, has down to the present been confined to municipal purposes, while the progressive, indirect, and subsidiary forms of the land-value tax are state and federal taxes.[1] Thus, it would seem, the purpose of the respective forms of the tax determines by what civic division it should be levied. Where fiscal considerations predominate, as in the case of the Canadian and Australasian municipal levies, land-value taxes are as yet strictly municipal taxes; where the purpose of the levy is primarily not revenue, but social-economic reform, the tax is levied by authorities of wider jurisdiction. It is significant in this connection, and in view of the apprehensions of some economists with regard to the results of separating the sources of public revenue,[2] that in both the Canadian and Australasian municipalities, where the tax is in operation, not only is the principle of separation in force, but autonomy, or rather local option, in taxation exists in a great measure.[3]

If it were necessary to justify the levy of the discriminatory land tax by the state or imperial governments, in accordance with the fiscal principle discussed above, it might be contended that the cause of the value increment of land is not wholly local, but that the expenditures of the

[1] The German "Wertzuwachssteuer" is an imperial tax in form only, the revenue accruing to the local bodies.

[2] For example, Professor Bullock, who is opposed to the principle of separating the sources of revenue partly because it will lead to local option in taxation. *Cf.* Seligman, *Essays in Taxation* (1913), p. 367.

[3] Nevertheless, the provincial government in Canada and the state government in Australasia control the local authorities in their tax legislation, while in Queensland the local tax on unimproved value is even compulsory, not optional.

larger and higher civic divisions affect the value of the land
as well. In the case of mines and other natural resources,
whose value depends and is generally attributable to a
more extended market than the immediate locality, the
imperial and state duties can indeed be defended theoretically from this standpoint. Or, it may be argued that the
fluctuating and indefinite yield of these indirect taxes,
which, if levied by the local authority, would be very
slight, becomes considerable when the base is broadened
by making them state or federal imposts.[1]

§ 4. The distinguishing features of the land-value tax,
and those which render its levy so popular with certain
groups of people are its underlying fisco-economic principles of incidence, amortization, and the taxation of capital *versus* rental value.

From the time the Ricardian rent theory [2] was promulgated to the present day, economists have been in
general agreement as to the theory of the incidence of a
tax on rent. Accepting the Ricardian theory of rent as a
surplus value, economic theory holds that a tax on rent or
on the differential value of land cannot be shifted. A sharp
distinction is drawn in this theory between land and other
commodities; land is non-reproducible; its supply is fixed
irrespective of the demand. Further analysis of distinc-
tions between land and other objects of value led economists to hold that the essential differentiating characteristics of land consist only in its qualities of extension and
situation. The principle that a tax on rental cannot be
shifted is held to be applicable only in so far as rent is due

[1] *Cf.* Seligman, *op. cit.*, p. 354.
[2] The credit of discovery of this principle belongs to a number of
writers who anticipated Ricardo. They were James Anderson (*An Inquiry into the Nature of the Corn Laws, with a view to the new Corn Bill
proposed for Scotland, 1777*), Sir Edward West (*An Essay on the Application of Capital to Land, etc., 1815*), Thomas R. Malthus (*An Inquiry into
the Nature and Progress of Rent, and the Principles by which it is regulated,
1815*), and Robert Torrens (*An Essay on the External Corn Trade, etc.,
1815*).

to the "location" or "differential site" value.[1] It is assumed by this theory that the landlord always exacts the highest possible rental from his tenant, a "rack" rent. Hence an additional burden, as a tax on rent, cannot be shifted to the occupier or lessee, but must be borne by the landlord himself.

Now, where conditions are as thus assumed,[2] this principle of incidence logically follows. But whether the tax on rent as ordinarily charged can be shifted or not has not yet been experimentally demonstrated. Indeed, Professor Nicholson[3] and others seem to have refuted the doctrine with respect to agricultural land in England by demonstrating that rating on agricultural land — values having declined so considerably during the last quarter of a century — is a tax on profits, and is borne by the tenant in part, as well as by the landlord. Does it mean, therefore, in so far as the tenant bears the tax, that the much maligned English landlord had not exacted the highest rack rent from the occupier after all? It is also to be noted that practical students do not accept the principle of rent unquestioningly. Thus, for example, in the conference proceedings of the "Verein für Sozialpolitik" the question of the incidence of the "Zuwachssteuer" was admitted to be

[1] According to Professor Davenport, unless the *fertility* differentials be separated from the *location* differentials, and unless the tax fall only on the latter, it will be shifted to the tenant who will in turn recoup himself by "skimming the soil" or exhausting the fertility. See his *Value and Distribution*, p. 249, note.

[2] Like many other assumptions of the classical economists, those under which the rent theory was worked out are preposterously inconsistent with the facts. Free competitive conditions do not exist; in the variety of the uses of land, the differential value cannot be computed except theoretically and diagrammatically; and, moreover, numerous other factors enter into the determination of rent besides the economic.

[3] Cf. *Rates and Taxes as Affecting Agriculture*, pp. 124 ff., 146. His explanation is, of course, that there exists little agricultural land subject to economic rent; that the rent paid is to a great extent profit on capital sunk in the land by the owner. This does not contradict the Ricardian theory, but illustrates how the theory is inapplicable to existing conditions.

unsolved.[1] To take another example, in the debates in the British Parliament on the mineral-rights duty the attitude of practical men with regard to the classical theory of incidence was very skeptical. Even among the supporters of the land duties, especially among the mining operators (not owners), the proposal to impose a tax on mineral rights, on the royalty, caused much apprehension that the price of minerals might be enhanced.[2] The evidence from the countries we have studied, furthermore, is equally inconclusive as regards the incidence of the tax. With respect to urban land, however, general observation seems to confirm the classical principle of incidence,[3] probably because of the great demand and the active competition for particular sites and because of the impersonal relationship that exists for the most part in cities between landlord and tenant.

In the generally accepted theory of the incidence of taxation on buildings and other improvements, is to be found the ground for advocating the exemption of improvements from taxation. Buildings and improvements are capital, reproducible and subject to decay. The value of reproducible commodities is held to approximate their cost of production. In the long run, therefore, a tax on buildings will tend to be shifted to the occupier.[4] The consequences of this theory will be further discussed in the following chapter. Here, it may be questioned whether the incidence of the tax on land and building respectively can be so nicely determined as the above statement of the theory suggests, or whether the two do not constitute a unit subject to a new law of incidence. The process of shifting

[1] Cf. Verhandlungen des Vereins für Sozialpolitik, Schriften des Vereins (1911), vol. cxxxviii, pp. 45–46, and elsewhere.

[2] Parl. Debates (1909), vol. ix, p. 415; vol. xi, pp. 1147 ff.

[3] Cf. Verhandlungen des Vereins für Sozialpolitik (1911) p. 46.

[4] Two conditions limit the application of this principle, namely, when the tax is imposed uniformly on all kinds of capital, and in the case of old buildings, when the owner may have to bear the tax.

an additional tax on buildings, for example, assumes a readjustment in the demand and supply of houses. That is, fewer new dwellings would be built until the rentals advanced sufficiently to cover the tax burden. The remission of the tax would similarly cause a readjustment in the demand and supply resulting in reduced rentals. Other factors enter, however, to complicate the problem of incidence, because the tax on land value may raise the tax on land, synchronously with the remission of the tax on buildings. To elucidate some of the frictional factors arising from this twofold change in taxation, its probable effects on building operations must be discussed.

§ 5. The recent developments in the economic theory revolving about the effects of the taxation of land value, called forth by the Single Tax agitation, are notable. It used to be consistent with sound theory to believe on the one hand that the remission of the tax from buildings, as from any reproducible good, would act as an incentive to their production; on the other, that the expectation of rising land value and of landownership was responsible for the development of new countries and new communities. Now, once we recognize that building too is inevitably bound up with land-value increments and landownership, and that, as Professor A. S. Johnson believes,[1] the latter are incentives to building operations, the antagonistic tendencies arising from the untaxing of buildings and from the appropriation of the value increment become apparent.

Before attempting to determine which tendency will be the stronger, it is necessary to point out the refutation on theoretical grounds of the doctrine that the owner is induced to build by the prospect of the future rise in land value. Dr. Anderson[2] has shown by a mathematical illus-

---

[1] *Cf.* "The Case Against the Single Tax," in *Atlantic Monthly*, January, 1914, p. 36.

[2] Anderson, "'Unearned Increments,' Land Taxes, and the Building Trade," in *Quarterly Journal of Economics*, vol. XXVIII, pp. 811 *ff.*

tration, on the principle that earnings in all lines of industry tend to become equalized, that the increment is an irrelevant factor in the determination to build. Whether his exposition accords with the facts or not, it would seem that in general the speculative character of the "unearned increment" would scarcely be conducive to building that was not capable of a return on the whole ground rent and interest on the investment. A distinction must be made between the ordinary investor in real estate and the speculator. The investor in urban property expects an annual income on his investments. The anticipated increment may make a smaller annual return satisfactory to the investor. This may also account for the fact that the deterioration of the building is often not amortised, and for the fact that the mortgagee often counts on the increment in making the loan.[1] But it seems clear that the influence of the future value increment can affect the rate of income only in communities where land values are based on actual rentals and where the rate of increment is constant and reflected from time to time in the higher rents. The investor in farm land, on the other hand, is the farmer himself, who is willing to forego an immediate return from his improvements, because of the prospective value increments.[2]

It is otherwise with the speculator, including the "land-poor" owner as well as the capitalist operator. Now in case of land not yet ripe for building, where the increment is more or less remote and speculative, an owner unable to pay the carrying charges on the land, i.e., taxes and special

[1] In the instance cited by Dr. Haig to show that realty operations also are financed on the expectation of the increment, it will be noted that it is a steady annual increment founded on the increase of the earning power of the land in New York City. *Cf.* "The Effects of Increment Taxes upon Building Operations," in *Quarterly Journal of Economics*, vol. XXIX, p. 831.

[2] It is interesting to point out in this connection that the money investment in the land by the pioneer, or the promoter of a new town is almost nil; hence his readiness to wait a long time for the inevitable increments.

assessments, might be tempted to build even when the rental did not promise a greater return than the interest on his borrowed capital,[1] and the carrying charges on the land. But such operations would be confined necessarily to outlying districts and new communities, and even there their scope would be limited. For the borrowing power of the "land-poor" builder, where the rise in value is remote is very much limited, and the rate of interest higher. The best proof, on the other hand, that the speculator with means is not induced to build prematurely is the large number of vacant lots in every city, and the large expanse of uncultivated rural land in the hands of absentee owners. And are they not deterred from building prematurely by the fact also that the low income would be a convincing proof to them, and to their creditors, of the true low value of their property? The importance of this psychological factor is seen in the usual practice of landlords to allow their apartments to stand vacant, or to offer "concessions" to the renter, rather than to accept a lower rental. It is scarcely credible that, taking any city as a whole, building operations could be based on the whims of speculators, rather than on actual values. Altogether then, whether he builds on leased ground, on ground which is not rising in value, or on ground which does promise an increment, the landlord "must extort from his tenants rental covering both the ground rent and interest on the investment."[2]

Now, grant that the development of a new country and that premature building, e.g., the "pay tax" kind of structures in Western Canada,[3] are attributable to the

[1] Disregarding the depreciation of the building to be covered by the anticipated "unearned increment."

[2] That there could be a difference in rentals according as the builder is the owner or lessee, if it does not invalidate the argument, at least shows that the number of operations that do not cover interest on the land investment can be but exceptional. *Cf.* Johnson, *op. cit.*

[3] Haig, *Exemption of Improvements from Taxation in Canada and the United States*, p. 47.

anticipated increment. They are not, however, the basis of our present agricultural progress or urban development, any more than speculation in stocks and produce, which assist general production and distribution, is the cause of the progress of the latter. The more than two million tenant farmers in this country, an ever-increasing class, not to mention the farm laborers, contradict the alleged efficacy of the "unearned increment" to preserve our agricultural population and progress.[1] So does the widespread leasing system in England discredit the potency of the "unearned increment" as the incentive to building operations. If, then, the cases where premature building is induced by rising land value are limited to the "land-poor" owners, the effect of the tax on land value on them, it has been pointed out,[2] will be a twofold one. First, as an increase in the annual burden on the land, the tax will have the tendency to induce early building; secondly, as an appropriation of more of the prospective increments, it will discourage building.

Now, turning to the influence of the untaxing of improvements on the building trade, the effect, it is generally held, would be to stimulate building. But in so far as this tendency would result merely from the exemption of one form of capital now disproportionately burdened by taxation, the stimulation would cease with the equalization of the rates of profit in competitive industries. Should, however, the demand for new buildings increase through other causes,[3] the building trade will continue active.

After these theoretical considerations, we may inquire whether the study of the tax does not elucidate the problem. Briefly, if it has been difficult or impossible to trace the great building activity in the Australasian and Cana-

---

[1] Cf. Johnson, op. cit., p. 34.

[2] Haig, in Quarterly Journal of Economics, vol. xxix, p. 838.

[3] Cf. supra, § 4, p. 311.

dian municipalities to the operation of the land tax, it can be said with confidence nevertheless, that no evidence of a restriction of building operations appeared anywhere. Nor could the inactivity in the building trade which followed the enactment of the land-value duties in England, and of the imperial increment tax in Germany, be charged to the tax on the "unearned increment." [1]

§ 6. The principle of "amortization" rests on the assumption that the land tax is not shifted. The argument runs as follows: Since the value of the land represents the capitalized annual net rental actually accruing or anticipated, and since the tax on this rental cannot be shifted to the tenant, the value of the land when the tax is imposed is reduced by the capitalized value of the tax. Therefore, the proprietor in possession, when the tax is levied, alone pays the tax, as is evident from the reduction in the selling value of his property. When the tax is thus capitalized, or "amortized," the purchaser of the land subsequent to the imposition of the tax is in reality exempt from its payment.

The process of "amortization" applies to the land tax in so far as the latter is an exclusive tax, i.e., not levied on other forms of capital, or income. The facility of capitalizing the tax depends upon the certainty of the levy, that is, the constancy of the rate of tax and of the assessed value. Provided the amount of the tax can be counted upon, the purchaser will deduct its capitalized value, for he will not pay more for the property than the capitalized value of the anticipated net rental. The fact that land falls in value on the imposition of a tax, therefore, corroborates the principle of incidence of a tax on land value. Theoretically the value of the improvements will not fall, for their value equals the cost of their production and it would seem as if their value could not fall below their cost. In other words, the tax on improvements is shifted to the tenant. Practically, however, especially when the structures are

[1] *Cf.* chapters IV and V.

old, the tax may affect their value. At any rate it is difficult to measure or trace the exact decline in the value of improvements in case of an imposition of a new tax on real estate.

In our American cities, with the general property tax, under which most forms of wealth except real property practically escape taxation, the "amortization" process is not only theoretically possible, but is the established procedure. In purchasing property every one takes into account the amount of taxes, deducting their capitalized value from the value of the capitalized rental of the property. Theoretically, then, the tax is no burden on the land owner who has purchased subsequent to the imposition of the tax. In this country, indeed, where the rate of tax is more or less constant the land tax essentially ceases to be a tax at all. The ease and certainty of this kind of taxation accords well, indeed, with American individualism, respect for private property, and general distaste for paying taxes. The "amortization" process may well be an explanation not only of the absence of full-value and uniform assessment, and of the general undervaluation of real estate, but also of the popularity of the real property tax in this country, as compared with other taxes.[1]

Whatever makes the ascertainment and computation of the untaxed value of the land difficult, checks or frustrates this process of "amortization." Not that the expectation of a tax will not always affect the value of the property, but by keeping the assessment at the actual value by frequent valuations, by graduating the scale of rates, by taxing the value increment, the landowner will at least be made to share the income from his value increment with the government to a greater degree than at present. Take,

[1] This is illustrated by the difficulties encountered with legislatures in revising the statutes to permit of a full-value assessment, in spite of the advantages it may have industrially in lowering the rate of tax, and broadening the basis for public loan purposes. A readjustment of values gives rise to apprehension among landlords. See *infra*, chapter x.

for example, the progressive urban communities where land tends to appreciate in value, as in western Canada, and where the untaxed value of the land one year may not represent the net value the following year. Again, by introducing a progressive scale of rates, how shall the purchaser estimate the capitalized value of the tax with any degree of accuracy? Even more does the tax on value increment defeat the process of "amortization" of the tax; for as the owner is taxed, not on the selling value, but on the profit or surplus likely to accrue in the future, the untaxed value of the land cannot be foretold. The amount by which such a tax may reduce the value of land becomes entirely speculative. Indeed, as the interest of both speculator and taxing authority is the same, namely, that the land appreciate in value, the value-increment tax may not have a severely depreciating influence on the value of the land at all. At any rate, the objection by some that the real property tax is no tax whatever because it is "amortized," does not apply so much to the tax on land value, especially to the value-increment form of the tax.

§ 7. The question whether the capital value, i.e., the capitalized net income, or whether the net income of the land (not deducting taxes) should be made the base of taxation is unimportant as regards the slight tax on land value at present in operation. Inasmuch, however, as critics of the Single Tax have pointed out the futility of attempting to raise revenue by a tax on the capital value of land and have employed the argument also against the proposal of land-value taxation,[1] it is necessary to analyze the point at issue. As a fiscal policy taxation on the capital value of land may be regarded as a paradoxical proposal, for by taxing land value you destroy the value by the amount of the tax capitalized. If, as has been pointed out,[2] the mar-

---

[1] For example, see E. R. A. Seligman, in *The Survey*, March, 7, 1914, p. 701.

[2] Mr. Pleydell, Secretary of the International Conference on State and

ket value declines by reason of the tax, there will be less
and less to tax as the rate increases. For example, suppose
the annual tax on land is two and one-half per cent. The
market value of a parcel of ground yielding an income of
$50 was before the levy of the tax $1000,[1] and after the imposition only $666⅔.[2] Instead of yielding a tax of $25 on
$1000, the tax on $666⅔ is only $16.66⅔, from the stand-
point of revenue a loss of about $8. Indeed, if the rate
of tax were sufficiently increased, in accordance with the
Single Tax proposal, the very purpose of the tax would be
frustrated. Thus, were the rate fixed at five per cent, and
were the capital value to remain the base of the tax, there
would be no value to tax, the capitalized tax having absorbed or destroyed all the income. The significant thing,
however, is that all this time the rental remains undis-
turbed.

In view of this situation it has been proposed[3] that the
annual rental rather than the selling value (the untaxed
value) be made the basis of assessment. Or, if *ad valorem*

Local Taxation says: "I was rather surprised to hear the advocates of
Single Tax speak in the same breath of taxing the unearned increment by
taxing a certain amount out of the value of land at the time of sale. All
attempts to deal with selling values in this way are dealing with what in
one sense is legal fiction. The only reason land has value at all is that you
can get a certain rental out of it. If you keep people from collecting rents
you destroy values. Now, how are you going to tax the unearned increment which disappears wherever you increase a tax on the rental value
is a problem I have not yet been able to understand. It is interesting to
see how that would work out. A man pays a certain amount of money for
his land based upon the estimated net return, but if he is deprived of a
certain amount of his net return by an increase in the annual tax, the
land will have its selling value reduced. The intricacies would amuse
one," etc. Quoted by Marsh, *Taxation of Land Values in American
Cities*, p. 49.

[1] At five per cent.

[2] Because two and one-half per cent of $666⅔, capitalized, plus the net
value $666⅔, make up the $1000 original value.

[3] See Davenport, "The Single Tax in the English Budget," in *Quar-
terly Journal of Economics* (1910), vol. xxiv, pp. 283 *ff*. Also Pleydell,
"The Incidence of Taxation," in *First Conference on State and Local
Taxation*" (1907), p. 432.

taxation is preferred, that the actual or anticipated rental be capitalized for purposes of taxation. From the standpoint of the proprietor certainly the change is of no consequence. Whether you tax the market value or the rental his net income will remain practically unaltered. From the point of view of fiscal policy, however, the change is important. Since, according to theory, the rent remains unaffected by the tax on land value, the government can always appropriate a portion of this economic rent by taxation, irrespective of market conditions.

For practical purposes, however important these suggestions may be for the Single Tax policy, the tax on land value may continue to be levied on the selling value without loss to the government. So long as confiscation is not proposed, through the regulation of the rate of tax the state can appropriate whatever share of land value it decrees by taxing the selling value.

More practical difficulties may be raised when the assessment is reduced by the decline in the value of the land. For, if a law exist limiting the rate of tax in the municipality, or if, as is customary, the amount of municipal indebtedness is restricted legally by the amount of the assessment of real property, the exemption of improvements, or any other cause of restricting the base of revenue, may necessitate a change in the statute. This is again a matter of administration, necessary to point out, but which does not vitiate the fiscal principle of the tax.[1] Moreover, full-value assessment and the tendency of appreciating land value will counteract the restriction of the base of taxation.

Another consideration important alike from the standpoint of the taxing authority and that of the taxpayer, is

---

[1] To circumvent the constitutional difficulties with respect to the legal limitation of the borrowing power of the city, the recent proposal for untaxing buildings in New York City retains one per cent of the value of improvements in the tax base. Thus, it is hoped, the total value of the improvements would continue to constitute part of the assessment value, by which the borrowing power of the city is limited.

raised by the value-increment duty. As the selling value is the basis of computing the increment, any change in that value occasioned by a change, not in income, but in the interest rate will contract or swell the taxable differential. Any fall in the rate of interest will, therefore, entail an unintentional hardship on the taxpayer; while a rise in rate will entail a loss in revenue. This difficulty, which raises a serious objection to the levy of the value-increment tax, could be obviated by making the gross rental the basis of computation.[1]

§ 8. This fine, even subtle, distinction in method of assessment for administrative purposes is not to be confused with the ordinarily understood difference between taxing the capital value and the rental of land. Historically the assessment on the basis of rents paid preceded that on the basis of capital value. In fact the latter method has only recently superseded, or is superseding, the assessment of rental income. With few exceptions,[2] the general assessment on the basis of the capital value of property is confined to the United States, Canada, Australasia, and (since the enactment of the land-value duties) to England. In Germany, the system of assessment "nach dem gemeinen Wert" has only recently begun to supersede the older method.

The advantages and causes of this change in method have already been reviewed.[3] The chief argument is that the taxation of rentals encourages the withholding of land from use. Land bought and kept undeveloped for speculative purposes is exempted from the tax provided no rent

---

[1] Cf. Davenport, in Quarterly Journal of Economics (1910), vol. xxiv, pp. 289–90.

[2] In some of the Swiss cantons, in Rome for building land, and in Holland for the property tax, capital value, rather than rental, is now also made the basis of assessment. Cf. Papers Bearing on Land Taxes, etc. (Cd. 4750), 1909, p. 50, and (Cd. 4845). The supplementary income tax in Prussia and some of the other states is levied on the capital value of property, while in Great Britain the death duties are so levied. See ibid.

[3] See supra, chapters v and vi.

is yielded; therefore, speculation is fostered. In urban communities the withholding of land from use has been said to promote congestion and unsanitary housing conditions. Furthermore, the exemption of vacant and poorly utilized land from taxation is fiscally inexpedient, for it becomes a means of escaping taxation. When it is considered also that the value of vacant land tends to appreciate equally, sometimes even more [1] than the improved lots, it will be admitted that the rent does not constitute a test of the taxpayer's ability to contribute, unless supplementary taxes are levied. For these reasons, the local authorities in England are desirous of adopting the proposed change from rental to capital value assessment.[2] And the purpose of the undeveloped land duty in England was to correct the inequalities resulting from the older system of assessment. Similarly in Canada, the wild-land tax and the method of superassessment have been resorted to, to offset the tendency of evading taxation by keeping the land undeveloped.

A word about the status of the absentee. Not all unimproved land is owned by non-residents; yet, in many communities much of the vacant land is the property of absentees. In the countries where vacant property is not liable to taxation, the general antipathy to the non-resident is comprehensible. But where taxation on capital value is in vogue, the non-resident contributes to the reve-

[1] For example, when a parcel of ground is sold, the building which may be out of date may be an impediment to the plans of the buyer. Thus, as the writer has been informed, the site on which the Masonic Temple is located in Chicago would be worth a great deal more if there were no building upon it.

[2] *Cf.* E. Porritt, "The Struggle over the Lloyd George Budget," in *Quarterly Journal of Economics* (1910), vol. xxiv, p. 257. "The mansions have been on the rate books at merely nominal rental values. They have stayed at such ridiculous valuations because no one in the parishes concerned cared to antagonize the local feudal aristocracy by objecting to the assessments."

The new system of land valuation which is being completed in England will help usher in the rating of capital value.

nue in proportion to the assessed value of his property.
He is also liable to special assessments, and special rates
for services by which he only remotely benefits. Nor, must
it be overlooked that he has no voice in the enactment of
measures pertaining to taxes and expenditures. The explanation of the discriminatory legislation against the ab-
sentee-owner lies in local conditions. Thus, in Canada, it
is the enormous increments that accrue to the absentee,
through the efforts of the settler in building up the community, that breed the spirit of opposition and discrimination. Then, it will be remembered that the Hudson's
Bay Company is classed with the absentees. And lastly,
in many towns half or more than half the area may
be owned by such a company, or other absentees, preventing the closer settlement and the growth of the community.

§ 9. It is necessary next to test the tax on land value by
the canons of taxation laid down by fiscal authorities.
Those canons are justice, economy, and fiscal adequacy.
To be just a tax must be equal, universal, uniform; to be
economical, it must accord with the criteria of certainty
and convenience; to be fiscally adequate it must be productive and elastic.[1] There is no tax in our complex system, however, which does not practically, if not theoretically, sin against these canons, especially those requiring
equality and universality.[2] Whether you make your standard of justice fit the "benefit" or the "faculty" theory, a
great deal of ingenuity must be employed to prove existent
taxes in harmony with the criteria of justice. The fact is,
as one writer has well expressed it, "expediency, not logic,

---

[1] *Cf.* Eheberg, *Finanzwissenschaft*, p. 165.

[2] We are aware that fiscal authorities have reconciled even the inheritance and corporation taxes with the canons of taxation. See Seligman,
Essays in Taxation (1913), pp. 126 *ff.*, for a justification of the inheritance
taxes according to equity. However ingenious such proof of the consis-
tency of the inheritance tax with the faculty theory may be, its adoption
was more a matter of fiscal expediency than of adherence to doctrine.

governs taxation." [1] So long as the ideal, a single tax, if such exist, is found impracticable, and it is necessary to have a multiple system in the hope that the inequalities of the respective taxes will offset one another,[2] the justification of a subsidiary tax on the basis of justice will be practically futile.

Now, the tax on land value is not only a subsidiary, but it is a discriminatory tax. But there is need of subsidiary taxes, and like the corporation, inheritance, business, and other imposts, the tax on land value may be made to perform a valuable function, wherever it is found expedient. As to its discriminatory character, all subsidiary taxes are discriminatory. Like the corporation tax, for example, the tax on land value is class legislation, an attempt of the dominant party to place an extra burden on the landowners. The excuse of course is that this particular group or class fails to contribute to the public budget in proportion to its ability.[3]

In calling the tax confiscatory, the opponents of the tax forget that all taxation is essentially confiscatory. A tax is no voluntary contribution, it will be recalled; it is "a compulsory contribution from the person to the government to defray the expenses incurred in the common interest of all, without reference to special benefits con-

[1] *First National Conference on State and Local Taxation* (1907), p. 219.

[2] Thus Cossa said, "by means of their variety rendering the burden less oppressive to the taxpayers." *Premiers Éléments de la Science des Finances*, p. 108.

[3] It is possible to argue that the landlord is better able to pay this extra charge because of his particular position of special privilege and because the growth of the community enhances the value of his land, so that his income is augmented over and above the interest on his investment. "Is it too much, is it unfair, is it inequitable, that Parliament should demand a special contribution from these fortunate owners towards the defense of the country and the social needs of the unfortunate in the community, whose efforts have so materially contributed to the opulence which they are enjoying." From Lloyd George's Budget Speech, *Parl. Debates* (1909), vol. IV, p. 536.

ferred." [1] Strictly speaking, every tax is an infringement
of the individual's property rights, therefore.[2] But there is
common agreement that the rights of the individual are
subordinate to the will of society. Society has the power
and, therefore, the right to single out one social group and
place a special impost upon it, provided such action is
proved expedient.[3]

§ 10. What, then, constitutes expediency in taxation?
The effects of the levy of a tax are far-reaching. Professor
Ely's[4] words are still valid: "Taxation may create monopolies, or it may prevent them; it may diffuse wealth or concentrate it; it may promote liberty and equality of rights,
or it may tend to the establishment of tyranny and des-
potism; it may be used to bring about reforms, or "foster
dissension and hatred between classes. . ." The importance of choosing the most suitable object for taxation is
thus made evident. If, then, besides satisfying the economic and fiscal canons, a tax is no more discriminatory and
confiscatory than the other existent imposts, and, furthermore, does not create monopoly, concentrate wealth, promote tyranny and social conflict, it is to be accounted
expedient.

Before discussing the expediency of the tax on land value
as judged from its operation, it is necessary to point out a
serious objection to its levy. The tax on land value, it is
claimed, is merely a pretext for the confiscation of property
for the purpose of promoting some social or economic reform; in reality it is no tax at all. It has been questioned
whether the government should exercise its taxing power

---

[1] Seligman, *Essays in Taxation* (1913), p. 432.

[2] *Cf. First National Conference on State and Local Taxation* (1907), p.
214. Those who protest against the introduction of a tax on the ground
that one class is discriminated against overlook the gross inequalities
tolerated under the present system of taxation.

[3] To a great extent legislation, when proved expedient, has had to be
reconciled to the standards of right and justice, or has even modified the
latter.

[4] *Taxation in American States and Cities* (1888), p. 55.

for other than fiscal purposes, i.e., to secure an adequate revenue.

Since Professor Adolf Wagner promulgated his "socio-political" theory of taxation, this question has aroused considerable controversy. But as regards many a contested theory, the opponents are nearer agreement than they will admit. Professor Seligman denies Wagner's thesis that taxation "is something more than a means of raising revenue, that it is also a means of correcting the distribution of wealth which results from competition." [1] Yet Professor Seligman reaches the same conclusion through reconstructing the conception of justice. [2] In setting up this socio-political point of view, Wagner was merely interpreting the new basis of justice, the socio-political *versus* the eighteenth-century competitive and individualistic basis. And that is what Seligman has done in constructing the "Social Theory of Finance." [3] Where shall the line be drawn between the socio-political theory stated in Wagner's own words above and the admission that the government should be able "to utilize the taxing power as a political or social engine?" [4] Nothing, indeed, shows this socio-political tendency more than progressive taxation and the English income tax, which distinguishes earned from unearned income. These may be explained on the assumption that they measure better the ability of the taxpayer than the proportional or ordinary income taxes. On this basis, however, the tax on land value can similarly be defended, for the profits accruing from land ownership can bear a heavier tax with less sacrifice on the part of the owner, it may be argued, than can earnings of labor. Nevertheless, in this age when, it will be agreed, wealth

[1] *Lehr- und Handbuch der Politischen Oekonomie: Finanzwissenschaft*, vol. II, bk. v, chap. 3, § 159.

[2] Seligman, "Progressive Taxation," *American Economic Association Quarterly*, vol. IX, pp. 130–31, and his practical admission of the standpoint in *Essays in Taxation*, pp. 316–17.

[3] *Ibid.*, p. 342.   [4] *Ibid.*, p. 78.

is being accumulated because of special privilege, as shown, for example, in the monopolistic control of industry, and when the laboring class is assuming greater power, the tendency of all legislation, including fiscal, to keep in view a more equitable distribution of wealth is inevitable.

The extent to which the tax on land value has been instituted as a reform measure, rather than as a source of revenue varies with its several forms. As has been discussed in the preceding chapters, the municipal land taxes in Canada and Australasia are purely fiscal in character. It will be recalled that in these cases the tax is a direct, proportional levy. Theoretically, this is explainable on the ground that for local purposes benefit, rather than faculty,[1] is the criterion of taxation; and that the degree of benefit to the individuals cannot be measured according to a graduated scale. Practically, it may be explained by the fact that the ratepayers are the voters, that in the above-mentioned communities opportunities are equal, and that the progressive tax is discriminatory, and would upset the stability of land values, the chief source of prosperity and income. In other words, the tax has no other purpose than to make every landowner pay toward the expenditures of government in proportion to the value of his land.

In a way, then, the progressive and value-increment taxes disclose the purpose of their levy. For the disintegration of large estates, indeed, the graduated scale is more effective than the proportional tax would be. So also, when the rate of tax in Germany varies with the length of ownership and condition of the land, the social purpose is clearly manifested. The English land duties, however, are an exception, for, although the predominant motive was nonfiscal, the rates of tax are proportional, not progressive. Either to avoid the additional complexity which the pro-

[1] Seligman, "Progressive Taxation in Theory and Practice," *American Economic Association Quarterly*, vol. IX, p. 301.

gressive scale of rates must occasion, or, what is more likely, to avoid the more strenuous opposition that would have been aroused by a departure from the traditional adherence to proportional land taxes, Lloyd George and his party contented themselves with proportional duties on land value.[1]

§ 11. There remains, then, by far the most important question, the fiscal expediency of the tax on land value. First, as to its productiveness. At the present rate of taxation, the conclusion from the data in the preceding chapters must be that the tax for state or federal purposes can supplement the sources of revenue but meagerly. Furthermore, the duties on increment, on undeveloped land, and on mineral rights are inelastic sources of revenue. Not only is the base of the tax limited, but the yield cannot be regulated. Fiscally, therefore, the value-increment duty and the other imperial duties are unimportant imposts. For local purposes, on the other hand, when all land is subject to a direct, proportional levy, the tax is not only productive but elastic. The experience with the tax in the Australasian and Canadian municipalities is evidence of this. Wherever the value of the land tends to increase enormously, so that the rate of tax can remain moderate, the yield of the tax on land value can be regulated so as to supply not only the major portion, but even the entire local revenue. The recent depression in Canada has not necessitated a change in the system even in "Single Tax" communities, but it is doubtful whether an additional source of income would not have facilitated the collection of revenue and relieved somewhat the landowners already hard hit by the collapse of land values. This would apply more strongly to older communities, where landowners constitute a small proportion of the population, and where landed property is not the chief source of wealth. The

[1] Instead of adopting the progressive scale as in Germany, the average rate of the increment duty in England, however, was made higher than under the German system.

fiscal expediency of the new system will vary with the conditions in the different cities; but the following facts must be borne in mind; that even today (1) the tax on real estate suffices for nearly the entire budget of numerous municipalities and partly also for state purposes; (2) full-value assessment is practically unknown; (3) the value of improvements does not increase so rapidly as that of the land.

Secondly, the convenience and certainty of the levy on land value compare favorably with other imposts. No arguments need be brought forth to substantiate this fact, but it is necessary to point out a few cases of economic hardship or inconvenience. In England, where taxation on capital value was practically unknown, attention has been called to the injustice or inconvenience of taxing the person who is in receipt of no income out of which to pay, as under the undeveloped-land duty.[1] Likewise, we have heard often of the hardship the tax would impose upon the widow, owner of her own old home. So also the owner of land whose value has depreciated has been commiserated. Again, it may be feared that the local option, where the tax on land value is in force at the option of municipalities, may endanger industry through the rivalry which exists between cities. Hardship has also been incurred by the retroactive feature of the "Zuwachssteuer" in Germany. It must be replied, however, that such instances of inconvenience and hardship can be cited in the case of almost every tax.[2] Of course in communities of rapidly rising land value, the land tax of a few per cent of the land value is easily discounted and is scarcely felt. The best proof that the tax is not oppressive in new countries is furnished in the adoption of the proportional form of the impost by such demo-

[1] Cf. Parl. Debates (1909), vol. XII, p. 516.

[2] Not to mention the hardship of the excise and import taxes on the poorest classes, the widow's case cited above is probably no worse than that of the German wage-earner who out of his 900 marks annual income pays a tax to the state.

cratic and virgin communities as in Australasia and in
western Canada. In these cases, the "leveling" factor, the
use of the tax to right a social evil, moreover, played little
or scarcely any part. As regards the other forms of the tax,
the exemption of a minimum increment under the value-
increment duty shields the less fortunate landowner from
the burden. It will be remembered also that the retroactive feature of the "Zuwachssteuer," however inconsistent with our standards of justice, was upheld by the
courts. It is improbable that the tax would have been
upheld, if, besides being unprecedented, it were oppressive.
This illustrates, indeed, how local conditions may influence
the criterion of justice, how expediency overrides abstract
principle.

Thirdly, in considering the discriminatory feature of the
tax on land value, the local tax must be again differentiated
from the imperial and state taxes. As subsidiary sources of
revenue the latter are no more discriminatory than the
corporation, inheritance, business, or even realty taxes.
But, when the tax on land value is made the only tax, the
expediency of exempting all other income from taxation
even for local purposes may be questioned. The fact is,
however, that setting against the apparent inequality
created by the exemption of other than the landowning
class from taxation the comparative difficulty of assessment and collection of other imposts, and considering, too,
that the value of the land depends so much upon the public
expenditure, the apparent injustice dwindles. Especially
is this true where the land constitutes the chief source of
wealth and income, as in the new communities where the
land tax is now in operation as the only source of public
revenue, and where the municipality itself, given the option, wills to exempt wage-earners and the capital invested
in industry from taxation. In that case only the non-resident landowner is discriminated against, and has cause to
complain.

Fourthly, it is evident both from the discussion of the underlying principles and from the operation of the tax, that it does not create a monopoly, nor concentrate wealth, nor promote tyranny, nor foster social conflict. The fact is that by this tax the community shares a little more of the value increment which accrues to the landowner than before.

§ 12. Aside from the above considerations, there is another criterion of expediency by which the tax must be tested, namely, the facility of its administration. In general, the prevalence of the realty tax is due to the comparative ease with which land and other real property can be assessed. Since an early period, the "cadastral" system of assessment has served a useful purpose. Not only for tax purposes, but for statistical, juridical,[1] political, and military purposes, the "Domesday Book" was of invaluable assistance to the government. In modern times, however, an extensive system of accurate valuation and registration of the land by the central government, so far as we know, exists nowhere. The reason is that such a valuation is very expensive and subject to change because of the frequent fluctuations in the value of the land. One of the results of the tax reforms in England has been to necessitate just such an extensive system, and the valuation of all the land in Great Britain is now under way.

It is difficult to say whether in England the fear of the tax on land value had for a long time prevented an accurate and separate assessment of the land and improvements respectively, or whether the accurate and separate assessment was feared as a consequence of the imperial land value duties.[2] At any rate, the most effective argument perhaps against the adoption of rating on land value and the argument which delayed its introduction in England, has been

[1] Namely, to guide the court in the division and adjustment of the estates of the deceased.

[2] That is, the increment and undeveloped land duties were opposed, because the latter at least would necessitate a valuation which might lead to the adoption of rating on land value.

the practical difficulty in the way of an accurate valuation of the site. Although some experts had declared such valuation practicable, public opinion generally opposed what was called a hypothetical valuation. Under the theoretical assumption that the tax on land value should fall on economic rent, and that, therefore, it was necessary to take account of all the capital ever sunk into the soil which might have affected the present value of the site, every one will readily admit the hypothetical character of such a valuation. The ascertainment of the exact "location" rental is an impossibility. Professor Seligman makes this clear in the following passage: [1] "Now, it is manifestly not so easy to assess the land values — that is, the bare value of the land irrespective of all improvements — as it is to assess the selling value of a piece of real estate. For instance, an acre of agricultural land near a large town may be worth $200; but if used for truck-farming, considerably more than $200 may have been expended on it during the last century or two. Who can tell how much of the $200 present value is the value of the bare land and how much is to be assigned to the labor expended? Under the present method we have at least a definite test — the selling value; under the new method we should have no test at all. There is every likelihood, therefore, that the difficulties of the present situation would be intensified."

If every reform had to be rejected on account of some theoretical objection little progress would be made. In the case of valuation, the experience in this country with separate valuations for land and improvements has demonstrated the practicability as well as the usefulness of the system. In fact, the theoretical objection seems unwarranted in the present advance made toward the more scientific valuation of land. Even admitting that improvements made a century or two ago have had an influence on the present value of agricultural and even urban land, that

[1] *Essays in Taxation* (1913), p. 77.

influence could be only slight on land whose value is due almost entirely to the growth of population. As for improvements made on land in recent years, their cost, in so far as they add to the value of the property, is deducted from the value of the site, and this suffices for all practical purposes.

One of the important effects of the adoption of the tax on land value will be the development of expert and more accurate, or even scientific, methods of valuation of the land separated from the improvements upon it.[1] This is because the system of taxing land value exempts improvements from taxation and requires full value assessments. But irrespective of this tax, considerable progress has already been made toward accurate valuation. So far as we have been able to ascertain, the best experiments toward a scientific method to displace the crude assessments based on estimate, have been worked out in a few American cities, for example, New York, Newark, Cleveland, etc.[2] In the United States, with the development of the assessment on capital value, some systematic method of valuation was inevitable. It is being realized that not only to avoid the present bickering between the county, state, and city authorities and to do away with the inequalities arising from underassessment, but for business purposes as well, full value assessment is necessary. As some one has pointed out, "if a person is seeking investment for capital he will not ask you what the standard of value is but what is the rate of taxation."[3] And by assessing property at its full value a reduction in rate is made possible. Moreover, such

[1] The agitation of the Single Taxers for a scientific valuation of the land and improvements and for full-value assessment has been especially influential and promises to eradicate some of the gross inequalities growing out of undervaluation.

[2] Montreal also is now experimenting with the new method. Cf. *Report of Assessment Department*, City of Montreal (1913), pp. 11–15. Cf. also *infra*, chapter x.

[3] *International Conference on State and Local Taxation* (1909), p. 348.

an assessment broadens the base on which the municipal loans may be contracted.

It is furthermore being recognized that to attain accuracy in assessment it is necessary to determine the value of the land and of the improvements separately.[1] The system of separate assessment is almost universal in the Australasian colonies and in Canada and is becoming so for England, Ireland, and Scotland. In this country only Indiana, Montana, North Dakota, Wisconsin, New York, and California provide for separate listing of land and improvements. It is also practiced in a number of American cities in other states.[2] The application of the more or less scientific principles, which have been evolved, to the ascertainment of the value of the site, is as yet confined to less than a dozen cities in the United States.[3]

§ 13. How does a scientific method of valuation differ from the present method? In general the assessment of property is now based on an estimate, for which there is more or less warrant, depending largely on the experience of the assessor, the time he can devote to this office, and on the political and personal influences at work. The assessor is guided by the selling price of land, by the rental, and by the assessment returns of the property owner. An expert, scientific valuation, on the other hand, must be based on certain principles of value which will assure uniformity and accuracy, and which will eliminate wholly the influence of personal and political considerations. The possibility of finding a more accurate value than the selling price may

---

[1] Such was the opinion of some of the expert valuers who testified before the different British Select Committees (*cf. supra*, chapter v), and such is the practice of realty appraisers in the United States. See also Webb, *Valuation of Real Estate*, p. 6.

[2] *National Conference on State and Local Taxation* (1907), pp. 131 *ff*. The following cities, besides those using the Somers system of valuation, also list the value of improvements and site separately: Washington, and the cities of New Jersey and Massachusetts. *Cf. Report of Commissioners of Taxes and Assessments of the City of New York* (1913), p. 120.

[3] See *infra*, §§ 13–15.

well be questioned. Indeed, if the selling price of every plot of land could always be had the difficulty of valuation would largely disappear. What is actually done is to compare the different lots on a block, for example, with one whose selling price happens to be known. It is the basis of this comparison that has been systematized and made scientific.

What a scientific valuation of real property comprises is summarized in the following resolution which was adopted unanimously at the conference of the International Tax Association in 1911: [1]

> Resolved, that as steps towards an equitable and scientific assessment of real estate we earnestly recommend: that the method of assessment *in rem* be extended to all districts in all states; the preparation and use of tax maps in each taxing district; the separate assessment of land and buildings; and the use of standard units of measurement as a basis of valuation for both land and buildings to assist the assessor in the exercise of his judgment, such standards of value to be determined for each locality by its officials with the greatest possible coöperation of its citizens, having due regard to local conditions.

First, then, the valuation must be impersonal, *in rem*, not *in personam;* [2] only those factors that influence the value of the site, irrespective of the owner's particular circumstances, irrespective also of the influence of the improvments on the site, must be taken account of by the assessor. Secondly, the essential apparatus for the valuation is a tax map. These maps "shall show the area, dimensions, and locations of the real property, and the various subdivisions of ownership." The maps shall be used alike in assessing city and country real estate, mining and forest land. In each case, however, the construction of the map will vary

[1] *International Conference on State and Local Taxation* (1911), p. 25.

[2] The assessment *in rem* does not take the owner into account, as it were, but only the real estate. It is an assessment of real estate geographically located, not in alphabetical order according to owner. *Cf.* Seligman, *Essays in Taxation* (1913), pp. 325–26.

according to the unit of measurement. Thus, the lot or block system for urban land is inapplicable for farm land, for which the acre constitutes a more appropriate unit.[1] Tax maps have been in use in the city of Newark, New Jersey, for forty years, in Milwaukee, Wisconsin, for nearly twenty years, in the Province of Quebec for even a longer period.[2] In 1907, a "timber cruise" was inaugurated in King County, Washington; maps were then employed which are expected to form an accurate basis for all future valuations.[3] Thirdly, the separate valuation of land and buildings is necessary, because the causes of their value are different. Fourthly, the selection of a unit of measurement and of a table to compute the relative values of other tracts of land is requisite to an efficient valuation. The two well-known systems for computing relative values for urban real estate assessment are the Hoffman-Neill Rule and the Somers system.[4]

§ 14. The function of the table employed to compute the relative values of different shapes and sizes of land is more important for assessment purposes than even the ascertainment of the accurate value of the unit, for it secures uniformity and equality in assessment; and uniformity and equality even exceed in importance the search after absolutely accurate values. The "Hoffman-Neill Rule"[5] is

---

[1] L. G. Powers has classified non-urban land into eight kinds for assessment purposes: (1) acres under cultivation, or being used for meadows; (2) land not under cultivation, but capable of being plowed; (3) land covered with a heavy growth of timber; (4) with orchards; and (5) acres properly classed as waste land because incapable of cultivation or of growing timber; (6) the number of acres of mineral land; (7) of quarry land; (8) land valuable by reason of oil, gas or other deposits. *International Conference on State and Local Taxation* (1909), p. 326.

[2] *Ibid.* (1911), pp. 347–48.

[3] It is interesting incidentally that the "cruise" cost $70,000, lasted a year, but resulted in an increased valuation of the timber land in the county of over $12,000,000., *ibid.* (1909), pp. 335–36.

[4] For other rules see *Manual on the Methods of Assessment of Real Estate in New York City* (1914).

[5] The "Rule," first used in New York, is known by that name because

a table showing the percentage of value for various depths of the unit, which is a 100-foot lot, as follows: [1]

Feet	Per cent	Feet	Per cent	Feet	Per cent
1.....	.0676	22....	.4123	53....	.6899
2.....	.1014	23....	.4232	54....	.6975
3.....	.1286	24....	.4339	55....	.7051
4.....	.1520	25....	.4444	56....	.7126
5.....	.1732	26....	.4548	57....	.7201
6.....	.1929	27....	.4650	58....	.7275
7.....	.2112	28....	.4751	59....	.7348
8.....	.2282	29....	.4850	60....	.7420
9.....	.2443	30....	.4947	61....	.7492
10.....	.2598	......	..	......	..
....	..	50....	.6667	98....	.9882
20.....	.3899	51....	.6745	99....	.9941
21.....	.4012	52....	.6822	100....	1.0000

Having determined the value of one-foot frontage, the assessor, with the help of the above table, is able to ascertain the value of the entire lot. The following is a description of a land-value map when completed: —

An outline map of the city is used, subdivided into such areas as may be convenient. On each side of each street, for each block, the unit value of the normal unit is entered. Thus the relation of value on one street with values on another street is at once apparent. Points showing high value will grade off towards the points showing low values, and everywhere the values on one street will interlock with the values on the next street in a way that can be seen, understood, and explained. Accuracy and precision will be introduced into an assessment. The disturbing in-

---

Judge Hoffman a half-century ago, in deciding a lawsuit before him, laid down the rule that the ordinary city lot fifty feet deep was worth two-thirds as much as an adjoining lot one hundred feet deep. *Cf. International Conference on State and Local Taxation* (1911), p. 351.

[1] Montreal has adopted the "Hoffman-Neill Rule" for determining the value of lots of a greater or less depth than one hundred feet. See *Report of Assessment Department*, City of Montreal (1913), pp. 12–13, where the whole table of which the above is an incomplete copy is given. See also *International Conference*, etc. (1911), p. 360.

fluences of abnormally high or abnormally low sales will be mini-
mized, and the assessor will be doing what he ought to do; namely,
exercising his judgment in assessing all lots within a given area in
their relative values to one another.[1]

The most difficult problem that the assessor encounters
under this system is the valuation of corner lots. It is obvious that a corner lot has more value than an inside lot.
There is no standard under the Hoffman-Neill Rule, however, as to how much greater the value is. "All that we can
at present say on this point is that the consensus of opinion
appears to be that corner influence varies according to the
use to which the property is put, being greatest in retail
business districts, and smallest in suburban residence districts." [2] The accuracy of this new system of valuation,
mechanical and hypothetical as it may seem, can be surmised from the fact that purchases and sales of property in
New York City are based on the same scale or rule as the
assessor uses.[3]

§ 15. Based on the same principle, namely, that there is a
mathematical relation between the values of the different
city sites affected by the same influences, but with a somewhat different method of computation of this relationship,
the Somers system of valuation has been devised.[4] This
system is more complete than the Hoffman-Neill Rule, for
besides the table of percentage of value of different depths
of lot, Mr. Somers has worked out a scheme of valuing

[1] *International Conference on State and Local Taxation* (1911), p. 353.
For a more detailed account of the "Rule" see Craigen, *Practical Methods
for Appraising Lands, Buildings, and Improvements.*

[2] *Ibid.*, pp. 353–54.

[3] In Chicago a similar plan for computing the value of urban land was
worked out, but according to the Manufacturers' Appraisal Company, for
whom Mr. Somers has become land valuation actuary and who have purchased control of his system, the Chicago plan is less scientific and less
accurate. *Cf.* Report of Manufacturers' Appraisal Company, *Analysis of
the Chicago Assessors' Plan of Computing Site Values,* etc.

[4] Somers, *The Valuation of Real Estate for the Purpose of Taxation.*
See also *The Somers Unit System of Realty Valuation* (pamphlet issued by
the Manufacturers' Appraisal Company).

corner [1] and alley lots, as well as other irregular and exceptional shapes and sizes of land. Very noteworthy also is the method of ascertaining the value of the "unit foot." "A unit foot is a frontage of ground one foot wide and 100 feet deep, located in the central section of a block at a distance from any street corner or other influence that might affect its value, other than which it obtains by reason of access to the life and business of the city through its own frontage." [2] To appraise the unit, persons with a knowledge of urban conditions, and of realty values are called in. Thus the system invites publicity and public interest. "There always exists in cities," says Mr. Somers,[3] "a Community Opinion that a certain street is the best for business and a consequent idea that land fronting thereon is the most valuable. From this most valuable street other streets of less value will be compared, a well-defined opinion being present that the property on the less valuable street is less valuable just in proportion as the street is less valuable, and the comparison will reach out from the center or best portion and embrace the entire city. . . ."

To appreciate the method of establishing the value of the unit by " Community Opinion " we quote the following procedure in the valuation of Cleveland: "The City Appraisal Board of Cleveland estimates tentatively the unit values of the various streets, beginning at the Public Square and working out in every direction to the corporation limits.[4] By means of maps and a campaign of pub-

[1] There is much skepticism among taxing authorities as to the principle underlying Somers' tables for computing the value of corner lots. Mr. Somers keeps his process secret.

[2] Vancil, *Somers Unit System of Realty Valuation*, p. 1.   [3] *Op. cit.*, p. 19.

[4] "The Board adopted the rule that property should be valued on the basis of the best use of it, i.e., a lot in the business section which was being used for residence purposes should be valued as business property. The owner and not the public, should bear the loss if the property were put to any other than its best use. Another rule followed was that thoroughfares, which were defined as the main channels of trade and travel, should be valued uniformly higher than the minor streets."

licity in the city newspapers, these tentative valuations
are scattered broadcast, and the community is invited to
discuss them. At a series of public meetings of the Board,
section after section of the city is covered, many parts being
gone over several times, until all interested persons are
given ample opportunity to appear before the Board and
submit evidence in favor of changing the tentative unit
values. After being thoroughly debated by the public in
this manner, the unit values finally agreed to by the majority are regarded as representing the consensus of opinion. These unit values are confirmed by the Board, and are
not open to further discussion." [1] When these unit values
have been thus agreed upon, the individual lots are then
valued in accordance with a systematic table or curve of
values. Corner lots and those abutting upon the alleys, and
lots near corners or alleys are appraised according to a
complicated table, whose underlying principle is that the
influence of corner proximity on the value of the lot ex-
tends both ways from the corner, growing less as the distance from the corner increases, until it disappears. In the
following table the application of this principle is illustrated
in part merely: [2]

Ratio of poorer frontage to better	Ratio of corner lot to middle lot	Ratio of second lot
.1	1.11	..
.2	1.14	1.02
.3	1.17	1.03
.4	1.22	1.03
.5	1.28	1.04
.6	1.36	1.05
.7	1.48	1.06
.8	1.60	1.08
.9	1.74	1.10
1.0	1.90	1.12

[1] Lutz, "The Somers System of Realty Valuation," in *Quarterly Journal of Economics*, vol. xxv, p. 174.

[2] *First National Conference on State and Local Taxation* (1907), p. 132.

The above table shows "the ratios assumed to exist between the values of the corner and second lots, and of the middle lots, where the lots are twice as long as they are broad and the corner lot has its shorter frontage on a street where the frontage is worth twice as much per foot as on the side street, these middle lots also fronting on the better street." [1]

The Somers system of valuation, of which the above description is brief and inadequate, was first put into operation by Mr. Somers in St. Paul, Minnesota, as early as 1896. Since then the following cities have tried the system: Columbus, Cleveland, Ohio, Philadelphia, Pennsylvania, Springfield, East St. Louis and Joliet, Illinois, Denver, Colorado, Houston and Beaumont, Texas.

The appraisal of buildings has also been systematized. Blank forms are used for gathering the data descriptive of the structures. The basis of the valuation is the cost of reproduction of the building minus the value of the depreciation. The cost and depreciation factors are based on the assessor's estimate, the valuation is then computed mechanically, the square foot of floor space being the unit of calculation. [2]

The advantages of a systematized method of assessment as compared with the haphazard guess-work of the prevailing system need no elaboration. More than that, the scientific, expert valuation on lines described above will exert a wholesome influence on the community socially. For example, one result would be the awakening of discussion and interest among the property owners, who will be urged and called upon to appraise the unit foot. Such participation

---

[1] For the determination of lots abutting upon the alley and of irregular shaped lots "where a high value from one street overlaps a lower value from another street," for example, other methods are employed. See pamphlets issued by the Manufacturers' Appraisal Company.

[2] *The Somers Unit System of Realty Valuation* (pamphlet issued by the Manufacturers' Appraisal Company), p. 10. See also *Report of Commissioners of Taxes and Assessments of New York* (1913), pp. 136–39.

cannot fail to arouse public spirit and interest in one of the most essential, but shunned, fields of legislation, taxation. The efficiency of the assessors and of the other tax officials will also follow; while the economic influences of the standardization of the value of real estate, upon contracting loans, and upon realty investment, for example, will likewise be advantageous. Moreover, the taxpayer will be able to compare his assessment made *in rem* with that of his immediate neighbors, which under the system of *in personam* assessment is not so simple.

§ 16. The classification, underlying principles, and fiscal expediency of the tax on land value having been discussed, there remains the consideration of the objections raised against its levy. The most vehement opposition which the new proposal has to brook grows out of its identification with the Single Tax.[1] The apprehension is current that the tax is merely the entering wedge to the Single Tax régime. Bearing in mind the differentiation made between the two proposals, however, most of the objections vanish. For example, such questions as the elasticity of the yield, which for the Single Tax is an all-important query, becomes insignificant for a subsidiary impost. So also with regard to the discriminatory, confiscatory character of the tax, and with regard to the generally accepted theory of justice in taxation. If the land-value tax be opposed on any such ground, any of the numerous excise duties, or the inheritance tax, must be similarly opposed. On the contrary, it has been argued that by the new land tax the government aims merely to shift or to impose a heavier burden of taxation, occasioned by the ever-increasing budget, on a class which is thought to be best able to bear it; just as is its purpose always in choosing one object, rather than another,

[1] It is almost entirely through fear of the adoption of the Single Tax that Professor Bullock opposes local autonomy in taxation, as is indicated strongly in his article in *International Conference on State and Local Taxation* (1911), p. 271. See also Professor Seligman, in *The Survey*, March 7, 1914, pp. 697 *ff*.

for revenue purposes; that, in exempting improvements
from taxation, the aim is to appropriate a greater share of
the profit arising from land ownership, and at the same
time relieve the capital invested in improvements and
buildings. Whatever the social and economic effects may
be, the proposal seems fiscally justifiable.[1] As to the ex-

[1] Professor Seligman brings forward certain objections to the Herrick-
Schaap Bill, a proposal to untax buildings in New York City, which it
may be profitable to touch upon at this point, in so far as they are fiscal
in character. (See *The Survey*, March 7, 1914, pp. 697 *ff*.) (1) Concerning
the fiscal theory of the tax it violates even the theory of "Benefits" inasmuch as the buildings which it proposes to untax derive benefit from the
public expenditures. Consider fire and police protection (p. 700). It is
noteworthy that in Canada this has been urged repeatedly against the exemption of improvements. But the theoretical objection had little weight
there, in view of the object to promote industry and business. It will
scarcely be denied that the high rent paid by retail dealers, for example,
enters more or less into the price of the commodities. Nor will it be denied
that in many urban communities the tax on buildings is heavier than on
other forms of capital. The consequence of this is that the tax is borne
not by the owner of the skyscraper, but by the general consumer, and as
Professor Seligman points out, by the big banks, the big lawyers, etc.
(2) With regard to the incidence of the tax he holds that so much of the
tax as does not fall on pure rent, but falls on improvements sunk *in* the
land, will be borne by the tenant, not by the owner (p. 698). Hence the
increased tax on that part of the land value will tend to be shifted in part
to the tenant. From a theoretical standpoint, in urban communities,
land-value increments are attributable primarily to the congestion of
population. But, whatever of the value added by the improvements sunk
in the land escapes exemption under a system of *expert valuation* may be
regarded as in the nature of old and fixed structures. The tax on such a
value would as likely fall on the owner as on the tenant, unless the investment for rock excavations, etc. were the general practice. From a practicable standpoint, the hypothetical difficulties in valuation have given the
assessors in western Canada and Australasia little concern. Land and
improvements are there assessed separately as a matter of course. (3) The
introduction of the tax on land value in New York City would result in a
decline in the value of the land as Professor Seligman points out (p. 701).
This would not only narrow the base of taxation, but would narrow the
base of assessment by which the amount of indebtedness that may be
incurred by municipalities is limited. It may be true that a constitutional
amendment would be necessary in the case of New York City, and the
tax may be, therefore, locally inexpedient. But the principle of the tax,
and its expediency elsewhere are not invalidated thereby. It is interesting to point out a few changes which the tax might occasion in New York

tent to which the share of the state should be increased, the community must be guided by local conditions, the rate of increase of value increment of land, the amount of revenue needed, the expediency of exempting other forms of income, and so forth.

There is, however, one serious objection which we have

City. Real estate is in this city assessed at very nearly the full value, and the land is listed separately from the improvements. Assuming that the rate of increase in the value of all the land, which the tax commissioners of New York City estimate at from four to five per cent annually, will counterbalance the fall in value as the result of the tax, the rate of tax will have to be raised through the exemption of all the improvements. Taking all five boroughs comprising New York City together, it is found that 37.9 per cent of the assessment in 1913 was on buildings. In order, then, to raise the same revenue as in 1913, the rate of tax would be increased from $1.81 on $100 to about $2.92. Whether the constitutional requirement which limits the rate to two per cent could be amended or not, it is interesting to note that in 1899 the rate was $2.48 for Manhattan and $3.27 for Queens. This reduction in tax rate on real property since 1899 means that purchasers of land before that year, and in fact before 1902 (see table on p. 92 of *Report of Commissioners of Taxes of New York*, 1913), according to the principle of "amortization," were granted a donation as it were. By raising the rate under the new system the long-time owners will have little cause to complain. It must, however, be borne in mind that the increased rate will not necessitate an increase in the amount of tax for all landowners. All those whose property has upon it structures of a value of at least 37.9 per cent the value of the site will find their tax bill either the same or reduced under the land-value tax; only those whose land is unimproved will bear a heavier burden. The fact that the value of the land in certain sections of Manhattan is nearly 70 per cent of the assessment corroborates the contention that the buildings there are not as they should be to accommodate the congested population. Brooklyn, the town of small dwellings, on the other hand, and which has called forth recently commiseration on account of the excessive assessment (see Cederstrom, *Unjust Taxation*) will be most relieved through the new system, because the value of improvements in Brooklyn exceeds the ratio existing between buildings and land values in Greater New York taken as a whole. For the probable redistribution of tax burden on the different classes of landowners resulting from the untaxing of buildings, cf. Haig, *Some Probable Effects of the Exemption of Improvements from Taxation in the City of New York*.

The changes proposed by the Herrick-Schaap Bill will be slighter than those incurred by the total exemption of improvements and will be discussed in chapter x. The non-fiscal objections of Professor Seligman to the tax are treated in the following chapters.

not yet discussed in this chapter, namely, the relative expediency of introducing the tax on land value in urban and rural communities. It is claimed that the tax would occasion a greater hardship on rural districts than on urban municipalities. The reason is that in the latter the value of the improvements and buildings exceeds the value of the site, whereas in the country the reverse is true. Now, if improvements are exempted from the tax, the rural communities will bear the heavier burden as compared with the cities. First, as to the facts with regard to the assessment. In New York City, in Boston, in Montreal, and other old cities the land value has been found to exceed that of the improvements. In Greater New York land value in 1913 constituted 62.1 per cent of the total assessment; in Montreal and Boston about the same.[1] In Brooklyn the percentage of building to land value was greater than in Manhattan (49.8 per cent to 34 per cent), in spite of the fact that the skyscrapers and mansions are in Manhattan. Statistics about other cities are unavailable because the land and buildings are not listed separately. But in Baltimore, according to Lawson Purdy,[2] the value of the buildings is fifty-six per cent of the total value. In the rural districts farm land has on the whole the higher value relatively to buildings.[3] Nevertheless, exceptions were found to this general characteristic in a number of counties in New England and east central states. In the following states the value of the buildings on farms exceeded that of the

[1] *Report of the Commissioners of Taxes and Assessments in New York* (1913), pp. 28–53; *Report of Assessment Department*, City of Montreal (1913), p. 4.

[2] *First National Conference on State and Local Taxation* (1907), p. 379.

[3] Taking the country as a whole, less than 20 per cent of the combined value of all the farm land and buildings represented the value of the buildings. Only in New England and the middle Atlantic states did the value of the buildings on farms approach near the value of the land. In New England, in fact, the buildings and the farm machinery and implements exceeded the value of the land. *Cf. Thirteenth Census of the United States* (1910), vol. v, Table 20.

land in 1910: Pennsylvania, in ten counties; New York, in ten; Maine, in nine (total number of counties, 16); Connecticut, in four; Massachusetts, in two; New Hampshire in one; New Jersey, in two; Vermont, in four; Rhode Island, in one.[1] Moreover, if farm machinery, implements, etc., were added to the buildings, — a legitimate assumption in view of the purpose of the tax to exempt all improvements, — the land would show the smaller value in many more cases.

But in the main we may assume that the value of the land in the country is higher relatively to that of the structures than in cities. What will be the burden on rural landowners? That will depend upon the method of levy and assessment. If the tax is raised for state or even county purposes, and is apportioned according to valuation,[2] the relative burden of rural districts may be inordinately increased under the taxation of land value. Thus, in Australasia, in those cases where the tax is obligatory, the rural districts were said to be proportionately more burdened than the urban municipalities. But where the principle of local option is instituted, local conditions will determine the expediency of the tax in the various districts. In those poorer communities where land even has not a sufficient value to yield any considerable revenue,[3] other taxes must be levied. It is noteworthy, nevertheless, that in both Australasia and in western Canada, among the localities that have optionally adopted the tax on land value are many rural communities.[4] In the country, when levied for

---

[1] *Thirteenth Census of the United States* (1910), vols. VI, VII.

[2] As compared with apportionment by expenditure or revenue. *Cf.* Seligman, *Essays in Taxation* (1913), pp. 359 *ff.*

[3] *Ibid.*, p. 85.

[4] A contributor to *The Public* (August 22, 1913) claims that the reform in taxation in western Canada is a farmers' movement. "These Canadian farmers are not satisfied, however, to have only municipal taxes levied on the land. Their organizations . . . have expressed themselves as in favor of levying all taxes, Dominion, Provincial, and Municipal on land values" (p. 800). The President of the United Farmers of Alberta spoke as fol-

local purposes, or even when levied for state or county purposes, provided the apportionment of the quota of the tax among the localities is made according to the *expenditure* of the respective localities,[1] the exemption of structures will not increase the rate of tax much over the present rate, because of the relatively small value of the buildings. The solution of the difficulty raised by the objection would seem to be local option in taxation, which the rural districts especially need to rid themselves of the tax on personal property as well.[2]

Finally, it may be asked which form of the tax is fiscally most expedient. Obviously the reply will differ according to the purpose of the tax and the conditions in the various countries. In the United States, where real estate taxation prevails, but where value-increment and indirect land taxes are unknown, and where progressive taxation was until recently practically non-existent and is yet unpopular, the annual, direct tax would seem more expedient than the European forms. Moreover, we lack the conditions of land tenure of England to seek the more discriminatory forms of the tax. For general purposes and for local revenue the exemption of improvements, scientific valuation, and full value assessment, would have the effect of taxing the "unearned increment" accruing from landownership, without introducing the novel system of value-increment and progressive rates.[3] Nevertheless, where the fiscal con-

lows in his Annual Report: "Few realize the importance of, and what Single Tax really will accomplish. Let me point out some of its most important recommendations. It will take the weight of taxation off the agricultural districts, where land has little or no value, irrespective of improvements, and put it on towns and cities where bare land rises to the value of millions of dollars per acre. . . . Thus the farmer would have to pay no more taxes than the speculator," etc. *United Farmers of Alberta, Official Report* (1912), p. 9.

[1] *Cf.* Purdy, *Local Option in Taxation.*

[2] Reasons for the social inexpediency of the tax on rural land is discussed *infra*, in the following chapters.

[3] It is doubtful whether certain fiscal authorities in this country would

sideration is not uppermost and where taxes are levied for special purposes, the value-increment tax has certain advantages: first, its collection is simple; secondly, it can be levied on future increment only, thus interfering less with the present owner's expectations of profit; thirdly, it lends itself better to the progressive scale of rates. In view of the system of realty taxation in this country, however, these considerations have less value for the United States.[1]

favor the value-increment tax in preference to the annual, direct tax on land value, if the spectre of the Single Tax régime were to them less imminent.

[1] The machinery for assessing and collecting the direct tax already exists in this country.

CHAPTER VIII

THE TAX AS A SOCIAL REFORM

§ 1. IF it is true of all taxes that the fiscal considerations are not to be divorced from the economic and other effects in judging of their expediency, it is especially important to consider the economic and social effects of the tax on land value. As a modified realty tax, the proposed changes involved in the tax on land value must be discussed in all their aspects. While no one will dispute the expediency and necessity of full-value assessment and of scientific valuation of real property, there is less unanimity of judgment with regard to the exemption of improvements from taxation. This is not strange when we consider that some fundamental social problems are involved in the proposal to exempt improvements. There is no agreement upon the meaning and prevalence of "unearned increment" and of speculation in land, nor upon the seriousness of the so-called housing problem in the various communities; while the whole problem of property in land will ever remain a logically controversial one. The best that can be done is to attempt to understand the nature of the above-mentioned problems in the light of the facts under the existent order; to examine certain social evils and the proposed reforms; and to test the efficacy of the tax on land value as a social reform by the effects of its operation where it exists.

It will be agreed that the most currently potent argument for the taxation of land value is that land rent is an "unearned" increment. The justification of this view is based on the rent concept explained in the preceding chapter. Now, the criticism generally directed by economists and laymen alike against the tax is that land rent is not the sole differential, that other incomes are likewise "un-

earned." Thus quasi-rents arising from capitalistic enterprises, from speculation in general, and even from natural ability [1] are likewise called "unearned" increments.
As commonly understood "unearned" increment is any
surplus value accruing to an individual not by virtue of
sacrifice or exertion on his part, but by virtue of his property right to a commodity. But it is also questioned whether
even a transaction in landed property does not involve some
labor on the part of the owner. Whatever view we admit,
so much is certain. There is a tendency in recent years to
differentiate between income accruing to labor in its widest
sense including entrepreneurship, and that accruing from
the investment of capital in any form. The latter is commonly considered the source of the enormous wealth accumulated by individuals which, it is evident, the modern
"Sozialpolitik" would prevent. Misleading as the term
"unearned" income may logically appear, it will probably
be retained, since English and German legislation has recognized the distinction between earned and unearned income.[2]

Just as in the case of monopoly and large scale capitalistic
production, legislation has been employed to check the
concentration of wealth in the interest of the social well-
being, so with regard to the land-value increments, it is
proposed to prevent some of the putative evils by means
of a tax. The fiscal expediency of the proposal having been
discussed,[3] the problem is now to discover (1) whether
those putative increments in land value are of widespread
occurrence, if they occur at all, (2) the causes and the
social evils that ensue therefrom, and (3) the effectiveness
of the tax to remedy the evils.

§ 2. What are the facts concerning the appreciation in
the value of the land? The difficulties encountered in at-

[1] *Cf.* Marshall, *Principles of Economics* (5th ed.), p. 579.
[2] *Cf.* the English income tax and the German "Wertzuwachssteuer"
where the term "unearned" is employed.
[3] See *supra*, chapter VII.

tempting an answer become apparent when we consider the several kinds of land, the lack of uniformity in the development of the several countries, the social, economic, and physical differences of communities, and the inadequate data due partly to insufficient information, partly to the practice of assessing, as a single class of property, both the land and improvements upon it.

To begin with, it will be necessary to classify land into three main categories: —

(1) Land used in the production of raw stuffs, i.e., agricultural land which forms the main source of human sustenance.

(2) Land necessary for dwellings and industrial purposes, i.e., urban land.

(3) Land containing the product in a form ready for use — in contradistinction to that requiring fertilization — i.e., mines and forests.

The following considerations make the distinction between rural and urban land apparent: First, agricultural production must be put in a class by itself. And it must be borne in mind that as yet the prevailing unit in agricultural industry is the small farm. Secondly, the transition from extensive to intensive farm cultivation has been very much retarded on account of the relative abundance of virgin soil. Thirdly, the demand for urban land is not merely for industrial purposes. The demand is composite; for it is a demand also for dwellings by a comparatively numerous population in a comparatively limited area. Fourthly, the unit of valuation of rural land is the acre, as compared with the lot in towns. The third kind of land, namely, natural resources in a limited sense, must be differentiated from the other kinds for many reasons. Unlike the other kinds, mines and forests belong in the category of wasting assets.[1] Upon their proper use or misuse, therefore, de-

---

[1] In a larger sense this is true also of agricultural land which may be used up through a careless, extensive cultivation.

pends the welfare of society. Hence in considering this
kind of land, the whole problem of conservation confronts
us.

In the following sections, then, we may expect to find
the tendency of values in the three kinds of land to vary
not only with regard to one another, but with regard to
the diverse conditions of place, population, and stage of
development.

§ 3. The discussion of agricultural values necessitates
a further division, for the lands under cultivation in the old
countries are not comparable to the virgin soils of Australasia and America. Bearing this fact in mind, we shall first
present some data regarding the European situation, and
then shall endeavor to show the tendency of value changes
in the newer countries.

TABLE SHOWING THE RENTAL OF AGRICULTURAL
LAND IN THE UNITED KINGDOM, 1750–1904 [1]

Year	Rental in millions (£)	Per cent of change in value
1750..........	16.6	..
1776..........	22.4	increase, 34.9
1800..........	32.6	" 45.5
1815..........	46.5	" 46.5
1843..........	54.4	" 17.0
1860..........	58.3	" 7.1
1870..........	64.1	" 9.1
1880..........	69.5	" 8.5
1888..........	61.2	decrease, 11.9
1894..........	56.2*	" 8.1
1904..........	52.0	" 7.1

* This figure was obtained from Mulhall, *Industries and Wealth of Nations*, p. 406.

From the above table we note that the rental value rose
steadily until early in the nineteenth century, held its own

[1] Mulhall, *Dictionary of Statistics* (1899), p. 341; the figures before 1870
are estimates; from that date, the figures are those taken from the Reports
of Inland Revenue. *Cf. Agricultural Statistics* (Cd. 3870), 1907, Table
XXIV.

until the eighties, although the percentage of increase diminished gradually, and since the eighties has declined considerably. The tendency of agricultural land values in the United Kingdom (1781–1880) to fluctuate about an average, showing comparative stability and appreciation in the price of the land, is illustrated also by the following table: —

AVERAGE PRICE OF FARM LAND PER ACRE[1]

1781–1800	£33.8
1801–1820	36.2
1821–1840	23.7
1841–1860	36.4
1861–1870	43.
1871–1880	51.3
Average price	£35.1

Evidence of the decline in agricultural land values in Great Britain since the eighties is abundant. For example, the Royal Commission on Agriculture of 1895 [2] quoted numerous illustrations of the decline in rental; in fact cases occurred where no rent could be paid. That this depression has continued to the present the following statement by Professor Nicholson [3] is evidence: "The conclusion, then, is that for the last half century instead of an *unearned increment* from agricultural land, there has been an unearned (and certainly undeserved) decrement."

Turning to France the situation regarding agricultural land values is similar to that in England. In France "land trebled in value between 1817 and 1879, but it has since fallen one-third." [4] This estimate is borne out by the following table showing the value of arable land in France: [5]

---

[1] Mulhall, *Dictionary of Statistics* (1899), p. 759. Average prices of estates sold in those years.

[2] See *Final Report of the Royal Commission of Agriculture, 1894–97* (C. 8540), pp. 207–08; also *Particulars of Expenditures and Outgoings,* etc. (C. 8125), 1896, pp. 40 *ff.*

[3] *Rates and Taxes as Affecting Agriculture,* p. 72.

[4] Mulhall, *Industries and Wealth of Nations,* p. 413.   [5] *Ibid.*

Year	Value in millions (£)	Per cent of change in value
1817..........	548	..
1879..........	2,301	increase, 319.8
1881..........	2,986	" 29.7
1895..........	1,386	decrease, 53.2

From another source of information, the percentage of decrease in the value of agricultural land in France was estimated at less than appears from the preceding figures.[1] This more conservative estimate was derived after a careful valuation of the land in 13,606 French communes, covering, therefore, a large part of the territory of France. From 1879 to 1884 the rural land in these communes was valued at 783,636,000 fr.; in 1909–10 the value had fallen to 616,540,000 fr., or 21.3 per cent. Another authority estimates the decline in the value of farm land at forty per cent.[2] Although the estimates of the extent of the depression vary, the fact remains that during the last generation the value of agricultural land has considerably depreciated.

Belgium has been likewise affected by the agricultural depression of the eighties. The average value of farm land per hectare declined from 4261 fr. in 1880 to 2838 fr. in 1895, about thirty-one per cent; the rental value declined during the same period from 107 fr. to 90 fr.[3] Ample evidence exists to show that this trend of values has been general throughout Europe.

The causes for this situation are not far to seek. They are to be found chiefly in the low prices of grain due to American and Australian competition, resulting from the

---

[1] *International Institute of Agriculture. Bulletin of Bureau of Economic and Social Intelligence*, vol. XVIII, April, 1912, pp. 220 ff. The author estimates the depression in the price of typical holdings from 600 fr. in 1856 to 210 fr. in 1908, or 65 per cent.

[2] *Cf. Congrès International de la Propriété Foncière* (1900), p. 561.

[3] *Annuaire Statistique de la Belgique* (1902), vol. XXXIII, p. 291.

improved facilities for transportation, and in the greater profitableness of manufacturing industries. An effect which is at the same time a proof of the general condition of agricultural depression in Europe is the marked decrease in the rural population. For example, the English rural population, which was 42 per cent of the total population in 1771, constituted 22 per cent of the total in 1841 and less since then; [1] the agricultural population in Belgium fell from 24.98 per cent to 18.79 per cent of the total population from 1846 to 1895.[2] In Germany too the percentage of those engaged in agricultural production decreased from 42.5 per cent in 1882 to 28.65 per cent in 1907.[3]

§ 4. But while value decrements, not value increments, characterize European farm land, the opposite tendency seems characteristic of the newer countries. Generally speaking, with the progress of the nineteenth century to the present, with the introduction of railroad and improved waterway transportation, the superior fertility of the soil in America and Australasia caused an extension of the grain market to a world market, while the growth in population had the same effect, an increased demand for agricultural land. The result has been a corresponding increase in the value of farm land as the accompanying table shows.

It is obvious that to determine precisely the real increase in the value of the land when farms and buildings are classed together as in the subjoined table is impossible. Nevertheless, as the ratio of the value of the buildings to that of the land in the country is small, the degree of error in estimating the percentage of increase can be but slight. It will be noted that while the number of farms since 1850 increased nearly 339 per cent, the value of the farm land

---

[1] Weber, *Growth of Cities in the Nineteenth Century, Columbia University Studies in Political Science*, vol. XI, p. 166.

[2] *Annuaire Statistique de La Belgique* (1902), vol. XXXIII, p. 272.

[3] *Handbuch der Politik*, vol. II, p. 263.

INCREASE IN THE VALUE OF FARM PROPERTY AND IN AGRICULTURAL PRODUCTION IN THE UNITED STATES [1]

Year	No. of farms	No. engaged in agriculture	Value of farms and buildings
1850...........	1,449,073	..	$3,271,575,426
1860...........	2,044,077	..	6,645,045,007
1870...........	2,659,985	5,922,471	7,444,054,462
1880...........	4,008,907	..	10,197,096,776
1890...........	4,564,641	8,565,926	13,279,252,649
1900...........	5,737,372	10,438,219	{ 13,058,007,995 * { 3,556,639,496
1910...........	6,361,502	12,659,203	{ 28,475,674,169 { 6,325,451,528

* The upper figure is the value of the farm land, the lower one that of the buildings.

and buildings increased almost 964 per cent. Furthermore, during the last decade, 1900–10, the increase in farm land *per se* was over fifteen billion dollars, or 118 per cent.

If we turn to the conditions in Australasia, it will be discovered that a similar trend of value increment exists there as appears from the data given in the table on page 356.

It would be possible to show the same tendency of rising value for farm land in the other Australian states and Canada [2] and wherever the development of the country and the demand for foodstuffs is growing.

§ 5. It may be expected that with the further extension of the cultivation of the soil and with the closer settlement of the country rural land will continue to rise in value in new countries and ultimately in the European countries. Nevertheless, it would be erroneous to assume that all farm land even in the newer countries tends to rise in value. The fact is that the value of farm land is subject to

[1] *Statistical Abstract of the United States Census* (1910), pp. 119, 121, 265; also *Report of the Twelfth Census*, vol. v, Table ix.

[2] *Cf. Statistical Year Books of Canada* (1904, 1910, etc.).

INCREASE IN THE VALUE OF RURAL LAND IN
AUSTRALASIA [1]

Year	Unimproved value of land in counties of New Zealand	Unimproved value of rural land in Victoria
1878...............	£48,212,290	..
1888...............	57,201,387	..
1891...............	57,880,233	..
1897...............	63,732,516	..
1902...............	71,747,758	..
1904...............	82,513,630	£77,557,628
1906...............	99,236,462	81,198,431
1908...............	114,301,726	91,025,874
1910...............	124,560,720	100,646,814
1912...............	138,813,886	106,752,622
1913...............	152,273,929	109,512,311

great fluctuation. In many parts of the United States, for
example, much country land has become impoverished and
abandoned. This impoverishment has been greatest in our
south central states, except Alabama, Kentucky, and Ten-
nessee. There has also been considerable impoverishment
and retardation in the southeastern states, especially in
West Virginia and Georgia; also in North Dakota, Nebraska, and Kansas land values have depreciated when
cultivation of the soil had to be abandoned. West of the
Mississippi four states reported a considerable reduction
in productivity. The total area of counties comprising impoverished land has been estimated as 307,730 square
miles or 10.3 per cent of the total land area of the United
States.[2] Moreover, 16,597 square miles, 0.6 per cent of the
total area, have been abandoned. Half of this abandoned
land is in southeastern United States.[3] Temporary fluc-

[1] *New Zealand Official Year Book* (1913), p. 860; *Victorian Year Book*
(1911–12), p. 223. *Cf.* also, Mulhall, *Dictionary of Statistics* (1911), p.
367.

[2] *Report of the National Conservation Commission* (1909), vol. I, p. 77.

[3] *Ibid.*, p. 78. It is not generally known that the oft-mentioned aban-

tuations frequently occur with the extension of production to our western prairie regions as well as with the exhaustion of the soil. Again, considered for short periods of time, through the introduction of improvements in the methods of cultivation and the substitution of intensive for extensive production rural land values are very often affected.[1]

Similarly, fluctuations are frequent in Australasia and Canada. Speculation in these countries has been and continues to be rampant, leading to "land booms" or to inordinate appreciation in land value, which later result in precipitate depressions. An illustration from Ontario, Canada, will make this tendency of rural land value to fluctuate more apparent. Consequent upon the opening up of Manitoba, the value of farm land experienced a decline in Ontario from $625,478,706 in 1884 to $587,246,117 in 1894.[2]

To conclude: (1) The extension of distant sources of grain supply due to the improvement of transportation facilities, along with social causes, e.g., dissatisfaction with rural life, changed conditions of labor, etc., has been the cause of the agricultural depressions and of the decline of rural land value in European countries. (2) In the new world, the extension of production, so detrimental to European agriculture, has not only been a boon to the farmers, but is also the cause of the appreciation in the value of rural land of the country as a whole. (3) The general upward trend of values is, however, not universal throughout the more newly opened countries, nor is the rise in value uniform. In many states and sections of the country, the value of rural land is subject to great fluctuation; in others the value remains constant. (4) Although,

doned farms common in New England have been largely reoccupied and rendered productive recently by Italian and French-Canadian farmers. (*Ibid.*)

[1] *Cf.* Fairchild, *Rural Wealth and Welfare*, pp. 300 *ff.*

[2] *Statistical Year Book of Canada* (1895), p. 303.

as free land is taken up and cultivated, as intensive super-
sedes extensive cultivation, and as the population increases, agricultural land will tend to appreciate in value;
for a long time to come, we may expect to find constant
values and decrements, more often than increments, characteristic of rural land.

§ 6. The problem of determining the trend of land value
in urban communities presents serious difficulties. The
rise and growth of cities in the nineteenth century have
been phenomenal and unprecedented in the history of the
world. And it is generally held that the movement of concentration of the population in cities will tend to continue.[1]
Cities, however, do not always progress in the same way,
nor to the same degree, the growth of some being far more
rapid than that of others. Their relative growth depends
upon such factors as differences in wealth, in the character
of the industries undertaken, in the number of population,
in topography, in transportation facilities, in climate, in
the platting system, and so forth.[2] All these factors in
urban growth likewise exercise an influence on the value of
the land. The value of urban land, indeed, is affected and
disturbed even by changes in the current rate of interest
(the capitalization rate for realty varies with the character
and use of the building and neighborhood, etc.), and by any
judicial decisions affecting property rights. Other influences
that are apt to depreciate land value are public or quasi-
public structures, as, for example, the elevated roads and
other so-called "nuisances." In studying the data presented below, therefore, showing the general movement of
values, it must not be overlooked that even in the most developed cities there are districts markedly retrogressive
and deteriorated.

The value of urban land is, of course, attributable to the

---

[1] *Cf.* Weber, *Growth of Cities in the Nineteenth Century*, in *Columbia Univ. Studies*, vol. XI, chap. IX.

[2] Hurd, "Distribution of Land Values," in *Yale Review*, vol. XI, p. 144.

fact that land is needed for residence and business purposes
and that the number of more desirable sites is limited. It
may therefore be laid down as a general principle that in
all countries, wherever the concentration of population
and progress are in evidence, the value of land will tend to
rise. Not to illustrate any abnormal growth in value, but
to show the general trend and to emphasize the extraordinary character of the increase especially in the larger
cities, the following statistics are presented.

In New York City the assessed value of real estate has
increased as follows: [1]

Year	Total real estate	Land	Improvements
1898.............	$1,856,567,923	..	..
1900.............	3,168,557,700	..	..
1902.............	3,332,647,579	..	..
1904.............	5,015,463,779	..	..
1906.............	5,738,487,245	$3,367,233,746	$1,959,179,364
1908.............	6,722,415,789	3,843,165,597	2,298,334,522
1910.............	7,044,192,674	4,001,129,651	2,490,206,348
1912.............	7,861,898,890	4,563,357,514	2,716,222,137
1913.............	8,006,647,861	4,590,892,350	2,796,344,754
1914.............	8,049,859,912	4,602,852,107	2,855,932,518
1915.............	8,108,760,787	4,643,414,776	2,884,475,851

In considering the above figures, it must be noted that
the assessed value of the land here given does not include
the value of the land owned by corporations, which is, however, included in the total value of the real estate; and that
until a few years ago the assessment was much below the
actual value, in some cases as much as thirty per cent below. Since 1906 the per capita value of the land itself has
fluctuated from between eight and nine hundred dollars.

[1] *Report of Tax Commissioners of New York City* (1915), pp. 20–21, 71.
The discrepancy in the figures between the separate and combined values
of real estate is accounted for by the separate classification of the real
estate owned by corporations and special franchises which are included
in the total value of real estate.

In 1915, the per capita value was estimated at $816. Allowing for the incompleteness of the data, the enormous increments in land value are, nevertheless, evident. In the decade, 1898–1908, the increase in the total value of real estate was nearly *five thousand millions* of dollars, or 262 per cent; since 1908, the increment has been again more than *one thousand* millions. To take a particular instance of the enrichment of private individuals by the enormous increments of land value, it was estimated by the assessors that the bare site on which Macy's store in New York City is located was worth, in 1907, $10,000,000 per acre.[1] And lest this be considered an exceptional case, attention is again called to the fact that for every additional member to the population of New York City the value of the land is enhanced about $800.[2]

Similar value increments have occurred in London, where it has been estimated that the increase in the value of the land from 1870–90 amounted to about £7,620,000, annually, and where every new inhabitant added during that same period more than $400 to the value of the land.[3]

Or take Chicago for illustration. The financial history of a quarter acre of land in Chicago, not unlike that in all the larger cities, has been traced as shown in the subjoined table.[4]

The correlation of land-value increments with the growth of population will be noted. In the same connection the

---

[1] *First Conference on State and Local Taxation* (1907), p. 401. There are sites in New York valued at $40,000,000 per acre.

[2] "The *bona fide* land values of New York City exclusive of expenditures by the owners or assessments by the city increase about $800 a year for every person who has been admitted to the population." (Marsh, *op. cit.*, p. 23.)

[3] Weber, *Ueber Bodenrente und Bodenspekulation*, pp. 128–29.

[4] *Eighth Biennial Report of the Illinois Bureau of Labor Statistics* (1894), p. 277. The enormous rise in the value of land in Chicago is even more astonishing than that in New York City and London because the territory comprised by Chicago is much greater in proportion to population than in the other two cities.

Year	Population of Chicago		Value of one quarter acre	Per cent of increase in value	Per cent of decrease in value
	Numbers	Increase per cent			
1830..........	50	..	$20	..	..
1831..........	100	100	22	10	..
1832..........	200	100	30	40	..
1833..........	350	75	50	67	..
1834..........	2,000	467	200	300	..
1835..........	3,265	60	5,000	2400	..
1840..........	4,470	37	1,500	..	70
1845..........	12,088	170	5,000	233	..
1850..........	28,269	134	17,500	250	..
1855..........	80,023	183	40,000	129	..
1860..........	109,000	36	28,000	..	30
1865..........	178,900	64	45,000	61	..
1870..........	298,977	67	120,000	167	..
1875..........	400,000	34	92,500	..	23
1880..........	503,298	26	130,000	40	..
1885..........	700,000	40	275,000	111	..
1890..........	1,098,570	57	900,000	228	..
1892..........	1,300,000	19	1,000,000	111	..
1894..........	1,500,000	16	1,250,000	25	..

following estimate quoted by Mr. Marsh [1] is impressive: "In 1818 the United States gave the square mile between State, Madison, Halsted, and Twelfth Streets (Chicago) to the State of Illinois to be held in trust for the support of the public schools and the education of the children of Chicago. Except for one block between Madison, Dearborn, State, and Monroe Streets, nearly all of this square mile was sold about seventy years ago for less than $40,000. Within fifteen years after it was sold this square mile was worth six million dollars. To-day its value is hundreds of millions of dollars (without improvements). The rent from this square mile of land would be sufficient to support for all time the entire school system of the State of Illinois without an additional dollar of taxation."

The development of German cities, likewise, has been

[1] *Op. cit.*, p. 109.

and continues to be extraordinary. From agricultural
values about 1870, land has risen many hundred fold in
value as the towns grew. Examples have already been
given of this oft-cited phenomenon.[1] A few more must suffice here. As in the other countries the metropolis, in this
case Berlin, leads and exemplifies this tendency best.

The approximate value of the area on Kurfürstendamm,
the principal thoroughfare of Charlottenburg, a comparatively new portion of Berlin, is shown below:[2]

Year	Value in million marks	Per cent of increase
1860...................	0.1	100
1865...................	1.0	1,000
1870...... :...........	2.5	2,500
1872...................	6.5	6,500
1885...................	14.0	14,000
1890...................	30.0	30,000
1898...................	50.0	50,000

The value of the land in Charlottenburg as a whole has also
appreciated enormously:[3]

Year	Value in million marks			
	Improved land	Per cent of increase	Unimproved land	Per cent of increase
1865.............	6	..	4	..
1880.............	30	400	20	400
1886.............	45	50	30	50
1897.............	300	566	100	233

From Professor Conrad's[4] illustrations of land-value
increments we quote the following: "In Frankfurt a. M. in

---

[1] Cf. chapter IV, § 7.   [2] Mangoldt, op. cit., p. 62.
[3] Voigt, P., Grundrente und Wohnungsfrage in Berlin und seinen
Vororten, p. 217.
[4] Grundriss Zum Studium der Politischen Oekonomie, vol. I, p. 128.

a period of fifteen years, 1880–95, the land had appreciated sixty per cent in value, while in Karlsruhe it had increased from 400 to 500 per cent in a period of thirty years."

In a paper delivered before the Congrès International de la Propriété Foncière, Professor Philippovich was cited as authority for the case of a piece of land in Vienna whose present value increment amounted to 3526 per cent of its original value in 1875.[1] Similar striking instances were cited at this conference. For example, a certain part of Paris was worth, less than a century ago, scarcely fifty centimes per square metre (5000 fr. per hectare); this land has since increased 699,900 per cent in value. "The value increment of unbuilt property in the environs of Paris, that is suburban land, has been estimated to have increased 1,793.07 per cent between the years 1851–79." [2]

The general trend of urban land values is unmistakable. The best proof of this is the fact that realty experts have been able to formulate an approximate scale of normal values per front foot like the following one,[3] "it being understood that the actual highest values in the various cities vary widely from any average scale, owing to the marked differences between these cities in wealth, character of industries . . .": —

City population	Best business per front foot	Best residences, per front foot
25,000..........	$300 to $400	$25 to $40
50,000..........	600 " 800	40 " 75
100,000..........	1,200 " 1,600	75 " 150
150,000..........	1,800 " 2,400	100 " 200
200,000..........	2,400 " 3,200	100 " 300
300,000..........	3,600 " 4,800	200 " 500
600,000..........	7,200 " 9,600	1500 " 2000
2,000,000..........	23,000 " 31,000	2000 " 3000
3,500,000..........	42,000 " 56,000	6000 " 9000

[1] *Congrès International de la Propriété Foncière* (1900), pp. 566–67.
[2] *Ibid.* Quotation translated from the French.
[3] Hurd, "Distribution of Urban Land Values," in *Yale Review*, vol. XI, p. 144.

According to Lawson Purdy, the president of the tax department of New York City, the annual rate of increase of real property in New York City should be from four to five per cent, since real property tends to increase somewhat faster than the annual increase in population, which is about three per cent.[1]

§ 7. In spite of the facts cited to show the upward tendency of urban land value, it must not be inferred that no decrements occur. Even in the most advanced urban communities, land does not increase in value always and everywhere. Some of the reasons have already been given for the occurrence of depreciation in value.[2] Changes in the development of the city or town are apt to depress values in certain districts. For example, when the utilization of land either for business or residence purposes declines, the value of the land likewise declines. Sometimes through changes in the internal structure of the city, e.g., when the residence section is superseded by industrial undertakings, or when a factory and a foreign population invade a neighborhood, values are adversely affected. Sometimes districts retrograde because of encroachments of public utilities or so-called "nuisances."[3] As a general rule retail property tends to follow the best residence section, while wholesale business replaces retail property or changes its location so as to be near the wharves and railroad terminals.[4]

Besides decrements that reflect changes in the city's development,[5] urban land has often experienced a deprecia-

[1] *Report of the Commissioners of Taxes and Assessment of the City of New York* (1909), p. 17; (1908), p. 7.

[2] *Cf. supra*, § 6.

[3] The improvement of transportation facilities, moreover, such as the construction of elevated roads, may cause a decline in land value by opening up suburban land. Some public improvements such as parks increase values generally. *Cf. Real Estate Magazine*, November, 1913, pp. 61 *ff.*

[4] *Cf. Practical Real Estate Methods* (1909), pp. 202–03.

[5] There are many other causes than changes in the population. The New York Tax Commissioners found that the owners' failure to replace

tion in value because of a previous overvaluation. For example, take the case of the quarter acre of Chicago land whose changing value has been tabulated.[1] Had the complete original table in which the annual changes were traced been reproduced, it would have been observed that in the sixty-five years, from 1830 to 1894, decrements in its value had occurred seventeen times.[2] Indeed, Chicago is an illustration of fluctuating values in real estate. As a result of the speculation and overcapitalization of land, Chicago real estate is said to be valued to-day on an 1889 basis,[3] for the expected rentals on which the value of the land was then based have failed to materialize. For example, in 1851 certain sites on Twenty-fifth Street were valued at $250 per acre; six years later the value had risen to $5000; after three years it sold for $25,000; in 1862 the value fell to $20,000, after which the property was improved, its value rising enormously until 1900, when it sold for only one-half its value twenty years earlier.[4] According to a real estate dealer this example is typical of Chicago property. "Real estate is now selling about on an 1889 basis. It reached high figures in the early seventies, too high for that time, and it required some fifteen or twenty years for the city to reach the values fixed in 1873; but while the city was growing to these values, the values themselves were falling back, so that somewhere about 1885 real estate was selling at about what it was worth. Another upward movement in the

their obsolete buildings with new ones resulted in lower returns and the depreciation of land value. See *Report of Commissioners* (1913), p. 8.

[1] *Supra*, § 6.

[2] These decrements, it is noteworthy, occurred in 1837, again in 1857, again in 1873, showing the effect of the panics and hard times on the value of realty.

[3] That is because, on account of the immense territory of Chicago and on account of the easy transportation facilities, the congestion of population is less imminent. This is shown by the comparative average value of land quoted in the Chicago *Tribune*, August 26, 1913, as follows: the average for Pittsburgh was $19,096; for New York City, $19,887; for Chicago, only $8138.

[4] Chicago *Real Estate News* (1909), p. 186.

early nineties carried values some ten years ahead of real conditions. The city began rapidly to overtake these values while the values themselves fell back to meet real conditions. This process has gone on now for fifteen years. Since the World's Fair a new city has been added to each of the sides of the river, wealth has accumulated, public improvements have been made, every token which goes to make a great metropolis has come into evidence, but the real estate pendulum has only begun to swing upward." [1]

In still another way are depreciations likely to occur for a shorter or longer period. Whenever the attempt to build artificial towns or cities, "paper towns," fails, the result is disastrous to the value of land. In Hurd's words: [2] "An apparent exception to the general law of no value in the site when the city starts occurs where cities are speculatively undertaken and the future is discounted, lots selling at comparatively high prices in advance of utility. The difference between price and value is usually demonstrated before many years, the swing of the pendulum carrying these lots as far below their value as prices were formerly above it. Thus lots in Columbus, Ohio, which sold in 1812 at $200 to $300, sold in 1820 at $7 to $20, and of recent instances there are many, such as the collapses in the early history of the speculatively started towns of West Superior, Wis., Tacoma, Wash., Everett, Wash., and Birmingham, Ala."

§ 8. With regard to the third class of land, namely, mines and forests, the problem is of a different character. We are here concerned with the problem of the conservation of natural resources. Mineral and forest lands are, moreover, distinguished from each other by the important fact that when exhausted or used up minerals cannot be replaced, while forests can be cultivated provided a suf-

---

[1] Chicago *Real Estate News* (1909), p. 186.

[2] "Distribution of Urban Land Values," in *Yale Review*, vol. XI, pp. 126–27.

ficiently long time is allowed. Nevertheless, as operated to-day forests as well as mines may be regarded as wasting assets. The United States Conservation Commission estimated that at the present increasing rate of production the coal supply of the United States will be near exhaustion before the middle of the next century, and that the high-grade iron ore will not last beyond the middle of the present century; so with the known supply of petroleum in the United States. "The consumption of nearly all our mineral products is increasing far more rapidly than our population. In many cases the waste is increasing more rapidly than the number of our people. In 1776 but a few dozen pounds of iron were in use by the average family; now, our annual consumption of high-grade ore is over 1200 pounds *per capita*. In 1812 no coal was used; now, the consumption is over five tons and the waste nearly three tons *per capita*." [1]

As regards our forests there are to-day over 200,000,000 acres less forest land than there were originally. "We take from our forests each year, not counting the loss by fire, three and one half times their yearly growth." [2] Of the countries exporting timber, only three, Russia, Finland, and Sweden, "have increased their exports to great extent without encroaching on their timber capital." [3] Yet, in spite of the substitutes for timber for various purposes, the consumption of timber has increased many fold.

In these circumstances the value of mineral and forest land has enormously appreciated. And taking these lands as a whole, the upward trend of values will continue as the opening of inferior mines is necessitated, and as the supply of timber is lessened. But the exhaustion of these natural resources, unless a policy of conservation is pursued, is inevitable. Moreover, as regards particular mines or forests, under ordinary circumstances, when the resources

[1] *Report of the National Conservation Commission* (1909), vol. I, p. 16.
[2] *Ibid.*, p. 58.   [3] *Ibid.*, vol. II, pp. 351.

give out the value increments do also. Great fortunes have been made through the increased value of natural resources and great fortunes will continue to be thus gained, but the process is limited. This class of land, then, is not only to be differentiated from the other two classes; but the problem presented by it is also of a different character from that which either the agricultural or urban land presents.[1]

§ 9. If we summarize the results concerning the three kinds of land we shall answer the inquiries: First, what gives land its value and its value-increment? Secondly, what factors distinguish one kind of land from each of the others? Thirdly, what problems does the phenomenon of increments and decrements present?

Scarcity, not of land as such, but of the various grades of land, depending upon the fertility, location, or richness of deposit, is the cause of the value of land. Land as a non-reproducible good becomes subject to monopoly price, whenever the demand for a certain quality or kind exceeds the supply. This demand, which is reflected in the high value or value increment, is created by an ever-increasing population and progress. By the latter are meant the changes in mode of life, pleasures, and comfort which occasion a proportionately greater demand for all products, including urban land. Granting that the population will grow and progress continue, we may assume that higher values will follow in all three classes of land. That, however, is a hypothesis concerned with the remote future. At present the problem is practically different for each kind of land and it is with the present conditions that we are here concerned.

To-day, in the case of agricultural land, the fact that decrements in value prevail in the older countries shows that there exists no world scarcity of farm land below a

[1] In essence there is less difference between agricultural land and forests, for example. Both need to be conserved. In the present era, however, the problem of conservation is not the same for both.

certain grade. And the fact that in new countries agricultural land tends to appreciate in value in some sections, but to depreciate in others, shows exceptionally favorable conditions of the soil which render the competition with foreign countries and with other parts of the same country profitable. Here, then, there is no problem of discriminatory legislation to divert to the coffers of the state the excessive profit accruing from the rise in the value of land. On the contrary, the government may find it expedient to promote the profit of the farm owners in the interest of greater and cheaper production.

With regard to urban land, on the other hand, the problem of monopoly value becomes more acute. Every person added to the urban population affects the value of the land more or less. The tendency of urban land value to appreciate is unmistakable. The result is that the owners of this commodity, land, reap the ever-increasing profit at the expense of the consumers, the tenants. The first problem, therefore, is that of the distribution of the value increment of the land. But the universal need on the one hand, and the scarcity of the commodity on the other, raises a second question, namely, does the present system of land tenure insure the best utilization of the land; since any misuse of the land by self-seeking individuals affects the social well-being. The evils charged to the present system of tenure are briefly: (1) speculation in land; (2) the so-called housing problem; (3) the misuse of natural resources.

The charges against speculation in land are that it fosters the monopolization of an indispensable commodity; that it artificially screws up the value of land; that it enriches one class at the expense of society in general. It is claimed that in cities a great deal of ripe building land is kept out of use by speculators who wait to pocket the profits arising from the appreciation in value. In this way they control or affect the supply like other monopolists, and through this practice rent in urban communities is unnecessarily exorbitant. As a further result, it is contended, the masses, upon whom the expenditure of rent falls most heavily as compared with the wealthier classes, are compelled either to resort to poorer dwellings, in the unsanitary and congested districts, or to give up a greater proportion of their income for rent, leaving other urgent wants unsatisfied. It is further charged that the private appropriation of land value breeds and perpetuates an idle class who contribute nothing to the improvement of the land or to social well-being. Such are the criticisms and problems which the phenomenon of urban land-value increments awakens.

As for mines and forests where speculation is also rampant, it is not so much the matter of distribution of the value, as the matter of conserving the natural resources, which calls for solution. Yet, it must not be overlooked that in this country, at any rate, the mineral and forest wealth is in the possession of a comparatively small group of persons, who practically control the prices of the natural products. The recent protests of the governments against the wasteful management of the natural resources which is a menace to social welfare is proof of the necessity for reform. As regards this class of land, therefore, the most expedient use of the resources must be considered.

All the above-mentioned problems fundamentally involve the expediency of private land ownership. Before, however, the latter is even considered, certainly before any conclusions can be reached, it is necessary to raise the questions: How rampant is speculation in land? What evils does it create? What are the extent and effect of bad housing? It is to the examination of these conditions that we now turn.

§ 10. That speculation in land exists needs no elaborate proof. The value of land is subject to change, and the essence of speculation in any commodity consists in the anticipated fluctuations in its value. Yet there is a marked distinction between the speculation in land and that in other commodities which deserves mention. We note that practically no real estate stock is sold on the stock exchange in this country,[1] and that no dealings in realty on the other exchanges occur.[2] The explanation for this lies in the peculiarity of land speculation, namely, that no short selling in land occurs. Land speculation is always "bullish." [3]

The fact seems to be that of all investments real estate is considered the safest and as yielding the most permanent income. "Nothing is more solid and permanent, more enduring in its nature and steadier in its value during cycles of time. Land cannot be destroyed, burned up, carried away by thieves, worn out or lost, nor can its real value be 'watered' by exploiters and impaired by the peculations and speculations of dishonest bank or corporation officials." . . . "It has been proved that the element of gamble in realty is less than in any other venture. Life itself is not so certain. . . . " [4] It is said that no commodity is so little affected in value during depressions as land. Some one has described the cycle of speculation somewhat as follows: At the beginning of a "boom" period there is but slight demand for real estate; at such times even realty dealers

[1] In New York, for example, the stock of only one real estate company is listed on the Stock Exchange. *Cf. Practical Real Estate Methods*, p. 273.
[2] So, too, guaranteed real estate mortgages are not attractive to speculators. *Real Estate Magazine*, October, 1912, p. 55.
[3] Dr. Eberstadt calls attention to this fact as follows: "Speculation in land is one-sided speculation; it differs decidedly from other kinds of speculation, such as, for example, speculation in stocks and grain. In the latter, the bids are up and down ('long' and 'short'), and in such transactions two parties try synchronously to further their diametrically opposed interests. In land, on the contrary, no one can speculate 'short'; without exception speculation tends to bring about a rise in price. Irrespective of the ownership, speculative land values are always 'bullish.' By this very fact speculation in land assumes a singular position as compared with all other objects of speculation." Translated from *Die Spekulation im neuzeitlichen Städtebau*, pp. 30–31.
[4] By an enthusiastic realty dealer. See Chicago *Real Estate News* (1909), p. 186; also Kirkman, " Real Estate," in *Business, Commerce and Finance* (1910), p. 319.

turn to the stock market. Everybody invests in personal property. Then the demand for realty improves, and so does its value. Although real property is the last thing to be affected, the speculative mania does finally set in, screwing up the value of land. The result is an overvaluation of property that cannot last long. As some one put it, "after real estate speculation comes the deluge." [1] It is these "fictitious" values that when the panic sets in need readjustment for the most part.[2] Aside from this element of safety and aside from the "bullish" character of the speculation in land, the fact that real estate security constitutes poor collateral for banks, makes this class of property a less attractive commodity for exchange speculation. Thus speculation in land must be placed in a class by itself.[3]

§ 11. Since the essence of speculation is to buy cheap and sell dear, we find the best examples of land speculation in new settlements where there is an abundance of free land, e.g., in the United States when first settled, the Australasian colonies, or western Canada. With the extended use of minerals in industry, mines formed an especially fertile field for speculators. And as urban communities assumed greater and greater importance, a further field was opened up for speculative operations. So long as free and cheap land existed, the speculator was generally an individual. All he had to do was to invest in a piece of land in

[1] Carney, *How to Buy and Sell Real Estate at a Profit*, pp. 202, 207.

[2] While stocks fell during 1907 more than half in value, real estate values were said to have depreciated very little and there were fewer foreclosures than in normal times. *Practical Real Estate Methods*, pp. 232–33.

[3] This anomalous character of the real estate market explains what to Mr. Cederstrom (*cf. Unjust Taxation*) seems irreconcilable, namely, the continued increase of real estate assessments in New York City during a time of a depressed market for real estate. The fact that people prefer some other investments to real property by no means signifies that real property has fallen in value. There is no overproduction or oversupply as in case of reproducible and perishable commodities. While the market activity, no doubt, in the case of real estate also, is an index to general values, yet the actual, stable value of land will rise without a market, provided the demand for dwellings and raw materials continues to rise. .

a district which he expected to develop, sit down and wait until the anticipated value was realized. For example, lots in the Bronx, New York, which sold in the eighties for $200 are now valued at $16,000 to $18,000 apiece. One who at that time invested $60 or $65, if he retained possession, can now sell the land for $6500 to $7000.[1] The returns, to be sure, were not immediate, but one of the cardinal traits of the land speculator is patience. Here is an actual illustration of a speculative transaction: In 1853 Morris sold to Nimphius a parcel of land, 150 feet front, for $300; in 1895 two lots of the parcel were sold for $9500. The following year the owner received from the city for exercising its right of eminent domain, for 9 feet, $40,000. In 1900 he received $70,000 for the balance of the land, making on his outlay of $300, $119,500, besides the usufruct of the property for fifty years.[2] Another person similarly realized, on an investment of $8000, $295,000 plus the rent of $4000 to $5000 annually. In this connection it may be pointed out that many of the millionaires owe their vast fortunes in part to land-value appreciations. The Astor fortune of $450,000,000 is a standard example. According to one writer [3] eighty-nine per cent of the millionaires started with real estate investments, and sixty per cent continue to invest in it largely.

But land speculation is no longer the same as it was even a generation ago. Of course, to this day, let the building of a railroad or a subway be contemplated and the surrounding ground becomes appropriated, to be sold at a profit in the future. Or, let a new mine be discovered, and not only the mine but the country round about is soon in the hands of promoters or speculators. "Long Island's waste land," quotes Marsh,[4] "is much of it held now by speculators

---

[1] *Practical Real Estate Methods*, p. 349.   [2] *Ibid.*, p. 354.

[3] *Real Estate News* (1909), p. 186. Quoted from Cincinnati *Real Estate Bulletin*.

[4] *Op. cit.*, p. 70.

who, paying no taxes to speak of and undoubtedly in many cases none at all, can afford to wait for the natural rise. . . ." In Brooklyn, where a subway is waiting construction, 20,000 lots, assessed at a value of $15,000,000, are in the hands of speculators, who are waiting for the value increments.[1] Speculation in suburban and vacant land to-day, however, is mainly in the hands of realty dealers or of "development" companies. Land speculation, according to realty men themselves, is a profession, the four requisites of the speculator being time, capital, courage and judgment.[2] "The real estate operator at one time was a drone in the community. He was really a real estate speculator, would buy and sell at a profit, but would do nothing himself to create increased value. To-day realty operating is a profession, and the speculative side is very unimportant." That is, the real estate operator must be familiar with the market situation, with the economic conditions which influence values, and he must recognize, too, the social forces which tend to build up the community.

In this country, speculators in land are in the main individuals, while realty corporations are comparatively few;[3] in Germany, on the contrary, the latter are said to control realty operations. In the German cities, especially in Berlin, professional realty speculation is said to flourish as nowhere else. These corporations resemble the so-called "development" companies of this country in that building forms part of their operations. It is claimed that the seventy-three or more "Terraingesellschaften" have practically controlled building operations in Berlin and its suburbs. In fact the magnificent apartment houses of un-

---

[1] Marsh, *op. cit.*, pp. 108–09. "It is stated that within five years after the completion of the Market Street subway-elevated road in Philadelphia the assessed valuation of the property within its sphere of influence increased in value by $130,000,000. The cost of the subway was in the neighborhood of $20,000,000." *Real Estate Magazine*, July, 1913, p. 84.

[2] *Practical Real Estate Methods*, p. 235.

[3] In Illinois realty corporations are forbidden by law.

iform size and structure in and around Berlin are attributed to the activity of these speculators. The extent and
character of these operations is shown in the following
statement by an American realty agent: [1] "I have great
respect for the magnitude of our realty operations in New
York, but Berlin can make us sit up and take notice when
it comes to buying undeveloped suburban land and taking
chances. Imagine a seventeen-million dollar deal in vacant
lots in New York. Recently a part of the Tempelhof
Parade Ground was bought by a syndicate from the government for 72,000,000 Marks." Then he tells how the
Schoenberg apartment-house quarter was founded by the
President of the Berlin Realty Company, which has paid
one hundred per cent dividends annually for years. The
president formed a syndicate and bought the site which
ten years ago had been farm land. "It took him several
years to get control of what he wanted and he then
started to lay out model streets on curved lines." This
land was afterwards sold to building contractors, but the
realty company retained control of the architectural designs. In this manner some sections of Charlottenburg,
Grünewald, and other suburbs were founded.[2]

§ 12. From the social standpoint it is questionable
whether this changed character of land speculation is an
improvement. To-day the professional land speculator
and the building operator are generally combined in the
same person. Or they form a corporation. The methods of
operation vary. In some cases the speculator borrows
money with the land as security to finance the building.
Or he may arrange with the building contractor for the
construction of the building, and thus undertake operations involving hundreds of thousands of dollars with only
a small sum of his own. In many cases speculators have
manipulated deals so as to get both the value of the lot

---

[1] Chicago *Real Estate News*, (1911) p. 169.
[2] See Voigt, *Grundrente und Wohnungsfrage in Berlin*, pp. 218 *ff.*

and house, the latter costing him practically nothing. This is said to be a common practice in New York State where he can exploit the workmen, because in New York State the mechanic's lien does not take precedence over a mortgage claim except when such a claim is recorded prior to the recording of the mortgage.[1]

In fact, between the speculator, the loan association and the building contractor, many kinds of frauds and socially disadvantageous operations are perpetrated. For example, some cheaply built, ill-equipped houses are often erected, advertised, and sold to workingmen for the most part at a price exceeding enormously the actual value of the property. Nor is this all; in most cases the terms of sale are so manipulated that after a failure to pay interest on the mortgage, the property reverts to the speculator, who repeats the deal, exploiting one person after another.

Through coöperation with building-loan associations enormous sums of capital are put at the command of land speculators, which must facilitate their control of the community's housing. Whole towns have been established, streets laid out and houses built by such operators, who reap enormous profits through the growth of settlements and of industry. A recent illustration is Gary, Indiana.[2] It is claimed, of course, that these land promoters, by developing the suburbs and erecting houses, are benefactors to the city population in relieving the congestion of the cities. This to a certain degree must be admitted. Nevertheless, when the importance of the commodities they deal in, i.e., land and houses, are considered, the expediency of putting the welfare of the community into the hands of money-making corporations may well be questioned.

[1] *Practical Real Estate Methods*, p. 217. This has been declared, by the decision rendered in Allis-Chalmers Co. *vs.* Central Trust Co. (190 Fed. Rep. 700), to hold everywhere.

[2] The Gary Land Company, the real estate department of the United States Steel Corporation, is described as the largest real estate corporation in the world. See Chicago *Real Estate News*, August, 1912, p. 141.

One kind of operation, for example, undertaken by the above-mentioned coöperative speculators and financed by banking or other loan associations, is the erection of the magnificent apartment houses in suburban districts. The timeliness, that is, the need for these is in question. According to some realty authorities these operations in New York City (the upper part of the city) have been losing ventures because untimely. In Germany the erection of these tenements or "Mietkasernen" has given rise to a great deal of controversy as to their social value.[1] The enormously rapid growth of speculative building operations in communities scarcely urban has been pointed out by Professor Eberstadt as a social evil. Quoting from a work entitled, "Viel Häuser und Kein Heim," he illustrates his theory that besides its untimeliness, speculative building drives up rather than reduces rents.[2] In the city of Cassel, according to him, a wealthy man bought up some land which would have yielded a good profit at twenty-five marks per square metre, if three-story houses with gardens had been erected thereon. But the landowner had tall tenements put up to yield him a rental from fifty to seventy-five marks per square metre. This resulted in higher rents to the tenants; but because of the oversupply of apartments, many of which remained vacant, the income of the landlord was no higher than if the three-story houses had been built. This violation of the law of supply and demand is illustrated also by the facts in our cities where, in spite of the unsatisfied demand for better dwellings, many apartments stay vacant indefinitely. A significant example of this is furnished by St. Louis. A few years ago it was esti-

[1] The chief contestants have been Dr. R. Eberstadt who holds that the "tenements" are socially injurious as well as the cause of high rent, and Dr. Andreas Voigt, who has defended the erection of these buildings in *Kleinhaus und Mietkaserne.*

Brentano asks: "Woher kommt jene Teuerung der Wohnungen, die sich gerade in den 90er Jahren in steigendem Masse fühlbar gemacht hat? Die Antwort lautet: Es ist die Folge der Wohlorganizierten Terrainspekulation." *Cf. Soziale Zeitfragen* (1904), vol. XVII, p. 7.

[2] Eberstadt, *Die Spekulation im neuzeitlichen Städtebau*, p. 15.

mated that about 11,000 houses and flats in St. Louis, exclusive of stores and offices, were vacant. Nevertheless, rents were said to have been higher there than in Chicago.[1] The reason is probably, as in the instance cited from Eberstadt, that it is to the advantage of the owner who is a speculator [2] to keep the houses vacant rather than to reduce the rent, for by reducing the rent the market or capitalized value of his property is depreciated.

§ 13. A graver charge even than those discussed above is that in urban communities land is kept from its best utilization by owners whose chief interest lies in the value increment which the property will in time realize. That the withholding from market and from improvement of land situated in the heart of a populous city causes unnecessary enhancement of rent is logical. The question is whether there actually are so many such undeveloped sites ripe for building as to cause concern to the community. Full data regarding this point are lacking. Upon an examination of the assessment roll of the downtown section of Chicago — the central business property from the river to Sixteenth Street and the river to Lake Michigan [3] — not counting the property owned and occupied by the railroads, nearly one hundred vacant lots with from twenty-five to two hundred feet frontage each were enumerated by the writer. The number of frame buildings, moreover, of trifling value was considerable, although most of these deteriorated structures were on the outskirts rather than in the center of this section. But taking Chicago as a whole, the proportion of vacant lots would undoubtedly be much greater than in the business center.

Valuable data in regard to vacant land in New York City are reproduced in the following table: [4]

[1] Chicago *Real Estate News* (1909), p. 136.

[2] There are few urban or other landowners who are not speculators, i.e., who do not anticipate an increase in the value of their property.

[3] See *Assessed Value of Property in Chicago*, compiled by Chicago Real Estate Index Company, issue 1908–12.

[4] *Report of Commissioners of Taxes . . . of New York City* (1913), p. 67.

Borough	Total number of parcels		Number of unimproved parcels		Per cent of vacant parcels		Assessd value of vacant parcels	
	1912	1913	1912	1913	1912	1913	1912	1913
Manhattan	96,496	95,654	7,622	8,211	8.0	8.6	$169,793,000	$182,598,890
Bronx	63,047	64,261	32,016	32,849	51.0	51.0	135,496,508	150,940,152
Brooklyn	206,279	211,038	49,144	50,173	23.8	23.8	161,892,217	154,644,027
Queens	126,065	131,382	79,681	82,221	63.2	62.5	142,722,081	142,392,400
Richmond	31,443	32,930	17,531	18,228	55.8	55.5	13,831,037	14,061,716
Total	523,330	535,265	185,994	191,742	35.5	35.8	$623,734,843	$644,637,185

With reference to the above table it is evident that there are relatively fewer vacant lots in Manhattan than in the other boroughs. In Manhattan, where property is so enormously high, rents so excessive, and the tax rate on improved and unimproved land alike so heavy, it is less profitable to keep land vacant than in Queens, where 62.5 per cent is unimproved.[1] The demand for dwellings is also less in the latter borough; perhaps much of the land is not yet ripe for building purposes in Queens. Nevertheless, the enormous value of this vacant land, over 142 million dollars in Queens alone, is significant. When it is considered that in all the boroughs about 645 millions represent speculative values, since the vacant property does not yield any annual income, the problem as to the regulation of private ownership of land in New York City is seen to be a serious one.[2] Moreover, the number of vacant parcels enumerated by the tax assessors does not include land with deteriorated and almost valueless improvements upon it.[3]

During the Lloyd George Budget agitation, the discussions with regard to undeveloped land revealed the conditions in Great Britain. For example, it was said that one-fifth of the land within the boundaries of the County of London lay vacant; that in Edinburgh 2000 acres of un-

---

[1] According to the report of the tax commissioners, vacant parcels were frequently acreage plots in the suburbs, so that the actual area vacant is greater than indicated in the table. See *Report* (1913), p. 64.

[2] The serious consequences of keeping land out of use and underdeveloped is recognized by the President of the Allied Real Estate Interests, Allan Robinson, as appears from the following exhortation to the ' real estate ground hog': " But the owner of underimproved property has a responsibility to the community in the same way that the owner of unimproved has. . . . Inertia and hoggishness on the part of real estate owners underlie the Single Tax menace. . . . With the removal of the causes which have brought about the Single Tax agitation and a changed point of view on the part of real estate owners and brokers as to the duties of land ownership, the Socialistic campaign aimed against real estate will die of its own weight." (*Real Estate Magazine*, October, 1913, p. 63.)

[3] "Every parcel which contains any improvement, however slight, is counted as improved." *Report of Commissioners of Taxes of New York City* (1913), p. 64.

used land excluding parks and gardens were kept unused, "until a clear feu-duty of £160 per acre per annum can be obtained." [1] It was estimated in 1892 that in Manchester the total area of vacant land (excluding gardens, roads, and other land unsuitable for building purposes) was 4200 acres. In Birmingham, out of 13,477 acres, 3500 were unbuilt upon. It was shown that in Bradford the density in some sections was 301 persons to the acre, although the average density was only 21; and that of 10,776 acres of the land in that city, 4512 acres available for building were still vacant. Indeed, two-fifths of the entire population of England and Wales, it is claimed, are crowded on about one eight-hundredth part of the total area of the country, another two-fifths occupy a little more than one two-hundred-and-fiftieth part, and the remainder are scattered over the rest of the land.

There is, however, more reason for the withholding of land from use in European countries than in the United States. In England unimproved land is not taxable under the rating system, and the land is largely inherited. In this country, to hold vacant or undeveloped land involves the payment of taxes and special assessments as well as the foregoing for a long time of the return on the capital invested. Real estate authorities confirm this opinion. "Where assessed valuation and taxes are both high, there is no money to be made in holding vacant land for an indefinite period. Every lot which is worth say $3000 and which is unimproved has annual charges against it of at least $200, not to speak of assessments. This charge is so heavy that it usually counterbalances the increase in value. Money made in vacant land accrues to purchasers who are shrewd or lucky enough to buy at just the right moment,

[1] Chomley and Outhwaite, *Land Values Taxation in Theory and Practice*, pp. 73 *ff.* In the Town Council it was said that Edinburgh contained 3000 acres rated at agricultural value. *Cf. The Budget, the Land and the People* (1909), pp. 68 *ff.*

and who capture a quick profit." [1] Or, as another one puts it: [2] "Unless a lot doubles in value every five years, its value will not keep pace with taxes, special assessments and interest." In cities, therefore, as in New York, where an earnest attempt is made to assess landed property at its full value and where the tax rate is considerable, speculation in vacant land is probably less prevalent than in other cities. Nor must it be thought that such speculation is always profitable. [3] Concerning vacant land that bears an *urban* value, so much may be said in conclusion: either the land is not yet ripe for building, or if ripe for building it is deliberately withheld from utilization. In both cases the purpose is speculative, but it is only in the latter that the practice is reprehensible. And yet the following consideration deserves attention. In a large, congested city, where land values are high but stable, [4] and taxes high, the ordinary investor will more likely find it profitable to build upon his land, if only to cover its annual cost. This holds true even of the land owned by the thirteen millionaire families quoted as the landed monopolists of Manhattan. For of the 205 or more millions of land value owned by them, less than ten millions comprise vacant land. [5] To be sure this does not take into account the *underdeveloped* land held by them.

§ 14. Another evil which speculation in land is known to foster concerns the investor. Of course it will be said that speculation of any kind is a game in which the investor

[1] Chicago *Real Estate News*, April, 1912, p. 53.

[2] Reed, *Science of Real Estate and Mortgage Investment*, p. 77. See also *Practical Real Estate Methods*, p. 242.

[3] "They do not hear of the thousands of unsuccessful prospectors or the many thousand proprietors of vacant property who wait for years for an improvement in values and finally see their profits disappear in interest charges and taxes." *Real Estate and Builders' Guide*, March 16, 1912, p. 540.

[4] Not constant, but in the sense of steadily increasing.

[5] From a statement by the Society to Lower Rents and Reduce Taxes on Homes.

consciously takes a risk, and must bear his losses. In land speculation, however, it is not a mistaken judgment in the investment so much as the system of mortgage which most often ruins him. The heavy indebtedness incurred by the purchaser results often in foreclosure, by which the mortgagee profits by more than the value of the mortgage. According to Professor Eberstadt,[1] six and one-half thousand million of the seven and one-half thousand million marks, the estimated value of the occupied land in Greater Berlin, were mortgaged. The general phenomenon of indebtedness and land speculation is described as follows by Professor Adolf Wagner:[2] "The factors which enter into this tendency are the fluctuations in the current rate of interest and of the rent. With the fall in the rate of interest and with the increase in rent, the capitalized value of land tends to rise. This induces the people, even with borrowed money, to invest in land. If the market price continues to rise as expected, the realization of profits is sought by continuing the sales, and this by means of more borrowed capital. The gratifying terms of credit which the banks offer at such times only draw more men on to such transactions. Then the market value changes, a higher rate of interest ensues, and, in consequence of the improved transportation facilities, the rent falls, tending further to decrease land values. The value of the land no longer covers the capital invested, there ensues a crisis in real estate, and mortgages falling due, the land is sold at auction, and once more the moneyed interests profit from the transactions." Occurrences of enormous gains in this country which have accrued to individuals as a result of such foreclosures could be readily cited. One example must here suffice. Mr. Hurd [3] tells of a piece of land 89 feet by 99 feet in Denver, Colo.,

[1] *Op. cit.*, pp. 54, 207. Land speculators are called by him "Prekaristen, die von der Gnade unserer Institutionen leben."

[2] *Grundlegung* der *Politischen Oekonomie* (1894), Pt. II, p. 389. (Translated freely from the German.)

[3] *Principles of City Land Values*, p. 131.

which had been bought on a tax title many years ago for $500. In 1890 it was leased for $14,000 annual net ground rent for a period of ninety-nine years. That made the land value $280,000 capitalized at five per cent. Every front foot of ground was thus worth $3150. A nine-story building was erected upon it in 1890 costing $325,000. In 1894 the net rents were about $17,500. The leasehold was mortgaged for about $75,000, and when the rent dropped, the building was surrendered to the mortgagee and then to the ground-owner, who thus acquired the building and the land, worth together $330,000, for an original outlay of $500.

Such losses, however, are attributable to miscalculations and short-sightedness such as appear in all speculation. Speculation in land cannot be condemned on account of this evil alone. And yet, when, as in Germany, mortgage indebtedness has proved a means of exploiting the farmer or peasant class, and a means also of concentrating farm land in the hands of the few, speculation in land which facilitates and creates indebtedness among the less wary owners should be subject to regulation.[1]

§ 15. Conclusions: Land speculation may prove socially injurious in four ways: (1) by preventing the best utilization of agricultural, mineral, and forest land; (2) by keeping land ripe for building out of use; (3) by controlling building operations; (4) by overcapitalizing the land.

It is evident that agricultural land no longer offers such a fertile field for speculative operations as formerly. The immense wealth amassed by individuals as a result of the generous land grants and speculative operations will not be duplicated anywhere soon, but should serve as a lesson to statesmen in their land policies of the future. Even yet, however, when this country has been almost all appropriated, agricultural land speculation in the United States has not ceased. Thus the hope of reclaiming some of our

[1] *Cf.* Buchenberger, *Grundzüge der deutschen Agrarpolitik* (1897), pp. 73 *ff.*

western prairies by means of irrigation has given rise to more speculation, resulting in the appreciation of from one hundred per cent to one thousand per cent in the value of some of our western farm land. Sites unsalable at $2 per acre ten or twelve years ago now command $10 to $15 per acre.[1] In general, nevertheless, it cannot be claimed that speculation has led to monopolization in agricultural land. For particular countries and localities, however, the appropriation and withholding of vacant land may entail social losses. The following illustration from Australia will show how this can happen:[2] "In every one of these colonies millions of acres of the richest agricultural land, with ample rainfall and near to markets and ports of shipment are used for mere grazing purposes. As a consequence most of the farmers were forced to settle on poorer land, farther from markets and ports, and where the rainfall is less abundant. Land fit only for grazing is thus used for agriculture, while the land fittest for agriculture is used for grazing only."

Enough has been said about the practice of keeping land vacant or partially utilized in the heart of large cities. It will be noted that several factors determine the extent and effect of this kind of speculation. While high carrying charges and taxation on capital value make the withholding of land unprofitable, they do not foster its best utilization. Nevertheless, the conditions of congestion are so various in this country, that there are comparatively few cities where the withholding of urban land is as yet a social menace. Only a careful study of the housing problem could decide in each case the harmful effect of uncontrolled building operations.

Although on the whole our American cities may be said to suffer from the *laissez-faire* housing system that prevails, attention must also be called to a species of controlled

[1] Chicago, *Real Estate News* (1910), p. 106.
[2] Hirsch, *Democracy versus Socialism*, p. 131.

building to be equally depreciated. We refer to the laying-out of towns by "development" companies. Gary, Indiana, is an illustration. The Gary Land Company not only graded, laid out, and subdivided the land and undertook the house building, but to this day it withholds the deed of sale from the purchasers of the lots until they shall have complied with the agreement to build within a certain time and on plans approved by the company.[1] However praiseworthy the intentions of certain of such undertakings, abuses of the power which such operations involve can easily be imagined.[2]

Overcapitalization of land, though a common phenomenon, varies in degree and extent. It is commonly known that suburban land is largely in the hands of speculators. Land near cities, the normal value of which for farming is from $50 to $100 per acre, and for gardening from $300 to $1000, may be held at $500 to $5000 per acre by speculators, who estimate values in accordance with the anticipated earnings of the land when it shall have secured the expected utilization.[3] As to the evil of inflated values, it would seem that this would affect only the less shrewd investor, who when values declined to the actual earning capacity of the land might be ruined. From his standpoint we might see nothing unusual in land speculation as compared with speculation in general. But just as over-

[1] Chicago *Real Estate News*, 1912, pp. 141–42.

[2] An interesting example in point is the Pullman City experiment. Mr. Pullman had erected, not only the dwellings for his workmen, but a library, hotel, church, etc. The latter remained vacant for some time, because there was no denomination large enough to pay the required rental. The arbitrary control which the Pullman Company might have exercised over the residents can easily be imagined. Indeed, the possibility of misusing the powers which the company had over the living conditions of its employees led to the decision of the court in 1899 requiring the Pullman Car Company to dispose of all its real estate holdings not used in the industry. *Cf. Report of the Commissioners of the State Bureaus of Labor Statistics on the Industrial, Social and Economic Conditions of Pullman, Ill.* (1884), p. 12; also Carwardine, *The Pullman Strike* (1894), p. 20.

[3] *Cf.* Hurd, *Principles of City Land Values*, p. 133.

capitalization in other industries indirectly may enhance prices; so to a greater degree as concerns dwellings, the choice of which involves so many factors besides rental, rents may very likely be affected. To take, for example, the value of land in Chicago; are we to believe that the landlords who bought their property on the 1889 basis, to which we are told the value of real estate is only now approaching, have been on the whole recipients of less than the expected interest on their investment until the present? Or, in spite of the law of competition,[1] did the landlord in many cases not find ample excuse for charging a higher rental because he had overpaid?

On the whole, therefore, as we contemplate the importance of the commodity which is made the object of speculative operations, when we consider that the speculator is guided by the possibilities of greatest gain to himself, a motive not always in accord with social welfare, when we recall that the problems of suitable housing and of the conservation of natural resources are involved, speculation in land is not an unmixed good.[2] On the other hand, considering that the complete suppression of speculation involves practically the abolition of private property, and considering the difficulties in the way of such abolition, even if found expedient, this solution is problematical. Government restriction, however, has been, and will undoubtedly continue to be employed in checking the abuses of speculation in land as they arise, and when and where they become a menace to the public welfare. The efficacy and expediency of the land tax in suppressing speculation will be considered in connection with the housing problem.

[1] The frictional forces that prevent the operation of this law will be discussed in the following chapter.

[2] The fact that in some countries, e.g., England, Germany, many municipalities have been compelled to purchase land and to undertake the building of houses for the working classes is a sign of the inadequacy of the present system of realty operations. *Cf. infra*, chapter IX, § 10.

CHAPTER IX

§ 1. THE growth of cities in the nineteenth century has given rise to numerous social problems, among which there is none more vital than the housing problem. It is unnecessary to point out that shelter constitutes one of the indispensable conditions of existence, nor that land is requisite for the provision of dwelling places. The latter fact shows the relation between housing and land values, for any influences that affect the value of land in any community will be reflected in the housing system of that community. Shelter, it need scarcely be pointed out, means more than protection from the physical elements; it implies all that we to-day regard as essential for the physical, moral and intellectual development of the individual. The home is the basis of the "sacred" family relationships, of physical efficiency, of sociability, of profitable leisure, and of character unfolding.

Social workers especially are well aware how the economic, moral, and social welfare of the greater part of the urban population, if not of the entire population, is affected by the housing facilities. We need only reflect that from twenty to thirty per cent of the income of the major portion of urban dwellers is expended for rent, and that the industrial development of a community, moreover, is dependent upon the accessibility to suitable locations, to understand how the economic interests of the population are rooted in the housing problem. How the social well-being of a community is hampered by such evils as congestion and overcrowding within the home, insanitary buildings, dark and poorly ventilated rooms, the lack of open spaces, has recently been shown in numerous treatises, in the reports of commissions and congresses, and in various hygienic and social exhibits.[1] It has been well established by statistical reports that health is greatly undermined and the death-rate enhanced by insanitation and overcrowding. The high death rate of infants has been attributed to these causes.[2] "It was the opinion of physicians who appeared before the commission that if the occupancy of the dark rooms now legally occupied is permitted, we shall continue to have in the city about 28,000 new cases of consumption, and 10,000 deaths from consumption every year." [3] When we consider that sickness means unemployment and means greater expenditure for medical treatment, the seriousness of the housing problem becomes more obvious. Of no less vital importance are the moral influences of insanitary, improper home conditions. It is claimed that the lack of suitable surroundings in and about the home where the child may play is responsible for much of the delinquency found in large cities. Crime too has been traced to a lack of proper home conditions. This was recognized by the eminent jurist, Liszt, who is credited with saying,[4] "A reasonable reform in housing is worth more than a dozen penal laws." Another grave evil due to overcrowding is the violation of the recognized standards of decency. In short as Damaschke puts it, "Schlafstellenunwesen, Prostitution, Alkoholmissbrauch, Zunehmen des jugendlichen Verbrech-

[1] To mention a few: The Ninth International Housing Congress held in Vienna (1910); the Tenement House Commission of New York (1900); the New York Commission on Congestion (1910); Housing Exhibits in Chicago and New York (1913); Hygienic Exhibit in Dresden, etc. See *The Tenement House Problem*, ed. by R. W. DeForest and L. Veiller.

[2] Dr. Meinert, a physician of Dresden is quoted as saying: " Wir suchen den Feind wo er sich nicht befindet. . . . Die Frage der hohen Säuglingssterblichkeit ist im wesentlichen eine Wohnungsfrage." quoted from Mangoldt, *Die Städtische Bodenfrage*, p. 392. See *Eighth Special Report of the United States Commissioner of Labor* (1895), p. 79, where the high death-rate in cities is attributed to housing conditions.

[3] *Findings of the New York City Commission on Congestion* (1910).

[4] Damaschke, *Bodenreform* (1912), p. 76.

ertums — das alles ist in seinem engen Zusammenhang mit Wohnungsnot und Wohnungselend heute in allen ernsten Kreisen bekannt!" [1]

§ 2. If these be some of the serious effects of bad housing upon health and social efficiency, we must ask where and why this evil has arisen. The "slum" constitutes to-day a definite section of most of the populous cities, but displays its worst features in London, Dublin, and in about half a dozen cities in the United States. The housing problem is, however, by no means limited to these cities. We may affirm that not only urban but also rural communities suffer from insanitary dwellings. In Berlin and the other German cities, for example, you look in vain for districts resembling Whitechapel, or the East Side (New York), yet investigations in German cities, some scarcely urban, have revealed startling conditions of overcrowding. A large percentage of families occupied but one or two rooms, while many homes were found in which more than six persons were living in a single room.[2] According to reports and statistics conditions are not better in English cities. To give a few examples: In Glasgow 100,000 persons, or one-fifth of the whole population, are reported as living in one-room dwellings. In Liverpool thousands of basements and alley houses in dilapidated and intolerable condition, without air and sun, are utilized as homes.[3] As regards overcrowding, conditions are nowhere comparable to those in Berlin and New York. In both cities the "skyscraper" predominates. But while it is claimed that three-fourths of the population of New York live in tenements, we find that of all the houses in Berlin 93.79 per cent are occupied by tenants, 2.57 per cent by proprietors, and 3.64 per cent by

---

[1] Mangoldt, *op. cit.*, pp. 396–97.

[2] Damaschke, *op. cit.*, p. 69. *Cf.* also Eberstadt, *Handbuch des Wohnungswesens, passim.*

[3] Fuchs, *Zur Wohnungsfrage*, pp. 118–19.

servants. The extent of congestion in Berlin is furthermore proved by the following fact: In London there were
found to be 7.93 persons to a building site, in Berlin,
76.9 persons.[1]

§ 3 The causes of these intolerable conditions are chiefly
economic and social. Few cities have originally been laid
out deliberately. For the most part their growth has
been haphazard. Building permits and sanitation laws
were later developments.[2] Contractors and owners had
houses constructed without regard to artistic design, or
uniform height, but after their own sweet will and with the
sole purpose of personal gain. It is this *laissez-faire* policy
which is responsible in part for the "slum" conditions.

A more fundamental cause is the economic factor as it
touches the tenant. If we study the population of the
"slum," we find that the south European immigrant predominates.[3] We know that his standard of living is much
lower than that of the country to which he emigrates, such
as the United States or England, and that his intention in
leaving his native country is to earn and save as much
money as possible, often with a view to returning to his
native country. Hence we should expect him to settle
where rent is the lowest. And so he does. If, now we inquire where rent is lowest, we find that it is generally in the
oldest part of the city, which on account of social changes
and of the industrial development has been abandoned by

[1] Pohle, *Die Wohnungsfrage*, vol. I, pp. 37, 43. The prevalence of
tenements is not always a sign of insanitation, but the congestion and
construction of the cheaper dwellings tend to make them insanitary as well
as to destroy the privacy of home life, and to hinder home-ownership.

[2] For New York the sanitation law of 1882 related to tenements and
lodging houses. A similar law was passed for London in 1891. *Cf. Eighth
Special Report of the Commissioner of Labor* (1895), chapter II.

[3] In St. Louis, for example, the poorest district was inhabited by Jews,
who constituted 28.4 per cent; by Italians, who constituted 27.5 per
cent; and by negroes who formed 15.7 per cent of the whole number of
residents. The Poles were 13.1 per cent and other various nationalities
15.3 per cent. *Report of the Housing Committee of the Civic League of
St. Louis* (1908), p. 84.

the native population for uptown residential sections. Here, where encroachments of all kinds are tolerated and where houses have become unfit for habitation, the immigrant makes his abode. If these insanitary structures are condemned by the building inspector, they are superseded by tenements. The large capital invested in these new structures and the great demand for houses in the "slum" district, cause rents to rise above the level in the suburbs or on the periphery of the town. Then the immigrant is compelled to take in more lodgers, to resort to the most insanitary, ill-equipped houses (unless the law condemns them all), and to make dwelling-places out of basements, garrets, and dilapidated rear houses. Viewed from another standpoint the low wages of the immigrant may be said to be responsible for the congested and otherwise insanitary conditions. It will be remembered that it is in the "slums" where the sweat shops are to be found. In those sweated industries the insufficient wage forces a lower standard of existence upon the worker.

Added to the economic is the social factor. The concentration of population is generally within the industrial center, where the workmen may be near their places of employment. This section corresponds to the oldest and most undesirable part for residential purposes. Now, when once settled, clannishness, that great social force, tends to keep the persons of one nationality and family together. The strength of this factor of sociability and family ties in engendering the "slum" district is seen in the unwillingness of tenement dwellers to move to cheaper and at the same time more desirable quarters in the city. That racial and social forces are responsible in part for the "slums" is further made evident by the fact that only where immigration has gathered a large number of foreigners does a Whitechapel or an East Side make its appearance.

§ 4. In view of these conditions it may well be asked, is

it the high rent which creates a lower standard of living among the immigrants, or is it the immigrant and his clannishness that raise rent? The relation between them is reciprocal. As Hurd says, the cause of rent for residences is social as well as economic.[1] It will be agreed that not only in the slums but in the city as a whole rent and land value tend to increase with the growth of population, that is with the increase in the demand for houses. On the other hand, for the reasons already given, the congestion per acre, the overcrowding per room, and resultant evils are not likely to be relieved much by the development of transportation facilities or by other methods of extending the available residential area. The seriousness of these conditions in our largest cities can scarcely be exaggerated. How, then, shall the urban housing problem be solved?

Obviously, a reduction in rent will not only afford relief to the poorer classes materially, socially, and even ethically, but, together with legislation regulating building operations and stricter laws of sanitation, may help to eliminate the slums. Before discussing the possibility of lower rents, it is necessary to point out the inefficacy of building regulations when unaccompanied by rent reductions.

That building and sanitation laws are the first steps toward the solution of the housing problem cannot be questioned. No government, in modern opinion, should permit the individual, even if he so desires, to occupy a dwelling that falls below the recognized standard of sanitation, comfort and decency. Adequate regulations limiting the height and area to be covered by the building, requiring the installation of sanitary appliances, fixing the minimum width of staircases, the height of ceilings, the size of rooms and windows, and so forth, should not only be enacted, but should be strictly enforced by the building inspectors. Indeed, it might be expedient for all cities to follow the

[1] *Principles of City Land Values*, pp. 77–78.

lead of German communities in promoting the "city beautiful" as well as the city hygienic. "German cities have taught us a valuable lesson in the matter of laying out suburbs. Improvement plans are furnished by the municipality, and architects are invited to compete in presenting designs. After it has been decided that a certain district shall be opened up, a jury is appointed to assess damages, terms are made with private owners, and the architect furnishing the most acceptable scheme is awarded the prize." [1]

What, however, must be the effect of such legislation? Evidently the enhancement of rent because of the increase in the cost of construction. Such has been the result in German cities. [2] Indeed, the increased overcrowding there is attributable to the high rents which expensive buildings and improvements tend to create. To keep rents down recourse will be had by those of a lower standard of living especially to increase the number of lodgers. In short, "the poorer classes want cheap houses, must have them; they understand what a saving of a sixpence a week in the rent means, but they do not understand yet the advantages of concrete foundations, properly jointed drain pipes or wash down water-closets. They do not mind taking a few lodgers into an already well-filled house, because they understand the advantages of a few shillings a week, but they do not understand that each inhabitant of a sleeping-room should have at least 500 cubic feet of air space." [3] Thus the method of solving the housing problem by restrictive building regulations may be rejected as futile.

In considering the possibility of reducing rents to relieve congestion, we may begin by analyzing the factors that enter into the determination of rent. And it will be con-

[1] *Eighth Special Report of the U.S. Commissioner of Labor* (1895), p. 93.

[2] Pohle, "Die Wohnungsfrage" in *Handbuch der Politik*, vol. II, pp. 522, 524.

[3] Thompson, *The Housing Handbook*, p. 173.

venient to classify these factors under ground rent and
building rent. Ground rents are affected by the population, by transportation facilities, by the industrial development, including the kinds of industries carried on, by
the system of land tenure and speculation, by racial ties
and other social considerations. Some of these tend towards
a reduction, others towards an advance in rentals. Friction
from offsetting and opposing influences may therefore be
expected. Thus, the tendency of improved facilities of
transit to draw the population to the periphery of the
town would be offset by the clannishness which has drawn
the foreigners to a particular neighborhood, generally in the
center of the town. The elements entering into building
rents are chiefly the various expenses of operation, determined by the conditions of the labor market, especially in
the building trades, the available capital for building, the
cost of materials, taxes, condition of the mortgage loan
market, etc. Under frictional influences may be classed
the immobility of invested capital, the leasehold and contract system, and above all the strong force of custom.
Relief of congestion through a reduction of rents may be
of two kinds, reduced congestion per unit of ground space,
e.g., per acre, and per room.

Viewing the housing problem thus from the economic
standpoint, its relation to the tax on land value becomes
clear. For the tax may be expected to affect a number of
the elements enumerated which make up rent. We have
now to examine the possible results on housing of the land
tax, as they have been deduced theoretically by the adherents of the tax on the one hand, and the adversaries on the
other.

§ 5. First, on the part of the advocates it is claimed that
the land tax would affect congestion in the following
manner: First, as the tax would make it expensive to keep
property unoccupied, vacant land would be forced into the
market. As a consequence, secondly, the market price of

land would tend to be reduced and land values would become more stable. This result would also follow, thirdly, when the lure of the value increment is in part removed; that is, speculation would be curtailed, and overcapitalization discouraged. Fourthly, the incentive to improvement would be created both by the high carrying charges on unimproved land, and by the untaxing of buildings. The latter would attract more capital into the building trades and would result in a larger number of available houses. Fifthly, the remission of the tax on buildings would benefit, not the builder (except indirectly), but the tenant, upon whom the tax ultimately falls.

In the platform of the United Committee for the Tax on Land Values in England it is stated,[1] "If urban and suburban land were taxed on its true unimproved value, irrespective of the use to which it happens to be put or not to be put; the iron girdle of land monopoly which now confines every large town and industrial center, every village, and every hamlet, would be broken through, and we should have more and cheaper dwelling houses, shops, offices, warehouses, and factories."

The reasoning by which the above deduction was derived needs no further elucidation. It is noteworthy, however, that the argument rests merely on the expediency of the tax on capital value *versus* that on rental value. Disregarding the assumption of monopoly in urban land, many will agree that the English rating system on annual value tends to encourage the withholding of land from use.[2] The passage quoted above, though it contains a grain of truth, is far too sweeping. Obviously, the degree to which the tax will be effective, even if the salutary influence be

---

[1] *Third Annual Report*, p. 64.

[2] "Lawson Purdy, the chairman of the Department of Taxes and Assessments for New York, expressed the opinion that were rates levied on actual capital value in London as in New York, nearly all Regent Street would be pulled down and a large part of the Strand." Chomley and Outhwaite, *op. cit.*, p. 78.

admitted, will depend upon the rate of tax, the prospects of its being increased, the amount of available vacant and undeveloped land, the counteracting forces, e.g., the increase in population, local improvements, and all other conditions that enter into building rents.

With regard to the stimulation of building operations the following passages are illustrative of the trend of thought: "Yet another argument which may be adduced in favor of the rating of site values, is that in consequence of urban land coming more freely into the market and building enterprises being stimulated, rent would be materially relieved; and this relief would come where rent is now at its maximum, i.e., in our large industrial centers. . . . Every opportunity given to the freer growth of the city in the suburbs will tend to reduce this congestion at the center." [1]

This quotation refers to the first method of creating an impetus to building, namely, by making the holding of vacant land "for a rise" unprofitable. In the following passage emphasis is laid on the effect of the untaxing of buildings: [2] "Again, we should be freeing buildings from the burden of rates. By levying rates on buildings, we make buildings dearer, and the inevitable consequence is that fewer are built. Under our present system of rating, builders cannot afford to build, because occupiers cannot afford to occupy so many or such good houses as they could if buildings were not liable to be rated. If we cease to levy rates on the value of buildings, we shall remove the first of the two main causes of the dearness and scarcity of houses."

Here, too, whatever truth the above claims may contain, they are vitiated by too general assumptions. For instance, they take it for granted that the demand for houses is

---

[1] Alden and Hayward, *Housing*, p. 94.

[2] Quoted by Thompson (*op. cit.*, p. 264) from a leaflet issued by the Liberal Publication Department.

elastic, that there are no limits to the available capital for building purposes, that mortgage loans will remain unaffected, that the effect of the overbuilding stimulus will not increase the cost of labor and materials, etc. To be sure, when these frictional forces are pointed out to the proponents of the tax they defend their position by more general statements. For example, they maintain that where rent consumes more than one-fifth of a family's income, crowding is the inevitable result. The reduction in rental, through the greater number of available dwellings would increase the demand for newer, larger accommodations, and would enable some of the large "lodging" population to establish homes of their own. As to the question of available capital, they point to the present excessive tax on buildings in comparison with that on other forms of capital. They urge further that under the present system of taxation, the cost of building is prohibitive except to meet the urgent demand for housing. That the effect on mortgage loans should be wholesome is deduced from the doctrine of capitalization. The value of the land under the tax would not fall below the capitalized net rental, either accruing or prospective. Land and buildings would, therefore, be safer securities than to-day, when the tendency is to overcapitalize the value of the land. With these important doctrines of the defenders before us, we shall next epitomize the arguments of the opponents of the tax system.

§ 6. The chief criticism of the theories concerning the consequences of the tax on land value, namely, that the numerous and offsetting elements that compose rents are lost sight of, as well as the frictional forces at work in social phenomena, gives the clue to the contentions of the opposition. First, consider the questions of vacant land and speculation. The prevalence of vacant land ripe for building is denied by some, while others even hold that building operations depend upon this speculative feature in realty holdings.[1] So long as there is a large number of vacant houses, it cannot be said that land is held vacant for speculative purposes; especially does this apply where the tax rates are high. The land must sometimes be kept in an unimproved or underimproved condition because of the possibility of change in the character of the neighborhood, and for other sound reasons. The validity of this position, however, cannot be decided theoretically. And yet, in studying the facts, the difficulty arises of fixing the standards of underdeveloped and appropriately improved land. These terms will probably have different meanings in different localities and countries, and the prevalence of such underdevelopment will probably vary from place to place.

Secondly, granting that the imposition of the tax will cause a decline in land value, and that it will induce the owner to build upon his land, might not this incentive and the untaxing of buildings lead to a more intensive use of the land? The dangers of an overutilization of the land from the standpoint of the housing problem are generally admitted. Not the congestion per room, but the greater congestion per acre is threatened thereby. If the improvement of the suburban districts only were stimulated by the tax, a general reduction of congestion in the city would be conceivable. But it is reasonable to expect that the more expensive the land, i.e., in the heart of the city, the greater would be the incentive to improve it. It is feared, therefore, that an overdevelopment might ensue, that the skyscraper would become more prevalent than the need of the community would warrant. The possibility of compact building, moreover, carries with it the utilization of the now available open spaces and even of garden space. The adherents of the new system admit the gravity of the charge with respect to lofty and compact building; they are less ready to admit the deleterious effect on garden space. To

[1] *Cf. supra*, chapter vii, § 5.

the first charge answer is usually made, that the intensive utilization of the land is a tendency which will continue irrespective of the tax. Indeed, the trend toward compact building may have been caused and furthered by the withholding of land from use. To overcome the dangers to good housing, the government will be compelled sooner or later to restrict and control building operations according to a well-laid-out town-planning scheme. It would seem, therefore, that legislation, at least restricting the height of buildings, would have to precede the introduction of the tax.

On the other hand, by opening up the suburbs, and by relieving the tenant in the center of the city, the necessity for tall buildings would be removed and the tendency toward more intensive utilization would be checked. Logically, it might even be reasoned that with the greater competition for tenants, the desires of the dwellers would be consulted in building more than at present. Furthermore, every one is aware that houses with gardens and open spaces are more desirable and valuable; and if the owner is looking forward to an increase in the value of his property in the future, he will prefer to keep it in a more desirable condition, fronting on a lawn or open space. It should be remembered, moreover, that the decline in the value of the land is expected to enable and encourage more persons to own their homes, especially in the suburbs. It is likewise expected that the reduced value of land will counteract the movement towards the more intensive use of the site.

Thirdly, the efficacy of the tax to promote building operations has also been questioned on various grounds. We are familiar with the theory that the curtailment of speculation, i.e., the reduction in prospective value increment, will tend to discourage building.[1] Another reason given to

---

[1] The untaxing of buildings would not necessarily relieve the owners who occupy their homes. The effect would depend upon the relative values of the building and site.

deny that a building "boom" will ensue is that the demand for houses is inelastic, that overbuilding could not
go on indefinitely. While, therefore, a decrease in rent
might have the effect of temporarily stimulating the
erection of new buildings, and of providing larger and
better accommodations, the tendency would check itself.
For, granted that modern types of buildings will tend to
supersede the older and inappropriate structures, and that
the latter will be torn down, the increased cost of constructing the new buildings will check the overbuilding
trend. Moreover, the incentive for capital to be employed in building, which will at first ensue, will be
checked when the rate of profit in that industry becomes the current rate in other industries. But, say the
adherents, even these assumptions insure a decided improvement in housing conditions.

Fourthly, with respect to the doctrine that the remission
of the tax on buildings would redound to the benefit of the
tenant in the shape of reduced rents, no account is taken
of the friction that may be expected to develop in the
readjustment. Aside from the reputed immobility of the
population, aside from custom which largely determines
the possible expenditure for rent, aside from existing leaseholds, the tax on land value may itself set in motion various
forces to enhance rents. Most important is the assertion
that owners of improved property count upon the prospective increments in land value to counterbalance the deterioration of the building. Thus rents are assumed to be
lower than if the owner had to provide a depreciation
fund. With the heavier tax on land value, such a reserve
fund would be necessitated, adding to the building cost.
This would result in higher rents. Again, by the decline in
land value, property would no longer be worth as much as
security for mortgage loans. Moreover, since the mortgagee takes the prospective increment into account in making the loan, the effect of the tax would be either to reduce

the amount of available capital for building, or to raise the interest rate,[1] in which cases rents would tend upward. These arguments assume, however, that building operations are a distinctive industry dependent upon land-ownership and land speculation. We have already pointed out how the widespread leasehold system in itself seems to contradict this theory.[2]

Lastly, in a dynamic society, further friction might be expected to arise to counteract the movement toward reduced rents. Assume the reduction of rent in one community, and would there not be an influx of outsiders to take advantage of the reduction? Moreover, the normal increase in population in a progressive community and the rise in the cost of materials and labor, if the stimulation in building becomes general, would tend to check the alleviating influences of the tax.

§ 7. Turning from the theoretical discussion of the effect of the tax on housing, we ask what are the facts? Our study has demonstrated the futility of attempting to determine precisely the influences of the tax in the presence of so many interacting social forces. Whether attributable to the fact that the growth of the community has offset the forces set in motion by the tax, or that the tax rate has been too slight to affect market values, or that the actual results of the tax on land and of the remission of the tax on improvements have not conformed with theory, the reports of the officials and the statistics for certain communities where the tax is in operation show that rent cannot have been materially affected by the tax.

On the other hand, the available data do reveal an activity in building operations in the Australian and Cana-

---

[1] A rather ingenious theory with respect to the effect on mortgage loans was propounded at the public hearings of the New York Committee on Taxation. The lower land value would mean less capital loaned on mortgages, with the result of a larger amount of available capital for building operations at a lower rate of interest.

[2] *Supra*, chapter VII, § 5.

dian municipalities which is generally attributed in part
to the exemption of improvements. There was no evidence
of overbuilding in Australasia; in Canada, on the other
hand, the excess in vacant buildings in some of the towns
in recent years has been charged to the operation of the
tax. Whether this condition of overbuilding existed during
the land "boom" period, when newcomers in some cities
had to resort to tents for shelter,[1] has not been established.
Nor is it possible to determine the effectiveness of the tax
on value increment to influence notably the land market
and building operations from the stagnant conditions in
both fields after the imposition of the taxes in England and
Germany. In the latter country, the unfavorable market
conditions, traceable, however, to the general depression for
which the tax legislation was not responsible, played a considerable rôle in the amendment of the law. The English duties on land value were likewise ineffective in preventing the
temporary slump in the building trades of London in 1911,
and failed to relieve the serious housing conditions there.[2]
But, in judging the tax, aside from the unfavorable effect
of the general industrial depression, it must be borne in
mind that the stimulation of building in the case of the tax
on value increment could not be expected to be the same
as in the case of a general untaxing of buildings. While the
influence of the tax on building operations is not traceable
in the extraordinary increase in structures in western
Canada before the depression, the general agreement
among the Canadian builders themselves, as to the efficacy
of the tax in stimulating building seems to substantiate
the generally accepted theory, rather than that which
holds that the tax will interfere with building operations.

Difficult as it is to assert any positive effect of the tax
on housing conditions, it is more difficult to discover its

[1] Cf. Haig, Exemption of Improvements from Taxation in Canada and
the United States, p. 273.
[2] See supra, chap. v, pp. 248 ff.

effect on speculation in land. We know that speculation is still rampant in the countries under the system of land-value taxation. And in the circumstances existing in western Canada, it would seem that the tax was introduced in part to further the speculators' interests.[1] In Australasia, the state land taxes, except in New Zealand, are not heavy. But in the latter colony, evidence of the disintegration of the large holdings exists, and the cause is generally found in the high graduated and absentee rates. On this question also, our conclusions in the absence of positive proof, must be qualified. We may assume that a tax levied on a commodity on the basis of its capital value will tend to discourage dealings in that commodity. Also that a tax on land, as is generally conceded, tends to encourage its utilization. Thus it would seem that the realty tax on capital value in American cities has made the withholding of land "for a rise" less profitable than in England. It follows, even, that were the tax high enough, as high as the transfer duties in Paris,[2] for example, realty operations would be greatly subdued. But where land rises rapidly in value, speculation will continue to thrive, irrespective of the tax. So much may therefore be assumed: since anything which lessens the anticipated income from a commodity will generally decrease the desirability of that commodity for speculative purposes, a discriminatory tax on land will put a damper on realty transactions and speculation. The degree of suppression will depend on the rate of tax and the trend of land-value increments.

§ 8. In the preceding chapter it was found that specula-

---

[1] *Cf. supra*, chapter vi, § 5.

[2] In Paris there is a tax of six per cent on the transfer of the deed and three and one-fourth per cent for other expenses, making a reduction of nine and one-fourth per cent of the value on every transfer. Of course the expectation even of an increase in tax rate suffices to give speculation in land a set-back. *Cf. Reports on City Real Estate Values*, compiled by Seattle Real Estate Association (1907). *Cf.* also *Congrès International de la Propriété Foncière* (1900), p. 109.

tion in land had its function in society under private
ownership, but like other social privileges it was capable of
abuse. The time arrives when the government is called
upon, or compelled, to check the abuses of social institutions. The proposals and the legislation already employed
to remedy the evils arising from landed property are many,
but chiefly ameliorative. The most radical proposal is the
public appropriation of the land. The question of the
expediency of land nationalization is, moreover, closely
allied to that of the tax on land value. For the underlying
motives of both proposals, as social reforms, are essentially
the same. Without entering into the theoretical inquiry of
the justice of private *versus* social property in land, the
facts and arguments for and against the practicability of
public appropriation will throw light upon the social expediency of the tax on land value.

Of the advocates of public ownership, there are those
who, like the Single Taxers,[1] favor the nationalization of
all the land; others who, like Professor Adolf Wagner,[2] have
pointed out the need of the municipalization of urban land,
not of the rural landed estates; others again, a more numerous class, who urge public ownership only of the natural
resources, mines and forests for conservation purposes.
In examining the reasons advanced in defense of these
positions the threefold classification of land of the preceding chapter will be of assistance. For it is evident that,
if the conclusions with regard to the trend of value of the
several kinds of land are valid, public ownership may be
less expedient in one case than in another.

[1] Of the noted economists who favored nationalization John Stuart
Mill and Léon Walras (see *Éléments D'Economie Politique*) have exerted
a great influence. The latter has even more persistently and tenaciously
defended the proposal for the Single Tax.

[2] How far Professor Wagner would go with regard to restricting the
private ownership of urban land is not certain. *Cf.* his *Grundlegung*, vol.
II, p. 470 *ff.*, as well as his speech on "Finanz- und Steuerfragen," in
Schriften der Gesellschaft für Soziale Reform (1904), Heft 15, pp. 28 *ff.*

§ 9. From the standpoint of the appreciation of land value no reason exists, generally speaking, for the public appropriation of agricultural lands, which are characterized by decrements and fluctuating value, rather than by increments. Nevertheless, large land holdings prevent the best utilization of the land and tend to impoverish the peasant.[1] The data showing the extent and significance of this concentration of land lend weight to the argument.

The experience of Australasia[2] with absenteeism and large landed estates is not peculiar. The conditions in most European countries (France and part of Germany excepted) are similar. The concentration of land holdings in England is notorious. From statistics of England and Wales in 1872–73,[3] it has been shown that 4917 owners (.5 per cent of the whole number) occupied each from 1000 to 10,000 acres, altogether 42.3 per cent of the whole area, and 21.8 per cent of the product. Of the whole area of England and Wales (London not included) 10,207 persons owned two-thirds; of 18,950,000 acres in Scotland, one person owned 1,376,000, while 1700 persons possessed nine-tenths of the whole area. In Ireland, 1942 persons ("these owners cannot even be counted among the inhabitants, for they are mostly absentee landlords!") owned out of the 20,160,000 acres, two-thirds of the whole.[4] "Two-thirds of England, nine-tenths of Ireland, and nineteen-twentieths of Scotland," says Mulhall,"[5] "are held in own-

[1] See Sering, "Die Innere Kolonisation in Östlichen Deutschland," in *Schriften des Vereins für Socialpolitik*, vol. LVI, pp. 26 *ff.*

[2] See *supra*, chapters II and III.

[3] Wagner, *Grundlegung* (1894), vol. II, p. 371: "Die colossale Concentrirung riesiger Grundstückscomplexe und Grundrentenbezüge in wenigen Händen lässt sich aber bestimmt nachweisen. . . . In Deutschland und England ist der ländliche Kleinbesitzerstand von der Staatsgewalt den grossen Grundherren preisgegeben worden." Then follows a description of the condition, the superseding of the small farmers, and that lawfully, by the big landed proprietors. See *ibid.*, p. 374.

[4] *Ibid.*

[5] Mulhall, *Industries and Wealth of Nations*, p. 64.

ership by a small group of persons." The following more recent statistics show clearly the concentration of English land in the hands of comparatively few individuals. Thus, while in France, of the 7,200,000 of the population engaged in agriculture, 1,638,000 were owners of land; in the United Kingdom out of an agricultural population of 2,530,000 only 19,275 were land owners.[1] But the difference in the size of the estates is equally noteworthy; in France the average estate was 56 acres, in the United Kingdom it was 3003 acres.

In Austria-Hungary the two largest landholders were said to be the Crown and the Rothschild family, the latter owning eight times as much as the royal family.[2] The following data appeared in "Vorwärts,"[3] the Socialist German daily: Fifty-two per cent of all the landlords owned somewhat less than three-fifths of the land in Hungary, while only .09 per cent of the proprietors owned 31.19 per cent, nearly one-third of the land. Or take Bohemia as an illustration of the concentration of the land. Here sixteen persons were said to own ten per cent of all the land.[4]

Serious as this charge against private land ownership is, it is highly questionable whether from the standpoint of production state ownership would be advantageous. To utilize rural land most efficiently private ownership is regarded as essential. It is an undisputed fact that where the cultivator is the owner under the existing system, the state of husbandry is most favorable. Whether under a

[1] These figures exclude estates of less than twelve acres. (Mulhall, *Industries and Wealth of Nations*, p. 115.) If, however, the small holdings from one to twelve acres are included, the total number of holdings in Great Britain owned by their occupiers was, in 1911, 60,217 or 11.73 per cent of all the holdings. "Since 1888 there has been an almost uninterrupted decline in the proportion of the acreage owned by the occupiers." *Agricultural Statistics* (Cd. 6021), 1911, pp. 9–10.

[2] Flürscheim, *Einziger Rettungsweg*, pp. 78, 161.

[3] April 11, 1909. The data were obtained from a current edition of *Jahrhundert* in Budapest.

[4] Flürscheim, *op. cit.*

leasing system by the state a sufficiently secure tenure could be assured the tenant to induce him to invest the same amount of capital as if he owned in fee simple is a matter of speculation. Not only from the standpoint of production, but also from that of administration state ownership would be a precarious undertaking. Added to these considerations the method of appropriation must be inquired into. The impossibility of purchasing all the land leaves only one course clear, namely confiscation, a measure justified in extreme exigencies only. In judging of the expediency of the nationalization of the soil, therefore, the evils of absenteeism, of large holdings, of peasant exploitation and pauperization in some countries must be weighed on the one hand; on the other, the responsibility that ownership would impose upon the state, the efficiency of public versus individual enterprise, the security of tenure under private ownership, the trend of depreciating and fluctuating agricultural values, and the revolutionary, confiscatory means to be employed. Nor must it be forgotten (1) that the concentration of agricultural holdings is characteristic only of certain countries,[1] and (2) that other legislative action has been proposed to disintegrate the large estates.[2]

The effectiveness of the tax on land value to overcome the deficiencies of private landownership, will depend chiefly upon the vigor with which the screw is tightened. The low tax rate which now prevails has had little effect in disintegrating large estates, for the expectation of a future value increment conduces to the payment of the

[1] In the United States about five-sixths of the farm land is in private hands. In forty-eight per cent of our area the size of farm holdings is increasing, in the remaining fifty-two per cent the size is either decreasing or there is no appreciable change. The tendency toward the increase in size of holdings is more pronounced in the newly settled western states. *Report of the U. S. National Conservation Commission*, vol. i, p. 84.

[2] *Cf.* in England, the Small Holdings and Allotments Acts; in Germany, the colonization laws (Ansiedelungspolitik).

tax rather than to relinquishment of the holding. But if made too discriminatory, the same objections apply as to public appropriation and confiscation with which it may become identical. To be most effective, the tax should be levied (1) according to a progressive scale of rates to strike hardest at the large and absentee landlord, (2) with a minimum exemption embracing most of the land under cultivation, and (3) by the state or central authority, that alone should retain the power to use the tax as a weapon of social reform. Thus far only New Zealand has found it expedient to apply the weapon vigorously. But at all events, by the levy of the wild land, the increment and graduated taxes, the government shares the value increment without imposing a very great burden upon the large holder, while exempting the small owner and cultivator altogether.

For local revenue, the expediency of a tax on land value in rural districts will depend upon other conditions. Levied in conjunction with the state or county rate, the imposition may put an extra burden upon the rural district, while it relieves the owners of urban property. For local purposes, on the other hand, with local autonomy, or with apportionment according to expenditure,[1] the tax on land value, provided it is sufficiently productive, would be a decided improvement over the present widely current general property tax, which taxes stock and agricultural implements. The exemption of all improvements, such as buildings, would occasion but a slight increase in rate because their value is small in comparison with that of the land. An additional rate on vacant and absentee holdings, as is practiced in Canadian rural municipalities, might in some cases more than recompense the loss in revenue through the exemption of improvements.

§ 10. In so far as professional land speculation is combined with speculative building operations, and in so far as

[1] *Cf.* Purdy, *Local Option in Taxation*, pp. 18–19.

speculative, overcapitalized values may, though indirectly, drive up rent (especially likely because so many factors enter into the choice of dwellings), the expediency of checking speculation in urban land may become urgent. But these abuses of private property rights have played only minor rôles in producing the acute housing problem which it is sought to solve. It is not to be wondered that the improvement in housing considered "as part of the great work of national regeneration with a view to secure the health, safeguard the pockets, and raise the housing standard of the working classes," [1] should be regarded by many as dependent primarily upon government control of building operations and ownership of the land. The advantages of municipal land ownership have been enumerated as follows: [2]

(1) More economical grouping of buildings instead of the odd and scattered houses of the "jerry builder" would ensue.

(2) Non-speculative land values would cheapen building sites.

(3) Buildings on a large scale erected by the municipality would reduce the expenses of construction.

(4) Or, if the land were leased to companies of working men or builders, and capital advanced to them by the public loan association at low rates of interest, a saving would result.

(5) The municipality would be satisfied with a smaller profit than the individual owner.

(6) The management of a large number of dwellings would reduce expenses.

(7) Capital could be borrowed at lower rates of interest.

[1] Thompson, *The Housing Handbook*, p. 151.
[2] *Ibid.* Mr. Thompson was not considering the municipalization of all the land, but the housing experiments undertaken by certain English cities. *Cf.* also, "Report of the Land Enquiry Committee," *The Land* (1914), vol. II, pp. 108 *ff.*

It will be noted that this assumes the municipality to be not only the landowner, but the contractor, builder, and loan agency as well. In view of the radical change which is here involved, we may ask to what extent the above advantages of municipalization may be expected to materialize. In the absence of any experience with municipal land ownership as a whole, it may nevertheless be of value to review the results of minor municipal housing operations. Germany and England furnish examples. The "Bodenpolitik" of German towns [1] is rapidly spreading. Many building experiments on town land have been tried. In Ulm, for example, where the government owns a large portion of the land, houses have been erected at public expense and the property sold to private individuals under restrictions, e.g., the government retaining the right to repurchase the property under certain conditions (Wiederkaufsrecht). Frankfurt a. M. and Leipzig, on the other hand, find it expedient to lease their land for building for a term of years, after which the property reverts to the cities (Erbbaurecht). Freiburg i. B. and Zürich, on the other hand, have experimented with the erection of houses on their town land which they rent directly to the occupiers.[2] As these undertakings have been in operation but a short time, and are of small scope, i.e., only a small percentage of the population have been accommodated, the evidences of success are inconclusive. According to Dr. Pohle [3] only a small proportion of the inhabitants have availed themselves of these houses and, generally speaking, no material reduction in rental has ensued.

Similar motives, the betterment of the housing conditions of the working classes, actuated the passage of the English Housing Acts of 1890 and 1900. Part III of the amended Act provides for the compulsory purchase by the

---

[1] See *supra*, chapter IV, § 8.
[2] Pohle, "Die Wohnungsfrage," *in Handbuch der Politik*, vol. II, p. 522.
[3] *Ibid.* See also his *Wohnungsfrage*.

local authority of land in the outskirts of the town to be built upon in any one of the following ways: [1]

(1) By the council.

(2) By leasing the land to companies, or builders, or to working men for the erection of workmen's dwellings; or

(3) By "any company employing workmen, or established for constructing or improving workmen's dwellings; or by any private person or persons entitled to a free-hold estate in land or to lease for an unexpired period of fifty-eight years who may borrow from the Public Works Loan Commissioners at low rates of interest for not more than forty years, half the amount required to erect dwellings for the working classes, and may supply water or gas to the tenants free of charge or on favorable terms."

Many local authorities have already taken advantage of the provisions of this Act, among which are London, Glasgow, Liverpool, and Manchester.[2] The following summarizes the "commercial" success of "sixteen municipal housing schemes involving a capital outlay of about £1,300,000":[3] "They show a gross return of about $6\frac{1}{3}$ per cent, and a profit of about $3\frac{1}{2}$ per cent. . . . In eight cases the profits have been more than sufficient, not only to pay interest on the capital outlay, but also to provide the whole of the sinking fund contributions. In nine cases the profits have been more than sufficient to pay interest on

[1] Thompson, *op. cit.*, p. 35.

[2] Under the amended Act of 1909, the supply of working-class dwellings by local authority and the purchase of land compulsorily have been greatly stimulated, as is shown from the subjoined data (*Report of the Land Enquiry Committee*, vol. II, p. 215):—

HOUSES AND TENEMENTS BUILT BY THE LOCAL AUTHORITIES IN , ENGLAND AND WALES, 1890–1913

Years	Houses	Tenements	Lodging-houses
1890–1899	822	772	3
1900–1909	3594	1955	3
1910–1913	4867	197	..

[3] Thompson, *op. cit.*, p. 171.

capital, but have only provided part of the sinking fund. In only three cases, Liverpool (blocks) and Manchester (blocks and tenements), have the profits been insufficient to pay all the interest on capital. When it is remembered that the workmen tenants of those dwellings contribute £21,157 a year to the rates and taxes, and over £10,000 a year to a sinking fund for the purpose of buying property for the community at large, it must readily be admitted that more reasonable financial arrangements ought to be supported by Parliament so as to enable the rents to be reduced."

When the dilapidated, insanitary housing conditions of a city become as threatening as in Glasgow and London, for example, unless other remedies can be found, the municipality [1] may be compelled to resort to public building operations, just as cities now operate other public utilities. In that case, however, the European experience tends to show that the anticipated economies of government ownership must be waived, for commercially speaking, such undertakings have seldom been remunerative.[2] With all the savings in the expenses of construction, the municipal building enterprises not only have not yielded a profit so high as that of the private landlords, but they have not even been instrumental in lowering the rental.[3] What they have accomplished is, nevertheless, of great importance, namely, the improvement of the standard of housing.

It must be admitted, however, that such partial experi-

----

[1] In the opinion of certain members of the National Housing Association the slums in English cities "while similar to those of Philadelphia and Baltimore are not as bad as the worst in the American cities." *The Survey*, October 31, 1914, p. 108.

[2] *Ibid.*

[3] Thomspon, *op. cit.*, p. 178. It may well be that the financial failure of public building operations is due to the present policy, which provides for the purchase of condemned or other property. The purchase price of the land is in many cases exorbitant and this may make impossible an average return on the capital invested. *Cf. Report of the Land Enquiry Committee*, vol. II, pp. 242 *ff.*

ments in municipal housing as have been attempted in Germany and England are far from conclusive evidence of the effect of total municipalization of land on rent and land value. Were this extreme reform practicable, it is readily conceivable how the public appropriation of land value might benefit the urban tenants, not alone in the better utilization of the land, so as to relieve the congestion of population, but also by expending the enormous value increment of urban property which now accrues to private individuals for public utilities and improvements. The question resolves itself into one of practicability.

What does the municipalization of the land involve? There are only two ways in which the community could get possession, first, acquisition by purchase, or secondly, confiscation. The first would unquestionably burden the community with a debt too enormous to contemplate, so that compensation for town land, except for new, recently settled communities, is not feasible. As for the second means, the confiscation of urban property, not only would it inflict a severe loss upon a single class of the population, but such a revolutionary measure would bring other consequences that might disrupt the entire social system. Moreover, society at present and for a long time to come will not tolerate such a course; nor should it be advocated in view of the present conceptions of justice and equality, except in the direst need of the state. For a long time to come, therefore, less drastic and more practicable measures must be found to help solve the urban problem which must be admitted to be grave and urgent.

From the tax on land value, however, little is to be hoped in the way of a solution of the housing problem, except as the supply of accommodations may be affected.[1]

[1] One of the causes of the acute shortage of houses in England was, according to the Land Enquiry Committee (see *Report*, vol. II, p. 87), the increased attractiveness of alternative investments. "New house property, then, is decidedly less attractive as an investment than it was a few years ago." Might not the untaxing of buildings remedy this?

Furthermore, the expediency of checking speculation in urban land by means of a tax might be doubted, if it were not for another consideration.

We have seen the inevitable upward trend of the value of land in progressive cities. This tendency even public ownership cannot prevent, except in so far as the unsystematic, wasteful use of land under private ownership and the screwing up of speculative values might cease. But it has been asked, why should the increments due to social influences accrue to private individuals? The need for social and recreational centers, for parks and play grounds, and other public utilities is increasing and these in turn tend to increase the value of land. Why not set aside these socially created values to meet the increasing public expenditures? If the argument is advanced from the standpoint of right or justice, the counter-argument is equally valid, namely, that other value increments are socially created and should be likewise appropriated for the benefit of the whole community. From the standpoint of expediency, however, in view of the foregoing reasons for reform, an additional tax on land, which would give the community a share in the increments accruing from land, is winning adherents.[1]

§ 11. In the case of agricultural land we saw that government ownership of the land was not expedient; in the case of urban realty, the expediency of the *method* of municipalization was questionable. Now, we ask, does the need of conservation of natural resources necessitate their appropriation by the state? The need of conservation in the face of the wasting character of these resources has already been discussed.[2] The reports of the commissions on conservation all agree that most nations have not acted

[1] *Cf.* Seligman, in *Proceedings of National Tax Association* (1914), p. 191.

[2] *Supra*, chapter VIII, § 9. *Cf.* also *Summary of the Commissioner of Corporations on the Lumber Industry* (February 13, 1911), part I.

very expediently in disposing of their forest and mineral land. The following data show the percentage of forest area under government ownership: [1]

Great Britain	2.2 per cent	
Italy	4.0 "	"
France	12.0 "	"
United States (national and state)	18.9 "	"
Norway	28.5 "	"
Germany { imperial 31.9 / crown 1.8 / municipal 16.1 }	49.8 "	"
Finland	61.2 "	"
Spain	84.0 "	"
Russia	87.3 "	"

Recognizing the need of conserving at least the existent forest land, for "forests exercise an influence on the water supply, on agriculture and on the general health of the people,"[2] there is a general movement in European countries to add to the public forest reservations by purchase. Since 1870 France has not only made no sale of forest land, but has each year consigned more land to forestry. France has spent nearly 200,000,000 francs in reforesting dunes and devastated mountain sides. Germany likewise spent, in the years 1867–95, over 22,000,000 marks in increasing her forest domain.[3] This policy is now being followed by Austria and Italy. The United States has only recently been aroused to the problem of conservation. Yet in this country, "in timber lands the tendency toward consolidation is strong and has gone far toward placing control of such lands in a few hands. It appears that the monopoly is partly in the interest of economy in logging, milling and manufacturing, but chiefly speculative."[4] The wastefulness of our forestry system has already been pointed out.[5]

The policy with regard to mines is not different. While the German States and France find it profitable not only to

---

[1] *Report of the National Conservation Commission* (1909), vol. II, pp. 280, 345.

[2] *Ibid.*, p. 281.   [3] Adams, *Science of Finance*, pp. 244–45.

[4] *Report of the National Conservation Commission* (1909), vol. I, p. 85.

[5] *Supra*, chapter VIII, § 9.

own but also to operate the mines, England and the United States have disposed of most of their mineral land. Moreover, the tendency of concentration in mine holdings is evident in this country. Especially is this true of the iron mines which is explained by the greater economy of large operations. In oil lands this tendency toward concentration is said to be apparently slight, while in coal lands it is intermediate.[1]

Now that these important resources have been disposed of by the government, the question of the expediency of repurchasing them arises. To devote a certain sum annually to the repurchase of natural resources as the European countries are doing, is a far different matter than either purchasing or confiscating all the land. Moreover, the operation of mines and forests is different from agricultural production. Especially is this true of forests. The forests under state management in Germany are said to yield considerably greater returns than those under private ownership;[2] the protection against waste and fires can be better undertaken by publicly trained officials than by the absentee speculator. But while the nature of forest cultivation permits of public ownership, the efficiency of government operation of the mines as compared with private enterprise is doubtful. Yet a few government-owned mines operated whenever the private monopolist unwarrantably raises the price of the mineral, or always operated in competition with the privately owned mines, might be highly advantageous to the consumer. Again we say, unless a sufficient amount of government control can be exercised to prevent the enormous waste and to break up the monopoly (the tendency toward the monoply of natural resources is well established[3]), public ownership through the policy of repurchase might be found expedient and feasible.

[1] *Report of the National Conservation Commission*, vol. i, pp. 84–85.
[2] *Ibid.*, vol. ii, p. 388.
[3] *Cf. Summary of Report . . . on Lumber Industry* (1911), vol. i, pp. 5–8.

In the case of forest and mineral land, the taxing authority must be governed by other considerations than the withholding of the land from use. To promote the conservation of forests, the levy should be such as to encourage reforestation, at the same time that it prevents a combination of owners of timber land from limiting and controlling the supply with the purpose of keeping prices high. A heavy annual tax on the value of the land only will not tend to encourage forest reserves; and yet, if assessed by expert valuers and uniformly, it would be an improvement over the present system which taxes the value of the trees under haphazard estimates of value. According to an authority on forest taxation, Professor Fairchild,[1] the best tax is one based on the yield at the time the trees are cut. This he thinks will encourage the growth of forests, although his discussion discloses numerous difficulties which the proposal involves. Some states, it must be noted, have even subsidized the owners of forests in the interest of conservation, instead of taxing them. Which, then, is the most expedient method? There seems to be one system, which without injury to the lumber industry in any way, and while aiding the conservation of forests, would yet secure to the state a share of the landowner's profits. That method is the taxation of the value increment at the time of transfer of the property. This is on the supposition that the value of the deforested land itself would show an increment over the purchase price.[1] Taxation, however, will not

[1] *Report of the National Conservation Commission* (1909), vol. II, pp. 615 *ff*. See also *Proceedings of the Sixth Conference on State and Local Taxation*, pp. 371–93.

[1] The supposition is, however, borne out as a fact in the *Summary of the Report on the Lumber Industry*, Pt. I, p. 37: "After all the timber has been cut from the great private holdings the value of the land alone will be enormous. Much of this cut-over land may be best adapted for new growth, in which case there may be a continuing concentration of timber ownership. A large part of the land, however, may be exceedingly valuable for agricultural purposes."

The system of assessment and collection of the tax could be modeled

solve the question of forest conservation. Only by the efforts of the federal government in getting control of a sufficient area on which to grow forests as the European nations are doing, and in this way to compete with the private holders of forest land can we hope that the concentration and private control of timber land will be broken.

The case is somewhat different with mineral land. The value of the mine, as of all land, depends upon a variety of social causes; but it also depends upon the amount and quality of the minerals it contains. Mines are for the most part exhaustible, and the expense of mining increases the deeper the veins are. For this reason the capital value of mines is determined with difficulty. Because of this peculiarity the new English duty calculates the capital value of mines by capitalizing the rental on the basis of twelve and a half years instead of at twenty or more as in the case of other land. Nevertheless, an approximately accurate valuation could be made of a working mine by following the method of rental payments. In England it is customary for the most part to lease the mine to an *entrepreneur* who pays a "dead rent" for a certain amount of minerals brought to the surface, and a royalty for the excess over that quantity, allowing also for shortages. According to Professor Marshall,[1] "the royalty itself on a ton of coal, when accurately adjusted represents that diminution in the value of the mine, regarded as a source of wealth in the future, which is caused by taking the ton out of nature's storehouse." Granted that the economic rent could be thus computed, this value could be found only when the mine was being worked. To levy a tax on the value of mines, therefore, some plan like the English duty must be devised.[2] But a tax will not assure the conservation of this

after the English value-increment duty. In case of a corporation, for example, the payment could be made every fifteen or more years.

[1] *Principles of Economics* (6th ed.), p. 439.

[2] Cf. *supra*, chapter v, §§ 10, 11.

class of land. To prevent the monopolization and waste of mines, the opinion is current, only public ownership can be effective enough.

§ 12. Having shown the inadequacy of the tax on land value seriously to check speculation, reduce rents, and ameliorate housing conditions, it is needless to dwell long on the further social benefits which have been loudly proclaimed. Thus, the tax it was claimed would affect industry and the general distribution of wealth. For the exemption of improvements would encourage building operations, and this stimulation in building would promote not only the building trade, but other industries as well. Not only would the employment of capital be aided by the remission of the tax on improvements, but labor too would experience a "boom"; the wages of building employees would tend to rise, the demand for other commodities would be enhanced, production in general would be stimulated, leading to a cheapening of many commodities, whereby the laborer as consumer would again benefit.[1] In this way the simple reform of taxing the value of land would have within itself the possibility of materially influencing the distribution of wealth, not only diverting some of the value increment, now accruing to the landlord, to the relief of the public budget, but uplifting the working class through better housing, cheaper rents, higher wages, lower prices.

Judging from our study, these hopes appear vain, on the whole. The reason, perhaps, for the failure of the tax to become a reform of wide-reaching influence lies in the harmless nature of the change. It is unreasonable to expect that a two or even three per cent tax on the value of land, or that

---

[1] *The United Committee for the Tax on Land Values, Third Report,* p. 64: "By the transfer of the burden of taxation on to Land Values production would be increased and the price of commodities lowered; the conditions of labor of all kinds would be improved; wages would be higher and employment more regular, and the foundation would be laid of equitable relations between man and man."

the remission of such a rate on improvements would, in our complex social system of interacting forces, bring forth the millenium. Nevertheless, as a fiscal measure, its influence towards reform, its tendency to check speculation in land, to relieve congestion, to appropriate some of the value increment for public purposes, and thus to relieve the burden to some extent from industry, outweigh the charge of discrimination against the landowning class, involved in the proposal to put a higher tax on them than they had anticipated at the time of their investment.[1] Not as a panacea, then, for all social evils and economic mal-adjustment, although its influence may be beneficial with regard to these, but as a tax must the expediency of the tax on land value be determined.

[1] "I have never been able to understand," says Seligman, "why a man who has invested in land should be exposed to the danger of having a part of his property taken away from him? When he invested his money in land it was on the basis of the accepted policy of social justice, that private property in land was to be treated like private property in other things." (The *Survey*, March 7, 1914, p. 700.) A student of the changes that have recently taken place in the policy of legislation should no longer wonder that the *accepted policy of social justice* is not permanent. The end, which is in this case social welfare, justifies the means.

CHAPTER X

EXPEDIENCY OF THE TAX ON LAND VALUE FOR
THE UNITED STATES

§ 1. THE inadequacy of the tax on land value as an effective means of reforming the social evils discussed in the preceding chapters reduces the consideration of the adoption of the tax to its expediency as a fiscal measure. The expediency of introducing a new tax must be determined: (1) by the need of an additional source of public revenue; or (2) by the efficiency or inefficiency of the existing system; or (3) by the special advantages of the proposed change. But even though by these criteria conditions were favorable to the adoption of a new tax, the opposition of interested parties, the conservatism of public opinion, as well as the constitutional barriers, would have to be reckoned with and overcome. What, then, is the situation in this country with regard to the new tax?

If proof were needed of the deep concern that problems of taxation are giving public officials as well as fiscal authorities, their interest in the conferences of the International Tax Association and the activity of the different state legislatures in creating tax commissions within recent years should be noted. The primary cause of this concern is the necessity of covering the ever-increasing budgets with revenue from the old and inadequate sources. This need does not appear in the budget of our national government which is supported adequately by excise and tariff duties, and by income and corporation taxes, nor in that of the state governments, whose expenditures even tend to decrease *per capita* of the population. The greatest fiscal need, as will be shown in the following section, is to be found within the local bodies whose rapidly growing expenditures must be met almost wholly from the selfsame sources.

A second cause of the interest which tax questions are arousing is the inequality of burden, and the general defectiveness of the existing systems of taxation. But the dissatisfaction is directed chiefly against the operation of the general property tax. And inasmuch as the local governments in this country rely almost exclusively on the general property tax for their revenue, the most needed reform is in local taxation.

Coming now to the tax on land value, the more fruitful and opportune inquiry will be concerned with its expediency as a local tax. This position is all the more justified, when we consider that the tax is best adapted for local purposes, if revenue be the object sought. Fiscally, both the German "Zuwachssteuer" and the English increment duties were found to be disappointing. Moreover, these indirect levies are the forms of the tax better suited for state and federal purposes. In this country, however, the conditions of landed monopoly are lacking which made progressive and increment taxes expedient in the other countries studied. Only with regard to forest taxation can the value-increment tax be considered for American conditions. Here too, however, conservation, rather than fiscal expediency, is the purpose to be held in view. On the other hand, to levy a proportional, direct tax on land value for federal or state purposes would be impracticable; it would be not only superfluous, but also against the recent tendency toward separation of the sources of revenue.[1] The choice, therefore, lies between the local increment and direct forms of the tax. The practicability of the increment tax for our municipalities is problematical. First, it is more discriminatory and less productive, i.e., it is less fiscal in character. Secondly, it is unprecedented in method of assessment. Thirdly, its administration presents

[1] *Infra*, § 6.

serious difficulties.[1] The adoption of the tax, if at all expedient, should, then, be for local purposes; the form of levy, the direct, proportional tax, such as we found it in the Australasian and Canadian municipalities.

With the inquiry thus limited, let us test the expediency of the tax on land value, in the light of the needs of the local governments, and the problems centering in local taxation.

§ 2. The tendency of local (including county) expenditure to increase is evident from the following table: —

TABLE SHOWING THE GROWTH OF TOTAL AND PER CAPITA EXPENDITURE BY LOCAL AUTHORITIES IN THE UNITED STATES *

Year	Cities, villages, townships, school districts		Counties, cities, villages, townships, school districts	
	Expenditures	Per capita	Expenditures	Per capita
1870......	$328,244,520	$8.51	$575,810,060	$13.38
1880......	724,427,848	14.44	848,532,875	16.91
1890......	780,941,558	12.47	1,025,989,603	14.79
1902......	1,433,505,091	18.24	1,630,069,610	20.74

* Adapted from table in *State and Local Taxation, Second Conference* (1908), p. 519.

The enormous increase in the outlays of the government in some of the largest municipalities in the country is seen from the tables on the opposite page.

In comparing the *per capita* expenditures in 1890 and 1912 as shown in the table, it should be borne in mind that the data for 1912 included interest on loan investments, and that there may be further discrepancies due to the change in classification by the Census Bureau.

One cause of the need for additional taxes is likewise seen

[1] *Cf. infra,* footnote p. 458.

INCREASE IN EXPENDITURES IN LARGE CITIES, 1900–1910 *

City	1900	1910	Percentage of increase
New York..........	$185,881,409	$513,225,555 †	176
Chicago............	30,141,134	50,878,547	68
Philadelphia........	30,625,246	47,750,049	55
Boston.............	28,959,312	33,237,816 ‡	14
St. Louis...........	8,953,106	16,322,348	82
Buffalo.............	6,967,419	18,014,574	158
Atlanta§..........	1,068,544	4,644,659	334

* Data taken from comptrollers' reports of these cities.
† Figures are for 1911, not for 1910.
‡ The expenditures include both ordinary and extraordinary. The figures were taken from *Boston Municipal Statistics* (Special Publications).
§ Figures are for 1901 and 1911.

in the increased indebtedness which the municipalities tend to assume. From over 27 millions in 1842, the indebtedness of the municipalities in the United States had grown to over 328 millions in 1870, to nearly 707 millions in 1880, to over 744 millions in 1890, and to over 1387 millions in 1902.[1] This enormous increase does not imply that the debts are assumed in lieu of taxation; but it results that the

COMPARISON OF PER CAPITA EXPENDITURES IN CERTAIN LARGE CITIES, 1890–1912 *

Per capita	New York	Chicago	Phila-delphia	St. Louis	Boston	Pitts-burgh	San Fran-cisco	At-lanta
1890: Expenditures except for loans and investments. ..	$24.56	$13.80	$13.10	$14.45	$32.63	$12.04	$18.86	$15.75
1912: Net governmental cost payments......	46.29	29.30	26.49	30.21	43.39	40.66	43.34	21.35

* Extra Census Bulletin No. 70, *United States Census* (1894); *Financial Statistics of Cities* (1912), p. 74.

interest on these enormous amounts must be met by taxation, thus adding another considerable item to the budget.

[1] *United States Census* (Special Report) *Wealth, Debt and Taxation* (1907), p. 131.

The socializing tendencies of modern communities, moreover, give assurance of the permanence in the trend toward increasing public expenditure. Unlike the growth in
the outlays of the federal government, due largely to the
army, navy, and pension expenditures,[1] that of the municipalities is attributable to the developmental needs of
government rather than to the protective.[2] The congrega-
tion of population in cities following upon the so-called
industrial revolution, and the other changes denoted as
progress, have made social problems out of what, less than
a century ago and to this day in certain remote, rural
communities, are considered matters primarily of individual concern, e.g., the education of the young, hygienic conditions of the home and neighborhood, etc. The departments of public education, health, public utilities, public
charities and recreation, as well as the police and fire
departments demand larger appropriations. The following
statistics regarding recreation and educational expenditures in certain large cities are worth noting: [3]

City	Expenditures for recreation			Expenditures for education and libraries		
	1903	1912	Per cent of increase	1903	1912	Per cent of increase
New York...	$1,516,057	$4,099,728	170	$22,923,375	$35,903,197	56
Chicago.....	1,046,799	2,828,816	170	6,703,217	10,719,484	59
Philadelphia	561,308	934,568	66	4,522,054	6,444,380	42
St. Louis....	160,280	391,555	144	2,083,054	3,488,917	67
Boston......	556,221	1,338,939	140	3,868,378	5,296,073	37

[1] Professor Bullock shows that, deducting the expenses for pensions
and army, the *per capita* expenses of the nation would not have increased
at all during the decade 1886–97. *Cf. Political Science Quarterly*, vol.
XVIII, p. 104.

[2] Terms used by H. C. Adams (*Public Finance*) to differentiate the
functions of government that uplift and further the social well-being by
promoting education, sanitation, public improvements, and public
utilities, from the protective functions which serve merely to defend life
and property.

[3] *Financial Statistics of Cities* (1912), Table XII; *United States Census
Report*, Bulletin No. 20 (1902–03), Table XXI.

In view of the increasing population in urban centers and the simultaneously increasing value of property and income, the above percentages of increase in expenditure may not seem extraordinary. The fact is, however, that the budgetary requirements outrun not only the growth of population, as shown by the higher *per capita* expenditure, but outrun also the increase in the assessed value of property.[1] And if the "social service" functions of government, as it now appears, continue to increase, the need of more sources of revenue will likewise continue.

§ 3. Further to emphasize the fiscal needs of the local governments, to which our inquiry is confined, it will be necessary merely to show the inadequacy of the general property tax which constitutes the prevailing source of local revenue in this country. Legally both real and personal property are taxable and both are assessable at their full value. The impracticability of this system, which at one time was almost universally prevalent, has led to its abandonment in almost all countries. And now this country too is waking up to the realization that property is no sufficient test of the taxpayer's ability to contribute to the support of government; and that the administrative difficulties in assessing personalty equitably are well-nigh insuperable.[2] So glaring are the inequalities of burden which the tax occasions, that even under the most efficient tax administrations little attempt is made to comply with the provision of the law in assessing personalty.

The effect of this inefficient system of taxation has been

[1] *Cf.* Gephart, "The Growth of State and Local Expenditure," in *Second Conference of the International Tax Association* on *State and Local Taxation* (1908), p. 524.

[2] There are, nevertheless, a few advocates of the general property tax who believe a graded property tax, with a low rate on certain kinds of personalty would be a productive source of revenue. It is true that, as in Baltimore and Pennsylvania, a low rate will result in an increased assessment of intangible personalty. It is in vain to expect, however, that under a system of self-assessment, which is alone practicable, an equality of burden will result.

to shift the main burden to real property. This will readily be seen from the fact that, taking the country as a whole,[1] in 1902, the assessed value of real estate was 78 per cent, of personalty only 22 per cent. In the city of New York, personal property contributed 35 per cent of the taxes in 1865, 29 per cent in 1870, 15.5 per cent in 1899, 12.5 per cent in 1903, and only 3.9 per cent in 1913.[2] In the State of Minnesota, of a total assessment of over a billion dollars, 84 per cent was on real and only 16 per cent was on personal property.[3]

In view of this circumstance it is interesting to inquire how real estate can support this heavy burden, and why a tax on realty arouses less complaint from the proprietors than an equivalent tax on income, for example.[4] Unquestionably, the explanation lies in the facts that the value of land tends to appreciate with the increase in the budget demands, that the tax is capitalized and largely amortized, and that the value of the property is generally underassessed. However necessary, therefore, fiscal authorities may deem it to supplement the realty tax by other imposts,[5] the relief of the landowner from a heavy burden is not a justifiable ground for such action.

§ 4. A further cause of disapproval of the general property tax is the failure to assess real property at its full

[1] *United States Census* (Special Report), *Wealth, Debt and Taxation* (1907), Table VIII.

[2] *Report of the Commissioner of Taxes and Assessment of the City of New York* (1913), pp. 90–91. Also, Purdy, *Taxation of Personal Property*, p. 9.

[3] *Minnesota Tax Commission, Third Biennial Report* (1912), p. 175.

[4] It must be remembered that a two per cent tax on selling value is equivalent to a thirty to forty per cent tax on the income, depending on the rate of interest. Where the land is undervalued, of course the tax is less heavy. Complaints of this burdensome impost are voiced chiefly in rural and village communities where land does not rise in value so rapidly, if at all.

[5] It is undoubtedly desirable that more than one class, that every individual in fact, should contribute something toward the public budget. Hence other taxes should supplement the realty tax.

value. In only seven commonwealths, Arizona, the District of Columbia, Illinois, Iowa, Kentucky, New Hampshire, and Vermont,[1] does the law provide for assessment at less than the actual value. In all the other states, with the possible exception of certain cities in Massachusetts and New York City, underassessment is the rule in spite of the legal requirement. "The habit of undervaluation is one of such long standing that in most assessment districts sets or series of arbitrary valuations *for assessment purposes* have become established. . . . As the years go by and the assessor continues in office a local system of assessment is developed that is more or less satisfactory to people who give the matter any attention, in that they are assessed on a minimum basis. The assessment thus made is usually copied from year to year and the injustices and inequalities therein existent are perpetuated." [2]

Underassessment in itself is not a serious evil. If the assessed value is thereby less, the rate will be higher; the burden, however, will not be greater. But the defect in the property tax is the failure of uniformity of assessment as between individual owners, between district and district, between rural and city property, between county and county. Such inequality in valuation causes one individual and one section to profit at the expense of another individual and another section. For example, a congressional report on the system of assessment in the District

[1] Arizona may assess property at seventy per cent for city purposes; the District of Columbia, at two-thirds of appraised value; Illinois, at one-fifth on all property (since changed to one-third); Iowa, at twenty-five per cent; Kentucky, at seventy per cent; New Hampshire, at fifty cents on $100; while Vermont is authorized to assess each $100 at $1. See *United States Census* (Special Report), *Wealth, Debt and Taxation* (1907), p. 628. To these states Minnesota must now be added. In 1912, the full value assessment was relaxed, so that property subject to the general property tax is assessed at forty per cent, while other classes of property are assessed at varying percentages. *Taxation and Revenue Systems of State and Local Governments* (1912), p. 124.

[2] *First Biennial Report of the Minnesota Tax Commission* (1908), pp. 6, 8.

of Columbia declares that areas occupied by small homes were assessed at sixty per cent of their true value, middle-class houses at fifty per cent, fine residences at thirty per cent, and suburban areas at twenty per cent of their value.[1] Again, in the United States there are many counties in which city and non-agricultural land (that is, suburban land not platted, nor laid out in lots) is assessed at a higher rate than farm property, and about as many more counties in which the assessment on farm property [2] is at a higher percentage of value than on urban realty.

While this undervaluation may be accounted a matter merely of administrative inefficiency, there is a more fundamental reason for its existence. So long as the assessment is the basis for a state or county levy as well as for municipal purposes, there will be a tendency for the local assessor responsible to the local body to underestimate the value of property in his district. "The departure from the full value probably has its origin in an effort to place valuations low enough to protect tax payers from paying more than a just proportion of taxes levied by the higher political organizations. When the departure is once made from the full value, the tendency is constantly downward, for the reason that the district assessments being made independently of each other, the districts which are assessed at a higher ratio of the true value than the average will be forced in the next assessment to a lower valuation in self-protection. In cases of rapid changes in value — either advancing by reason of increase in population or business, or decreasing from any cause — the assessors will naturally try to protect the interests of their constituents by quickly recognizing any decrease in value, and by being correspond-

[1] *Report on Assessment and Taxation of Real Estate in the District of Columbia* (1912, House, No. 1215), p. 5.

[2] *United States Census* (Special Report), *Wealth, Debt and Taxation* (1907), p. 5.

ingly slow in recognizing an increase, and thus accelerate the downward tendency." [1]

As for the inefficiency and incompetency of the assessor, the fault lies with the present system under which, as an elective official, the assessor becomes responsible to a local constituency, and under which, too, the remuneration is often insufficient to enable him to devote all his time to his office. Until expert, civil service employees are engaged to make the valuation, arbitrary guesswork, not scientific accuracy, will continue to be the basis of realty assessment in this country.

§ 5. With regard both to the need for more revenue and to the defects of the general property tax, there is general agreement among fiscal authorities. It is also generally admitted that the first step toward reform is to amend the state constitutions so as to make changes in the tax system possible. Flexibility in legislative powers, in view of the evolution of social institutions, is essential; it is most essential, too, in that very important function of government, the taxing power. Yet there are only three states (excluding the District of Columbia), Connecticut, New York, and Rhode Island, that have no constitutional restrictions upon the taxing power.[2] In all but thirteen states restrictions, more or less far-reaching, obstruct reform in taxation.

To abolish the "uniform *ad valorem* system," the taxation of *all kinds of property* at the same rate, amendments to the constitution are still required in most of the states.[3]

[1] Somers, *The Valuation of Real Estate for the Purpose of Taxation*, pp. 3–4.

[2] *Cf. Proceedings of the Third International Conference on State and Local Taxation* (1909), p. 73.

[3] In spite of the difficulty of passing a constitutional amendment, about a dozen states have succeeded in so doing and more are ready to follow their example. The constitutions of Arizona and New Mexico now permit of classification, while those of New Jersey, Vermont, Maryland, and Iowa never prevented the classification of property. In Pennsylvania, Idaho, Delaware, Virginia, Minnesota, Oklahoma, Iowa, Michigan,

The nature of the amendment can be seen from the provision in the Minnesota constitution (1906) that "taxes shall be uniform upon the *same class* of subjects." [1] A system of classification of property with varying rates for each class is thus made possible.

With this obstruction to legislation removed, some of the states have instituted changes in taxing personalty that are productive of more revenue and distribute the burden upon a larger proportion of the people. Thus, for example, in Maryland, Pennsylvania and West Virginia, a mere reduction in rate on certain forms of intangible property has resulted in a larger return of personalty for taxation than ever before. Other states, after classsifying the different subjects included under personalty, have adopted special taxes for each class. Thus, mortgages, bonds and other forms of credit may now be subject to a recording or registration tax payable once, that is, when the deed or bond is recorded. In New York state the taxpayer is not even required to make a return of his personal property. [2] Yet, through a system of classification of personalty, the assessment of intangibles has increased. [3]

But even these special taxes have little to recommend them, except that they are more practicable and less burdensome than the old system of taxing personal property. As for an equitable distribution of burden among the taxpayers, objections may well be raised against these special taxes, first, because the taxation of mortgages and bonds generally involve double taxation, and secondly, because all the personal property cannot be reached even when the rate of tax is slight. While, therefore, many to whom

New Hampshire, New York, and Wisconsin the ad valorem principle has been amended. *Ibid.* (1909), p. 73; (1911), pp. 56–58.

[1] *United States Census Report, Taxation and Revenue Systems of State and Local Governments* (1912), p. 120.

[2] *Ibid.*, p. 162.

[3] See *Report of Commissioners of Taxes ... in New York City* (1913), pp. 11, 102.

expediency is all-sufficient favor this change in method of assessment, there are others who would prefer to see certain forms of intangible property exempt altogether, and other systems of taxation supersede the antiquated general property levy. For the latter, then, classification of property for purposes of taxation, although admittedly an improvement, is not an adequate reform.

The substitution of other taxes for the personal property tax would necessitate further amendment of the state constitutions. Wisconsin has successfully substituted an income tax,[1] while in Canada, where the municipalities have greater freedom of action in budgetary matters, business and habitation as well as income taxes have largely replaced the old general property tax. Without entering into the relative merits and defects of these imposts, it will be generally admitted that each one could be made not only more productive, but also more widely distributed than the personal property tax. But like the modified personalty taxes discussed above,[2] the income tax could still be evaded, while the habitation, license, or business taxes would fail to distribute the burden equally and equitably.[3]

§ 6. Aside from the legal and economic difficulties in the way of the elimination of the personal property tax in the manner indicated above, there is evident in this country a trend of tax policy which may make a state income, habitation, or business tax together with the personalty tax, unnecessary. This tendency is toward the separation of the state from the local sources of taxation. Already in ten states, California, Connecticut, Delaware, New Jersey, New York, Ohio, Vermont, Pennsylvania, Wisconsin, and West Virginia, the separation is more or less complete.[4] In

[1] See Fourth International Conference on State and Local Taxation (1910), pp. 87 ff., also Census Report, op. cit., p. 261.

[2] See supra. p. 432.

[3] Cf. Fourth International Conference on State and Local Taxation (1910), pp. 89, 90.

[4] In some of these states, as in New Jersey, subsidiary levies, as for

others, the dependence of the state upon the general property tax is growing less.[1] An analysis of the sources of income for state purposes, moreover, confirms belief in the continuance and further development of this practice.

These sources are public utility and other corporations, inheritances, insurance companies, banks, express companies, while some states derive large sums of revenue from licenses, especially liquor licenses, from mortgages, bonds, notes and other secured debts, and also from fees of various kinds. The success of the levies on public utilities, corporations and on inheritances, and the recent unfriendly attitude towards monopolies and large fortunes, especially expressing itself in the improved methods of assessment, will tend to make these sources of income more and more productive. Thus the separation of state from local taxation will be furthered.

What will be the effects of this policy? First, according to many,[2] separation presents the best remedy for the underassessment of realty.[3] This we saw [4] was one of the defects of the present system of taxation. Secondly, it will facilitate local option in taxation. At first sight the relation between separation of sources for state and local revenue and local option seems remote. But when once the

schools, are the only taxes on general property. In Pennsylvania vehicles and intangibles only are taxed for state purposes. In California and Delaware the separation is complete. *Cf. Census Report, Taxation and Revenue Systems of State and Local Governments* (1912).

[1] For example, Massachusetts, Oregon, and Minnesota derive a considerable proportion of their revenue from other sources. *Cf. Ibid.*; also *Fifth Conference on State and Local Taxation* (1911), p. 238.

[2] There are those who still hold that coöperation between state and local authorities in assessment will solve the evil of underassessment. *Cf. Second Conference on State and Local Taxation* (1908), pp. 113 *ff.*

[3] Another practicable remedy is the apportionment-by-expenditure system. In 1901 this principle was embodied in an Act passed in Oregon, but the reform was never put in practice, largely because of some defective features in the Act. *Cf. ibid.* (1911), pp. 237 *ff.*; also Purdy, *Local Option in Taxation,* p. 32.

[4] *Supra,* § 4.

general property tax is relegated by the state to the local authorities, the interest of the state in the local assessments would diminish and there would therefore be less incentive to oppose local option when the latter is demanded by the municipalities.

The problem of "home rule" in taxation is a serious and vital one just now, first, because of the strong division it has created among fiscal authorities, and secondly, because of the far-reaching changes it may effect in taxation. That the municipalities desire local option in taxation is in harmony with democratic government; it is of a piece with the general movement of cities to govern their own affairs.[1] And as was admitted in part by an opponent of local option,[2] cities like New York, Chicago, Philadelphia, etc., are commonwealths in themselves and may well be left, within limits, to govern themselves. The special importance of freedom in taxation, furthermore, grows out of the constitutional restrictions and the conservatism of the legislature. To await reform in taxation through the slow legislative procedure is in many states hopeless. Hence the demand for the initiative and referendum and for local autonomy, or local option. The consequences of this policy will be treated in the following section.

§ 7. Local option, it must be remembered, is but a means for overcoming the inflexible framework of our state and federal government, and the political interests which thwart reform. It is, furthermore, a method of adapting the laws to the prevailing variety of conditions. Yet, although local autonomy sounds consistent with the ideal of democracy, it has, just as too much liberty has, great dangers. The history of the struggle in this country

[1] The agitation in Chicago to be given power to control the public utilities corporations, etc., is an illustration of the same movement.

[2] Professor T. S. Adams in *Fourth Conference on State and Local Taxation*, p. 107 (footnote).

between state rights and centralization, and of the victory of the latter is sufficient vindication of concentration of authority. But as shown in our history there are limits to this policy. Legislation that is state-wide, for example, is apt to be more effective; nevertheless, in matters purely local this rule has no force. And most large cities that are without a liberal charter are often hampered in their development through the indifference, ignorance, and self-interest of legislators from remote sections of the state.

Admitting the desirability of local autonomy in certain matters, it may, nevertheless, be asked whether taxation is a fit subject for local control. Surely not, when the state is dependent upon the same sources of revenue; nor even if the revenues were all for local purposes, would full power in taxation be justified. We need only to call attention to the evils growing out of the lack of uniformity among the states under our present system and to the recent proposals of inter-state comity, to reject the principle of local autonomy in taxation. Moreover, because of the far-reaching influences of taxation, and the general spirit of rivalry which prevails among the local bodies, it would be dangerous, it is held, to delegate to them full control of the tax system. The power to exempt and discriminate against certain classes of taxable objects might be employed by the towns to attract industries away from other localities, for example. The business chaos that might be expected to ensue from such policies may well be imagined.

Local option, however, does not imply complete autonomy. To argue against the latter in opposing "local option" is willfully to evade the issue.[1] The legislature is

[1] Professor Bullock points out the inconsistency of the Oregon referendum for local option in taxation, to which was attached the provision that no poll tax should be levied in Oregon. If the position of the present writer is correct there is no inconsistency at all. What the people of Oregon voted for was to empower the municipalities to exempt *certain kinds* of property if they chose, at the same time that they were held subject to other general state laws. See, *Fifth Conference on State and Local Taxation* (1911), p. 287.

always well aware of, and the Act always specifies the particular question, in this case, the particular tax or subject in taxation which the municipality may adopt or reject. So with the local option provisions in New Zealand and in Canada.[1] The employment of local option is to give the municipalities a choice of action, and often the power to rescind this action goes with it. In this way local conditions are taken into account. Both in New Zealand and in western Canada a two-thirds vote is generally required to carry a petition on a local option measure. The important fact to notice, however, is that the legislature, moved by a strong public opinion that a certain measure is desirable, yields to what appears a harmless compromise. And this concession will be all the more readily made as the separation of state from local taxation becomes complete.

Where, then, lies the danger in local option, which has called forth such great opposition on the part of fiscal authorities?[2] It is alleged to be the shortest route to the Single Tax. Few would regret the abolition of the personal property tax by the municipal bodies. But, if given the power to exempt personal property, what if the municipality should demand the power to exempt improvements and to abolish all other taxes than the tax on realty? Whether this fear is well founded and justified will appear from a review of recent events.

There is unmistakably a movement in certain of our states to seek local option in taxation. It accompanies the propaganda for the initiative and referendum. The curious thing, however, is that these radical propositions encounter less opposition from the state legislatures than from the people themselves. For example, the California amend-

[1] For example, in British Columbia the Municipal Act (Statutes, 1892, sec. 148) granted power to municipalities to pass by-laws for assessing improvements not in excess of fifty per cent of their actual cash value, or to exempt all improvements from taxation.

[2] *Cf. Conferences on State and Local Taxation* (1907), pp. 515 *ff.*; (1911), pp. 271 *ff.*

ment empowering "any county, city and county, city or town to exempt from taxation for local purposes in whole or in part, any one or more of the following classes of property,"[1] etc., passed both houses of the legislature in 1912 only to be defeated by the popular vote in November, 1914. In Oregon, it is said, the local option amendment to the constitution was adopted [2] in 1910 chiefly because of the provision for the abolition of the poll tax.[3] The measure accomplished nothing, since the power to regulate taxation and exemptions, according to the amendment, was "subject to any general law which may be hereafter enacted." But this amendment was subsequently repealed, with the exception of the clause prohibiting the levy of a poll tax.[4] The conservatism of the general public is further evidenced by the defeat in three counties of Oregon, Clackamas, Multnomah and Coos, of a proposal of the Graduated Specific Tax Exemption League (a Single Tax body) to levy a graduated supertax on land value exceeding $10,000 in a single holding. Another proposal for the adoption of the Single Tax for local purposes also met defeat.[5] At the same time, the following amendment to the Wisconsin constitution was passed in 1913 by both houses of the legislature: [6] "The legislature shall have power to

[1] These classes were: improvements in, on, and over land; shipping; household furniture; live-stock; merchandise; machinery; tools, farming implements; vehicles; other personal property except franchises. See *The Public*, May 23, 1913, p. 492; also New York Tax Reform Association, pamphlet No. 552 (1914).

[2] *Sixth Annual Conference on State and Local Taxation* (1912), pp. 47–48; (1911), pp. 245 *ff.* The vote stood 44,171 for, and 42,127 against, with 33,950 not voting. (*Ibid.*, p. 248.)

[3] *Ibid.*, p. 249.

[4] Art. IX, § 1a. See *Census Report, Taxation and Revenue Systems* (1912), p. 191.

[5] *Cf. The Public*, October 25, 1912, p. 1010; December 11, 1914, p. 1184.

[6] To become a part of the constitution, this proposed amendment had to be readopted by the next legislature before it could be put to a popular vote. *Cf. ibid.*, May 30, 1913. In view of the recent defeat of the progressive

authorize counties, towns, cities and villages, by a vote of
the electors therein, to exempt from taxation, in whole or in
part, designated classes of property, including the buildings and improvements on land, but not the land itself;
but the value of such exempt property shall be included in
the assessment and equalization for State and county
taxes." Nothing more has been done with it, however.

This evidence of recent legislation would tend to indicate that there is not much reason to fear the popular
judgment of the American people even in matters of taxation. Indeed, that the initiative petitions for local option
have aroused the interest and general intelligence of the
people in one of the most important of civic questions has
in itself been a most wholesome influence.[1] In view of the
present defective system of taxation and the many difficulties under which our society is laboring to improve the
system, there is to many no more hopeful outlook than this
movement toward "restricted" local option in taxation.[2]

§ 8. Whatever direction reform in local taxation may
take in this country, it may be confidently assumed that
real estate will continue to constitute the most substantial
source of revenue. The first and most essential step, therefore, must be to eliminate the defects in that system of

party in Wisconsin (November, 1914) there is little hope for the adoption
of the amendment.

[1] See *Fifth Conference on State and Local Taxation* (1911), p. 251.

[2] It is significant that the opposition to "home rule" in taxation has
been awakened by the attempts of the Single Taxers to use local option as a means to submit their doctrines to a popular vote. In 1907,
the National Tax Association adopted without much opposition the
following resolution: "That state and local systems should be so far
divorced that by general laws the appropriate local governing bodies may,
if deemed expedient, be granted certain limited and carefully prescribed
powers over the licensing of occupations and the selection of subjects of
local taxation and the rate of assessment upon such subjects." At the
fifth conference of the Association, in 1911, on account of the diversity of
opinion among the members that had arisen since 1907 on the question of
local option, the above-quoted resolution was withdrawn. *Cf. Proceedings
of the Fifth National Conference* (1911), pp. 425 *ff.*

taxation, which are chiefly administrative. The importance of a more efficient system of valuation and assessment can scarcely be exaggerated, since it would not only tend to equalize the burden of taxation, but would, in a great measure, make special and additional taxes in our localities unnecessary. Moreover, any proposed new tax will presuppose a more expert method of administration than at present employed.

Already a number of American municipalities have taken action to improve the administration of the realty tax. The movement in general is toward expert valuation of property, toward full-value assessment, and toward annual revaluation. What is meant by an expert, scientific method of appraising real property has already been described.[1] The first requirement for a fairly accurate system of valuation is the separation of the value of the land from that of the improvements; the second is the employment of maps and rules for relative values; the third, good administrative machinery, trained valuers holding office by civil service appointment and responsible to a head taxing authority.

The progress already made in this country toward such scientific valuation is a strong argument against the halfway schemes to patch up the assessment roll which are advocated in some states. The recent attempts by the Tax Commissions of Wisconsin and Michigan to ascertain the actual value of real property by a comparison of a number of recorded sales with the assessed value of the same property and under the untenable assumption that the same discrepancy that existed between the sale and assessed value in a relatively few cases will apply to all property,[2] are futile and inadequate to overcome the flagrant inequalities in assessment. Even though the assessed value of real property has by this method risen

[1] *Supra*, chapter VII, §§ 13 *ff.*
[2] *Cf. Second Conference on State and Local Taxation* (1908), pp. 120 *ff.*

enormously, the process of attempting an equalization of the admittedly incompetent original assessment, is scarcely commendable. And added to this fundamental defect is that arising from the fact that the recorded values are often nominal and fallacious and that the number of sales transactions in any one year are comparatively few. There remains, therefore, no doubt that the more scientific and in the end more practicable method of valuation is that endorsed by the committee of the National Tax Association on Real Estate Assessment, and practiced in New York City, a *cadastral* valuation based on the principles already set forth.

The second change in our administrative system, namely, full-value assessment, will automatically result from an expert valuation. Whether underassessment is legally required,[1] or is the outcome of a defective system, it is to be condemned. Enough reasons have already been given elsewhere [2] in favor of full-value assessment. We repeat that from a purely business standpoint its influence is most favorable, since underassessment, even when uniform (which is contrary to experience), means a higher tax rate.[3] Yet a low rate will all the more readily attract residents and business to a community.

As to annual assessments, inasmuch as it is the tendency of land to fluctuate and especially to appreciate in value, the valuation must be frequent enough to reflect such fluctuations. And without a revaluation, even annual assessments have proven ineffective. Already assessments are made annually in twenty-four states for all taxing

---

[1] As in Illinois and several other states.

[2] See *supra*, § 4.

[3] The recent reform in Ohio, the chief feature of which consisted in adopting full-value assessment, has shown the value of the change. The maximum rate limit for all local purposes in Ohio has been fixed at fifteen mills, while in Chicago for practically the same purposes the tax rate for 1915 is about fifty mills. (In Chicago, however, property is legally assessed at one-third of its actual value.)

purposes, and in seven more for local purposes only,[1] thirty-one states in all. In most of these cases, however, the assessment of the previous year with or without changes is readopted for the current year. To be effective, then, an annual revaluation of the property is necessary.

§ 9. The need of administrative reform being generally acknowledged, the more disputed question presents itself, as to what new sources of revenue are available for local purposes. Speaking generally, local tax reform tends to take one or more of three forms: (1) the classified general property tax, or (2) the realty tax supplemented by special taxes on business, corporations, and possibly income, or (3) the realty tax relegated exclusively to the local authorities. The adoption of any one of these systems will require in most states a constitutional amendment. The preference, then, rests on the basis of relative expediency, for opinion is divided with regard to the relative equity of the proposed substitutes for the general property tax.[2]

If there is some truth in the adage, "every old tax is good, every new one bad," the introduction of new and untried taxes into the local system in this country should and probably will proceed slowly. The conservative tendency toward reform in the United States bears out this statement. For this reason the course of reform is greatly in favor of the classified property tax which involves only slight innovation. The classified property tax, moreover, is preferred to the separation of the revenue sources of state and local governments respectively, because of the far-reaching consequences which the latter may involve. Indeed, the opposition against separation seems to be actuated by the fact that it will lead to local option, local option to the tax on land value, and land-value taxation to the Single Tax.[3]

[1] *United States Census* (Special Report), *Wealth, Debt, and Taxation* (1907), p. 627.

[2] See *supra*, §§ 5, 6.

[3] In reference to the experience of Pennsylvania and Maryland (see

Nevertheless, the expedient of dividing the revenue sources between the state and local governments is making progress.[1] With the modern movement toward the levy of specific taxes on public utility and other corporations, on inheritance, insurance, and on mines for state purposes, the separation of sources will grow more feasible.[2] In fact the tendency is for separation to follow classification. Iowa and Virginia exemplify this movement. In both of these states classification is not restricted by the constitution, and departure from the uniform *ad valorem* property tax has been tried. In 1913, an amendment passed the legislature of Iowa, providing for a separation of the sources of revenue.[3] In Virginia a partial [4] separation was enacted in 1915. Another noteworthy enactment, a halfway measure, perhaps, between classification and separation, is the plan adopted by Connecticut of apportioning the state direct tax against the towns in proportion to their revenue, instead of proportionately to their assessed valuation.[5]

The replacing of the personal property tax in our local bodies by business and income taxes, as has been the devel-

supra, § 4) with the classified property tax, Professor Bullock asks: "Is it not possible that these commonwealths have found a practicable, if not an ideal, method of removing the worst evils in American state and location taxation?" See *Second Conference on State and Local Taxation* (1908), p. 137. How much the inevitable movement toward local option which Professor Bullock desires to ward off is responsible for the sentiment quoted above can only be surmised.

[1] *Cf. supra*, § 6.

[2] The most serious objection to separation, the lack of elasticity of the state system of taxation (*cf.* Seligman, *Essays in Taxation* (1913), pp. 358 *ff.*), has not interfered with the method in Delaware, for example, where it is of long standing.

[3] The amendment must be passed again in 1915, before it can be submitted to the people. *Cf.* New York Tax Reform Association, pamphlet No. 547 (1913).

[4] *Ibid.*, pamphlet No. 560 (1915). Partial separation, because realty is relegated to the local bodies for all purposes, except for the school tax rate of ten cents which is to remain a state levy.

[5] *Ibid.* (1915). *Cf. supra*, p. 434, footnote 3.

opment in Canada, is for practical reasons remote. The inexpediency of the business tax for large cities lies fundamentally in the difficulty of finding a measure of even relative uniformity to ensure equality of burden. The experience with this tax even in the smaller communities of Canada affords evidence of its defects. It is readily seen that to make the actual rental the basis of levy is to inflict an inordinate hardship upon the retail merchants, for example, whose rental is comparatively higher on account of the better location and size of their premises. In most cases, therefore, floor space has superseded rental as the unit of measure for the tax. But this has necessitated generally an elaborate classification of the various businesses, with a variety of rates or assessed valuations of the different classes. In Winnipeg, for example, where both methods of assessment have been tried, there is dissatisfaction with the present system, which makes an *assumed* rental the basis of assessment.[1] The complications which would arise in any large American city, from a classification which must be more or less arbitrary, are alone a sufficient deterrent to the introduction of the business tax. As for the local income tax, the diffidence shown in this country with regard to its levy even for state purposes,[2] and the inexpediency of taxing income locally, because income is no longer local in character, argue strongly against its introduction.[3] From the administrative standpoint, therefore, the most feasible of the proposed new taxes is perhaps the habitation tax. But because of its "regressive" and its unprecedented character in American communities its institution will probably depend upon the

[1] *Cf.* Haig, *The Exemption of Improvements from Taxation in Canada and the United States*, pp. 22 *ff.*

[2] Only seven states have enacted income tax laws. *Taxation and Revenue Systems of State and Local Governments* (1912), p. 10.

[3] The last objection would of course lose its force if the tax was administered by the state or central jurisdiction and the revenue apportioned among the local governments.

urgency of the fiscal stress, and the effectiveness of the other changes, namely, classification and separation, to relieve the pressure of the growing budgets.

§ 10. There is, however, one alternative method of raising more revenue. That is to increase the tax on real property. That the latter is already heavily burdened has been shown above.[1] But the increase of burden would occasion less opposition, were it not for the fact that the charge falls as heavily on the tenant as on the landowner. To raise the rate of impost is, therefore, to hinder building operations and to aggravate the general condition of congestion in urban communities. Hence the growing popularity of the tax on land value.

The tax on land value is in reality, then, no new source of revenue; the untaxing of buildings is intended rather to free the way to put a heavier charge upon the land. To the extent that this is confiscatory and too discriminatory its adoption in this country is remote. In so far, however, as the tax on land value involves the untaxing of buildings without over-burdening the landowner its expediency will appeal to the general public. Now, under what circumstances is the proposal in the latter sense feasible?

First, the relation of the separation of the state and local sources of revenue to the tax on land value has been pointed out. The dependence of the two reforms is reciprocal. While the separation of sources tends to facilitate the introduction of the tax on land value, the latter presupposes and would be inexpedient without separation. The reason is as follows: the exemption of improvements from taxation would impose an unequal burden upon land owners in rural and urban communities respectively. As a matter of fact, since the relative value of the land and improvements varies in the different counties, cities, villages, and rural districts, a state tax on land value, unless apportioned among the local governments according to

[1] *Supra,* § 3.

expenditure,[1] would have no possibility of enactment. For example, in Minnesota, the remission of the tax on structures, according to the Tax Commissioner's estimate,[2] would necessitate an average increase in the tax rate of 12.6 per cent in the rural districts (where the land far exceeds the improvements in value), and an increase of 103.75 per cent in the cities. It is evident how onerous such an exemption of improvements would be, if a uniform rate were struck for state purposes.

If, however, the municipalities should receive the quota from the property tax now accruing to the state, the tax rate under the new system could be reduced to that degree. That the relief from separation will not be significant will appear from the following considerations. In 1902, about eleven per cent of the total receipts from the general property tax in the country constituted the state levy.[3] But it must be remembered that the exemption of personalty which may be expected to accompany the proposal to untax buildings will largely offset this source of relief. Moreover, this relief will not apply to the states where separation is now wholly, or approximately, in force. To what degree separation will prevent an additional burden from falling upon site value will depend upon the conditions in the various communities.

For this reason, the desirability of local option has been advocated. Aside from the unequal distribution of burden upon rural and urban districts to be thereby obviated, there is a further reason for local option. There are municipalities where the value of the land tends to increase rapidly. These are the local bodies where the untaxing of the buildings could be instituted without the imposition of

---

[1] *Cf.* Seligman, *Essays in Taxation* (1913), pp. 358 *ff.*

[2] *Third Biennial Report of the Minnesota Tax Commission*, pp. 178–79.

[3] Taking the United States as a whole, 51.7 per cent of all the state revenue in 1902 consisted of the general property tax yield. *United States Census* (Special Report), *Wealth, Debt, and Taxation* (1907), p. 968.

a heavier burden on the land. And if there be a grain of truth in the contention that the untaxing of buildings will stimulate business and industry and attract population, this tendency of rising land value will even be accelerated to the advantage of the landowner. Here, indeed, we must call attention to the fear expressed by some that under local option the tax on land value might be employed by municipalities as a means to attract business and population from rival cities. Without denying the possibility of misusing complete home rule in taxation, the argument is, nevertheless, an admission of the wholesomeness and expediency of the new system. The movement to exempt machinery from taxation in American cities[1] is dominated by the same motive, namely, to attract and encourage industry. And why should not a wholesome tax system, or in fact any civic institution, be used as a bonus to outside industry, just as an endowment by leading citizens is often used to lure an industry to a city? If business will thrive better where improvements are not taxable, the latter, if other considerations allow, might be exempted with advantage. Least of all has the landlord great cause to complain, for whatever enhances the industrial prosperity of the town causes his land to appreciate in value.[2]

A third consideration bearing upon the problem of the untaxing of buildings without levying an excessive tax on land arises from the underlying requirements of the new

[1] See *infra*, § 12.

[2] It is interesting in this connection to show how readily the business world and especially the realty operators respond to a reform which promises to promote prosperity. This explains, perhaps, the great and often favorable comment on the so-called Single Tax in realty journals, such as the *Real Estate Magazine*. For example, there appeared in the *Wall Street Journal* (May 14, 1914) an article in praise of the Houston (Texas) Plan of Taxation because of its effect on "boosting" the town. The plan is partially the tax on land value (see *infra*, § 12). In view of the agitation concerning the tax in New York City, however, the article could not stand unassailed. Hence Allan Robinson's very effective criticism of the Houston experiment in the *Wall Street Journal* of May 23, 1914.

system, namely full-value assessments and annual revaluations. In view of the prevailing underassessment of real property for taxing purposes, expert valuation and assessment at full market value would swell the assessment roll; and if revaluation were made frequently enough, preferably annually, the increments of land value in urban communities would also augment the proceeds of the tax.

Fourthly, it might be found expedient to reduce the rate on buildings as compared with that on land, or to untax buildings altogether, covering the deficit in revenue through the levy of other taxes. If the choice lay between the old realty tax and the new proposed additional tax on habitation, business, or income, few would decide for the latter, for the reasons already set forth. If, however, the tax could be removed from buildings, by the substitution of special and franchise taxes, and of a more extended licensing system, much could be said in favor of such exemption.

§ 11. Speaking generally, however, there are but few municipalities in this country where the tax on land value would not impose a heavier charge on the property-holder than under the realty tax. The relative value of land and buildings will determine the amount of added burden. In general it may be said: (1) that there are few urban and rural communities where, if the reform were complete, an increase of one hundred per cent in the tax rate would be necessary, since such an increase would imply that the value of the improvements exceeds the value of the land; (2) that there are only a few localities, where the rise in land value, and the relatively greater value of the land than the buildings would occasion no increase in the tax rate; (3) that in the majority of local governments, some advance in rate would be needed, the increase varying from a few mills to one or two per cent.[1]

[1] In the case of New York City, we estimated an increase in the tax rate of over eleven mills. *Cf. supra*, p. 343, footnote.

Again we must call attention to the fact that, in spite of the higher tax rate, the landowner will not necessarily find his tax bill higher. The distribution of the shifted charge will fall unequally. A little reflection shows that the tax on land value puts a premium upon improved land. The proprietor, therefore, who has expended more on improvements than on the value of the site, will profit at the expense of the owner of vacant property. Since the ground owner in this country is in most cases the proprietor of the improvements as well, it is evident that many of them might be relieved by the change rather than burdened. This assumes, however, that the proprietor is also the occupier of the building, or that the remission of the tax on buildings will not fall to the benefit of the tenant in reduced rents.[1]

Take New York City, for example.[2] Less than six per cent of the families in Manhattan live in their own houses. In the other four boroughs the percentage will of course be much greater. Some of these owner-occupiers in Manhattan would probably enjoy a reduction in taxes; these would comprise the owners of the finest residences in that borough. The occupiers of the average single family house, according to Dr. Haig, would find their tax bill increased, because the value of the land in Manhattan is excessive as compared with the cost of the ordinary dwelling house. In the other boroughs, however, the owner of his residence would generally have less taxes to pay. The relief accruing to such owner, however, might be counterbalanced by the reduced value of his property which is another probable effect of the introduction of the tax. The last consideration

[1] Frictional forces, we have seen, may prevent the shifting from taking place.

[2] Dr. Haig has worked out the probable distribution of burden that the reduction of the tax on buildings by fifty per cent would occasion in New York City. In this section we reproduce his conclusions. *Cf.* Haig, *Some Probable Effects of the Exemption of Improvements from Taxation in the City of New York*, pp. 128 ff.

does not seem important in the case of the home-owner who in general may be expected to remain in possession.

In the case of the owners who let their houses the reduction of the tax on buildings should theoretically fall to the profit of the tenant; but to the extent that friction will hinder the transmission of the benefit, the remission of the tax will rather relieve the landlord, provided the value of the improvement on the land exceeds the average ratio between the site and building values for the whole taxing jurisdiction. Now, in New York City, where rented apartments and houses are the rule, the landowner would find his tax bill reduced or increased according to the value of the improvements on the site. On the average the value of the building tends to exceed the value of the land in the three boroughs, Brooklyn, Bronx, and Richmond; for Manhattan and Queens the contrary is true. In the latter borough the large number of vacant and undeveloped parcels of land, in Manhattan the proportionately greater land value, will increase the burden of the property holder. "Houses in Manhattan would usually pay higher taxes while those in other boroughs would pay lower ones. In Manhattan the more expensive parcels in the samples would receive decreases; in the Bronx the less expensive ones. Tenements in one portion of Manhattan would pay greater taxes while those in other sections would pay smaller." [1] The important conclusion, as pointed out by Dr. Haig, is this: In so far as indirect benefits may be expected to follow the new system and to raise the value of the land, and in so far as the owner is the occupier or user of improved property, he will gain; but as ground owner he will have higher taxes to pay on his *land*. Therefore, unless other changes in the tax system accompany the untaxing of buildings, the landowner alone will be discriminated against by the change.

§ 12. Until recent years, the proposal of the tax on land

[1] Haig, *The Exemption of Improvements*, etc., p. 134.

value, confounded with the Single Tax, remained a dead issue in this country. Only with the widespread reaction against the existing system of taxation is the question coming to the front. At this time, indeed, when the more immediate and urgent tax measures are pressing for adoption, the activity of the Single Taxers in the propaganda of the tax on land value, insignificant as their organization is, is noteworthy.[1] Their advocacy of the tax on land value is entirely opportunistic; that is, the Single Taxers view the land-value tax as the entering wedge. It may well be, however, that the Single Tax bugbear will retard rather than promote the adoption of the tax on land value.

Nowhere in this country thus far has the attempt been made to introduce the tax on land value in its entirety. Most of the legislation which sought to exempt improvements gradually has met with failure. Only a few instances of success in introducing the partial exemption of improvements are recorded as the following summary of the legislation will make clear.

That attempts to introduce the tax should be made in states having the initiative and referendum is not strange. The reform was made part of the election campaigns in Oregon, Washington, and Missouri, and the referendum propaganda was assisted by the Joseph Fels Fund[2] organized for the promotion of Single Tax legislation in the United States. The defeat of the measures in Oregon have been mentioned.[3] In Washington it was no different. In accordance with a constitutional amendment in that state, cities are empowered to draft their own charters. In 1911,

---

[1] It is to the credit of the Single Taxers that, more consistent than some of their opponents, they do not urge the immediate adoption of their utopian system *in toto;* but they are confident that the success of partial exemption of improvements, full-value assessments, etc., will further their complete system.

[2] Mr. Fels contributed a sum equal to all the other contributions to the Fund. *Cf. Joseph Fels Fund Bulletin* (1913).

[3] See *supra*, p. 438.

accordingly, an amendment to the city charter of Everett was proposed and adopted providing for the exemption of improvements for local purposes to the extent of twenty-five per cent of their value in 1912 and 1913, to fifty per cent in 1915, to seventy-five per cent in 1916 and their total exemption thereafter.[1]   In spite of the affirmative vote, the city commission of Washington decided to exclude the amendment from the new charter, but to submit it as a supplementary proposal to the charter. This amendment, submitted to a referendum vote in March, 1912, was defeated. At the November election of the same year, however, the proposal was carried in every ward, the vote standing 4200 in favor to 2200 against.[2] The amendment to the Seattle charter fared differently. Adopted by the city council in December, 1911, the measure was submitted to the people the following March only to be defeated by a vote of about 12,000 to 28,000. Another proposal for the gradual exemption of improvements introduced by Councilman Erickson met the same fate as the first.[3]

In Missouri the attempt of the Equitable Taxation League[4] and of the Civic League of St. Louis,[5] in 1912, to

[1] *The Public*, November 24, 1911, p. 1194; May 3, 1912, p. 422; November 15, 1912, p. 1091.

[2] The fate of this measure is undecided. The officials declaring it to be unconstitutional have not put it in operation. *Cf.* Haig, *The Exemption of Improvements*, etc., p. 258.

[3] *The Public*, January 15, November 22, 1912; March 14, 1913.

[4] This league was instrumental in obtaining 30,000 signatures to the initiative petition. See *ibid.*, August 23, and July 12, 1912.

[5] *Report of the Municipal Finance and Taxation Committee of the Civic League of St. Louis on the Taxation Amendments to the State Constitution of Missouri to be submitted November, 1912.*

Section 1 of the proposed amendment provided: that "all property now subject to taxation shall be classified for purposes of taxation and for exemption from taxation as follows: —

"Class one shall include all personal property. All bonds and public security of the State, and of the political subdivisions and municipalities thereof, now or hereafter issued shall be exempt from all taxes and all personal property shall be exempt from all taxes, State and local, in the year

amend the constitution providing for the gradual exemption of improvements and the exemption of personal property failed. After a vigorous campaign, the measure was
defeated by a large majority.[1]

While this referendum and active propaganda terminated
in defeat, the first step toward the taxation of land value
has been taken by a few municipalities, without the
publicity of which we have just spoken. In Houston,
Texas, the tax commissioner, J. J. Pastoriza, a disciple of
Henry George, upon assuming office in 1911 decided to
introduce some changes. Texas is hampered by the constitutional provision which requires uniformity in the
taxation of all property, tangible and intangible. Pastoriza's predecessors had violated this provision, and Pastoriza
decided that he would also, but in another way. First he
had the Somers' system of valuation introduced and then
fixed the assessment, so that land was assessed at its "fair"
value,[2] and improvements at twenty-five per cent of their
actual value, or cost of reproduction. Personal property

1914 and thereafter, provided that nothing in this amendment shall be
construed as limiting or denying the power of the State to tax any form
of franchise, privilege or inheritance.

"Class two shall include all improvements in or on lands, except
improvements in or on lands now exempt from taxation by law. In the
year 1914 and 1915, all property in class two shall be exempt from all
taxes, State and local, to the extent of one-fourth of the assessed value of
such property; in the years 1916 and 1917, to the extent of two-fourths;
in 1918 and 1919 to the extent of three-fourths; and in the year 1920
and thereafter, all property in class two shall be exempt from all taxes,
State and local; provided, however, that in the year 1914 and thereafter,
the improvements to the extent of $3000 in assessed value on the home-
stead of every householder or head of a family shall be exempt from all
taxes, State and local." *The Public*, November 1, 1912, pp. 1035–36.

[1] The amendment was opposed most strenuously by the agricultural
population of the state. *Cf. The Public*, September 13, and November 15,
1912, p. 1091.

[2] That is Pastoriza's statement. See *The Public* (February 20, 1914),
p. 179; (June 12, 1914), p. 557. Fair means about seventy per cent.
The buildings were assessed at thirty-three per cent of their value in
1912 and 1913, and at twenty-five per cent in 1914. *Cf.* Haig, *The
Exemption of Improvements*, etc., p. 244.

continued to be taxed, but no attempt was made to reach it. Bank deposits, credits, and house furnishings were not taxed. The reform consisted, therefore, in establishing an expert and more equal valuation of the land, and in reducing the rate on buildings to about 36 per cent of that on land.

According to the Tax Commissioner [1] and the Single Taxers, very noteworthy results have ensued. First, the total assessments were raised from 64 million dollars in 1910 to 94 millions in 1912; and it is claimed that by this change the tax rate had been reduced from $1.70 to $1.50. As a result of the readjustment in valuation and assessment over 5000 owners paid less taxes in 1912 than in 1910.[2] Secondly, building operations have been enormously stimulated. The number of building permits during the first six months of 1912 showed an increase of 55 per cent over the corresponding period in 1911.[3] Thirdly, Mr. Pastoriza claims that the partial exemption of improvements has lowered house rents.[4] Fourthly, the general

---

[1] In spite of the agitation among his opponents, Mr. Pastoriza has been twice reëlected by a large majority. According to J. Pastoriza the population of Houston since 1910 had increased by 25,000. (See *Wall Street Journal*, May 14, 1914.) His friends set it even higher. (*The Public*, January 9, 1914, p. 31.)

[2] *The Public*, June 21, March 29, August 23, 1912.

[3] *Ibid.*, June 12, February 20, 1914. The reports of the building inspectors present even a more favorable showing than the statement quoted. The following shows the valuation of building permits before and after the adoption of the Houston Plan. (Statement of financial statistics furnished the writer by J. J. Pastoriza.)

Year	Valuation	Year	Valuation
1910	$3,695,145	1913	$5,432,265
1911	3,585,468	1914	4,044,367
1912	5,142,352	1915	2,418,693

[4] These are his words: " The exemption of buildings from taxation to the amount of seventy-five per cent of their value has had the effect to lower rents, which is only another way of saying that it has raised wages. The following is a short list of houses (there are many more) showing the amount of reduction in rent since the Houston Plan of Taxation has been in existence. The plan has caused many new houses to be erected, thus

progress of the city is thought to owe something to the
Houston Plan of Taxation.[1] Statistics, indeed, bear out
the statements of Pastoriza, but they do not reveal the
cause of the remarkable progress made by Houston. The
popularity of this illegal reform, nevertheless, indicates its
general soundness.[2] This interesting experiment has, however, been cut short by the recent court decision declaring the method of taxation in Houston illegal.[3]

Another example of reform in the same direction was
the enactment of the Stein Bill [4] in Pennsylvania providing
for the gradual exemption of improvements from taxation
in second class cities, i.e., in Pittsburgh and Scranton.
Especially significant is this legislation for Pittsburgh,

creating competition and changing the condition which existed before
the Houston Plan of Taxation was inaugurated. Before that time there
were two or three tenants for every house that was newly built; as a result
house rent jumped to the skies. Now there is never more than one
tenant after a house when it is completed, and sometimes not that. The
result is that the owners of houses, being anxious to rent, have reduced
the rent until the revenue derived from improved property does not
exceed very much the interest which you can get for money in the open
market. I will ask if this is not a good thing for the people of our city? "
Quoted from *The Public*, June 12, 1914, p. 557.

[1] Allan Robinson, President of the Allied Real Estate Interests,
attempted to refute some of the claims of Pastoriza with regard to the
effects of the tax. (*Wall Street Journal*, May 23, 1914.) To the statement that the bank deposits had increased in Houston about seven
millions of dollars from 1911 to 1912, Robinson quotes figures to prove
that other cities in Texas show similar gains. Taking all the facts into
consideration Houston does show remarkable progress for a city of its
size.

[2] " The people have expressed themselves universally as being satisfied with the Houston Plan of Taxation, and I believe that if the matter
was submitted to a vote of the people, over 90 per cent of them would
vote in favor of it." (From *Report of Tax Commissioner* (1914), in *City
Book of Houston*, p. 97.) Although this estimate may be judged extravagant, yet Mr. Pastoriza has been elected again and again on the platform
of retaining the illegal system he has introduced. *Cf.* Haig, *The Exemption of Improvements*, pp. 243, 251 ff.

[3] Decision rendered by Judge Read, of the Texas State District Court,
at Houston on March 2. *The Public*, March 12, 1915, p. 260.

[4] H.R. 967. Passed in May, 1913; approved May 15. Pennsylvania,
1913, No. 147.

where until 1911 property was assessed according to a classification made in 1867, the land being divided into three categories, agricultural, rural, and full city land.[1] The Act of 1913 provides that the assessment on buildings shall be reduced to ninety per cent of their actual value the first year, to be followed by a further reduction of ten per cent every third year, until after fourteen years the exemption will be only fifty per cent. If not repealed, this legislation may after a few years' operation serve as an object lesson to other states.

A few more isolated instances where the principle of exemption of improvements is in force could be mentioned, as for example, Pueblo, Colo., and Modesto, Cal. The latter is an irrigation district. A few more irrigation districts in the San Joaquin Valley took advantage of the California state law to pay for the irrigation projects by a special assessment on land value. The results of the new system there are said to be noteworthy.[2] In Pueblo, the initiative petition to amend the city charter providing for

---

[1] The first kind paid one-third of the prevailing tax rate in the ward, the second kind two-thirds, the last kind the full tax rate. With revaluation of the land in a growing city like Pittsburgh, the effect of such a system can readily be imagined. "Property for some distance along one side of Center Avenue, and also along Fifth Avenue has been classed 'full,' paying the full tax rate, while at the same time, that on the other side of the street has paid but two-thirds of the rate" — "it was found that the low rates have been paid almost entirely by large 'agricultural' holdings and expensive residence properties while the high rates have been saddled upon small business realty, small residences, and congested tenement neighborhoods." *The Survey*, July 1, 1911, pp. 477, 479.

This "fiscal anachronism" as some one has well called the system was abolished in 1911, and in the same year the legislature passed an Act exempting machinery from taxation in Pittsburgh and Scranton for municipal purposes. It is claimed that Mayor Magee saw the possibility of the tax in stimulating industry and therefore had the Canadian system investigated. The Pittsburgh Civic League aided and supported him. Cf. *The Public*, February 14, 1913, p. 151. In a pamphlet, *An Act to Promote Pittsburgh's Progress by Reducing the Tax Rate on Buildings forty per cent*, examples were cited showing that the change would occasion an increase in rate only from fifteen mills to eighteen mills.

[2] *The Public*, February 27, 1914, pp. 205–06.

the partial reduction of the tax on buildings was adopted
November 5, 1913, by a majority of 540. In 1914, fifty
per cent of the value of realty improvements and buildings
was to be exempt; in 1915, ninety-nine per cent was to be
exempt for local purposes.[1] After being in operation two
years, the measure was repealed on November 2, 1915.
The vote for adoption, in 1913, was 2711 for, and 2171
against; in 1915, the vote cast was larger, 3042 against, to
3255 for repeal.[2]

In New York City two thus far unsuccessful attempts
have been made to tax land value. The movement is
the outcome chiefly of the agitation for better housing.[3]
The Congestion Commission of 1910 recommended a
decrease in tax rate on improvements and an increase of
the rate on land value. This recommendation was embodied in the Herrick-Schaap Bill providing for the gradual
exemption of improvements to the extent of fifty per cent.[4]
The second proposal was the levy of a value-increment
tax. This tax was recommended by the Commission on
New Sources of City Revenue appointed by Mayor
Gaynor in 1911.[5] Among other taxes advocated by this
Commission was an annual increment tax of one per cent
"to be perpetual upon all increments of land values as
shown by comparison with the assessed valuations of the

[1] *The Public,* November 14, 1913, p. 1089; Haig, *The Exemption of
Improvements,* etc., p. 253.

[2] *The Public,* November 19, 1915, p. 1122.

[3] The housing exhibit held in New York City was an attempt to bring
home to the people the necessity of the proposed tax reform. *Cf. The
Survey,* March 15, 1913.

[4] *Cf. Report of The New York City Commission on Congestion of Population* (1911), p. 32. The Bill of 1915 proposed the untaxing of buildings gradually so that after a period of ten years the exemption would
be practically complete.

[5] *Report of the Commission on New Sources of City Revenue, City of New
York* (1913), p. 6. The untaxing of buildings was again made the subject
of investigation by the Mayor's Committee on Taxation in New York
City in 1915. *Cf. Final Report of the Committee on Taxation of the City
of New York* (1916).

year 1912, and to be in addition to the general tax levied upon all real estate." [1]

These few attempts to introduce the partial untaxing of buildings may be classified into three general categories. The Oregon, Washington, Colorado, and Missouri movements were instigated largely by the Single Tax propaganda. These states are a fertile soil for agitation because of the referendum possibilities. The Houston, Pittsburgh, and Scranton experiments must be attributed rather to the widespread tendency in this country to underassess improvements, machinery, etc. For example, in Minnesota "a custom has been developed in the state of assessing land and improvements at different percentages of actual value. Especially is this true in the newer parts of the state. The argument has been advanced that a heavy assessment is a fine on improvements." [2] Under the present defective system of assessment such illegal undervaluation of improvements may be assumed to be general. Moreover, the same trend is evident in the recent legal exemption of machinery and tools from taxation in Pittsburgh and Scranton (1911) and more recently in Philadelphia (1915).[3] The purpose in all such cases is probably to lighten the burden on industry. The agitation in New York, on the other hand, may be regarded as the outgrowth (1) of the housing reform movement, and (2) of the search for new sources of revenue to cover the colossal budget.[4]

[1] In addition to what has been said in disapproval of a local increment tax (see *supra*, § 1), it must be pointed out that the great discontent in New York City with the assessed values in recent years makes the above proposal of an annual increment tax, at least until conditions in the realty market change, very undesirable and inexpedient. If levied on the occasion of sale as in Germany the computation of the increment would be much simpler and the tax more equitable.

[2] *First Biennial Report of the Minnesota Tax Commission*, p. 56.

[3] Pennsylvania (1915), No. 346.

[4] The activity of the Society to Lower Rents has helped bring this proposal before the various tax committees.

As yet, with the exception of a few isolated instances, reform in local taxation in the United States is still in its infancy. The prospect of the institution of the tax on land value is, therefore, remote. The momentum of the agitation to introduce the tax will quicken, however, as the fiscal exigencies of the cities assert themselves. But judging from the conservatism displayed by the people with regard to the referendum measures mentioned above, the adoption of the tax on land value can only be the outgrowth of the general fiscal reform movement, not the vindication of the Single Tax doctrines.

THE END

BIBLIOGRAPHY

I. GENERAL AND MISCELLANEOUS REFERENCES

Adams, H. C. Science of Finance. New York, 1898.
Anderson, James. Enquiry into the Nature of the Corn Laws; with a View to the New Corn Bill Proposed for Scotland. Edinburgh, 1777.
Armitage-Smith, G. Principles and Methods of Taxation. London, 1910.
Assessment of Real Estate for Purposes of Taxation, The. City Club Bulletin (Phil.), v. 6, March 4, 1913, pp. 321 ff.

Bastable, C. F. Public Finance. 3d ed. London, 1903.
Bellom, M. L'Impôt sur la Plus-Value des Immeubles. In Séances et Travaux de L'Académie des Sciences Morales et Politiques. N.S., v. 75, 1911, pp. 379 ff.
Bericht über den ersten allgemeinen deutschen Wohnungskongress in Frankfurt a. M., 1904. Göttingen, 1905.
Bericht über den zweiten deutschen Wohnungskongress in Leipzig, 1911. Göttingen, 1912.
Bernhard, A. D. Some Principles and Problems of Real Estate Valuation. Baltimore, 1913.
Bowen, D. The Taxation of Mines in Various Countries. In Transactions of the Institution of Mining Engineers, v. 44, pp. 560 ff. London, 1913.
Buchenberger, A. Agrarwesen und Agrarpolitik. Leipzig, 1892.
Buchenberger, A. Grundzüge der deutschen Agrarpolitik. Berlin, 1897.

Carney, W. A. How to Buy and Sell Real Estate at a Profit. Los Angeles, 1905.
Cederstrom, S. Unjust Taxation. Brooklyn, 1913.
City Planning. Hearing before the Committee on the District of Columbia. Sen. Doc. no. 422. 1910.
Clamageron, J. J. Histoire de l'Impôt en France. Paris, 3 vols., 1867-76.
Cohn, G. System der Finanzwissenschaft. Stuttgart, 1889.
Congrès International de la Propriété Foncière, 1900. Paris, 1901.

Cooley, T. M. A Treatise on the Law of Taxation including the Law of Local Assessments. 2 vols., 3d ed. Chicago, 1903.

Craigen, G. J. Practical Methods for Appraising Lands, Buildings and Improvements. New York, 1911.

Dawson, W. H. The Unearned Increment: or Reaping without Sowing. London, 1890.

De Forest, R. W., *and* Veiller, L., *editors*. The Tenement House Problem. 2 vols. New York, 1903.

Eberstadt, R. Handbuch des Wohnungswesens und der Wohnungsfrage. Jena, 1909.

Eberstadt, R. Das Wohnungswesen. Jena, 1904.

Eheberg, K. T. Finanzwissenschaft. 11th ed. Leipzig, 1911.

Eheberg, K. T. Steuerreformen. Handbuch der Politik, v. 2, 1912, pp. 104 *ff*.

Ely, R. T. Taxation in American States and Cities. New York, 1888.

Ensley, E. The Tax Question. New York, 1901 (abridged).

Esslen, J. Das Gesetz des abnehmenden Bodenertrages seit Justus von Liebig. München, 1905.

Fels, Joseph, Fund Bulletin. (Monthly Information for Contributors to the Fels Fund and Single Taxers Generally.) Cincinnati, 1915.

Fetter, F. A. The Passing of the Old Rent Concept. In Quart. Jour. of Ec., v. 15, 1901, pp. 416 *ff*.

Fillebrown, C. B. A, B, C of Taxation. New York, 1909.

Fillebrown, C. B. Henry George and the Economists. Boston, 1914. Pamphlet.

Fillebrown, C. B. A 1912 Single Tax Catechism. 7 ed. Boston, 1912. Pamphlet.

Flürscheim, M. Der einzige Rettungsweg. Dresden und Leipzig, 1890.

Fowler, W. The Present Aspect of the Land Question. In Cobden Club Essays, 1871. Ser. 2, pp. 117 *ff*. London, 1872.

Fuchs, C. J. Zur Wohnungsfrage. Leipzig, 1904.

George, H. The Complete Works of Henry George. 10 vols. Garden City, N.Y., 1906–11.

Godwin, W. Enquiry concerning Political Justice and its Influence on Morals and Happiness. 3d ed. London, 1798.

Gossen, H. H. Entwicklung der Gesetze des menschlichen Verkehrs und der daraus fliessenden Regeln für menschliches Handeln. 1st ed. Braunschweig, 1854.

Grice, J. W. National and Local Finance. London, 1910.

Haig, R. M. Some Probable Effects of the Exemption of Improvements from Taxation in the City of New York. New York, 1915.

Harrison, S. M. Getting Down to Tax in Pittsburgh. In The Survey, July 1, 1911, pp. 476 *ff*.

Hertzka, T. Die Gesetze der sozialen Entwicklung. Leipzig, 1886.

Hertzka, T. Das soziale Problem. Berlin, 1912.

Hollander, J. H. The Concept of Marginal Rent. In Quart. Jour. of Ec., v. 9, pp. 175 *ff*.

Housing of the Working People, The. Eighth Special Report of the U.S. Commissioner of Labor. Washington, 1895.

Hurd, R. M. Principles of City Land Values. New York, 1903.

Hurd, R. M. The Distribution of Urban Land Values. In Yale Review, v. 11, 1902, pp. 124 *ff*.

Jaeger, E. Grundriss der Wohnungsfrage u. Wohnungspolitik. Berlin, 1911.

Jaeger, J. Die Wohnungsfrage. Kempten und München, 1909.

Johnson, A. S. The Case against the Single Tax. In Atlantic Monthly, January, 1914, pp. 27 *ff*.

Johnson, A. S. Rent in Modern Economic Theory. In Publ. of Am. Ec. Assoc., November, 1902.

Kirkman, G. W. Real Estate. In Business, Commerce and Finance. Chicago, 1910.

Kleinwächter, F. Das Wesen der städtischen Grundrente. Leipzig, 1912.

Land, The. The Report of the Land Enquiry Committee. 2 vols. London, 1914.

Land Value Maps. Department of Taxes and Assessments of the City of New York. New York, 1909.

Laveleye, E. De la Propriété et de ses Formes Primitives. 4th ed. Paris, 1891.

Lotz, W. Fiskus als Wohltäter. Betrachtungen über Nebenzwecke bei der Besteuerung. Vortrag. In Volkswirtschaftliche Zeitfragen. Heft 219. Berlin, 1906.

Lutz, H. L. The Somers System of Realty Valuation. In Quart. Jour. of Ec., v. 25, 1910, pp. 172 *ff*.

Mangoldt, R. Die Städtische Bodenfrage. Göttingen, 1907.

Marsh, B. C. An Introduction to City Planning. Democracy's Challenge to the American City. New York, 1909.

Marsh, B. C. Taxation of Land Values in American Cities. New York, 1911.

Means, D. M. The Methods of Taxation Compared with the Established Principles of Justice. New York, 1909.

Mill, J. S. Principles of Political Economy with some of their Applications to Social Philosophy. Book II. London, 1891.

Mill, J. S. Land Tenure Reform Association. Report of the Inaugural Public Meeting, Mr. John Stuart Mill in the Chair. London, 1871.

Mulhall, M. G. Industries and Wealth of Nations. London, 1896.

New York Tax Reform Association. Pamphlets. 1902, 1913–15.

Nicholson, J. S. The Relation of Rents, Wages and Profits in Agriculture, and their Bearing on Rural Depopulation. London, 1906.

Ogilvie, W. An Essay on the Right of Property in Land, with respect to its Foundation in the Law of Nature and the Rights of the People! London, 1780.

Olshausen and Reincke. Ueber Wohnungspflege in England und Schottland, 1897.

Oppenheimer, F. Freiland in Deutschland. Berlin, 1895.

Oppenheimer, F. Grossgrundeigentum und Soziale Frage. Berlin, 1898.

Peters, A. H. The Depreciation of Farming Land. In Quart. Jour. of Ec., v. 4, 1889–90, pp. 18 ff.

Pohle, L. Die Wohnungsfrage. In Handbuch der Politik, v. 2, pp. 517 ff.

Pohle, L. Die Wohnungsfrage. 2 vols. Leipzig, 1910.

Post, L. F. The Taxation of Land Values. In Canadian Law Times. March, 1913.

Post, L. F. Taxation of Land Values. 5th ed. Indianapolis, 1915.

Practical Real Estate Methods for Broker, Operator and Owner. By Thirty Experts. New York, 1909.

Public, The. Chicago, 1897–1915.

Purdy, L. The Burdens of Local Taxation and Who Bears Them. Chicago, 1901.

Purdy, L. Local Option in Taxation. New York, 1901.

Purdy, L. Progress Toward Local Option in Taxation. Reprinted from Public Policy, September 14, 1901.

Putney, M. Real Estate Values and Historical Notes of Chicago. Chicago, 1900.

Real Estate Magazine, The. New York, 1912–.

Real Estate News. Chicago, 1906–12.

Real Estate Record and Builders' Guide. New York, v. 90, 1911–.

Reed, H. Science of Real Estate and Mortgage Investment. Kansas City, 1899.

Reiners, H. Zur Frage der Besteuerung am städtischen Boden in Oesterreich. Wurzberg, 1906.

Reitzenstein, F. Das kommunale Finanzwesen. In Schönberg's Handbuch der politischen Oekonomie, v. 3, 4th ed. Tübingen, 1898.

Report on Assessment and Taxation of Real Estate in the District of Columbia. 62 Congress. House Report no. 1215. 1912.

Report of the Commissioners of Corporations on the Lumber Industry, Summary of. Department of Commerce and Labor. Washington, 1911.

Reports of the Commissioners of Taxes and Assessments of the City of New York. New York, 1907–15.

Reports of the Conservation Commissions of Various States and of Canada, 1909–12.

Report of the National Conservation Commission. Sen. Doc. no. 676. 3 vols. Washington, 1909.

Reports of the National Lumber Manufacturers' Association. Chicago, 1912–13.

Report of the Commission on New Sources of City Revenue, City of New York. January 11, 1913.

Report of the New York City Commission on Congestion of Population. New York, 1911.

Report of the Municipal Finance and Taxation Committee of the Civic League of St. Louis on the Taxation Amendments to the State Constitution of Missouri, to be submitted November, 1912.

Reports of the California State Board of Equalization. Sacramento, 1912–14.

Reports of the Minnesota Tax Commission. St. Paul, 1908–12.

Reports of the Wisconsin Tax Commission. Madison, 1910–.

Rumbold, C. Housing Conditions in St. Louis. Report of the Housing Committee of the Civic League of St. Louis. 1908.

Samter, A. Gesellschaftliches und Privateigentum als Grundlage der Socialpolitik. Leipzig, 1877.

Samter, A. Das Eigentum in seiner sozialen Bedeutung. Jena, 1879.

Schumpeter, J. Das Rentenprinzip in der Verteilungslehre. In Jahrbuch für Gesetz., Verwalt. u. Volksw., v. 31, 1907, pp. 31 *ff.*

Seligman, E. R. A. Essays in Taxation. New ed. New York, 1913.

Seligman, E. R. A. The Shifting and Incidence of Taxation. 2d ed. New York, 1899.

Seligman, E. R. A. Progressive Taxation in Theory and Practice. 2d ed. In Am. Ec. Assoc. Quart., v. 9, 1908.

Seligman, E. R. A. Halving the Tax Rate on Buildings. In The Survey, March, 7, 1914, pp. 697 *ff.*

Seligman, E. R. A. The Theory of Betterment. In Staatswissenschaftliche Arbeiten. Festgaben für Karl Knies. Berlin, 1896, pp. 57–84.

Sering, M. Die Innere Kolonisation in Oestlichen Deutschland. In Schriften des Vereins für Sozialpolitik, v. 56, 1893.

Sering, M. Die Agrarfrage und der Socialismus. In Jahrbuch für Gesetzgebung, Verwaltung und Volkswirtschaft. N.F., v. 23, 1899, pp. 1493 *ff.*

Shearman, T. G. Natural Taxation. 2d ed. New York, 1898.

Single Tax Review, The. Ed. by J. D. Miller. New York, 1901–16.

Slater, G. English Peasantry and the Enclosure of Common Fields. London, 1907.

Somers, W. A. The Valuation of Real Estate for the Purpose of Taxation. St. Paul, 1901. Pamphlet.

Somers, W. A. The Valuation of Real Estate for Taxation. In National Municipal Review, v. 11, 1913, pp. 230 *ff.*

Somers Unit System of Realty Valuation, The. Cleveland.

Somers System of Valuation: —

Letter by the Manufacturers' Appraisal Company of Cleveland to the Comptroller of St. Louis, Mo., describing the Somers System and the Application to Two Blocks in St. Louis. September 10, 1911.

Analysis of the Chicago Assessors' Plan of Computing Site Values and Comparison thereof with the Methods of the Somers Unit System of Realty Valuation. Report of the Manufacturers' Appraisal Company, Cleveland, February, 1911.

Vancil, B. The Somers Unit System of Realty Valuation. Pamphlet.

Spahr, C. B. The Single Tax. In Pol. Sc. Quart., v. 6, 1891, pp. 625 *ff*.

Spence, T. The Meridian Sun of Liberty; or the Whole Rights of Man Displayed and most accurately Defined, in a Lecture read at the Philosophical Society in Newcastle, November 8, 1775, etc. London, 1796.

State and Local Taxation. Addresses and Proceedings of Conferences held under the auspices of the National Tax Association. New York, 1907–15.

Stöpel, F. Der Grundbesitz. In his Soziale Reform, v. 4, 5. Leipzig, 1885.

Stöpel, F. Theorie und Praxis der Besteuerung. In his Soziale Reform, VIII. Leipzig, 1885.

Symposium on the Land Question, A. By A. Herbert, . . . M. Flürscheim, Herbert Spencer, etc. Ed. by J. H. Levy. London, 1890.

Systems of Land Tenure in Various Countries. Series of Essays Pub. under the Sanction of the Cobden Club. Ed. by J. W. Probyn. London, 1881.

Taxation. Eighth Biennial Report of the Illinois Bureau of Labor Statistics, 1894. Springfield, 1895.

Thompson, W. The Housing Handbook. London, 1903.

United States Census Reports: —

    Bulletin 105. Abstract of Annual Report of Statistics of Cities. 1907.

    Bulletin 20. Statistics of Cities Having a Population of over 25,000. 1902–03.

    Wealth, Debt, and Taxation. Special Reports of the Census Office. 1907.

    Taxation and Revenue Systems of State and Local Governments. A Digest of Constitutional and Statutory Provisions Relating to Taxation in the Different States in 1912. 1914.

    Thirteenth Census of the U.S. 1910. Agriculture, v. 5, 6, and 7.

Vandervelde, E. Das Grundeigentum in Belgien in dem Zeitraume vom 1834 bis 1899. In Archiv für Sozialgesetzgebung u. Statistik, v. 15, pp. 419 *ff*.

Veiller, L. Housing Reform. New York, 1910.

Wagner, A. Finanzwissenschaft. 3 vols. Leipzig, 1880–89.

Wagner, A. Grundlegung der politischen Oekonomie. 3d ed., v. 2. Leipzig, 1894.

Walker, F. A. Land and its Rent. Boston, 1883.

Wallace, A. R. Land Nationalisation. London, 1882.

Walrus, L. Études d'Économie Politique. Paris, 1898.

Walrus, L. Élements d'Économie Politique. Lausanne, 1889.

Webb, C. A. Valuation of Real Property. London, 1909.

West, M. The Distribution of Property Taxes Between City and Country. Pol. Sci. Quart., v. 14, 1899, pp. 305 ff.

Weston, S. F. Principles of Justice in Taxation. In Columbia Studies in Hist. Econ. and Public Law, v. 17, no. 2, 1903.

Wohnungsfürsorge in deutschen Städten. Beiträge zur Arbeiterstatistik. N. 11. Berlin, 1910.

Wolf, J. Sozialismus and kapitalistische Gesellschaftsordnung. Stuttgart, 1892.

Zahn, Friedrich. Die Finanzen der Grossmächte. Berlin, 1908.

II. WORKS WITH SPECIAL REFERENCE TO THE GERMAN SYSTEM OF TAXATION

Adickes, F. Kommunalabgabengesetz vom 14 Juli 1893 und Gesetz wegen Aufhebung direckter Staatsteuern vom 14 Juli 1893. Berlin, 1893.

Adickes, F. Ueber die weitere Entwicklung des Gemeinde-Steuerwesens auf Grund des Preussischen Kommunalabgabengesetzes vom 14 Juli 1893. In Zeitschrift für die gesamte Staatswissenschaft, v. 50. Tübingen, 1894, pp. 410 ff., 583 ff.

Adickes, F. Die sozialen Aufgaben der deutschen Städte. (Zwei Vorträge) Leipzig, 1903.

Aehnelt. Das Zuwachssteuergesetz in seiner Bedeutung für bebaute Grundstücke u. baureife Stellen. Berlin, 1912.

Aereboe, F. Die Taxation von Landgütern und Grundstücken. Berlin, 1912.

Altmann, S. P. Der Kampf um die Besitzsteuer. In Archiv für Sozialwissenschaft und Sozialpolitik, v. 29. Tübingen, 1909, pp. 84 ff.

Amtliche Mitteilungen über die Zuwachssteuer. Hrsg. im Reichsschatzamt. Berlin, 1911–12.

Ballod, C. Zur Frage der Gewinnen der Terraingesellschaften. In Jahrbuch für Gesetzgebung, Verwaltung und Volkswirtschaft. N.F., v. 32, 1908, pp. 51 ff.

Bendixen, F. Die Reichsfinanzreform. Hamburg, 1909.

Berthold, O. Ergebnisse der Wertzuwachssteuer und die Wirkungen der Steuer auf den Grundstücksumsatz. Berlin, 1914.

Besteuerung des Grund und Bodens in Frankfurt a. M., Die. Frankfurt, 1905.

Beusch, P. Die Reichsfinanzen und die Steuerreform. Gladbach, 1909.

Birnbaum, B. Die Gemeindlichen Steuersysteme in Deutschland. Berlin, 1914.

Boldt. Die Wertzuwachssteuer, ihre bisherige Gestaltung in der Praxis als Gemeindesteuer und ihre Bedeutung als Reichssteuer unter Beteiligung der Gemeinden. 3d ed. Dortmund, 1909.

Bredt, J. V. Der Wertzuwachs an Grundstücke und seine Besteuerung in Preussen. 1907.

Bredt, J. V. Nationalökonomie des Bodens. Berlin, 1908.

Brooks, R. C. The German Imperial Tax on the Unearned Increment. In Quart. Jour. of Ec., v. 25, 1911, pp. 682 ff.

Brunhuber, R. Die Wertzuwachssteuer zur Praxis und Theorie. Jena, 1906.

Brunhuber, R. The Taxation of the Unearned Increment in Germany. In Quart. Jour. of Ec., v. 22, 1908, pp. 83 ff.

Damaschke, A. Aufgaben der Gemeinde ("Vom Gemeinde-Sozialismus"). 5th ed. Jena, 1904.

Damaschke, A. Die Bodenreform; grundsätzliches und geschichtliches zur Erkenntnis u. Ueberwindung der sozialen Not. 6th ed. Jena, 1912.

Damaschke, A. Geschichte der Nationalökonomie. 5th ed. Jena, 1911.

Diefke, M. Die Wertzuwachssteuer. Im Auftrage des Verbandes der deutschen Terraininteressenten. Berlin, 1908.

Eberstadt, R. Städtische Bodenfragen. Berlin, 1894.

Eberstadt, R. Die Spekulation, ihr Begriff und ihr Wesen. In Jahrbuch für Gesetzgebung, Verwaltung und Volkswirtschaft, v. 29, 1905, pp. 1489 ff.

Eberstadt, R. Entwurf einer Bauplatzsteuer. In Preussische Jahrbücher, v. 74, 1893.

Eberstadt, R. Die Spekulation im neuzeitlichen Städtebau. Jena, 1907.

Eheberg, Das Reichsfinanzwesen. Bonn, 1908.

Ehlert, R. Zur Wertzuwachssteuerfrage. In Jahrbücher für Nationalökonomie und Statistik. N.F., v. 32, 1906, pp. 333 ff.

Ephraim, H. Zur Einführung der "Steuer nach dem gemeinen
    Wert" in Oldenburg. Zeitschrift für die gesamte Staatswis-
    senschaft, v. 66, 1910, pp. 144 *ff*.
Epstein, J. H. Zur Verteidigung der Zuwachssteuer. Soziale
    Zeitfragen. Heft 33, 34. Berlin, 1907.

Fragen der Gemeindebesteuerung. In Verhandlungen des Ver-
    eins für Socialpolitik in Nürnberg, 1911, v. 138. Leipzig,
    1912.
Freudenberg, F. C. Die Wertzuwachssteuer in Baden. Karls-
    ruhe, 1908.
Fuisting, B. Das Gesamtsteuersystem in Reich, Staat und
    Gemeinde in Verbindung mit der Reichsfinanzreform. In
    Finanzpolitische Zeit- und Streitfragen. Heft 2. Berlin, 1906.
Fuisting, B. Die Preussischen Direkten Steuern. 4 vols. Berlin,
    1899–1902.

Gemeindefinanzen. In Schriften des Vereins für Sozialpolitik,
    v. 126. Leipzig, 1908.
German Increment Tax Law of February 14, 1911, The. Trans-
    lated by R. F. Foerster. In Quart. Jour. of Ec., v. 25, pp. 751 *ff*.

D'Hara, F. Die Uebertragung der Grundrente an die Gesell-
    schaft. Berlin, 1904.
Hartmann, F. Die Bewertung städtischer Grundstücke in Preus-
    sen. Eine Studie über Taxmethoden. Berlin, 1907.
Hauser, A. Einführung in die Städtische Bodenreform. Soziale
    Zeitfragen, xvii. Berlin, 1904.

Jahrbuch der Bodenreform. Vierteljahrshefte. Hrsg. von A.
    Damaschke. Jena, 1905–14.

Kausen, H. Die Reichswertzuwachssteuer, Besprechung der
    Kommissionsbeschlüsse zweiter Lesung. Köln, 1910.
Keller, K. Die Besteuerung der Gebäude und Baustellen. Ber-
    lin, 1907.
Das Kommunalabgabengesetz von 14 Juli 1893.
Kommunale Steuerfragen. In Schriften der Gesellschaft für
    Soziale Reform. Heft 15. Jena, 1904.
Kommunales Jahrbuch. Jena, 1909–14.
Köppe, H. Die Aufgaben der Reichsfinanzreform und die ihr
    drohenden Gefahren, vom Finanz- u. sozialpolitischen Stand-
    punkte. In Annalen des Deutschen Reichs, 1909.

Köppe, H. Das Schicksal der Reichszuwachssteuer. In Annalen des Deutschen Reichs, 1910, pp. 670 *ff.*

Kumpmann, K. Die Wertzuwachssteuer. In Zeitschrift für die gesamte Staatswissenschaft. Ergänzungsheft 24. Tübingen, 1907.

Leuckart v. Weissdorf, H. Entwicklung und Ergebnisse der Wertzuwachsbesteuerung im Königreich Sachsen. Borna-Leipzig, 1911.

Linschmann, H. Die neuen Reichssteuern. In Burschenschaftliche Bücherei, v. 3, Heft 2. Berlin, 1909.

Linschmann, H. Die Reichsfinanzreform von 1909. Berlin, 1909.

Lützeler, I. Die Schätzung von Grundstücken für die Beleihung. In Jahrbuch für Gesetzgebung, Verwaltung und Volkswirtschaft, v. 26. Leipzig, 1902.

Meyer, A. Das Princip der Communalsteuern. In Preussische Jahrbücher, v. 18. Berlin, 1866, pp. 166 *ff.*

Meyerstein, E. Zur Frage der Wertzuwachssteuer unter besonderer Berücksichtigung der Vorlage des Berliner Magistrats vom 11 Januar, 1906. In Deutsche Wirtschaftszeitung, 1906, nos. 7 and 8.

Miller, C. Reichsgesetz über die Zuwachssteuer. Tübingen, 1911.

Neumann, F. J. Zur Gemeindesteuerreform in Deutschland mit besonderer Beziehung auf Sächsische Verhältnisse. Tübingen, 1895.

Neumann, F. J. Vermögenssteuern u. Wertzuwachssteuern als Ergänzung der Einkommensteuer, insbesonder in Württemberg. Tübingen, 1910.

Nieden, W. Zur Gebäudesteuer und Wohnungsfrage in Preussen. In Jahrbuch für Gesetzgebung, Verwaltung u. Volkswirtschaft, v. 24, 1900, pp. 1 *ff.*

Pabst, F. Zur Beseitigung der kommunalen Grund- u. Gebäudesteuer. (Betrachtungen eines Hausbesitzers.) In Zeitschrift für die gesamte Staatswissenschaft, v. 56, pp. 113 *ff.* Tübingen, 1900.

Peisker, E. Reichswertzuwachssteuer. Das geltende Recht und die Ziele seiner Reform. Berlin, 1912.

Reichszuwachssteuergesetz, Das, v. 14, February, 1911.

Rothkegel, W. Die Kaufpreise für ländliche Besitzungen im Königreich Preussen von 1895 bis 1906. Staats- u. sozialwissenschaftliche Forschungen. Heft 146. Leipzig, 1910.

Sardemann, G. Die Steuer vom Grundbesitz. Ein Beitrag zur Lösung der Wohnungsfrage. Marburg, 1904.
Seibt, G. Kleinhaus und Mietkaserne. In Jahrbuch für Gesetzgebung, Verwaltung und Volkswirtschaft, v. 29, 1905, pp. 1106 *ff*.
Steiger, J. Die Wertzuwachssteuer in Deutschland und in der Schweiz. Zürich, 1910.
Stumpff, F. Die Gemeindesteuer-Reform in Württemberg, in Zeitschrift für die gesamte Staatswissenschaft, v. 60, 1904, pp. 749 *ff*.
Südekum, A. Die Wertzuwachssteuer, Reichsgesetz vom 14 Feb., 1911. Berlin, 1911.

Voigt, P. Grundrente und Wohnungsfrage in Berlin und seinen Vororten. Jena, 1901.
Voigt, A., u. Geldner, P. Kleinhaus und Mietkaserne. Berlin, 1905.

Wagner, A. Die Abschaffung des privaten Grundeigentums. Leipzig, 1870.
Wagner, A. Rede über die soziale Frage. Berlin, 1872.
Wallach, M. Umsatzsteuer oder Wertzuwachssteuer? Berlin, 1908.
Warschauer, O. Zur Reform der direkten Steuern in Preussen. Leipzig, 1889.
Weber, A. Ueber Bodenrente u. Bodenspekulation in der modernen Stadt. Leipzig, 1904.
Wehberg, H. Die Bodenreform im Lichte des humanistischen Sozialismus. München u. Leipzig, 1913.
Weissenborn, H. Die Besteuerung nach dem Wertzuwachs insbesondere die direkte Wertzuwachssteuer. Berlin, 1910.
Weitpert, K. Die Steuern vom Immobiliarbesitzwechsel in den deutschen Staaten. Erlangen, 1908.
Weyermann, M. Die Reichszuwachssteuer von sozialpolitischen Gesichtspunkten. In Jahrbuch für Gesetzgebung, Verwaltung und Volkswirtschaft, v. 36, 1912, pp. 283 *ff*.
Weyermann, M. Die Ueberwälzungsfrage bei der Wertzuwachssteuer. In Annalen des Deutschen Reichs, v. 43, 1910, pp. 881 *ff*.
Wohnungsnoth der ärmeren Klassen in deutschen Grosstädten,

Die. In Schriften des Vereins für Sozialpolitik, vv. 30 and 31, Leipzig, 1886.

Wolf, J. Die Reichsfinanzreform und ihr Zusammenhang. Leipzig, 1909.

Wygodzinski, W. Die Besteuerung des landwirtschaftlichen Grundbesitzes in Preussen. Jena, 1906.

Zuwachssteuergesetz vom 14 Feb., 1911, Das. Erläutert von C. Becher, u. H. Henneberg. Berlin, 1912.

III. Works with Special Reference to English Conditions

Baumann, A. A. Betterment, Worsement and Recoupment. London, 1894.

Baxter, R. D. Local Government and Taxation, and Mr. Goschen's Report. London, 1874.

Beken, G. The Taxation of Site Values and Cognate Subjects. London, 1905.

Blanch, W. H. Shall I Appeal against my Assessment? London, 1890.

Blunden, G. H. Local Taxation and Finance. London, 1895.

Boas, W. P. A Guide to the Duties Imposed upon Land and Mineral Rights. London, 1910.

Briggs, T. Poverty and Taxation, and the Remedy: Free Trade, Free Labor; or Direct Taxation the True Principle of Political Economy. London, 188-(?).

British Parliamentary Debates.

British Parliamentary Papers: —

First Report of Her Majesty's Commission for Inquiring into the Housing of the Working Classes, 1885 (C. 4402).

Report from the Select Committee on Town Holdings, 1890 (341). Same, 1892 (214).

Report on Local Taxation in Scotland, 1894 (C. 7575).

First Report of Her Majesty's Commissioners appointed to inquire into the Subject of Agricultural Depression, 1894 (C. 7400).

Final Report of the Commissioners appointed to inquire into the subject of Agricultural Depression, 1897 (C. 8540, C. 8541).

Memoranda chiefly relating to the Classification and Incidence of Imperial and Local Taxes, 1899 (Cd. 9528).

Minutes of Evidence taken before the Royal Commission on Local Taxation, 1899 (Cd. 9150, Cd. 9319).

Final Report of the Royal Commission on Local Taxation in England and Wales, 1901 (Cd. 638).

Report and Special Report from the Select Committee on the Land Values Taxation, etc. (Scotland) Bill, 1906 (379).

Memoranda and Extracts relating to Land Taxation, prepared for the Chancellor of the Exchequer, 1909 (Cd. 4845).

Finance Act 1909–1910. Bill 144 of 1910.

Instructions issued by the Inland Revenue Department to Valuers, 1911 (283).

Report of Commissioners of Inland Revenue, 1911 (Cd. 5833).

Dispatches from Consular Officers Respecting the Taxation of Land Values in New York, Boston, San Francisco, and Cleveland, 1909 (Cd. 4578).

British Taxpayer and his Wrongs, The. (Including an Analysis of a Typical Year's Imperial and Local Taxation, with Remarks on the Budget Proposals of 26 March, 1888, and an Appendix). By "Finance." London, 1888.

Brodrick, G. C. English Land and English Landlords. London, 1881.

Budget, the Land, and the People, The. Issued by Budget League. London, 1909.

Castle, H. J. Practical Remarks on the Principles of Rating, as Applied to the Proper and Uniform Assessment of Railways, Gasworks, Waterworks, Mines, Cemeteries, etc. 2d ed. London, 1869.

Chapman, S. J. Local Government and State Aid. London, 1899.

Chomley, C. H., and Outhwaite, R. Land Values Taxation in Theory and Practice. London, 1909.

Chorlton, J. D. The Rating of Land Values. Manchester, 1907.

Cox-Sinclair, E. S., and T. Hynes. Land Values. . . . London, 1910.

Cox-Sinclair, E. S., and Hynes, T. Some Problems in Land Values. In Law Magazine and Review, v. 38, 1912–13.

Davenport, H. Single Tax in the English Budget. In Quart. Jour. of Ec., 1910, pp. 279 ff.

Davenport, H. J. The Extent and the Significance of the Unearned Increment. Bull. of Am. Ec. Assoc., Ser. 4, v. 1, 1911, pp. 322 ff.

Davitt, M. The Land League Proposal: A Statement for Honest and Thoughtful Men. Glasgow, 1882. Pamphlet.

Dowell, S. History of Taxation and Taxes in England. 4 vols., 2d ed. London, 1888.

Edgeworth, F. Recent Schemes for Rating Urban Land Values. In Ec. Jour., v. 16, 1906, pp. 66 *ff*.

Eve, C. G. Systems of Land Valuation in the United Kingdom. 2 Pts. In Monthly Bulletins of Economic and Social Intelligence of the International Institute of Agriculture, December, 1913, January, 1914. Rome, 1913–14.

Fox, A. W. Rating of Land Values. London, 1908.

Giffen, R. Economic Inquiries and Studies. 2 vols. London, 1904, v. 1, pp. 253 *ff*.

Gomme, G. L. Local Taxation in London. In The Journal of the Royal Statistical Society, v. 61, pp. 442 *ff*. London, 1898.

Goschen, G. J. Return on the Increase of Local Taxation. 1870.

Goschen, G. J. Reports and Speeches on Local Taxation. London, 1872.

Graham, J. C. Local and Imperial Taxation and Local Government. 4th ed. London, 1906.

Hallgarten, R. Die kommunale Besteuerung des unverdienten Wertzuwachses in England. In Münchener volkswirtschaftliche Studien. N. 32. Stuttgart, 1899.

Konstam, E. M. Land Values. London, 1910.

Konstam, E. M. Rates and Taxes: A Practical Guide. London, 1906.

Land Duties and Negative Values. In Solicitors' Journal, v. 56, pp. 478 *ff*.

Land and Real Tariff Reform. Pub. by Joseph Edwards. London, 1909.

Land Union Pamphlets, The: —

    Report of the Speeches Advocating Repeal of the New Land Taxes. Delivered at Inaugural Meeting. May 5, 1910.

    The New Land Taxes. Pamphlet No. 1.

    Land Union Guide to Property Owners Called upon to Fill up the Government Valuation Forms.

Land values. (Monthly.) London and Glasgow, 1894–.

Lange, M. E. Local Taxation in London. London, 1906.

Lightbody, F. H. The Valuation of Undeveloped Land. Edinburgh and London, 1910.

Lloyd George. The Lords and the Budget. In Independent, v. 67, 1909, pp. 1340 *ff.*

Local Rating. Memorandum on the Proposal of the Departmental Committee on Local Taxation that the Assessments for Local Rates should be made by the Valuation Staff of the Inland Revenue Department. Compiled by a Body of Surveyors. London, 1914.

London County Council. Valuation for Rating Purposes. Report of the Local Government and Taxation Committee, 1902.

Lovat-Fraser, J. A. Duties on Land Values. London, 1910.

Marum, E. P. Mulhallen. Taxation and the Taxable Bases of the United Kingdom. (Imperial Taxation, including Colonial Taxation. Local Taxation, including Bottomry Taxation.) Dublin, 1890.

Moffet, T. Land Taxes and Mineral-Rights Duties. London, 1910.

Murray, D. The Valuation Roll in Scotland and the Proposal to Enter Land Values upon It. London, 1907. Pamphlet.

Napier, T. B. The Valuation Scheme of the Land Clauses of the Finance Act, 1910. In Law Quart. Rev., v. 27, 1911.

Napier, T. B. The Land Clauses of the Finance (1909–10) Act, 1910. (Some Ambiguities, and Two Recent Decisions.) In Law Quart. Rev., v. 28, 1912.

Napier, T. B. The New Land Taxes. London, 1910.

Nicholson, J. S. Tenant's Gain, not Landlord's Loss. Edinburgh 1883.

Nicholson, J. S. Rates and Taxes as Affecting Agriculture. London, 1905.

Noble, J. Local Taxation: A Criticism of Fallacies and a Summary of Facts. London, 1876.

O'Meara, J. J. Municipal Taxation at Home and Abroad. London, 1894.

Orr, J. Taxation of Land Values as it Affects Landowners and Others. London, 1912.

Palgrave, R. H. I. The Local Taxation of Great Britain and Ireland. London, 1871.

Pamphlets published by United Committee for the Taxation of Land Values: —

"Form IV": What Next? by Frederick Verinder. 1911.

The United Committee for the Taxation of Land Values. Annual Reports. London, 1907–.

Rural Land Reform. 1911.

A Plea for the Taxation of Ground Rents. Prepared for the "United Committee" by Sidney Webb. With Preface by the Right Hon. Lord Hobhouse. 1887.

Land Values and the Budget Manifesto by the United Committee for the Taxation of Land Values. 1909.

Perin, R. Die Englischen Bodenwertsteuern. In Finanz-archiv., v. 30, 1913, pp. 96 *ff*.

Porrit, E. The Struggle over the Lloyd-George Budget. In Quart. Jour. of Ec., v. 24, 1910, pp. 243 *ff*.

Raine, G. E. Lloyd George and the Land. London, 1914.

Rathbone, W., Pell, A., and Montague, F. C. Local Government and Taxation. London, 1885.

Rating of Ground Rents and Ground Values, The. A Study in Local Taxation. London, 1888 (?). Pamphlet.

Rhodes, C. T. Taxation of Land Values, The Case Against. London, 1901.

Row-Fogo, J. An Essay on the Reform of Local Taxation in England. London, 1902.

Sargent, W. L. Taxation, Past, Present, and Future. London, 1874.

Sargent, C. H. Urban Rating (being an Inquiry into the Incidence of Local Taxation in Towns). London, 1890.

Schooling, J. H. Local Rates and Taxes. London, 1905.

Smart, W. Taxation of Land Values and the Single Tax. Glasgow, 1900.

Storey, H. The Economics of Land Value. London, 1913.

(Tennant, C.) The People's Blue Book: Taxation as It Is, and as It Ought to Be; with a practical Scheme of Taxation. London, 1862.

Urquhart, W. P. Dialogues on Taxation, Local and Imperial. Aberdeen, 1867.

Wedgwood, J. C. Land Values. Letchworth, 1907. Pamphlet.

Williams, W. M. J. The King's Revenue. Being a Handbook to the Taxes and the Public Revenue. London, 1908.

Wright, R. S., and Hobhouse, H. An Outline of Local Government and Local Taxation in England and Wales. London, 1884.

Wylie, J. The Duties on Land Values and Mineral Rights. London, 1910.

Zimmerman, L. W. Taxation of Land Values. (Introduction by C. P. Trevelyan, M.P.) Manchester, 1913 (?).

IV. REFERENCES ON THE AUSTRALASIAN TAX SYSTEM

A, B, C of Queensland. Statistics, 1913. Brisbane: A. J. Cummings, 1913.

Anderson, H. C. L. Statistics. Six States of Australia and New Zealand, 1861 to 1905. Compiled from Official Sources. Sydney, 1907.

Australian Economist, The. (Monthly.) Journal of the Australian Economic Association. 1888–90.

Australasia. London, 1900.

Australasian, The. Melbourne, 1869–1909.

Australasian Tax System, The. By the Revenue Commission of Colorado. Senate Doc., v. 15, 1901.

Boothby, J. Statistical Sketch of South Australia. London, 1876.

British Parliamentary Papers: —
　　Papers Bearing on Land Taxes and on Income Tax, etc., in Foreign Countries (Germany, France, Australia), etc., 1909 (Cd. 4750).
　　Similar Papers with Regard to Queensland, 1908 (Cd. 3890).
　　Papers relative to the working of Taxation of the Unimproved Value of Land in New South Wales, 1908 (Cd. 3761).
　　Papers relating to the working of the Unimproved Value of Land in New Zealand, New South Wales, and South Australia, 1906 (Cd. 3191).

Census of Commonwealth of Australia. April, 1911. Census Bulletin no. 17.

Chomley, C. H. Protection in Canada and Australasia. London, 1904.

Clark, V. S. Labor Movement in Australasia. London, 1907.

Coghlan, T. A. A Statistical Account of Australia and New Zealand. 1903–04. Sydney, 1904.

Coghlan, T. A. A Statistical Account of the Seven Colonies of Australasia. Sydney, 1890–1900.

Commonwealth of Australia: —
  Monthly Summary of Australian Statistics. Melbourne, 1912–14.
  Parl. Debates. 1910.
  Statutes —
    No. 21 of 1910 (Land Tax Act, 1910).
    No. 22 of 1910 (Land Tax Assessment Act, 1910).

Epps, W. Land Systems of Australasia. London, 1894.

Facts about New Zealand. Issued by New Zealand Government Department of Tourist and Health Resorts. Wellington, 1907.
Fenton. Queensland Official Year Book. (1901) Annual Report and Guide Book issued by Lands Department.

Hall, W. H. Statistics. Six States of Australia and New Zealand, 1861 to 1904. Compiled from Official Sources. Sydney, 1905.

Jenks, E. A History of the Australasian Colonies. Cambridge, 1896.

Land and Income Assessment Acts, The. 1891–92. Wellington, 1902.
Land System of New Zealand. In Law Magazine and Review, 1909–10, pp. 279 ff.
Lloyd, H. D. Newest England. New York, 1900.
Lusk, H. H. Social Welfare in New Zealand. New York, 1913.

Monthly Statistical Abstract for Western Australia, 1907. Compiled in Gov't Statistician's Office. Perth, 1907.

New Zealand: —
  Journal of the Department of Labor for 1911. Wellington, 1912.
  Official Year Book. 1890–1913.
  Parl. Debates. 1891–96.

Official Statistics. Commonwealth of Australia. Bureau of Census and Statistics. Finance Bulletins. Melbourne, 1901–13.
Official Year Book of the Commonwealth of Australia, 1901–11.
Official Year Book of South Australia, 1913, by D. J. Gordon. Adelaide, 1913.
The Official Year Book of N.S. Wales, 1911. Sydney, John B. Trivett, 1912.

Public Accounts of Western Australia for 1910. Prepared by Hon. the Colonial Treasurer.

Reeves, W. P. State Experiments in Australia and New Zealand, v. 1. London, 1902.
Report of the Results of a Census of the Colony of New Zealand, 1901. By E. J. Von Dadelszen, Registrar Gen'l. Wellington, 1902.
Report on Results of Census of New Zealand, 1911.
Le Rossignol, J. E. and Stewart, W. D. State Socialism in New Zealand. New York, 1910.
Le Rossignol, J. E., and Stewart, W. D. Taxation in New Zealand. In University Studies of the Univ. of Nebraska, v. 9, pp. 249 ff. Lincoln, 1909.

Settlers' Handbook of New Zealand, The. Compiled by Direction of Hon. Minister of Lands. Wellington, 1902.
South Australia. Statistical Register, 1909.
Statistics of the State of Tasmania for 1913–14. Compiled from Official Records. Tasmania, 1914.
Statistics of the Colony of Queensland, 1897. Finance, Part. iv, Brisbane: Gregory, Government Printer, 1898.
Statistical View of Fifty Years' Progress in New Zealand, 1854–1903. Wellington, 1904.
Statistics of the Dominion of New Zealand, 1910. Wellington, 1911.
St. Ledger, A. Australian Socialism. An Historical Sketch of its Origin and Developments. London, 1909.
Statutes of the Various Australasian Colonies.

Turner, H. G. The First Decade of the Australian Commonwealth. A Chronicle of Contemporary Politics, 1901–10. Melbourne, 1911.

Victorian Year Book. Melbourne, 1895–1914.
Vigouroux, L. L'Évolution Sociale en Australasie. Paris, 1902.

Western Australian Year Book for 1902–04. By M. Fraser, Government Statistician. Perth, 1906.
Walch's Tasmanian Almanac for 1907. London.
Walker, H. Australasian Democracy. London, 1897.
Wise, B. R. The Commonwealth of Australia. Boston, 1909.

V. References on Western Canada

Agriculture in British Columbia. Official Bulletin 10. Pub. by Authority of Legislative Assembly. Bureau of Provincial Information. Victoria, 1912.

Annual Report of Department of Public Work of the Province of Alberta, 1911. Edmonton, 1912.

Annual Report. City of Calgary, Alberta, 1912.

British Columbia: —
  Royal Commission on Taxation. Synopsis of Report and Full Report, 1911. Victoria, 1912.
  Year Book, 1911, 1912.

British Columbia Federationist. Vancouver, 1912-.

British Parliamentary Papers. Papers relative to the Working of Taxation of the Unimproved Value of Land in Canada, 1908 (Cd. 3740).

Bullock, C. J. Single Tax in Vancouver. In the N.Y. Evening Post, Saturday, June 27, 1914.

Canada and its Provinces. A History of the Canadian People and their Institutions by One Hundred Associates, vv. 19–22.

Canadian Municipal Journal. Official Organ of the Union of Canadian Municipalities. Montreal, 1909–15.

City of Edmonton, Alberta. Ninth Annual Report to December, 1913. Financial and Departmental.

Commercial Handbook of Canada. Ninth Year, 1913.

Consolidated Statutes for Upper Canada. Toronto, 1859.

Dixon, F. J. The Progress of Land Value Taxation in Canada. Winnipeg (pamphlet), 1913 (?).

Enock, C. R. The Great Pacific Coast, New York, 1913.

Financial and Departmental Reports. Corporation of the City of Vancouver, British Columbia, 1912-.

Five Thousand Facts About Canada. Toronto, 1910–14.

Haig, R. M. The Exemption of Improvements from Taxation in Canada and the United States. (A Report prepared for the Committee on Taxation of the City of New York.) New York, 1915.

Handbook of British Columbia. Bureau of Provincial Information. Bulletin no. 23, 1913.

Harpell, J. J. Canadian National Economy. Toronto, 1911.

Hillam, W. A. The Magic of Single Tax. (Reprint from British Columbia Magazine, April, 1911.)

Immigration Situation in Canada, The. Report of the U.S. Immigration Commission, Senate Doc. no. 469. Washington, 1910.

Land Values in Canada. Review of Business Conditions during 1912. Issued by the Canadian Bank of Commerce.

Lawson, W. R. Canada and the Empire. Edinburgh and London, 1911.

Lighthall, W. D. Canada, a Modern Nation. Montreal, 1904.

Municipal Government in Canada, ed. by S. M. Wickett. In University of Toronto Studies, History and Economics, v. 2. Toronto, 1907.

Municipal World, The. Ontario, 1909–.

Nock, A. J. Why Nature's Way is Best. In American Magazine, July, 1911, pp. 335–38; *ibid.*, pp. 76 *ff.*, 221 *ff.*

Official Handbook of Alberta, An. Compiled under direction of Hon. W. T. Finlay, Minister of Agriculture. Edmonton, 1907.

Official Handbook of Information relating to the Dominion of Canada, An, 1897. Ottawa, 1897.

Ordinances of North West Territories. Regina, 1894–.

Public Accounts of the Province of Saskatchewan, 1912. Regina, 1912.

Public Service Monthly, The. Regina, 1913.

Reports of Assessment Department, City of Montreal, for 1912 and 1913. Montreal, 1914.

Report on Strikes and Lockouts in Canada, 1901–12. Ottawa, 1913.

Report of the Ontario Assessment Commission, 1901. Toronto, 1901.

Report on Taxation of Improvements by Assessment Commissioner of Toronto. 1912. Pamphlet.

Revised Statutes of British Columbia, 1897, c. 179.
Revised Statutes of North West Territories, 1898.
Revised Statutes of Ontario, The. 2 vols., v. 2. Toronto, 1877.

Statistical Year Book of Canada. Ottawa, 1895–1910.
Statutes of the Western Provinces.

Vineberg, S. Provincial and Local Taxation in Canada. In Columbia Studies in Hist., Ec. and Public Law, v. 52, no. 1. New York, 1912.

Wade, F. C. Experiments with the Single Tax in Western Canada. In Eighth Annual Conference on Taxation, September 11, 1914.
Wade, F. C. The Single-Tax Failure in Vancouver. (Letter to Vancouver Sun, January 7, 1914.) Pamphlet.
Wade, F. C. The Single Tax Humbug in Vancouver. (Letter to Vancouver Daily Province, January 2, 1912.)

VI. REFERENCES ON KIAO-CHAU

Denkschrift betreffend die Entwicklung des Kiautschou-Gebiets. Berlin, 1901–09.

Gaul, J. Finanzrecht der deutschen Schutzgebiete unter besonderer Berücksichtigung der Steuergesetzgebung. Leipzig, 1909, pp. 162–72.

Köbner, O. Einführung in die Kolonialpolitik, pp. 191 *ff*. Jena, 1908.

Landordnung von Kiautschou, Die. In Jahrbuch der Bodenreform, v. 1, 1905, pp. 56 *ff*.

Preyer, O. E. Aus der Praxis der Landordnung von Kiautschou. In Jahrbuch der Bodenreform, v. 4, 1908, pp. 126 *ff*.

Schrameier, W. Die Landpolitik im Kiautschougebiet. In Jahrbuch der Bodenreform, v. 7, 1911, pp. 1 *ff*.; v. 8, 1912, pp. 1 *ff*.

INDEX

Absenteeism, 6, 23, 30, 31, 58–59, 257–58, 268, 276, 291; definition, 39–40, 48, 321–22; effect of tax on, 81.

Administration, in Australia, 62–67, 95; in Germany, 160–63; in Canada, 274–77; in England, 234–38; of property tax in United States, 431, 440–42.

Agricultural land, 195, 350; exempt from increment tax, 215–16; valuation of, 243; expediency of tax on, 344–45, 346, 409, 445–46; values, 351–58; 368–69, 385.

Alberta, 18, 254, 255, 257, 260–61, 262–63, 265, 270–71, 289, 301.

Amortization, 13, 192; principle of, 315–17.

Annual value, 4 *n.*, 30, 36, 52, 70, 129, 195, 252, 320–22, 396.

Australasia, chaps. II, III; land tenure, 6, 20–23, 30, 96 *ff.*; absenteeism, 6, 23, 30, 31; finances, 26–28, 34; local government, 28, 29, 90 *ff.*; building and housing conditions, 107–15.

Australian state taxes, 41–42; characteristics, 23–24, 34, 36 *ff.*, 27–28, 59–60; prevalence, 34; rate of, 41–42; exemptions, 42–43, 103–05; assessment roll, 65–66; publicity, 66; assessment, 68–69.

Benefit principle, 30, 49, 91, 122, 124, 141–43, 160, 251, 252, 269, 306, 326.

Berlin, rental tax, 123; transfer tax, 126; congestion, 138, 390–91.

British Columbia, 17, 254, 255, 257, 258–61, 262, 266, 270, 275, 301.

Building, effect of tax on, 107–12, 248–49, 292–96, 298–99, 311–15, 397–98, 399, 400, 402–03, 420.

Building regulations, inefficacy of, 393–94.

Building-site tax, in Bremen, 125, 128, 130; recommended by Housing Committee, 197.

Business tax, 251, 271, 273, 444.

Calgary, 265, 273, 278, 282, 283, 286, 290, 293, 294, 297.

Canada, Western, 3, 6, 17–18; local taxation, chap. VI; land tenure, 254–56; social conditions, 253, 292; municipal ownership, 269.

Canons of taxation, 322 *ff.*

Capital value, tax on; definition, 70; 125, 128–29, 157, 223, 252, 317–18, 320–22.

Capitalization. *See* Amortization.

Classification of tax, 304–08.

Classified property tax, in Germany, 130; 431–32, 442, 443.

Cologne, 132–33 *n.*, 164, 168, 170, 175, 181.

Commonwealth of Australia, federal tax, 17, 36, 55–59, 60; Labor Party, 55–56; absenteeism, 56–57, 58; leaseholds, 57; mortgages, 58; rate of tax, 58–59, 84–86; valuation, 76; revenue from tax, 83–87; effect on holdings, 98–99.

Congestion, 108–10, 112–14, 120, 138, 385, 386, 388–91; no problem in Canada, 296; in Great Britain, 390–91; in Berlin, 390–91; causes of, 391–93; remedies proposed, 410, 411–13, 414; relation to tax, 395 *ff.*, 398, 399–400, 420.

Conservation of natural resources, 366–68, 370, 415–20; effect of tax on, 418–20.

Cost of collection, of federal tax, 86, 88; in New Zealand, 88, 95.

Differential rating, 90–91, 116–17, 345–46, 445–46.

Direct and indirect forms of tax, 7 *ff.*, 210, 224.

The Riverside Press

CAMBRIDGE . MASSACHUSETTS

U . S . A